Dryden Press Professional Books in Education

PHILOSOPHIES OF EDUCATION

IN CULTURAL PERSPECTIVE

Theodore Brameld

PROFESSOR OF EDUCATIONAL PHILOSOPHY

NEW YORK UNIVERSITY

THE DRYDEN PRESS · NEW YORK

Parts of this book have appeared under the title *Patterns of Educational Philosophy*, copyright 1950 by World Book Company.

Second Printing, May 1956

Preface

Dear Student:

THIS VOLUME IS AN EXTENSIVE AND INTENSIVE REVISION OF THE first half of an earlier work, *Patterns of Educational Philosophy*. (The second half is also published as a revised and separate volume.) In this book I have tried to provide an interpretation that will acquaint you with the most conspicuous points of view now influencing American education.

You are, I assume, planning to become a teacher. I wish it were somehow within my capacity to express to you my own great pride in our profession. It seems to me beyond doubt the greatest of all professions; and I trust you are entering it with a sense of adventure, of opportunity for public service, and with every intention to remain in it as a lifework.

If you wish to be a first-rate teacher, you know that you will need the most thorough training you can obtain and that this training can never terminate so long as you remain a teacher. The philosophy of education is intended to provide some of that training. More than any other field of learning, philosophy goes to the roots of things. It explores the basic sources and aims of life. It asks and tries to answer the deepest questions that man can ask or answer.

When philosophy does its job, it disturbs anyone it touches. I hope that you will be disturbed by this book. If you are not, then the book has not succeeded in compelling you to subject your beliefs to re-examination, perhaps to modification, possibly even to rejection or drastic reconstruction. Unless you are willing to take the risk that this will happen, you can scarcely expect to qualify as a thoroughly trained teacher—as one whose beliefs about education and about the culture it serves have been weighed and tested.

Perhaps it would help if I were to make a few suggestions. First, try your best to avoid impatience toward the ideas you will consider. If they are truly significant, there is no short cut to understanding them. Consequently, you cannot expect to read this book with the speed or ease with which you may read many others. You should plan to read slowly, carefully, underlining main points, jotting comments in the margins. Above all, try to read actively, not passively. The more you react to every discussion—disagreeing and questioning wherever you wish—the more firmly is philosophy probably beginning to take hold. But allow enough time: the more time you allow and the more critically you read, the greater the likelihood that early confusions will begin to disappear, that principal concepts will begin to be clarified. Also, to help you further you will find fairly extensive summaries throughout the book. These should be useful *after* you have studied the main text; they are not a substitute.

If you have hitherto had no formal work in philosophy or in the history of education, some of the terminology and names of individuals may be new to you. Whenever possible, every technical term is defined when first used, and individuals are identified in terms of their chief contributions to a specific period. A second suggestion to help you further, however, is that you do additional reading in such sources as are indicated both in the footnotes and in the Appendix.

The names of many prominent thinkers listed in the Index are followed by their life dates; these dates ought to assist you in situating important individuals within their respective historic settings. Finally, there are in the text many cross references to other pages of this book; by following them you will be able to observe the close relations among various parts of the developing presentation.

You may be interested in the further suggestions I have written to your instructor below. If you, yourself, care to offer any suggestions either to him or to me, please feel free to do so. I should be happy to have you write to me, for I consider this book yours as well as mine.

The chief thing I wish to say to you, however, is much more important than these academic matters. I wish to speak to you as a citizen rather than merely as a student. If you have not yet reached voting age, you soon will. Even if you have not, you are a young adult, and the burning problems of our period are *your* problems. In some ways, they are yours even more than they are your elders'; for it is upon you that those of us who are older must rely for many of the grave decisions that now impend both in education and in society.

My book is your concern because it discusses you, the kind of world you live in, the kind you can help to shape in the future. It contends that education is of crucial importance to you; that you are of equal importance to education; and that you have a solemn responsibility to determine the policy and the program of education during the next half century.

I readily admit that the task is arduous. Issues as basic as those education now confronts can never be resolved hastily or superficially. If you are willing to go forward with me, you will find that we shall need assistance from the most profound minds of history: Plato, Locke, Hegel, James, Freud, and a great many others. We shall need, further, to consider questions and situations that often create bitterness, even violence. Nothing less than a willingness to study and act upon them as honestly and forthrightly as possible will suffice.

For you and I live at a grim and fearful juncture of history. Events of grave significance have occurred within our lifetime. You know of these events, but I shall review them for you again in later pages. It is necessary to do so again and again, for we have scarcely begun to estimate their monstrous impact upon all of us. Especially, we have not begun to appreciate their revolutionary meaning for education.

The task of this book is to investigate that meaning. In the degree that it does so, it is compelled to ask what we, as citizens, should demand of education. Our right is to demand. For the schools and colleges of America—of many other countries, too—are or could become *our* schools and colleges. We have a right to make of them what we believe they should be. We cannot, however, justify our demands until we understand much more clearly in what respects the schools and colleges are now inadequate and what kinds of change are required in order to meet the highest standards we may set for them.

But such purposes cannot be attained until you and I regard them as purposes we are utterly resolved to attain. Education in a democracy is not confined to books and teachers, students and classrooms. Fundamentally, it is the instrument by which the people learn how to manage themselves and their environment in their own highest interests. Moreover, in our time of crisis we cannot wait for the young to grow up; either lay adults of the community must join hand in hand with members of our profession, or education must fail.

I do not believe that you wish it to fail. I believe, rather, that you are in essential agreement with what I have tried to express here. This is why I expect you to recognize with me that only an analysis that is philosophic in character can equip us to go forward concertedly with hope of success.

Very sincerely yours,

April 1955

THEODORE BRAMELD

Dear Instructor:

IF YOU AGREE WITH MY COMMENTS TO THE STUDENT, I HOPE THAT you will stress them while adding others of your own. I should be grateful, too, if you were to keep in mind one distinction regarding the structure of the book. Part I is intended chiefly for those making their first, or nearly first, acquaintance with the kind of concepts and problems that are central to philosophy, education, and culture in their interrelations. Hence it is geared to readers of limited background. To a lesser extent, the same intention governs the largely expository chapters in subsequent Parts (Chaps. 4, 5, 7, 8, 10, and 11) dealing with progressivism, essentialism, and perennialism. In terms of your own scholarly interests, therefore, you may be most concerned with the evaluative chapters (Chaps. 6, 9, and 12). At the same time, I must point out that the evaluative chapters rely so heavily upon the foundation laid in the more expository treatment that any careful reading of them would require exacting attention to the latter also.

Of considerable interest to you, perhaps, is the section of the Appendix entitled "Aids to Learning and What to Read." This section provides a series of possible activities designed to dramatize or illustrate many of the relatively abstract ideas presented in the text. It is my conviction, which I am certain you share, that philosophy can be made quite as exciting and concrete as any other subject in the college curriculum —even more so when it concerns itself, as of course it should, with the most urgent questions facing our generation. In so far as possible, therefore, the activities proposed extend beyond typical classroom routines. Many of them take you and your students into the community; others provide opportunities for experimentation and intergroup participation within the school or college.

The more these "Aids to Learning" are employed, the more meaningful educational theory should become. Certainly it is not expected, however, that all of the suggestions should be followed in any one course of study. With the help of your students, you will want to select from among them and to add others of your own, just as you will want to do so with the "What to Read" paragraphs.

You will recognize at once that all the chapters owe much to other writers in philosophy, education, the social sciences, and other fields. I have tried to indicate this indebtedness through the footnotes, but these do not begin to reveal the influence of innumerable colleagues, students, and personal friends who have encouraged and advised me in the writing of both the original volume and this revision. I have particularly benefited from the constructive criticisms of my own students, one of whom, Professor Richard Morland, of Stetson University, devised the diagram in Chapter 3.

At the same time, it is important to emphasize that no one but myself can be held finally responsible for the interpretations here offered. You will be particularly aware that my evaluations of the three prominent philosophies anticipate an educational point of view that differs, at least in degree, from any one of these. In the Epilogue I have tried further to prepare the way for careful study of this point of view, which is elaborated in a companion volume. Its guiding assumption, which permeates this volume also, is that all contemporary philosophies of education, including my own, are interpretations in some form of our precarious and bewildered culture—philosophies serving either to debilitate or to vitalize and redirect that culture. In an age such as ours, threatened by the total annihilation of mankind, the scholar and instructor have a responsibility to fulfill that is doubtless greater than at any time since the end of feudalism and the rise of industrial civilization. Each of us can assume some slight share in that responsibility.

Very sincerely yours,

April 1955 THEODORE BRAMELD

Contents: An Overview

(For a complete table of contents, see pages xiii-xvii)

Contents

PROLOGUE

Part One

PHILOSOPHY, CULTURE, AND EDUCATION

Part Two

PROGRESSIVISM:
Education as Cultural Transition

Part Three

ESSENTIALISM:
Education as Cultural Conservation

Part Four

PERENNIALISM:
Education as Cultural Regression

EPILOGUE

APPENDIX

PROLOGUE

CHAPTER I

A Time of Great Debate

AT NO PERIOD IN AMERICAN HISTORY, NOT EVEN IN THE EARLY decades of the nineteenth century, when public schools were first established as a permanent institution of our culture, has education stirred such heated public controversy as in the years of the midcentury. Traditionally, the American people have tended to be rather complacent about education, honoring it, perhaps, more widely than any other people, but also taking it for granted. They have left the responsibility of what to teach and how to teach to those professionally responsible.

Today the public's attitude toward education has radically changed. Far from being taken for granted, education is more likely to be discussed in language colored by a wide range of emotionally toned judgments, which disclose strong feelings at least as often as a knowledge of facts. In hundreds of local communities, from Scarsdale, New York, to Pasadena, California, citizens have taken sides—sometimes angrily—for or against a specific school program or proposal. Such organized groups in the community as labor unions, churches, chambers of commerce, and patriotic bodies have come to regard education as their special concern. Never before, moreover, have magazines with vast circulations considered education to be a subject certain to arouse its readers and to attract countless new ones. In hundreds of articles and scores of issues, these magazines as well as others of smaller circulation but of great influence continue to feature the conflicting positions on a wide variety of educational problems. Newspapers with nationwide circulation, books and pamphlets, radio and television networks, public forums, powerful national organizations, even state legislatures and the Congress of the United States—all have joined in the debate.

What deeper social trends and conflicts lie behind this bitter and persistent public controversy? The question is easier to ask than it is to answer. Actually, many answers might be suggested—some of them worthless, others convincing; some superficial, others profound; some inconsistent and confused, others logical and clear. In one sense, the first purpose of this book is to try to answer the question by placing education in a wider perspective—in the perspective of the contemporary American culture and, to some extent, of cultures historically and geographically beyond our culture. It is not enough, however, to attempt even this large task. It is necessary, in addition, to find a way whereby culture and the educational processes within it can be effectively examined and interpreted. This, we believe, is the chief role of philosophy.

For philosophy, as we shall show, is most properly defined as the effort of any culture to become conscious of itself—to face honestly and stubbornly its own weaknesses as well as strengths, failures as well as achievements, vices as well as virtues. Contradicting the common notion that philosophy at its purest is an aloof, intellectual discipline unsullied by either the miseries or the joys of everyday life, we shall develop the thesis that it is the supreme instrument man has fashioned by which, through the ages, he comes to terms with himself as he struggles to organize his existence within culture. It follows that, because education is indispensable to that struggle, even within the simplest of cultures, the only way we can hope ultimately to understand education is to subject it to philosophic scrutiny.

To prepare for this task we might find it helpful to observe four aspects of the great debate in education. We shall not be able to analyze them in detail, and we shall certainly not assume that our selections include all major issues that now perplex and divide citizens. Our purpose is merely to build a kind of stage setting within which the real drama of contemporary education may be enacted—a drama of both foreboding and hope about the deepest functions and purposes of human life as these are expressed through cultural self-awareness.

Here then are our examples:

1. How should American culture support and control education?
2. How and what should our youth learn?
3. How much and what kinds of academic freedom can we justify?
4. How should the community relate to the school?

Support and Control. We begin with the issue of support and control of education because it has been uppermost in the minds of millions. Parents who at another period might have been little concerned about education have become alarmed at the failure of their communities to provide adequate facilities for their children. It is common knowledge that schools in many parts of the country are overcrowded, that double sessions are chronic, that teaching staffs are short-handed and undertrained, and that such essential equipment as textbooks, laboratory materials, and desks are frequently insufficient, obsolete, or both. Figures compiled by the U.S. Office of Education show that the rapid increase in the birth rate since World War II has left the schools of the country tragically unprepared. For example, there was an increase of 13 percent in the elementary school population in the four short years 1946 to 1950; and it is estimated that by 1958 seven million additional children must be accommodated by our public schools. New buildings have been constructed far more slowly than the need requires, and the teacher shortage has become more alarming with each passing year.

Although the absolute expenditure on education has been higher in the years after than in the years before World War II, the dollar is worth much less, and most taxpayers spend less on education in proportion to their income than they did when the need was not so acute. It is astonishing to discover that the percentage of personal income spent on education was 2.2 in 1950-1951 as compared with 3.2 in 1937-1938 and that the great majority of states now devote a smaller percentage of their total income to education than they did during the great depression of the 1930's. Meanwhile, although teachers' salaries have risen sharply, so, too, has the cost of living. No wonder that young adults hesitate to enter teaching as a life career.

Now, there has been little disagreement among most people in America that this is a disgraceful situation (disgraceful, for example, that America continues to spend a substantially larger percentage of its total budget on alcoholic beverages than it does on education). True, a few extremists have wished to see public education almost if not entirely abolished. Some educators of standing have suggested that colleges and universities admit only a fraction of the number now admitted. Nevertheless, a remarkably wide consensus has prevailed that "something ought to be done" to expand facilities.

To be sure, "something" has been done. The National Citizens' Commission for the Public Schools, the National Education Association, the National Congress of Parents and Teachers—these and many other organizations, including local community groups all over the country, have worked hard and long, without, however, any assurance that they would find an even partial solution to the problem that so gravely distresses them.

Granting that workable solutions would not be easy at best, we must nevertheless recognize that the problem has been made infinitely harder by uncertainty and confusion as to how to approach it. Part of the difficulty has stemmed from a financial dilemma: although most parents would unquestionably endorse a better education for their children they have too often been unwilling to authorize even the small increases in local taxes essential to such improvement. For them, education—like virtue—has appeared fine in the abstract but not so fine when it reaches into their pocketbooks. In addition, they have not been at all agreed on the meaning of a "better" education. Influenced by the propaganda of taxpayers' leagues, which have operated in every corner of the country, they have often been persuaded that what the schools need is more efficiency, not more money; a heavier load for the present corps of teachers, not a larger corps; more inexpensive, conservative teaching methods, not more "new-fangled," expensive ways of learning.

The most controversial aspect of our first issue, however, has focused on the role of the federal government. Our public schools have a long tradition of local or, at widest, state autonomy. Federal aid for the public schools, except for special funds earmarked for special limited purposes (such as the free-milk program), has never been provided by the Congress. To be sure, bill after bill to provide such funds has been introduced. And fact after fact has been presented to prove the necessity for federal aid—particularly, that the poorer states simply cannot afford nearly the per capita expenditure on education that the richer states can, even though they spend a larger percentage of their total income for education. South Carolina is fairly typical. Recently it spent annually on education nearly a third more of its income than New York did. But at this time the proportion of the student population enrolled in high schools was less than half that of the country as a whole. Meanwhile, every federal-aid bill introduced in Congress has been decisively defeated.

Why have we failed to correct such inequities by the only feasible means, according to most experts—namely, by federal support? There are several reasons that relate to but extend beyond the general tradition of local or state authority. One is the strong objection of most Southern states (South Carolina is again conspicuous) on the ground that federal money would probably be allocated only on a basis of equality for white and Negro children. They fear federal aid would thus threaten still further the pattern of segregated education that the Supreme Court already weakened by its momentous decision on desegregation. Another is the opposition of some religious groups, who have insisted that, if federal aid is provided at all, it must be provided for parochial schools, too. But the most commonly offered reason has been advanced by many school leaders: they have feared that support by the federal government would lead inescapably to its control of education and, thus, to dictation of courses of study as well as of other policies that must be kept free from "bureaucratic encroachments."

Advocates of federal support have not been at all unanimous in their answers to such objections. Some have been willing to make concessions to supporters of segregation, to religious groups, or to both. Others have argued that federal aid need not involve federal control, so that this alleged danger would be avoided. Still others have not only admitted that some degree of control must accompany aid but have welcomed this necessity. The national government, they have maintained, has a right to share in determining the general conditions of so important a national institution as the public school.

But the issue of educational control is not confined to the role of the federal government. The responsibilities of control by authorities on all levels of the educational structure, right down to teachers, students, and parents, have been debated. We have traditionally assumed that school boards and administrators are the proper custodians of this control—or, on the college level, boards of trustees, presidents, and deans. But this assumption has come to be challenged. Who, after all, *should* have a right to educational authority if not those most immediately involved? Teachers have organized, a few of them into trade unions affiliated with labor organizations, for the express purpose of bringing their influence to bear not only on salaries, budgets, and conditions of service but on almost every phase of education. Students in some schools and colleges have formed councils that have had a considerable voice in the affairs of their institutions. Parents, too, have become more active: through their PTA's, through advisory councils, through community groups, they have insisted that the schools' policies and programs are their legitimate concern.

Amidst these conflicting trends we are left unsure of the locus and degree of control that are *really* legitimate. Not only has the question produced a variety of answers with regard to the responsibility of government but experts in school and university administration have failed to agree even on the principles that should prevail at the individual school level. One expert may resist encroachments by organized teachers; another may welcome their interest and newly found power. One would have students and parents and even teachers be merely the recipients of rules established at the top; another would encourage much more of their participation and authority.

In short, the problem of educational control, like that of support, not only remains unresolved but probably is now more widely contested than ever before in the history of our schools.

What and How to Learn. If our first issue is one of common concern, our second—what and how to learn—has generated even more excited controversy. The antithetical slogans that first occur to us as symbolizing this issue are much too simply called the "three R's" and "progressive education."

Is it not true, as so often charged, that our children learn the fundamental skills and the basic facts of history, science, and foreign language, far less adequately than our parents and grandparents learned them? Is it not true that young people today are less disciplined, less orderly, less respectful of law, custom, and morality? Is it not true that schools waste time and money on all kinds of frivolous if not meaningless activities?

And on the college level, do we not hear the charge that standards have declined, that classical, liberal education is being replaced by a sorry mixture of "practical" subjects and techniques that do anything but genuinely educate? Are not thousands of young adults every year receiving degrees, sometimes even doctorates, in highly specialized or vocational fields, having had scarcely any exposure either to the basic sciences, biological or physical, or to the humanities, philosophy, religion, literature, and the other arts? Finally, are not colleges of education themselves largely responsible for the decline of learning on the lower levels? Because these institutions have been captured by the "educationists," who are themselves "anti-intellectual," are not the teachers whom they train bound similarly to be "anti-intellectual"?

The state of conflict in American education is highlighted by the fact that for each of these heavily loaded accusations both lay citizens and professional educators have raised another accusation equally loaded but of opposite tenor. Are not children still forced to study a great number of subjects in which they have not the slightest degree of interest—to which, indeed, they respond with the most appalling boredom? Why is it, if this is not the case, that students so frequently detest every day of school, even to the point of committing widespread vandalism and worse delinquency? Is it not true, also, that the first objective of most secondary schools is to meet the requirements for college entrance (regardless of how many of their students plan to go to college) rather than to provide students with learnings relevant to the pressing problems and tasks they must confront as human beings living in a time of rapid change?

Further, can we deny that countless young people are seldom if ever exposed in their classrooms to the most serious disturbances of our contemporary world—to the tensions, for example, between capitalism and communism? Can we deny that many, though surely not all, teachers still consider that the only way to persuade students to learn is to punish them with low grades or other pains if they do not learn, and reward them with high grades or other pleasures if they do? Can we deny that again very many teachers conceive the "ideal" student to be the one who mirrors their own status in society and thus their own standards of "good" manners and "proper" behavior? Can we even deny that innumerable students, not only in the lower schools but in the schools of higher learning, are still evaluated primarily by their ability to reproduce from memory the contents of lectures, textbooks, or laboratory manuals?

Who, then, is right? The answer can be derived partly from objective evidence—evidence that research into school curriculums and methods is equipped to provide for citizens who are dispassionate enough to examine it. At another level, however, the answer cannot be derived from objective evidence, for it rests upon conflicting basic attitudes toward education. Here the cleavages are often very deep-seated. Usually they are only half articulate, and nearly always they resist purely logical analysis. Moreover, they are not confined to attitudes toward education alone. More fundamentally, they are cultural, deriving from the habits, the practices and routines, the implicit values that every person acquires from his human environment, that react in turn upon that environment, and that are an integral part of the institution of our culture called the school.

What is far from accurately regarded as the three-R's outlook, which has been so vocal and so vehement in American life, thus reflects an outlook much wider than the outlook on education. So, too, does the equally vocal and vehement outlook that we associate with an amorphous movement called "progressive education."

Academic Freedom. Our third issue, academic freedom, is, of course, closely related to our second. Nevertheless, those who align themselves on opposite sides of the curriculum-and-learning issue do not invariably align themselves on comparable sides of the academic-freedom issue. Some, though by no means all, of those educational leaders who firmly support a more conventional or even classical type of education also support the right of teachers and scholars to pursue and to believe the most heretical ideas. Conversely, some, though again by no means all, leaders in the "modern" group seem more ready to restrict or compromise their defense of academic freedom under the pressure of social circumstances. The alignments demonstrate that we cannot easily generalize the whole educational position from one element in it. The problem is too complex for that.

Academic freedom is not a recent problem. It has plagued American education throughout its history—and education everywhere long before the founding of the Republic. Nevertheless, in the decade since the close of World War II it assumed proportions and stimulated quarrels both within the profession and in the community at large which, like the first two issues, have seemed quite unprecedented.

In a number of communities, for example, hundreds of "questionable" books have been removed from library shelves. Magazines and textbooks formerly studied by millions of students have been placed on the forbidden list. Teachers and professors have been warned not to discuss certain controversial subjects in their classrooms, though the vast majority scarcely needed warning. Generously financed investigations by Congressional committees and by state legislatures across the nation have sought to ferret out "disloyal" teachers. Books written by distinguished university authorities have been banned from American libraries abroad. Films dealing with human birth and growth have been outlawed in certain schools at home. Study of the United Nations Educational, Scientific, and Cultural Organization has been virtually banned in at least one of the large school systems in America. Our largest educational organization, the National Education Association, has been accused by our largest patriotic organization, the American Legion, of "un-American" tendencies. Some educators of high rank have insisted, to be sure, that teachers are as free as ever to discuss controversial questions; yet surveys by the New York *Times* have revealed that few teachers conduct such discussions and that many of those who have conducted them have done so too innocuously to stir the thinking of young citizens. Indeed, the most serious aspect of the situation has probably been not the avalanche of direct attacks upon education or even the dismissals and other penalties that followed them but rather the negative effects of these measures: the reluctance of schools to study material or to try experiments that might be considered objectionable. For hundreds of school leaders, it has apparently seemed wiser to "play safe."

The issue of academic freedom raises searching questions about which Americans are no less at odds than they are about other educational issues. Is one school superintendent on solid ground when he insists that children must be "indoctrinated" in "the American way of life" in order to protect them against the poisonous effects of the "Communist" way? Is another superintendent closer to sound policy when he opposes indoctrination of any sort—when he argues that the first task of education is to provide the young not with preconceived answers or with doctrines acceptable to influential sections of the community but with opportunities to examine, to criticize, to consider "all sides" of every vital problem?

Shall we support the position of the National Education Association that Communists must under no circumstances be permitted to teach in our schools? Or is the view of the American Association of University Professors more defensible when it takes a stand in behalf of any teacher proven to be professionally qualified, regardless of legal political affiliation? How shall we evaluate the distinction that some educators make in protecting the right to express "heresy" in classrooms but not the right to engage in "conspiracy"? If scrupulously tested by the professional behavior of the so-called conspirators who have already been penalized, is this distinction sound? Or does its application inevitably generate suspicion, as other educators argue, and thus weaken academic freedom for all teachers, the "heretics" included?

We must conclude from these random questions that the meaning of academic freedom in particular is tied firmly to the meaning of human freedom in general. It is thus tied to the Bill of Rights, especially to the First Amendment—which guarantees freedom of speech without recrimination—and to the Fifth Amendment—which protects the accused citizen, and hence presumably the teacher, from being compelled to testify against himself. It is tied to the Cold War and to the terrifying fear of a hot war between the Western nations and the Communist bloc. It is tied to the complex problem of human reasonableness—of how far, in the long run, individuals freely exposed in the market place of "evil" as well as "good" ideas can be trusted to repudiate the former and embrace the latter. It is tied to the role of the community—to the power of pressure groups to affect school policy and to the correct role of education in responding to that power.

Relation of the Community to the School. Thus, we have reached our final issue in the great debate. Discussion of the role of the community offers an opportunity also for recapitulation of the first three issues. The first issue is related to it because the question of how far we shall support and control education is clearly one that involves the financial and political responsibilities of citizens all the way from the one-room country school in Missouri or Maine to the Office of Education in Washington. The second is related because the nature of the curriculum and the methods by which knowledge shall be communicated bear directly upon what most parents doubtless consider the prime obligation of the school: to prepare children for effective life in their own small or large communities. And the third issue is related because academic freedom is inextricably involved not only with the nature of curriculum and methods but also with the ideas about human freedom assumed more or less clear-mindedly by these communities.

We may conclude that since the first three issues provoke diverse reactions so also must our fourth. Let us consider, as an example, the role of pressure groups, mentioned above. How shall the school respond to them? Shall it simply refuse to recognize them? Or, if this is impossible, shall it deliberately encourage pressure groups of every kind—from reactionary to radical—to express their special interests? But how shall they express them? Through membership on school boards? Through faculty representation? Through speeches in assemblies, distribution of literature in classes, membership in PTA's? Through invitations to students to work in their own groups?

With this last question, the issue broadens still further. It now becomes a matter not only of how far the community should enter the school but of how far the school should enter the community. Some educators believe that the classroom should be widened to include study of and direct experience with every phase of the environment: with nature itself (through studies like biology and geography), and also (through studies like sociology and the arts) with race relations, factories, farms, mines, social agencies, theaters, and the United Nations. Other educators are militantly opposed to this approach. The school, they contend, must not usurp the functions of other institutions. Social studies and similar courses properly have little if any place on the lower levels. On the upper levels, the primary responsibility of education is to train the mind, not to clutter it with such trivialities as "current events" and "work experience." For these educators, the whole plan of "modern" schools to widen the educational circumference—to impinge, let us say, upon family life—is wrong. It will lead, they insist, to the ruin of education.

The issue of school-and-community becomes even more distressing when we observe the controversy over the place of religion in American public schools. Although religion is certainly one of the dominant aspects of community life and although, in deference to this dominance, the doctrine of separation of church and state has never been strictly observed in our public schools, as evidenced by required Bible reading, celebrations of religious festivals (notably Christmas), and similar widespread practices, nevertheless, religion has traditionally been considered outside the scope of public education. In recent years, new pressures by religious organizations in many communities have made additional inroads against this tradition: released time from regular school hours permits many thousands of children to receive weekly instruction under theological auspices; formal religious exercises in public schools appear to be increasing; and religious groups have often been successful in censoring courses of study, winning decisive positions on school boards, and otherwise influencing formally secular policies.

But even those who would zealously guard these secular policies do not agree on the school's role in regard to religion. They do agree, to be sure, that the public school must not indoctrinate in any sectarian creed. They disagree, however, on the question of what, if anything, should be done to inculcate "moral and spiritual values," which, more and more educators admit, have a rightful place in the schools. To give these values a place in the curriculum various educators advocate teaching "about" the religions of the world without advocating any. Some college teachers who support this position conduct courses that enable students to compare the great religions by firsthand contact with leaders, doctrines, and ceremonials of different religious groups. Other teachers believe that even study of comparative religion would set a dangerous precedent, and they limit their definitions of "moral and spiritual values" to experiences that, presumably, are independent of any religious faith.

An ironical alignment emerges from the related issues of school-and-community and school-and-religion. On the one side are many organized religionists, who often criticize the schools for usurping community functions, who believe that the schools should confine themselves to teaching academic subjects, precepts, and skills, who therefore almost invariably oppose the inclusion in the curriculum of such problems as sex education (on the grounds that these problems are solely the responsibility of the family) but who are nevertheless eager to draw closer the ties between the school and the religious community. On the other side are many leaders of "modern education," who endorse closer school-community cooperation but who continue to oppose the schools' cooperation with one of the community's most influential institutions—organized religion itself.

We are forced to conclude that on the broad issue of community and school relations we in America are not more agreed or more consistent than we are on other educational issues. On this question the policies we endorse and the practices we employ are sometimes opportunistic, sometimes vacillating, sometimes merely vague. Whether American education should immerse itself more and more fully in the life stream of the people or whether it should isolate itself for the purpose of performing a function that can somehow be defined as "distinctively and purely educational" is a question that we seem thus far unable to decide.

What shall be said of these broadly sketched differences, considered in themselves and in cultural perspective? The fact that the issues overlap has been made clear by our discussion. That still other issues could be selected for attention should also be clear. The significance of the issues chosen is that they reveal both healthy and unhealthy symptoms in the education of our period. The healthy symptoms are: growing vitality of public interest, growing public discussion, growing concern over the activities and purposes of a great institution—an institution that, after all, the people have themselves created and have thus far more or less conscientiously maintained. The unhealthy symptoms are: increasing strain, bewilderment, suspicion, and uncertainty in regard to both the means and the ends of education in America.

Both kinds of symptoms exist in the culture at least to the same degree that they exist in education. For, as stated above and as we demonstrate in subsequent chapters, it is the culture in which education germinates and flowers. It is the culture, also, upon which education exerts, in turn, a nourishing or debilitating influence. Thus, the problem of aid and control is grounded not only in the broad cultural dilemma of centralized versus decentralized authority but in the specific political dilemma of more or less federal control. The problem of curriculum-and-learning is part of the much more inclusive problem of education's essential role in the American culture: granted that it is always partly both, is this role *primarily* one of transmitting cultural habits and skills, of teaching individuals to adjust to their heritage; or is it *primarily* one of teaching individuals how to cope critically and actively with their total environment, how to change and guide their culture as it evolves through succeeding generations? The problem of academic freedom is inseparable from the wider question of the rights of citizenship: considering the obligations involved in his relations with the entire community, to how much "freedom" of speech and other behavior has the teacher a right? Finally, the relations of school and community are but one aspect of the interrelations and interdependence of the parts of a much larger cultural whole: to what extent and in what ways should the school, as an important one of these parts, isolate itself from or relate itself to that larger whole? Through all these issues, moreover, runs a simple but still more searching problem: what, after all, do we *mean* by "good" education?

Expressed in these terms, the four issues we have raised by way of illustration are shown to be, at root, philosophic issues. We do not say that philosophy can resolve all of them—certainly not to everyone's satisfaction. We do say that without philosophy there is no hope of their being resolved at all. For philosophy requires us to express the beliefs and the grounds for the beliefs upon which ultimately rest all theories of authority, all theories of social change, all theories of freedom, all theories of the community, all theories of the good life.

To undertake the philosophic task we must, however, have at our command certain conceptual tools with which to analyze and formulate the meanings that constitute the substance of all theories. In the pages that now follow, our central aim is to select and sharpen some of the most useful of these tools.

PART ONE

PHILOSOPHY, CULTURE, AND EDUCATION

CHAPTER 2

Philosophy: Its Import and Its Functions

PHILOSOPHY DEALS WITH MATTERS OF LIFE AND DEATH. IT SEEKS to ask and to answer questions that are the most stubborn, baffling, and disturbing in the history of the human race. Yet they cannot be avoided. So long as cultures are confronted with perplexities, obstacles, choices, men must think as well as they are able, and they must act in terms of their thinking. And when are men not so confronted?

Education, too, shares these perplexities, obstacles, choices. In some form, education is infused with all phases of all cultures, simple and complex alike. Therefore, it can no more escape philosophy than cultures can escape it.

But philosophy can be used in many ways—inefficiently or efficiently, vaguely or clearly, haphazardly or systematically. If we are to move forward from our starting point, we should try to make the second choices among these pairs of alternatives our way. That is, we should bring philosophy to bear upon the problems of education as efficiently, clearly, and systematically as we can.

Let us, then, consider some of the more elementary characteristics of this powerful discipline. As we proceed our philosophic definitions and classifications are to be *used*. They are to function throughout the remainder of this book as tools of analysis, criticism, synthesis, and evaluation.

If we are to be in a position to grasp their significance for the philosophy of education it is especially important that these definitions and classifications be placed within the *setting of culture*. Since this is the principal task of Chapter 3, the present chapter should be regarded as integral with it. Each needs to be understood in relation to the other.

Three main topics are considered here:

1. philosophy: the expression of beliefs;
2. philosophy: its branches; and
3. the relations of philosophy.

Philosophy: The Expression of Beliefs

When Do We Philosophize? You and I have often tried to phrase, in terms of our own experience and background, certain beliefs that concern us dearly—beliefs about religion, love, freedom of speech, politics, labor unions—each involving questions important to thinking, maturing people everywhere. In fact, most typical groups of people, whatever their interests and ages, include individuals of varying opinions who, from time to time, wish to express their beliefs concerning some basic policy. Whether we call it philosophy or by some other name, *we all philosophize whenever we try to express the things we believe about our lives and about our relations to the rest of life.*

Educators are certainly no different from others in holding beliefs and utilizing them. When they philosophize about the schools they simply concentrate upon one very important area, an area in which people not only have strong views but are also exceptionally quick to tell them to one another. Most of the time such expressions of belief are not *called* philosophy. Often they are made by practical-minded school executives or by certain professors of the "science" of education who love to assert that philosophy is an outworn subject.

Philosophy, then, is inseparable from living experience. However implicit, unexpressed in definite terms, our particular philosophy may be, it is always in the background, helping to shape and being shaped by the tangible means through which we carry on our day-to-day responsibilities. In every phase of life—material, spiritual, lay, professional—we believe certain things about the activities we perform. And these beliefs, usually to a far greater extent than we realize, not only reflect our day-to-day activities but in turn mold and direct these activities.

As a matter of fact, we could not do without our beliefs. A businessman would fail if he did not assume and act upon the legitimacy of making a profit from his enterprise. A conscientious preacher would suffer severely if he felt that he ought to re-examine his faith every Sunday morning before services. A school principal might accomplish little if he thought that his school rested upon a crumbling foundation of beliefs. There is nothing more necessary to mental health, to personal and social harmony, to consistency of action and purpose than to be fairly well satisfied with the beliefs that underlie everyday conduct. They constitute a type of habit-pattern that enables us to proceed with some degree of efficiency, orderliness, and confidence in what we are doing.

Conflicts in Belief. If, however, it is true that we take our beliefs for granted much of the time, it is equally true that few of us can take them for granted all of the time. Either or both of two main causes may jolt us into sudden questioning of what, up to this point, we have been inclined to accept without much question.

The first cause is the discovery that one's cherished patterns conflict with someone else's patterns, a discovery that is frequently made by individuals in interaction with other individuals. Sometimes it is made by reading a provocative book, seeing an exciting play; occasionally by contact with a stimulating teacher or by participating in the far from trivial pastime of college "bull sessions." Most often the discovery is made when we are thrust into a different environment where, whether we welcome them or not, we must make economic, moral, or other readjustments in order to fit harmoniously within the new configurations demanded by the new group.

The second cause is the discovery, often a powerful one, that our beliefs are in contradiction not so much with those of another person as with one another. Then we are rudely awakened to an internal inconsistency by finding that what we believe is not consistent at all points with how we behave. This is another way of saying that what we *profess* to believe and what we *really* believe simply do not harmonize.

Often we make this second discovery after having made the first one—that is, by perceiving acute differences of belief between ourselves and other people. Whatever the exact steps, the important point is that something like this happens at one time or another to most of us. At first, no doubt, we are just a little annoyed because if the differences become meaningful enough they disturb our sense of tranquillity—our satisfaction with the beliefs we have hitherto accepted as adequate to our accustomed pattern of life.

Levels of Belief. Whether we welcome the task or not, many of us, nevertheless, are compelled to decide, more or less deliberately, what we shall do about some disequilibrium of our beliefs. This decision is not simply a choice between agreement and disagreement, between Yes and No. Theoretically, we face a number of levels of choice:

1. We may refuse to allow a disturbance of belief to affect us after the first moment of reaction. Instead, after begrudging it a minimum of attention, we may settle back upon the old comfortable cushion and pray that nothing will happen to upset us again. Typically, we tend to resent any disturbance of our belief habit-pattern; and, the more deeply entrenched it becomes, the more we are resentful. This, the least reflective level, may be called the *complacent* choice.

2. We may feel compelled to analyze our beliefs with some care—to ask why they seem to be in conflict either with other beliefs of our own or with those of different individuals—but this examination will not necessarily lead to resolution of the conflict. It ends with the examination itself so that, in a sense, we have taken apart our beliefs but have not put them back together. This is the *negative* choice.

3. We may decide that our entire body of major beliefs is now open to such severe question that the most honest course to take is to doubt them. This takes us one step beyond mere negativism in that we are now definite in our *dis*belief. This may be termed the *skeptical* choice.

4. We may reach the opinion, after careful examination, that it is simply impossible to accept one set of beliefs in preference to another. We cannot decide whether they are true *or* false. Neither affirming nor denying, we remain as neutral and noncommittal as humanly possible. This is the *agnostic* choice.

5. We may fasten together many different beliefs, not fusing them into a harmonious pattern but keeping them as separate pieces, ready to shift about into different positions as the need arises. This is the *eclectic* choice.

6. We may decide, despite or perhaps because of our analysis, that our original pattern of beliefs is on the whole sound and worth conserving against any significant change. As against choice 1 above, we make this judgment not before but *after* careful consideration. This is the *conservative* choice.

7. We may decide to test out degrees of rearrangements of the pattern as a whole—a process that involves some trimming of its original elements, some gradual improvement and modification. This is the *liberal* choice.

8. We may conclude that what is needed is to substitute for the pattern in which we have been putting our trust another pattern—one that was widely followed in some earlier age. We return to this pattern, however, not because it is old but because it is to us more permanently satisfying than any other. This is the *regressive* choice.

9. We may decide, finally, to substitute a fairly new pattern—new not merely in the sense that it is reconstructed in a thoroughgoing fashion from the one we have been holding but in the sense that it is different from any that has been commonly held thus far by other people either in our own period or in past periods of history. This may be called the *radical* choice.

Qualifications Among Choices. These main choices, which we are compelled to weigh, are not, of course, as mutually exclusive as they seem when stated as generalizations. Of course, they overlap in actual experience; at best, they are rough approximations of alternative emphases. Also, we may shift from one level to another or possibly combine two or more. Strictly speaking, the final choice above—to consider one—is possible only theoretically. Since no one is able to invent a completely original pattern of beliefs, it is possible to contend that the "radical" overlaps with at least one or two other choices—the "liberal," for example. Again, the "regressive" choice is, in one sense, "new" if the person who accepts it is not yet aware of its ancestry. Equally true is the fact that even the most far-reaching change one individual makes in beliefs will in all probability be made at about the same time by other people. Beliefs, as we shall note further, are *results as well as causes* of social and other environmental changes to which whole populations are subject more or less at once.

Yet, after every qualification has been considered, we return to the crucial fact that whenever we are shocked into awareness of our beliefs we cannot escape responding to our awareness. In the last analysis, this simply means that we must choose, with varying degrees of deliberation, among such levels as we have summarized above.

How often we do so depends both upon our sensitivity to the impact of conflicting beliefs and upon the frequency or force of that impact. In times of severe tension and rapid change, such as the present period, the compulsion to do so is greater than in times of comparative stability. The probabilities are, however, that most of us do not make any far-reaching choice more than once or twice in our whole lives, if we do so at all. Moreover, the number of times we are deeply concerned tends to diminish as we grow older, as our patterns of belief become increasingly fixed. Typically, we are more and more often drawn to settle upon the *first* level of choice (the complacent), less and less often upon the *last* (the radical).

"Expression" Defined. We have now enriched our earlier statement about the meaning of philosophy as the expression of beliefs. The term "expression" covers a number of factors, all of which, in the last analysis, are important. Taken together, they point to the recognition that philosophy is the art not merely of *having* beliefs regarding life, or even of *articulating* them, but of deliberately inquiring into the nature of beliefs and thus of *judging* them in order to determine whether they are worth holding.

Philosophy, to put the point differently, operates on more than one level of significance. The truism that everyone has a philosophy of life means no more than that everyone holds certain beliefs about the things and events relating to his experience. This remains a fact however often —or seldom—his beliefs are expressed to anyone's satisfaction. But as he develops awareness of differences, of clashes or inconsistencies, the philosophy that has thus far lain largely on an implicit level tends to become more and more explicit. Thus, the need increases for searching analysis, perhaps for amendment, even for drastic reorganization. The entire process, though it may eventuate in sharply diverse results for different individuals, is in the richest sense the art of philosophy.

Educational Philosophy: Its Need and Function. Just as philosophy is by no means the prerogative of professional theorists, so the philosophy of education is by no means the private domain of specialists in this field. Educational beliefs are the unavoidable concern of everyone connected with the schools. And, since almost every individual in America is at some time or other connected with them, almost every individual is at some time concerned with their correlative philosophies.

This common situation has both its fortunate and unfortunate results. Fortunate, because in a democracy, if anywhere, all citizens deserve not only to possess beliefs about so universal an institution as the school but also to voice them as often and vigorously as they wish. Unfortunate, because, although everyone feels he is entitled to express his beliefs, too few do so with much discrimination or respect for the beliefs of others. An immense amount of philosophizing is expressed in our halls of learning by people who profess impatience with philosophy—but who never recognize that philosophy is what they are practicing. Here is one reason why educators are accused of so much confusion and superficial talk.

The moral to be drawn is that, *since nearly all of us philosophize about education anyway, we should try to do as good a job of it as we can.* Assuming that you and I are genuinely concerned with the welfare of the schools, the least we can try to do is to become aware of and intelligently satisfied with our beliefs about them. Instead of hugging them tightly to ourselves or expressing them with too much dogmatism, we might well inquire into the structure of our educational philosophies. We might compare them with one another. We might ask whether education would not profit by thorough diagnoses leading to consideration of alternative results.

To accomplish this better job, however, it is not enough to exhort ourselves to do so. A main reason why we often philosophize badly is that we do not know how to philosophize well. It is one forward step to recognize that—in some sense and at some time—virtually all human beings perform that function. It is another step to recognize that there are a number of levels of belief among which we may—indeed *must*—choose. Several steps remain, however, before we are rightly qualified to philosophize about the schools in any adequate way.

As we climb the stairs toward a more substantial conception, let us remember that we are at no time departing from our original conception. We shall simply try to widen and deepen it—to understand more thoroughly what we do when we analyze and synthesize our patterns of belief about learning, teaching, the whole complex of habits, attitudes, and practices embraced by education.

Philosophy: Its Branches

Ramifications of Meaning. One of the rewards of the study of philosophy, for those who are willing to be patient, is that as we move slowly along we find that philosophy develops ever wider ramifications of meaning. The degrees of sophistication and critical awareness, of agreements and disagreements in the expression of our beliefs, vary sharply among the most highly trained theologians, artists, and scientists as well as among ordinary individuals.

The same plurality of meanings applies to the nature of "belief." That we all have beliefs of some sort is undeniable. But what it is we imply when we say we believe something can hardly be taken for granted unless we are willing to be satisfied with a naive philosophic attitude. If you have ever attended a large political rally, you have no doubt been impressed by the earnestness of the speakers. Each seemed to be quite convinced of his own views. For him, they were certainly *real,* and not only real but *true,* and not only true but, in the most earnest sense of the word, *good.* Whether each speaker was equally sincere or equally able to defend his reasons for so regarding his views may have been difficult to determine from the brief record of their meeting. But that each speaker did thus regard them, or at least wanted you thus to regard them, must have been apparent.

Such beliefs are not peculiar to philosophers, however. Is it not a common observation that the beliefs ordinarily professed seem true to us who hold them—seem so true that, whether we are followers of the Republican Party, of Christian Science, or of the college elective system, we are inclined to look upon disbelievers as victims of the false? Is it not apparent that the institutions of culture, the structures of nature, the practices and faiths of men seem real to their participants—so real that to think anything else is to be deceived by sheer illusion? Is it not an observation, also, that we often regard certain of these institutions, structures, practices, and faiths as essentially good—so good that those who maintain very different beliefs about them seem to be nothing less than believers in the bad?

What Are the Grounds of Belief? Yet, when we have said this much about the nature of beliefs we have scarcely done more than remove their outermost skin. The core of the problem is obviously to determine *why* we are justified in calling one belief false and another true, one bad and another good, one illusory and another real. What does "X" mean educationally when he announces that an experiment with Negro students proves the *falsehood* of the hereditary theory of intelligence? What does "Y" mean when he declares that a certain community-oriented school is concerned with the *concrete* world? Or "Z" when he insists that the study of Latin is definitely *wrong*? "X," "Y," and "Z" are hardly entitled to ask others to agree with them if they can offer no better reason than simply their own inscrutable wisdom. This is the way too many people, including some educators, are inclined to meet inquisitors. *What* are their grounds? *Why* are they sure?

Through the many centuries of philosophy's history, the attack upon these plaguing questions has been made from a number of fronts. Philosophy has been divided into specialized branches, methods, and divisions, each of which concentrates upon one major area of belief. This is an admission, perhaps, that the question is simply too complex to be treated as a whole. As to the number of such divisions philosophers have differed among themselves—some speaking of four or five, others of as many as eight or nine.

For our purposes we consider but three, regarding others as subsidiary to them. These are: (1) study of the principles of reality; (2) study of the principles of knowledge; and (3) study of the principles of value.

The historic labels we shall use for these branches of philosophic investigation are *ontology, epistemology,* and *axiology*. The task of these branches is to clarify as far as possible our underlying criteria or principles of belief about the areas of reality, truth, or value respectively. Each is indispensable to education not only in theory, but in practice as well.*

Study of beliefs about reality—ontology

Let us suppose you are gazing intently for a moment at an object that you take for granted so much of the time as seldom to think of its existence at all—the floor in the room where you are reading this book. Suppose you ask yourself to describe its simple characteristics: well, it is

* The beginning student in philosophy should look beyond this chapter for the meaning of philosophy in general and of such divisional terms as "ontology," "epistemology," and "axiology" in particular. For suggested supplementary reading, he may consult the list of sources cited under "What to Read" in the Appendix.

solid, flat, and smooth, you say; its color is brown; whether concrete or wood it surely is a substance of a thoroughly material quality. This is what almost anyone would mean, no doubt, by calling the floor *real.*

Suppose, however, that at this point a teacher of physics enters the room. You ask him the same question that you asked yourself. He replies that, strictly speaking, the floor is made of molecules; that molecules consist of atoms; atoms of electrons, protons, neutrons; and these, finally, of electrical energy alone. Thus the *real* floor—the "energetic" floor—is to him not at all identical with that which a layman apparently perceives.

Or, let us consider the floor from another point of view. The color of the floor, he tells you, is merely light waves of a certain length striking your retina, being then translated through your optical nerve into visual response. Do you not in this case, therefore, contribute something *to* its nature through a nervous system which, after all, is peculiarly yours?

Thus, it would seem that you are standing on at least three floors rather than one. The *first* is "out there" in the material world. The *second* is the construction of the scientist—certainly not the one you perceive directly with your eyes. The *third* is the product of external fact *plus* your own nervous response. Which, then, *is* the floor—or are all three blended into one? *This is the task of ontology: to determine what is real about any and all aspects of the world.*

Ontology in Education. It should be apparent even from this simple illustration that schools, too, are confronted with problems of reality. For they deal at every level with countless objects of nature—inanimate and animate, subhuman and human—and the scope of their ontological concern reaches as far as the kind of universe they wish children to accept. We may recall the profoundly hostile conceptions of reality that divide Catholic parochial schools from public schools; the widespread influence of such superstitions as astrology and palmistry upon millions of "educated" adults; the inability of many teachers to articulate the most elementary traits of existence (for example, what it means to say that nature everywhere *evolves*) as these have been brought to focus by the microscopes and telescopes of science. Such are the products of an educational system that too seldom thoroughly examines its own body of ontological beliefs.

It is commonly claimed that the schools do not prepare the young to face the "real world." This is in a measure true. Curiously, however, those who shout this accusation loudest are often themselves victims of ontological myopia. They gaze upon reality with vision distorted by prejudice, propaganda, worship of custom, or other influences of which they may not even be aware. Often they are more in need of diagnosis than the schools they criticize.

"Education for what is real" is, then, a statement of one major obligation.* We can hope to meet it successfully not by yielding to warped conceptions of the real but by utilizing constantly the service that philosophy, particularly ontology, is best qualified to give us.

Metaphysics and Cosmology. We are now ready to take another step. The general study of reality can be approached by means of even more specialized terms, two of which—*metaphysics* and *cosmology*—are widely used in philosophic discourse.

The first is defined in various ways, sometimes as a synonym for ontology itself. Literally, however, metaphysics means "beyond the physical"; and even today many people associate it with some sort of elusive, esoteric art—with an attempt to discover "realms of being" quite outside the realm of everyday experience. In this sense, metaphysics is strictly *one kind* of ontology, an "other-worldly" as opposed to a "this-worldly" kind. Ontology, as such, does not prejudge the question of what the principles of existence may turn out to be. Rather, it searches for them wherever they are and whatever their forms—be they physical or spiritual, one or many, fluctuating or permanent. If some philosophers believe that reality at its most real is metaphysical—that it transcends the fleeting events of everyday experience—others are just as emphatic in holding that such "fleeting events" are the only ones that exist.

Cosmology centers attention upon those characteristics of reality that are cosmic in scope, that seem to disclose a universe of system and order. No doubt, the aim of most ontological quests in intellectual history has been for a cosmology. There are exceptions, however. One may conceivably be satisfied to determine the character of particular things and limited spheres; in this regard cosmology, too, is subsidiary to ontology. For the latter is equally interested in *both* the particulars and the universals of reality. It does not assume, necessarily, an all-embracing cosmos any more than it assumes, with metaphysics, the primacy of an "other-worldly" realm.

How, then, are these subsidiaries of ontology also important to the schools? They are important whenever children or adults are taught to

* See Earl C. Kelley, *Education for What Is Real.*

believe in a realm of eternal existence beyond the here-and-now. Important whenever they learn that the world of which they are part is a vast, ultimately perfect harmony of order and law. Important when, on the contrary, they are told that neither eternity nor cosmic harmony is a demonstrable fact. Important, in short, whenever or however their minds are conditioned to such beliefs of metaphysics or cosmology as assure them that here, indeed, is the only *real* reality.

Study of beliefs about knowledge—epistemology

So far as education is concerned, the problem of knowledge with which epistemology deals is at least as crucial as the problem of reality. Reduced to elementary terms, *it is epistemology that gives the teacher the assurance that he is conveying the truth to his students*. Are there principles upon which he can rely when going about the crucial business of developing that most precious of possessions—human knowledge? Or, must he simply trust his "intuition," his sensations, the opinions of his superiors, faith in some "infallible" document, or still other tests that happen to be conveniently at hand?

In relation to the questions we have just asked, we may note these four familiar remarks:

1. "You can't kid me, brother; I *know* a crook the moment I see one."
2. "Of course I *know* she was cribbing; I saw her."
3. "Certainly I *know* what I'm talking about; doesn't the Constitution say so itself?"
4. "We *know* the bridge is safe because six of us just crossed it."

In each of these instances, the speaker "knows." In each instance, however, his reason for knowing is obviously different from the other instances. The first rests upon "common sense" or some other judgment that is fairly spontaneous and personal: plainly one does not rely solely upon observation in such a case; one does not literally *see* a crook unless in the very act of committing a crime. The second instance, on the contrary, is based upon direct observation: the speaker asserts a truth precisely because his senses have reported to him what he sees. The third rests upon prestige and authority, upon a revered document—hence, not directly upon either "common sense" or observation. The fourth instance suggests that knowledge is the product of tested experience, in which sense perception is an ingredient but in which the effect of what happens is the basic measure of truth. Behind each instance (and it is easy to add others) lies some kind of belief about how and when we know in contrast with how and when we do not. In short, we believe "truths" because, consciously or not, we hold certain epistemological criteria *of* belief.

We cannot escape such criteria. Suppose we accept a belief as true at face value. If we do we are probably following the line of least resistance, satisfied with the lowest level of philosophic expression—complacency. If we do not we are faced with the necessity of analyzing our principles to determine whether we can accept as true what, thus far, we have accepted without doubt.

Logic and Semantics. We shall have occasion to note how closely epistemology is related to the other two main branches of philosophy, ontology and axiology. In this section we are more concerned to note how *logic* and *semantics,* though sometimes regarded as distinct branches of philosophy, may be regarded as subsidiary to epistemology, just as metaphysics and cosmology are regarded as subsidiary to ontology.

Logic is concerned with the reasoning *process* and may be used to demonstrate that, however accurate a person's reasoning may be, he does not thereby necessarily attain the truth. One authority may argue, for example, that since children have low intelligence quotients because of bad environments, therefore Johnny has a low I.Q. because of a bad environment. In this case, the observer is reasoning with complete logical accuracy, but he is not *necessarily* telling the truth about any of the facts. Thus, the precise relations between logic and epistemology are not simple. But if, by careful attention to *how* we think, we are enabled better to detect strengths and weaknesses in *what* we think, logic becomes a useful technique in the determination of knowledge. It establishes rules for connecting links in a chain of thought so that they can be depended upon to hold fast. These rules enable us to recognize flaws and weaknesses that may appear in the chain.

The two traditional types of logic—deductive and inductive—both illustrate this function. *Deductive logic* proceeds from general premises to particular conclusions (the illustration regarding Johnny's intelligence is a common form). *Inductive logic* proceeds from particular data to general conclusions (the fourth remark above, concerning men crossing a bridge, is typical). Logic helps to make us more conscious of how we reach sound or unsound beliefs about the true or false; in this respect it is not only a legitimate but an indispensable aid to epistemology.

Semantics, which has elements in common with both epistemology and logic, has become something of a fad in America. Centering upon the problem of what words signify, it examines the connections of languages with events, the relation of concrete terms to abstractions, the devices that serve to conceal facts behind confusing and deceptive smoke screens of words, and other difficulties that block common understanding. Some semanticists, like some logicians, might object to regarding their field as a subdivision of epistemology; and no doubt the connections between the two are far from elementary. Nevertheless, it would not be difficult to demonstrate that semantics is also concerned with beliefs about knowledge. How, for example, can we discover measures by which to determine: first, whether what we try to communicate coincides with what we *mean;* and, second, whether what we mean coincides with the facts or events that our words *represent*?

That logic and semantics, like epistemology, are necessary tools in education can be easily illustrated. To learn how to reason from step to step, to detect common fallacies in thinking, to practice the inductive method of arriving at results in laboratories and classrooms, to appreciate the necessity of cautious reliance upon past deductions—all these are logically indispensable. Equally useful to education is the way in which semantics helps to clarify our meanings—for example, to detect words so vague or abstract as to have no relation to actual experience, to appreciate how language is colored by the milieu in which it is used, the social class to which the user and his audience belong, or the perhaps unconscious motivations of a speaker or writer. All of these and still other contributions that the study of beliefs about knowledge makes to effective schooling are demonstrated many times in subsequent pages.

Study of beliefs about value—axiology

Axiology, the last major branch of philosophy, is a term including the study of beliefs about value. It is subdivided into three fields, in each of which values are predominant: (1) moral conduct, (2) esthetic expression, and (3) socio-political life. Problems of each of these fields have been treated ordinarily by three special disciplines: (1) *ethics,* (2) *esthetics,* and (3) *socio-political philosophy*. We have chosen, however, to regard them as having one denominator in common—that of value itself. Thus, they may be regarded as subsidiary to axiology, as logic and semantics are regarded as subsidiary to epistemology.

The problem of axiology is to clarify the criteria or principles by which we determine what is good in human conduct, what is beautiful in art, what is right in social organization, and, finally, what these have in common as well as what distinguishes them from one another. The significance of axiology for education is, then, *to examine and integrate these values as they enter into the lives of people through the channels of the school.*

What Is "Good"? The way in which the axiologist determines what is "good" is by no means always simple. Just as those who have not explicitly philosophized may suppose that anything we "know" is in some sense "true," so at first glance it is quite easy for us to suppose that anything we "value" is in some sense "good." On second thought, however, we discover that "good," too, has a wide range of meaning. Let us consider the implications of these remarks made casually in the course of a day by an imaginary child:

1. "Gee, this ice cream's *good.*"
2. "All right, mama, I'll be *good* and obey you."
3. "That was mighty *good* medicine; it cured me in no time."
4. "Boy, wasn't that song *good*?"
5. "What're you reading, Dad? Oh, 'The *Good* Society.'"

The implications contained within these and other apparently simple meanings of one word have led to the development of elaborate philosophic doctrines. Thus, the first statement suggests a theory technically called *hedonism*—the theory that only what is pleasurable can really justify the label "good." No doubt the hedonist can argue a strong case, but he would be challenged by consistent believers in the value epitomized by the second statement. In that case good conduct is judged by the standard of someone in authority, a standard that may extend so far beyond the home as to circumscribe the conduct of millions of subjects in a state. The third statement illustrates what ethicists sometimes call an *instrumental* good, a means to some desired end. The fourth implies two criteria rather than one: an *immediate* good (as an end in itself rather than as a merely useful means) and an *esthetic* good, a certain kind of "taste." The final statement signifies a *social* valuation; the author of such a book is writing not of the good of individuals alone but of the good or goods relating to the organized associations of many people at once.

This final example helps us to understand why we have need for such a comprehensive term as axiology; here *both* ethical and social values are included under one caption. How completely the values we hold interweave with values of the home, neighborhood, city, and state is a fact no teacher, for example, could possibly ignore. To consider the values of art in isolation is also unsound. We must ask whether they, too, do not arise in social media—whether the painter, composer, poet, or architect is not always conditioned by the interrelations of human experience at the same time that he *re*conditions these interrelations.

Thus, like the issues arising in the first two branches of philosophy, the issues of axiology carry us far afield. Moreover, as we detect the complexity of values, we seek their overlapping as well as their distinctive qualities. In the case of education, we ask and try to answer such questions as these: What are the grounds upon which schools confidently and traditionally teach that certain rules of morality are good and others are bad? That certain kinds of literature are beautiful and others are ugly? That certain forms of government are right and others are wrong?

The Relations of Philosophy

Were we to continue now the process of dividing and subdividing, we should be misrepresenting philosophy. We should be giving the impression that it is solely a series of specializations rather than equally a subject concerned with *connections among* beliefs.

If, in recent years, philosophy has seemed more and more to confine itself to the less and less, the same trend is noticeable in other fields of scholarship and research. Like many experts, philosophers have seemed to delight in narrowness rather than breadth; in a "trade" vocabulary rather than ordinary language; in the life of the "ivory tower" rather than that of the market place. In some respects this is perfectly legitimate; as our knowledge of the modern world has increased, the criteria by which we judge it have also become increasingly complex and technical.

The history of philosophy attests, however, to its age-old concern with the totality of life—in fact, as intimated by our brief reference to cosmology, even with the totality of the universe. In terms of our original conception of philosophy, we are concerned not merely to express many *heterogeneous* beliefs but to determine how far these are *homogeneous.* This is all that is meant by "system" in philosophy. It is an effort to bring all important human thought into some kind of design, to create what is aptly called in German a *Weltanschauung,* a unified view of the world.

The reader will observe frequently throughout this book that the philosophy of education is as much interested in such an effort as it is in utilizing such specialized tools as axiology. In this chapter, however, we discuss primarily philosophy in its general sense, by considering: (1) its *internal* relations (those *inside* the boundaries of philosophy as such); and (2) its *external* relations (those that relate it to *outside* major fields, like science or art).

Philosophy's relations: internal

Philosophy's *internal* relations may be approached through a twofold question. (1) How is *each branch* of philosophy concerned with the question of its own homogeneity—that is, with whether there is *truth* or an indefinite variety of *truths, value* or many *values, reality* or many *realities*? (2) Are epistemology, axiology, and ontology separated by insurmountable walls, or do they overlap and join into an inclusive pattern?

"Oneness" or "Manyness"? The problem of the "oneness" or "manyness" of each major area—reality, truth, and value—is as ancient as philosophy itself. The levels of belief that we called skeptical and agnostic tend to question whether any solution of this problem can be found. Nevertheless, the farthest reaches of antiquity disclose, in fragments of Greek philosophy, how Thales, Anaxagoras, Parmenides, and others hoped to discover a principle of reality that would reduce all physical objects to such basic "substances" as water or fire. Today, with the aid of vast cumulations of scientific knowledge, the search continues in the effort of cosmologists—Albert Einstein is the most famous—to encompass the seeming disparities of the earth and the heavens under a single universal formula of mathematical physics.

The philosophic terms commonly used in reference to this problem of oneness or manyness are *monism, pluralism,* and *dualism*. Thus, a monist in the area of knowledge is one who believes he has found some all-inclusive criterion by which he can judge the truth or falsity of every idea. A pluralist insists that various criteria are essential, depending upon the nature of the ideas we are dealing with, the time and place in which they are expressed, and similar qualifications. A dualist in epistemology believes that the plurality of types of knowledge is limited to two. He might hold, for example, that science produces one type and religion a second; each is regarded as reliable in its own sphere, neither being reducible to the other.

The problem of oneness and manyness is equally important in the area of values. Many of us are troubled, for example, by the appearance of dual sets of values in family and business relations: the devotion and generosity that a father shows his children may seem quite opposite from the competitive spirit and acquisitiveness with which he runs his office or store. Likewise, in the past half-century we have asked, with increasing anxiety, whether the nations of the world can find a common standard of right and wrong or whether each must be left free to be its own supreme judge and sovereign authority. If the latter should continue to be the case moral standards on the explosive plane of international affairs will continue to be pluralistic, as well as dangerously antagonistic.

Relations Among Major Areas. The answer to the second half of our question (Are the branches of philosophy, in their concern for reality, truth, and value, related to one another?) is implied by our answer to the first. One who tends toward a monistic pattern of belief in the area, let us say, of reality, is likely to wish to extend that pattern to embrace knowledge and value also—to encompass all three by some single sweeping principle. Typically, although not invariably, the same rule holds for pluralists and dualists: a pluralist in axiology is likely to be pluralistic in epistemology and ontology; a dualist in epistemology tends to find reasons for dualizing his beliefs in ontology and axiology.

A few additional philosophic terms help to point up these generalizations. In the long history of thought, the terms *empiricism* and *naturalism* refer, respectively, to philosophies of this-worldly experience and of nature. The terms *idealism* and *transcendentalism* refer, respectively, to philosophies of spiritual existence and of other-worldly perfection. Each pair of terms suggests a kind of partnership of beliefs: thus, the empiricist and naturalist tend to be theoretically closely allied, as do the idealist and the transcendentalist. Each pair of terms also suggests others that we shall find important. To illustrate, the empiricist and the naturalist may find themselves allied with *materialists* (who believe in the universality of "matter" as the basic reality); while the idealist and transcendentalist tend to find themselves allied with *absolutists* (who often believe that the key to reality is to be found in a final, immutable, eternal Being).

Such abstractions may be irksome to the student of educational philosophy. They are as important, however, to the great conflicting choices among beliefs about life and education in our time as they have ever been throughout human history. At this point in our discussion they are most important because they serve to *join together* the three chief branches of philosophy. Thus, a naturalist would hardly find in nature a sufficient ground for his beliefs about value if he looked to some transcendental realm for his beliefs about truth. On the contrary, we shall find that a belief-pattern may be thoroughly naturalistic from beginning to end. A system of beliefs about knowledge and value may be rooted in an interpretation of reality that is viewed entirely as animate and inanimate nature, and as explicable wholly by the several natural and social sciences. Such philosophies as idealism also cut across reality, knowledge, and value and combine all three into patterns of belief that sometimes attempt to be even more unified than naturalistic patterns.

PHILOSOPHY'S RELATIONS: EXTERNAL

Philosophy is concerned with much more than the relations that help to supply its own internal homogeneity. It probes inquisitively into the assumptions and purposes of every field, revealing, indeed, that it has no fixed boundaries at all. Hence, to speak of *external* relations is really only a convenient means to differentiate its outreaching characteristics from those relations that bind it within.

The philosopher, far from regarding other fields as isolated from his, has a special responsibility to become familiar with them. To philosophize in the broad field of science he must have a serious understanding of physics, biology, geology, sociology, psychology; in the field of art, an understanding of painting, music, poetry, the dance, the theater; in the field of education, an understanding of the curriculum, teaching methods, the principles of learning and administration. And to philosophize about the interrelations among these fields he must have an understanding of science, art, and education.

Is the Relational Task Too Forbidding? It may be argued that such wide knowledge is not possible for any one man in our time. It was possible, perhaps, for a man of ancient Greece or Rome, let us say, to possess all available knowledge; the civilized earth was narrow, and what men knew of it was meager. Today, however, not only has most of the earth been brought under man's direct observation but also our knowledge of it and the surrounding universe has increased enormously. Shall we not, then, be satisfied to specialize and give up the ambitions of philosophy to organize relations external to itself?

The answer, for several reasons, is definitely *No*.

In the first place, the very scope and depth of modern knowledge constitute an urgent reason why philosophy should attempt to relate the major fields to one another and to itself. Where mutual understanding is missing the activities of men result in confusion, cross-purpose, complacency, skepticism, negativism. Such a phenomenon is only too commonplace among nations, in politics, religion, art, and science, among professional educators, and still more in the contempt in which academicians too often hold such educators. *In the necessary and fruitful but also dangerous growth of specific knowledge only one discipline seems to remain that specializes in non-specialization: philosophy itself*. Far from diminishing, the need today is increased by the very difficulty of meeting it.

In the second place, achievement, although arduous, is not unattainable. There is a difference between being familiar with all important facts and events known at a given period (an achievement possible for Aristotle in his period but impossible for any man in ours) and being familiar with the major summarizations, implications, and presuppositions of those facts and events. The most that a single student can accomplish is to master the outstanding premises, issues, conclusions, laws about which the experts are concerned within their own fields. This in itself is no minor task.

In biology, for example, the philosopher need not—indeed cannot—retrace the steps of intricate laboratory experimentation to understand its development or to appraise the principal beliefs from which it operates. He need not be a priest in order to appraise the foundations of a church, nor a professional politician to weigh the import of the principal laws enacted by a senate, nor a superintendent to evaluate the main objectives of a school. If he has had experience in these fields so much the better; if he is acquainted with their guiding beliefs and richest results so much the better still. Ralph Barton Perry, the eminent Harvard philosopher, makes the point effectively. The philosopher, he says, must

> enter fields in which specialists have already staked their special claims, and where the philosopher finds himself an amateur among professionals. He cannot hope to do their special work better than they do it, but only to incorporate their results and add items and relationships. The philosopher is accustomed to this somewhat shameless role. He does not, however, undertake the task arrogantly or overconfidently. For it is the philosopher who, having undertaken the task, is most acutely aware of the difficulty.[1]

In the third place, the success with which anyone can understand the position or significance of various fields is always a matter of degree, differing very widely even among highly trained philosophers. A few contemporary thinkers—such as Croce, Dewey, Russell, Maritain—possess such large funds of information about the content and achievements of major fields that they become guides and interpreters for many lesser practitioners of philosophy.

It is, nevertheless, a mistake to think of the philosopher exclusively in this professional sense. Just as anyone who expresses his beliefs is thereby practicing philosophy in a minor way, so anyone who expresses beliefs concerning the ordered connections of experience is practicing philosophy in a more substantial way. He is doing so, moreover, whether he is called a philosopher or is a political leader, scientist, artist, or educator functioning as a philosopher. What conscientious classroom teacher can totally ignore such questions as the role of schools in politics, the bearing of history upon art, or the connections of atomic energy with peace? This service of philosophy, in studying relations, becomes an imperative of education at the same time as the common and organic aspects of life take their places along with the more specific and atomistic aspects.

In the last place, that teachers are often intimidated by the prospect of synthesizing knowledge, of helping young people to obtain an ordered outlook upon their culture, may be caused not so much by inability as by intellectual conditioning. The schools themselves have been victims of specialization. Subject-matter compartments—English, science, mathematics, foreign languages—are not conducive to the development of integrated education. Teachers so frequently concentrate in single departments that, if they succeed in building a broader conception, they do so in spite rather than because of their professional preparation. In short, we should be unfair to doubt the competence of teachers to encourage beliefs that rest upon appreciation of life's relations so long as they themselves lack the experience and training that would help them to understand those relations.

Philosophy Within One Field. Thus, we return to our contention that, despite the undeniable difficulty of the task and the imperfection of accomplishment, philosophy is today properly concerned with wholes as well as with parts, with connections *among* facts as well as with facts as such. Of course, it may choose to focus upon relations within one rather than another major field. The "unity of science" movement, which has recently attracted wide attention, is an example of how the philosophy of science delineates the basic similarities of the physical, biological, and social sciences. The philosophy of religion, in the Occident, is concerned not only with the common beliefs of various Christian creeds but also with how these may or may not harmonize with Oriental creeds.

In this relational function, moreover, philosophy may utilize any of the concepts and branches introduced above. Thus, some philosophies of religion are dualistic, in that they predicate a separation of "body" and "soul." (This is also true of certain transcendental types of idealism.) Philosophies of science are usually empirical and pluralistic, and frequently naturalistic. In any case, we can expect axiology, epistemology, and ontology to serve as indispensable tools of analysis and of synthesis precisely to the extent that value, truth, and reality are indispensable areas of study within each field.

Philosophy Relates Major Fields. Let us note, finally, that, just as these branches and concepts are not merely principles of connection *within* philosophy itself but also *between* philosophy and art, philosophy and science, philosophy and education, so they are useful as links among *all* such fields. Thus, axiology becomes important everywhere; it is a bridge connecting the islands of history *and* science *and* education *and* art. Moreover, if such concepts as idealism and empiricism or monism and dualism are fundamental to single fields, they become even more fundamental to great systems of philosophy—to sweeping views of the universe.

The philosophy of education exemplifies all such relations. It is concerned with those characteristics that unite the innumerable aspects of education into one great field and also with the manner in which these reach out to encompass other fields. In either aim the philosophy of education is less comprehensive than philosophy taken as a whole. Yet the philosophy of education may on occasion—and, indeed, should more often—function as *a complete philosophy of life viewed from a particular perspective*—from a hilltop overlooking the plains of the world. As the great American philosopher John Dewey has said: "The most penetrating definition of philosophy which can be given is, then, that it is the theory of education in its most general phases." [2]

A TYPICAL EXAMPLE: EDUCATION, SOCIAL SCIENCE, AND PHILOSOPHY

We now review, as a kind of summary interpretation, some of the more important points of this chapter. To do so we examine briefly one typical belief that is taught to millions of children and adults in our communities and schools—the belief that competition for profits is the mainspring of economic life in a system of free enterprise.

How Epistemology Functions. Let us begin by illustrating how *epistemology* is a bond between the two fields especially relevant to this belief—education and social science. Each seeks knowledge not only of itself but of the other as well. Education is concerned to *know* many things about American society—facts and laws, structures and operations, history and aims. Social science is concerned to *know* the important social institution of the school—how population trends, economic levels, and other phenomena affect education and how education affects them.

The relational service of epistemology is, however, only one of its services. Its chief interest, obviously, is in the nature of beliefs by which educators and social scientists determine that they are speaking the truth. If, for example, it investigates the basis of the belief in a competitive struggle for profits it finds that, although this belief is widely regarded as a general truth, a number of qualifications must be stated. Let us list four: (1) tens of millions of individuals never engage in such competition directly, for they are entirely dependent on wages or salaries; (2) huge sections of industry are owned by corporations that fix prices and determine productive policies without competition of any kind; (3) government subsidizes and controls business in various ways; (4) free competition, therefore, applies, at least in our period, largely to a theoretical rather than actual economic system.

Why, then, if the truth of this belief is found upon examination to be so qualified, should social science and education, working in partnership, continue to assert it at all? Is it, perhaps, because free competition was at one time in America—especially during the era of Andrew Jackson and the freehold farmer—successful and really dominant? If so, then does not the record of our past become the measure of truth in the present?

How Axiology and Ontology Function. But epistemology is not a sufficient test for the truth of this belief. Indeed, to assert that the past is the measure of truth does not tell us in what sense the past is *better* than the present. Thus, we resort to a second division of philosophy. If we do not any longer assert that competition *is* the mainspring of a free economy in the sense that it is a true description of what actually occurs but nevertheless do assert (on the basis of past experience) that this is the direction American economic life *ought* to take, then we are utilizing axiology. We are saying that the values expressed in the Jacksonian period of our history were so admirable that they deserve to be the standard of what should be desirable today and in the future. We are implying, in short, a norm by which we may be guided toward the good—in this case, a renascence of a genuinely competitive economy.

Having established this norm, we are confronted by another question. *Why* are these values admirable, why is this norm the one we ought to follow? One influential answer (toward which we shall be critical below) leads straight to a third branch of philosophy, namely, *ontology*. Since before the time of Adam Smith the answer frequently given has centered on the nature of man's existence. The chain of argument is broadly formulated thus: Man *is* innately, permanently competitively selfish. Self-interest *is* a law of human nature. Every law of human nature *is* the expression of everlasting laws of nature as a whole. The good *is* the product of just these laws, which exist also as the basis of knowledge. Thus, free enterprise—that system motivated by man's materialistic self-interest in profits—is made to rest impregnably upon existent laws of nature. Therefore it is *real*. Therefore it is *good*. Therefore it is *true*.

And if the epistemologist persists in demonstrating that free enterprise does not operate today as fully as many people are taught to believe by our schools (and other mind-shaping agencies), this still need not vitiate the position of the free-enterprisers who argue as we have indicated above. They insist that it *would* operate well if left alone, that in allowing interferences by government and other agencies we do violence to what is ordained by existence itself. Hence, they argue, the only solution to our economic problems is to put free enterprise back under the rule of its original laws of nature and so once more allow unhampered competition full play. This is the kind of economics, moreover, that all citizens should learn. Other kinds are evil and false because unreal.*

The Need for Critical Judgment. Our illustration could, of course, be carried much further. It has not been our purpose to analyze extensively the issues it raises. We have attempted to demonstrate simply that: (1) *beliefs* are expressed throughout the illustration; (2) such beliefs are often *taught* in the classroom; (3) they pertain to *several different fields:* history, economics, psychology, and education itself; (4) the several fields are related not only by the interworking of *all three branches of philosophy* but also by a *naturalism* that is, in this case, fairly *monistic* and *materialistic;* and (5) after so expressing these beliefs, *we are in a stronger, clearer position to pass critical judgment upon them.*

Now it is item 5, especially, that calls for further attention. After exposing a favorite criterion of one widely held belief we may legitimately ask whether that criterion (basically an ontology of an acquisitive, egoistic human nature) is any longer indisputable. We may inquire, for example, whether the evidence of anthropology, sociology, psychology, and other sciences supports today an ontology so largely the product of earlier modern centuries. We may peer into history to see whether any successful economies have been based upon cooperative enterprise or only upon competitive enterprise. We may insist that young people have the opportunity to examine such traditional beliefs and their alternatives.

Above all, we may ask whether cultural forces do not influence the choice of alternative ontologies, axiologies, and epistemologies; whether philosophy, like art, does not mirror, in degree, an age and a culture; whether, therefore, the leading American philosophies of education are not themselves partially, perhaps chiefly, results of the total environment in which they are conceived and in which they grow to such maturity

* For a contemporary example of this kind of reasoning, see Beriah Sellers, "All for One, the Corporation Is All," *The Nation,* October 2, 1954.

of influence as to aid in shaping that environment—including its schools. In short, without in the least diminishing the necessity of articulating our beliefs about the good, the true, and the real, we may ask whether *these should not be judged not merely by or for themselves but in relation to the rapid movements, conflicts, and reconstructions of contemporary culture*. This is the important question to which we now turn.

Notes

The Bibliography supplies complete publication data for all the references cited in the footnotes, the text, and the "What to Read" sections of the Appendix.

The Appendix contains, in addition to suggestions for further reading, a set of "Aids to Learning."

[1] Ralph Barton Perry, *Realms of Value,* p. 14. Copyright 1954 by Harvard University Press and reprinted with their permission.

[2] John Dewey, *Democracy and Education,* p. 386.

CHAPTER 3

Culture: The Context of Philosophy

THUS FAR, PHILOSOPHY HAS BEEN VIEWED "FROM THE INSIDE out." Proceeding from the definition that it is the attempt of any person to express his beliefs as clearly and honestly as possible, we have seen how philosophy seeks to determine the reliability of any person's premises and standards about: (1) reality, knowledge, and value; (2) the relations of these areas to one another; and (3) the relations of these areas, in turn, to all other fields.

As our interpretation moved outward toward point 3, we were already, then, becoming concerned with the "external" relations of philosophy—that is, with the crosscurrents of meaning between this discipline and science, art, politics, religion, society, education, taken either as separate or as interconnected fields.

Our purpose in this chapter is to explore these external relations further by viewing philosophy more fully "from the outside in." As is suggested at the conclusion of Chapter 2, we need next to consider how philosophy is a creation of its surroundings. Such a view is not in contradiction with our previous implication that philosophy is also a creator of its surroundings. One conception merely counterbalances the other: philosophy is seen as *both* effect and cause, *both* created and creator.

The context within which philosophy functions and from which it draws its sustenance is considered under two captions:

1. the culture we live in; and
2. philosophies of education in a crisis-culture.

The Culture We Live In

The meaning of culture

The Concept Defined. That *culture* is one of the most fruitful, quite possibly the single most fruitful, of all the concepts that have lately emerged in the social sciences is a proposition in which at least a considerable majority of scholars in these fields would surely concur. We say "lately emerged" because, while the term itself is very old, its delineation by the discipline most directly concerned with it, namely, anthropology, is comparatively new. Indeed, the first influential scientific definition of culture, and still by far the most often quoted, was made in 1871. In this year, the great Englishman Edward B. Tylor wrote at the very opening of his *Primitive Culture* that "Culture or Civilization . . . is that complex whole which includes knowledge, belief, art, morals, law, custom, and any other capabilities and habits acquired by man as a member of society."[1]

Let us examine the components of this definition. In the phrase "complex whole" Tylor is hinting that any culture, however numerous or diverse its parts, still possesses unity, perhaps some kind of pattern or configuration. Also, it embraces innumerable psychological activities along with their objective manifestations. Morals, for example, are in one sense invisible or covert, but in another they attain overt expression through the behavior of families, through courts, legislatures, churches, schools, and other institutions. Again, Tylor implies by the terms "law," "custom," and "habits" that culture connotes regularities of human behavior rather than idiosyncrasies or accidental occurrences—regularities upon which, be it carefully noted, he passes no judgment of approval or disapproval, of better or worse. All characteristics of culture, moreover, are acquired; they are not inherited, not carried by the genes or other biological equipment from generation to generation. Finally, the individual cannot create culture by himself; he does so only in so far as he lives and works with other men—that is to say, socially.

A good case could be made for the contention that Tylor's successors down to the present day have devoted most of their energies to refining, elaborating, and testing his famous definition.* Virtually every word has

* See, for example, Ralph Linton (ed.), *The Science of Man in the World Crisis;* M. J. Herskovits, *Man and His Works;* A. L. Kroeber, *Anthropology.*

been subjected to scrupulous analysis and has generated endless debate and vast research. Let us consider the term "society." What is its precise relation to culture? Are culture and society synonymous? If not, why do even anthropologists still so frequently interchange the two terms in their own writings? Part of the answer lies in the fact that anthropology is, relatively speaking, a young discipline and that its terminology, therefore, still is less refined than the terminology of, say, economics or political science. Part of the answer, also, is that, by fairly wide agreement among experts, society is one very important aspect of culture; hence, when they are talking about that aspect they quite properly use the term "society." For anthropologists, a human society is the situation in which people find themselves when they are associated together, as in a family or club or village. A society assumes the character of culture when it acquires habits, values, institutions, skills that are held in common and are cherished and transmitted to successive generations.

The other terms in Tylor's definition are equally provocative. Habit, for example, demands careful psychological interpretation. Thus, the most influential anthropologist in American history, Franz Boas, defines culture as follows: "Culture embraces all the manifestations of social habits of a community, the reactions of the individual as affected by the habits of the group in which he lives, and the products of human activities as determined by these habits." [2]

Or let us consider the term "civilization," which Tylor regards as equivalent to culture. Many authorities continue to follow his lead here, also. They do not contrast "civilized" with "uncivilized" cultures, preferring to regard all cultures, however different from one another, as civilized within their own context of beliefs, habits, and practices. For this reason, authorities also increasingly reject as misleading the term "primitive." When they wish to distinguish between a culture such as the American or French and a culture such as the Australian aboriginal they more often use the terms "literate" and "nonliterate," the latter merely denoting that the culture possesses no written language. This terminology is not universally accepted, however—especially not among some historians and philosophers of culture.

The present status of thought regarding the meaning of culture is interpreted most authoritatively in *Culture: A Critical Review of Concepts and Definitions* by two of America's outstanding anthropologists. Alfred L. Kroeber and Clyde Kluckhohn. Their review demonstrates that, despite a wide range of emphases and perspectives on the central idea, there is also now a high degree of consensus on its core meaning. They recognize, of course, that the older, honorific notion of culture as cultivation—"to achieve or impart refined manners, urbanization, and improvement"—is still entirely legitimate so long as we are clear that this is what we intend. As used by social scientists, however, culture is at least that "set of attributes and products of human societies, and therewith of mankind, which are extrasomatic [not bodily or organic] and transmissible by mechanisms other than biological heredity, and are as essentially lacking in sub-human species as they are characteristic of the human species as it is aggregated in societies." [3]

The concept becomes especially useful when applied pluralistically rather than monistically. Consider for a moment the *variety* of cultures existing upon the earth—all of which have something in common, but each of which is distinguished from the others, as a "way of life," by its own qualities of internal consistency and harmony. Some cultures have disappeared, except in historic memory or in the important respect that certain of their features have been absorbed by later cultures. Thus we speak of ancient Egypt and Greece as having once had great cultures, which, however, no longer exist. We can also apply the term pluralistically to our own period of history. Though it is true that peoples of various races and nationalities are today in closer contact than formerly, profound dissimilarities exist between the institutions, customs, and beliefs of, let us say, the Orient and the Occident—or between those of Europe and North America and those of central Africa and Madagascar. Still further, we recognize the existence of *sub*cultures within a single culture. It is not improper to speak of our American culture as different in certain ways from the European, although both belong to "the West." Nor is it improper to regard such subcultures as those of the American Indian as having their distinctive patterns. What we should keep in mind is that the totality, culture, carries many smaller "totalities" within it—smaller clusters of institutional and behavioral experience, which, while capable of differentiation, are also interwoven within larger clusters at innumerable points.

It is as though we were looking through a picture frame at the culture created by modern man. Sometimes we hold it so close to our eyes as to take in almost the whole of the earth. Sometimes we place it at arm's length, so as to view smaller, yet still ordered, segments of the whole.

More than any other, the panorama that we wish to behold through our frame is the culture of America. To appreciate it comprehensively, however, we must look at America's past, at its future, at its subcultures, at its relations with still wider cultures. Later pages consider how certain phases of American civilization are affected by such current subcultures as the Southern Negro and how other phases are affected by cultures as remote in space and time as the Age of Pericles.

But most of all we need to consider the present period in broad outline. Our task is to provide a frame through which we can appraise the significance of American philosophy and education today. For philosophy, and education too, are cultural experiences. They spring from the culture; they develop and mature within it; they react upon it. They cannot be understood without it.

What Is the American Culture? Merely to inquire into the nature of the American culture is to reveal how difficult—nay, impossible—is any one definition. Historians, sociologists, philosophers, novelists and other artists have been seeking a definition almost since the moment America was born, and they are still seeking. This is not unfortunate. America is boundlessly rich, not only in natural resources but in spirit and stamina. It is young, as cultures go, and certainly complex. No wonder that it is seen differently through different eyes, or that the view is changed by the viewers' different emotions and characters.

How do American anthropologists view America? They are only beginning to apply their special competencies to their own culture. Unfortunately, the majority has, until recently, concentrated on simpler or nonliterate cultures. An increasing minority, however, is beginning to operate nearer home. Not only do they study fairly distinct subcultures, such as Indian tribes, Negroes, or other minority groups, but some have examined whole American communities. The works of Helen and Robert Lynd on "Middletown," though more often formally classified as sociological, utilize effective anthropological techniques; so, too, do those on "Yankee City" by W. Lloyd Warner and his associates. Occasionally an anthropologist may study a particular institution in America: Hortense Powdermaker's work on the motion-picture industry is an example. More rarely, an expert may view anthropologically the whole of Western culture and America's place in it: Bronislaw Malinowski's stirring *Freedom and Civilization* may be cited here.*

* See Robert S. and Helen M. Lynd, *Middletown, a Study in Contemporary American Culture;* W. L. Warner and P. S. Lunt, *The Social Life of a Modern Community;* Hortense Powdermaker, *Hollywood, the Dream Factory;* Bronislaw Malinowski, *Freedom and Civilization.*

An interesting brief example of how an American anthropologist regards his own culture is offered by Clyde Kluckhohn. He finds that Americans are characterized by, among other traits, a capacity for generosity, laughter, and optimism; a faith in the rationality of the common man; a high moral sense; a glorification of action and work; a dramatization of the individual; a worship of success; a faith in "progress"; a tendency to conform to majority standards; a warm regard for recreation; a consciousness of diversity in cultural and biological origins; a "relatively strong trust in science and education and relative indifference to religion"; a love of gadgets and bigness; a high degree of restlessness and insecurity.

It is significant, in relation to the special problem of this book, that Kluckhohn finds, in common with many other social scientists, a sharp divergence between the theory and practice of American culture. Thus, in support of our illustration at the close of Chapter 2, we may cite his statement that "it is only the *tradition* of economic independence which truly survives. For all our talk of free enterprise we have created the most vast and crushing monopolies in the world." Further illustrations of such divergence are, first, the "intolerable contradictions" in our creed of equality and our treatment of minorities, and, second, the existence of a status and class structure that tends to stratify people to a far greater extent than is so blandly assumed by our long-held belief in freedom of movement and opportunity. "Americans are at present seeing social change of a vastness difficult to comprehend . . . the depression and World War II appear to have destroyed the old equilibrium beyond repair."[4]

Is Ours a Crisis-Culture? Kluckhohn's last-quoted observation raises the question of whether the American culture can be diagnosed as a culture-in-crisis. Despite such observations, however, he probably does not regard this as a paramount question. Other anthropologists are even less likely to think in these terms, continuing to deal more typically with narrow problems. Nevertheless, one finds frequent reference in their works to the abnormal rate of change that they find to be characteristic of most cultures today. A number of them have also been enlisted in the difficult task of assisting underdeveloped peoples to adjust to rapid technological advances with their accompanying tensions.†

One of the ablest interpretations of an underdeveloped people in

† See Margaret Mead (ed.), *Cultural Patterns and Technical Change.*

America is Laura Thompson's *Culture in Crisis,* a study of the Hopi Indians of northern Arizona. Her definition of culture-crisis is "the manifestation of critical imbalance in one or more essentials of a culture structure in environmental setting." [5] The anthropological theorist David Bidney has defined culture-crisis as "a state of emergency brought about by the suspension of normal, or previously prevailing, technological, social, or ideological conditions." [6] And H. G. Barnett, a cultural anthropologist, has explained that in a state of culture-crisis

> a familiar universe of associations and sanctions has been distorted or destroyed, and must be reorganized. The wrenching away of any control mechanism . . . requires a reorientation. Unsettlement for any cause creates a fluid condition in which the old values are no longer operative. With the old sanctions and compulsives gone or of doubtful validity, the way is open for the creation and the acceptance of new interpretations.[7]

Such definitions are probably fairly acceptable to those historians and philosophers of culture who believe that the present age is one of profound crisis.† The Englishman Arnold Toynbee is one of these.* Another is the American Lewis Mumford, who has written:

> The period through which we are living presents itself as one of unmitigated confusion and disintegration: a period of paralyzing economic depressions, of unrestrained butcheries and enslavements, and one of world-ravaging wars: a period whose evil fulfillments have betrayed all its beneficent promises. But behind all these phenomena of physical destruction we can detect an earlier and perhaps more fundamental series of changes: a loss of communion between classes and peoples, a breakdown in stable behavior, a loss of form and purpose in many of the arts . . .[8]

We propose, then, to designate the man-made environment of the present period of American history as a crisis-culture. On the basis of the definitions and explanations of culture-crisis given above, our use of the designation crisis-culture implies that our institutions, habits, symbols, beliefs, and faiths are almost all infected by chronic instability, confusion, bifurcations, and uncertainties.

† For a helpful diagnosis of our crisis-age, see William O. Stanley, *Education and Social Integration,* Chaps. 2-5.

* See Arnold J. Toynbee, *A Study of History,* Vols. 7-10.

At the same time, we recognize that the crisis through which much of the world is now struggling has by no means struck every facet of the culture with equal force. Recalling that many people live on what we have termed a complacent level of belief (see pp. 21-22), many would deny the assertion that ours is a crisis-culture in any way. Various institutions and faiths, including some schools and churches, tend to build in their members habits of acquiescence in, rather than a feeling of concern about, the current of events. It is true, of course, that these events cannot disturb all of us, at every moment. We tend to go about our daily routines, accepting, as far as we can, those attitudes and practices to which we have grown accustomed, from which we draw security, and upon which we depend. If for no other reason than that the constant strain upon us would be unendurable, we often overlook, or deliberately ignore, many symptoms of abnormality in the culture. It is reasonable to suppose that even some experts in culture, who are also humanly preoccupied with their own interests and ambitions, might overlook these symptoms.

This "normal" tendency to conceal "abnormality" is peculiarly characteristic of the American people. More than any culture of modern times, perhaps of any time, ours is an optimistic culture. We have enjoyed an abiding faith in the inevitability of progress.† We have possessed limitless confidence in our youthful virility, ingenuity, resources—our "bounce." Most important, we have thus far escaped the worst effects of the epidemics that have swept so much of the earth—the epidemic of war, especially. Although parts of our land have suffered terribly (the Civil War occurred less than a century ago), our cities have hitherto escaped bombing, our fields and farm lands have not been ravaged, our civilian populations have not been scourged. Nor have we been threatened too seriously, thus far, by the totalitarian movements of Europe and Asia. We entered World War II to destroy fascism, but few of us feared it could conquer America. True, the period of the Cold War has subsequently generated new fears—this time of Soviet totalitarianism. Many of us have continued to believe, nevertheless, that the "democratic way of life" is quite invincible—that the ideals of "liberty" and "equality," though never quite attainable, are secure forever.

Granting that the United States may be less directly affected by our crisis-culture than are other regions, we cannot assume that ultimately

† See J. B. Bury, *The Idea of Progress.*

it is less involved. On the contrary, by comparison with many nations it is *more* involved. As the leading world power it can set, not only its own course, but, to a great extent, the course for lesser powers. Its post-war foreign policy, indeed, has frequently expressed this power, notably in its program of foreign economic assistance. Thus it may deepen the crisis of our time, or it may greatly relieve, perhaps resolve, that crisis. It may hasten the complete collapse of civilization, or it may contribute immeasurably to cultural rehabilitation and reconstruction.

But if America is to assume the solemn responsibilities thrust upon it by its own dominance, one of the first tasks of its thinking citizens is to look critically and honestly inward to examine the condition of their culture. Can it be, for example, that the habit of many of us to gloss over our frailties and to shy away from sharp analysis of our personal and social instabilities—the easy optimism with which we like to believe that opposing forces can be persuaded to act reasonably and to cooperate amicably—is itself symptomatic of cultural disturbances? We can begin to answer this question only if we are first able to demonstrate that internal conflicts, tensions, hostilities do permeate the fiber of our culture.

In the language of psychiatry, our culture may be diagnosed as, in grave respects, a "schizophrenic" culture. The personality elements of a schizophrenic individual are not only in conflict but are totally unrelated. The term is applied to culture with the awareness that it has the defects of every analogy, for a culture cannot be schizophrenic in the strict sense that a person can. Our own culture, moreover, lacks the extreme manifestations of this disease in the degree that its areas of conflict have still some relation to one another. These areas of conflict have, indeed, a long American history, and it would be inaccurate to imply that any of them have developed only within the last decades. Qualifying the analogy in these ways, let us note several symptoms which are, nevertheless, especially critical in the present period.

Our "schizophrenic" age

Self-Interest versus Social Interest. Traditionally, American culture, borrowing much from modern Europe, has been concerned to promote the self-interest of its individual members. This is manifested not only in the shibboleths of competitive enterprise, but also in the daily conduct of countless persons. Self-aggrandizement, self-display, self-promotion; an ethic that rewards and praises those who practice shrewd dealings; the elevation to civic dignity and authority of individuals who win pecuniary success by such dealings; the feeling that family loyalty precedes if it does not deny all wider loyalties—these are common to our way of life.

Yet, while they are common, they are not exclusive. Side by side with these attitudes and habits of self-interest are others that reveal a strong social-interest.‡ Admiration for the gifts of philanthropists; the generosity with which people of small income "chip in" to support public causes; an ethic that praises service to others, the ideal of brotherhood, and honesty in business; the eagerness with which groups ranging from Rotary Clubs and Boy Scouts to organized labor and farmers' unions join in good fellowship and cooperative effort—these, too, are characteristic of American communities.

Inequality versus Equality. What Gunnar Myrdal calls "an American dilemma" * is another example. The term refers to our failure to provide full civil rights, fair job opportunities, and respect for millions of citizens at the same moment that we subscribe officially to "equality for all." Myrdal is concerned with the 10 percent of our population that is Negro. But, as Kluckhohn and others have pointed out, other minorities should also be included: Mexican-Americans of the Southwest, American Indians, Orientals—not to mention millions of white citizens who, for one reason or another, are denied economic, social, educational, or other privileges. Jews constitute one instance; women in business, professions, and politics, another.

Nor is the dilemma confined to our failure to practice what we preach. The truth is that, even as an ideal, American culture is by no means universally committed to equality. Recall the first conflict noted above: when success is measured by the "ability" with which a man wins over others in the struggle for financial gain, the implication is clear that individuals should either be condoned for their superiority or blamed for their inferiority. In this context, it is not equality that deserves praise so much as the kind of inequality that enables one to stand economically well above the average.

Again, however, inconsistencies appear in practices and attitudes. Legislative efforts to provide equal privileges for Negroes and other

‡ See Robert S. Lynd, *Knowledge for What?* pp. 60ff.
* **See Gunnar Myrdal, *An American Dilemma.***

minorities indicate that inequality is *not* generally approved. The long series of Supreme Court decisions declaring unconstitutional segregation of Negroes in public accommodations, including public schools, has given powerful sanction to that disapproval. Still more significant is a growing insistence that economic failure is not necessarily the mark of inferior ability. In an industrial system as huge and complex as ours a person may be victimized by circumstances wholly beyond his control. Hence equality of security, if not of opportunity, must be guaranteed by social insurance, cooperative agencies, and other public services.

If it be asked whether such illustrations do not muddy the concept of equality, the reply is that, even if they do, there is no avoiding them. The culture itself has muddied it. The fact is that, if judged by its behavior, America does not agree with itself as to what equality means.

Planlessness versus Planning. Does our culture agree any more harmoniously as to the need for, or meaning of, social-economic planning?

To some, the very term *planning* smacks of "communism," "socialism," or other obnoxious "un-American" proposals. To others, not only is careful planning desirable in such an intricate social order as ours, it is an unavoidable necessity.

The advocates of "planlessness" are often those who are governed by self-interest and who profit by economic inequality. They want their businesses, families, and personal lives to function as independently as possible, without interference "from the outside." If they have theorized about their beliefs at all, they doubtless contend that such "independence" will, in the long run, produce the greatest welfare for the most people.

Yet it is startling to observe with what difficulty even the most rugged of "rugged individualists" square their verbalizations with concrete actions. Recognizing that recurrent depressions with their heavy toll of suffering are undesirable, even the professed opponents of planning are reluctantly willing to plan within particular localities or states, but they look with suspicion upon trends toward centralized control or federal direction. And although they opposed the economic and social planning of the New Deal and the Fair Deal and labeled such projects of regional development as the Tennessee Valley Authority "creeping socialism," such huge corporate enterprises as the Du Pont "empire" are themselves magnificent demonstrations of *planned* efficiency—not only of technological integration but also of interlocking directorates, hierarchical supervision, price-setting policies. Nor are they averse to regulation by government—so long as such regulation strengthens their power, their right to plan as *they* see fit for *their* own ends. Tariffs, to cite another example, are carefully designed to reduce foreign competition; yet we seldom hear objection to them from the most vociferous foes of planning.

But the advocates of wider social-economic planning are not without their own contradictions or uncertainties. They are not agreed on how much and what kinds of political controls over economic life should be approved. Some are willing to settle for a curious conception termed the "mixed economy." The economy they tend to endorse is "mixed," not only in its wavering proposals for planning here but no planning there. It is too often a confession of mixed attitudes as well—another significant symbol of a culture that tends to conceal its bifurcations from itself by patchwork, compromising remedies.

As one instance of this confusion, we may consider the attitude of organized labor toward planning in America. Though in certain other countries—in England, let us say—labor has taken the lead in encouraging national planning by democratic means, our own powerful unions hesitate to propose any measures that might jeopardize ultimate domination by the captains of commerce. True, labor is not timid in pressing for higher wages. True, too, it sometimes supports partial measures of planning—for example, health insurance, unemployment compensation, retirement benefits. A few labor leaders have even begun to ask whether the organized working people must not build strong political-economic programs less dependent upon the aims and interests of the businessman. By and large, however, such questions are raised less frequently today than they were twenty years ago. Struggle between the two great forces of capital and labor is confined primarily to determining how they shall divide profits accrued from the traditional economic structure, which both accept and both endorse.

Nationalism versus Internationalism. Hans Kohn, the historian, has written of this conflict in deeply disturbing terms:

> . . . the "one world" of the twentieth century offers the apparent paradox of an unparalleled intensity of economic and cultural intercourse between peoples . . . and at the same time a

> completely novel bitterness in conflicts between nations . . . A unified humanity with a common cultural design seemed to emerge at the beginning of the twentieth century, but at the same time the divisions within mankind became more pronounced than ever before; conflicts between them spread over wider areas and stirred deeper emotions. Cultural contact had engendered and intensified conflict between nationalities.[9]

In this statement, we see how the crisis from which we suffer extends beyond the boundaries of America; how, in our kind of world, cultural illnesses cannot possibly be confined in some "isolation ward." They are contagious illnesses.

Our century is the first in history in which not merely one, but two, world wars have been fought—and these less than a quarter-century apart. Moreover, the brand of nationalism that has developed under the labels of fascism and nazism has been unprecedented in its fanatical fury and hatreds, its techniques of creating mass hysteria, the shocking speed with which it replaced democratic-libertarian practices with autocratic-authoritarian practices. Soviet communism, too, has become more nationalistic, much less concerned to promote the Marxian ideal of an international socialist democracy than to strengthen the Russian "Motherland," and increasingly ruthless in its punishment of those who dare to question Party rule.

Nor is the spirit of nationalism by any means lacking in America. Here are familiar symptoms: the almost complete exclusion of Orientals from our shores; rigid and shockingly callous immigration laws against other nationalities and races; tireless agitation by isolationists against not only the United Nations but "internationalists" of all kinds; a huge and costly armaments program that deprives educational, health, recreational, and other services of desperately needed funds; a foreign policy that speaks more often for national than for world economic interests and still more often acts as though our nation alone were innocent of wrongdoing.

Though familiar, these trends, too, are offset by others. Communication among large-scale cultures has increased more rapidly in the past few decades than in the whole of preceding history. The airplane and radio have brought all parts of the globe into closer proximity than was formerly dreamed to be possible. Rapid infiltration of Western customs and industrial methods is transforming great areas which, only a few years back, were primitive and barbaric. Recognition that war has become infinitely more destructive than ever before has brought persistent demands for world government with enforceable authority over individual nations, demands that signalize the possible emergence, at last, of a "unified humanity."

In terms of our crisis-culture, the danger lies in the grim possibility that these dichotomies between nationalism and internationalism will not be resolved in time. Force, not only in atomic and bacterial weapons but also as a rationale for collective behavior, has become stronger at the same moment that the power of communication and skills in collective arbitration have become stronger. The insistence that might makes right, the superstition that some races are inherently destined to rule over others, just as some individuals are inherently superior to other individuals—these are not the heresies of a few "crackpots." They are widely maintained, in foreign lands where fascism in some form is still openly or subversively practiced and even by many individuals and groups in the United States. They are maintained side by side with equally fervent convictions: reason above force, the equal worth of nationalities and races, and a peaceful, ordered world.

Absolutism versus Experimentalism. Permeating all these cultural cleavages, yet extending beyond them, is the more subtle struggle between absolutism and experimentalism. On the whole, and granting exceptions, we may say that self-interest, inequality, planlessness, and nationalism tend in our culture to be absolutist in spirit and action; whereas social-interest, equality, planning, and internationalism tend in our culture to be experimentalist in spirit and action.

Thus we saw, in our closing illustration of Chapter 2, how advocates of private enterprise may attempt to ground the assumption of self-interest in an absolute law of nature. The same attempt might seek to justify, not only the right of the "superior" to unequal privilege, but also a "free competition" which alone, friends of planlessness insist, guarantees a workable economic system. Absolutism is also a familiar feature of nationalism; common examples are the inviolable sovereignty of each nation, the supremacy of a leader or a racial elite, the use of dogma, and the play upon passions.

At the same time, experimentalism, typified by the promotion of social-interest through the New Deal period, has been powerful in its own motivations. We may recall the experiments of the 1930's with federal works projects; such successful planning ventures as TVA and social security; the later programs in interracial housing, employment, recreation, all of which enhance equality; the abortive but pioneering League of Nations after World War I; and the more hopeful United Nations after World War II. It is clear that the whole spirit and method of social science have gained immense prestige and influence. It is clear, also, that the experimental approach to new, more inclusive, more humane cultural arrangements makes a prodigious impact upon our century.

Whether experimentalism makes a greater *total* impact than absolutism, however, is by no means equally clear. For one thing, the natural sciences have been under attack in recent years. Nuclear physicists create such fiendish devices as hydrogen bombs, which have the force to destroy their creators, along with everyone else. Other experts invent jet-propelled airplanes and rockets which, while knitting the world together, also preclude adequate defense against enemy invaders; they build radios, television sets, movies, automatic printing and recording devices, which create unprecedented opportunities for world enlightenment and, at the same time, give to those who control them a stranglehold on public opinion and mass mentality. For another thing, science is held to be weak in moral or social responsibility and purpose. The fact that its creations are so often used to destroy or maim rather than to build or improve life is evidence enough for many of its critics.

This is not to say that absolutism provides what experimentalism thus far lacks. On the contrary, absolutism is itself open to grave charges. We may consider its religious forms. American culture, like virtually all cultures, nonliterate or literate, is saturated with supernatural faiths. The dominant creeds—Catholic, Jewish, Protestant—are more or less alike in their acceptance of a Supreme Being, Who is Himself perfect, Who is the source of natural and moral law, and to Whom mortals should look in facing the travails of this earthly realm. All three creeds unite likewise in their stand that science is inferior to religion as a final source of protection and authority.

Here, however, religious unity ends. Not only do sects differ as to how much and what kinds of science are permissible, they dissent bitterly in their interpretations of religion itself. They disagree on social, political, and other policies. Some disclose sympathy with nationalism, self-interest, inequality, planlessness; others tend toward internationalism, social-interest, equality, planning. No wonder that, in the face of these internal disorders, experimentalists criticize religious absolutists for their escapism, anarchism, and dogmatism quite as severely as the latter criticize them. No wonder that, as against the absolutist's dependence upon some secular or divine, but always unquestionable, power, the experimentalist holds that men, their skills and their intelligence, are the sole reliable guide to their own destiny. No wonder that he insists that moral confusions must be solved and purposes fashioned not by less but by *more* experiment, and that all absolutisms are finally of a piece, in the respect that all tend to build cultures that are closed and static rather than open and dynamic.

In the years of the Cold War, the conflict between absolutism and experimentalism has centered on still another issue: the scope and limits of free speech, assembly, and other privileges guaranteed by the Bill of Rights. Those of experimental temper have generally insisted that these privileges must be scrupulously protected, because they are essential to the rational and scientific exploration of every sort of human problem. Those of absolutist temper tend to support political and other maneuvers that would restrict the right of dissent, the right to belong to unpopular parties, and especially the right to advocate beliefs "contrary to the public interest." On this issue religious groups are again divided—some strongly supporting civil liberties because of their concern for religious liberty itself, others tending to define religious liberty in terms of their own absolutist creeds. But experimentalists are themselves often unclear or inconsistent: in recent years, many, as we shall point out in Chapter 6, have taken equivocal stands on the question of the kind and degree of freedom that they would grant to those political minorities who, they contend, once in power, would destroy all freedom. True, the fears and intimidations generated by the mutually hostile attitudes and policies of the Soviet Union and the United States are mainly responsible for these vacillations and confusions. The question that has not yet been resolved, however, is whether the extreme restrictions that are proposed for combating "communism" (a term not always well defined) will not lead to the same absolute ruthlessness of suppression and the same conformity in behavior that characterize totalitarian policy.

Man-against-*Himself versus Man*-for-*Himself*. The final illustration is a kind of recapitulation of the preceding ones, observed now from the vantage point of human nature. In our culture, man seems to be his own worst enemy quite as often as his own best friend. It is enough to remind ourselves that America's sanitariums are filled to overflowing; that the number of qualified psychiatrists falls short of the need by thousands; and that millions of men, women, and children who should receive treatment are not receiving it. To denote the extremes of mental illness we now use the term "schizophrenic" in the more strictly scientific sense of the mental disturbance of split personalities. But the tendency to schizophrenia, which we may characterize as "schizoid," is so insidious and so widespread that no one can say how many people are in varying stages of mental illness from the conflicts besetting them.

The kinds of disturbances from which individuals suffer in our culture are, of course, numerous. Psychiatrists and psychoanalysts today are by no means agreed, either in theory or practice, on how far Freud was right in tracing mental illness so exclusively to malfunctioning of the sexual drive. They do more fully agree that until inner conflicts are removed, until an equilibrium is established in the patient, he cannot hope to be "happy." Typically, they explore the patient's emotional behavior—especially his unconscious motivations—with the expectation that if he can be made aware of such motivations he will be able to face his problems and adopt a pattern of behavior that is internally harmonious.

However helpful this kind of psychotherapy may be in particular cases, the difficulty is that it usually leaves untouched the *status quo* of the patient's cultural environment. It seeks to remove conflicts within, but it does little to remove conflicts without. It insufficiently concerns itself with the problem of whether many individuals can achieve *internal* harmony so long as they do not struggle with other individuals and groups to achieve *external* harmony. If man is against *himself*, the question is whether, more basically, the culture is not against *itself*. If countless individuals suffer from emotional frustration, from violation of "normal" rules of sexual conduct,† or from other troubles, can it be that these are caused by instabilities or cleavages in the institutions, customs, beliefs with which man has surrounded himself? Can the cause be, for example, that, while the supernaturalism of much traditional absolutism frowns upon sexual expression as a necessary evil, the naturalism of a social-experimental way of life looks upon it as life-affirming and a necessary good? Can it be that the economic system that man has been taught to accept forces him to behave acquisitively, in support of self-

† See Alfred C. Kinsey, *Sexual Behavior in the Human Male;* and *Sexual Behavior in the Human Female.*

interest and inequality, at the same time that he wishes to behave generously, in support of social-interest and equality? Can it be that the nationalism that exploits so many hatreds and fears, that threatens his very life in time of war, that produces such political diseases as fascism, is in mortal combat with an internationalism that encourages man to regard all peoples with friendliness and trust and that promises him peace?

To the extent that psychiatry and allied sciences do not squarely face such questions—to the extent that they are governed by a "psychological" approach rather than by one that is equally "sociological" and cultural—they themselves perpetuate those bifurcations of culture that are reflected in the human beings who make up culture. Fortunately, however, the nonsubjective approach has its own quota of able advocates.‡ Erich Fromm is among those who defend "man for himself"—the kind of man who as often as possible says "Yes" rather than "No" to himself and his children; who seeks to satisfy rather than to deny the largest range of his deepest wants; who appreciates that abundant self-expression requires equally abundant and hopeful social-expression; who dedicates himself accordingly to a purposeful, expanding program of life-fulfillment for himself and the widest possible circle of his fellow men.

A TIME OF CULTURAL REVOLUTION

One further interpretive view needs to be added to our cultural portrait. The examples selected to illustrate the hypothesis that ours is a crisis-culture do not adequately reveal that, in various ways, the tensions set up between polar institutions, behaviors, attitudes, are already past the breaking point. That is to say, the energies dammed within them are bursting through the floodgates into the open. The result is that ours may also properly be called a time of cultural revolution.

The concept "revolution" should be defined. It is the shifting of cultural patterns at such accelerated rates that patterns that have hitherto been dominant begin rapidly to collapse, to be replaced by others that have never before been tried. According to this definition, revolutions

‡ See Erich Fromm, *Man for Himself;* Karl Menninger, *Man against Himself.*

may embrace huge areas of the earth; or they may be confined to smaller cultures, to subcultures, even to aspects of a single culture. They need not generate overt violence, although sometimes they do. Nor can we say that revolutionary events inevitably produce fresh cultural patterns. Sometimes they simply collapse; at other times they become *counter*revolutionary, in which case the direction of change is reversed toward patterns still older than those presently disintegrating.

It is true, of course, that change is always occurring, even in the most static of cultures. Indeed, it is often a matter of interpretation whether a particular movement is *evolutionary* (meaning "in a state of gradual transition") or *revolutionary*. That numerous evolutionary changes are taking place in present cultures, including America's, is obvious. What is not so obvious is that many of these slower movements are also cumulations of cultural strain, carrying within them the potentials of revolution. They are connected beneath the surface with streams of energy flowing from and to all parts of the globe—in some cases, energies exploding into volcanic transformations and hence into radically new cultural patterns in place of the old.

Utilizing the kind of evidence provided above, three illustrations may be cited in behalf of the contention that we live in a time of revolution.

Technology. The first illustration is the swift realignments caused by the partnership of science and industry, realignments that have produced social changes greater than any since the Renaissance.*

The single most dramatic symbol, atomic energy, has already changed our outlook on war—its practices, its horrors, its destructive force. And, while atomic energy has not yet succeeded in bringing about a sufficiently strong world government to control its dangers, it has stimulated the need for such a government as have few events in history.

Meanwhile, the technological revolution has reshaped the character of our culture in other ways. The automobile has transformed rural life, especially in America, to such a degree that the former isolation of farm families has almost disappeared. The same isolation has been drastically reduced by mass media of communication—magazines, newspapers, telephone, telegraph, movies, radio—the last of which has brought the voices

* See Robert Jungk, *Tomorrow Is Already Here;* Harrison Brown, *The Challenge of Man's Future.*

of the most remote people of the earth within a split second of one another. Television has even more amazing potentialities as an instrument of cultural contact.

New methods of production and distribution are equally revolutionary. The use of electric power makes it possible to decentralize industrial production and to raise its efficiency manyfold. Under the pressures of global war, quantity production via the assembly line has increased swiftly within the span of a few years. Certain commercial enterprises (General Electric is one) have acquired resources greater than all those of some whole states of the union. The speed of commodity distribution, which multiplied rapidly with the coming of railways, has now reached the stage where it is not unusual to hear of herds of cattle being shipped from continent to continent by air freight. Atomic energy has boundless potentialities, not only for revolutionizing the manufacture of industrial power, but for medicine, transportation, and other fields as well. Already it has reached the stage of practical constructive use. What it will make possible in the future defies imagination.

Economics-Politics. The twentieth century is also signalized by economic-political revolutions that are interrelated with the technological revolution. The most dramatic of these is the Russian—a revolution that not only overthrew a semifeudal order but also replaced it with the first system in history in which the main instruments of industrial and agricultural production are owned and controlled by a nation-state. If we recall that, since 1917, a predominantly illiterate population much larger than that of the United States, and occupying far greater territory, has become literate; that the Union of Socialist Soviet Republics is already the second most powerful nation in the world; and that communism is spreading through other parts of the world, notably the Orient—if we recall such facts we cannot deny, however much we may dislike some of them, that the Russian Revolution is one of the most earth-shaking events in modern history.

While authorities in politics and economics disagree about the extent to which the U.S.S.R. has regressed, in certain respects, to cultural habits reminiscent of czarism, there is less disagreement about the regressive character of fascism and nazism. True, certain of these movements also overthrew earlier regimes. But they replaced them with systems that were largely counterrevolutionary. As against the Communist belief in equality of race or sex, for example, they restored the ancient and medieval pattern of strict inequality—a pattern still influential in Germany, Italy, Argentina, Spain, South Africa, even in parts of America. At the same time, in its exploitation of propaganda methods, in its encouragement of state programs of recreation, and in other ways, fascism, too, has disclosed revolutionary symptoms.

Changes less violent and sweeping in character, but still far-reaching, have occurred, or are occurring, in parts of the British Empire, in Mexico, in the Scandinavian countries, and elsewhere. In all of these, despite temporary attacks and compromises, the shift is toward democratic socialization and public ownership of major industries and natural resources. The patterns that will emerge are not, however, at all clear. Probably they will be different from any now prevalent.

The United States, of all the great countries, is thus far least affected internally by the revolutions of other countries. Yet, even here there have been rapid changes since the 1930's. Some authorities predict that in the event of another depression these changes may well produce new social institutions similar to those of England and other democratic-socialist countries—if they do not produce an Americanized fascism. The increase of public ownership of electric power, the growth of consumer cooperatives, the rise of federal agencies responsible for old-age security and other public welfare—these developments are of enormous significance. Yet the trend is neither consistent nor universally supported. In the years since World War II, popular choice has alternated between political leadership that favors an extension of governmental public responsibility and leadership that strongly disfavors it. And the pendulum may continue to swing.

Abundance. By abundance, our third and last illustration, we mean the economic, social, and esthetic transformations through which the peoples of the world might be provided with resources of healthful, creative, cooperative living. This revolution is in large part the effect of our technological and economic-political revolutions—not wholly an effect, however. As abundance is made possible for hitherto impoverished people—medical care, adequate nourishment and shelter, instruction, art —they, in turn, become powerful causal agents of rapid change in, say, industrial productivity.

The third revolution has not yet, of course, reached vast areas of the earth. In this sense it is, perhaps to a greater extent than the others, potential rather than actual. What is not potential is our increasing awareness that abundance *can* be provided if we are wise enough. Not only does medical science know that the sick and ill-nourished, wherever they may be, can be made healthy and well nourished. Not only do psychology and the related sciences know that the average illiterate, whoever he may be, can learn to read, write, cooperate, and operate machines. The applied arts and sciences (chemistry is one) know that plastic, nylon, and other new synthetic products can be shaped into thousands of useful articles, from household appliances to clothing.

Nor is the fact that the world's population is steadily increasing necessarily fatal. Actually, the declining rate of infant mortality and the rise in life expectancy are largely the consequences of more abundant health and economic opportunity. Various scientists insist, moreover, that abundant sources of food have never yet been tapped—in the oceans, for example, or the arctic regions. At the same time, the need to control population growth in countries like India is considered by many authorities to be paramount—a need that will require enormous study and experimentation.‡

More deep-cutting than any of these potentials of a revolution in abundance are the potentials within man. Frustrated as he has so often been by life-denying customs, by ignorance and superstitions, by cleavages in loyalty and other values, man has never come into full command of his own energy, creative intelligence, and strength. He has been ruled over more often than he has ruled. He has been starved, hoodwinked, exploited, cajoled, intimidated, frightened more often than he has been decently fed, well informed, respected, encouraged, aroused. With all the weaknesses that remain for him to conquer, "the next development in man"* is the mature social development of man himself. This revolution, too, is already under way.

Philosophies of Education in a Crisis-Culture

Philosophy and education, we have said, permeate every fiber of our culture. Philosophy does so because every culture, literate and nonliterate

‡ See Bertrand Russell, *New Hopes for a Changing World.*
* See L. L. Whyte, *The Next Development in Man.*

alike, has a pattern of basic beliefs, which provides those who accept that culture with greater or lesser articulation and significance.† Education does so because every culture provides formal or informal symbols and trainings, which aim to translate its philosophy into habits and skills by showing its members how to serve it most fruitfully. If philosophy expresses the beliefs of a culture, education helps to carry them out and, in so doing, builds additional habits and skills useful to that expression.

Whether judged in terms of sophistication, worth, or adequacy, it is equally apparent that neither philosophy nor education is always of the same serviceability. Nor is this true only of nonliterate cultures; literate cultures and subcultures also differ to an astonishing extent. Oriental philosophies and programs of learning are very unlike Occidental ones. The Soviet Union constructs its entire system upon a definite philosophy called "dialectical materialism" and builds its educational institutions, from nursery schools to universities, with conscious insistence that everything they teach shall demonstrate that philosophy. Fascism and nazism expressed views of the world, *Weltanschauungen,* that were transplanted into their schools. Although less logical and profound than those of the Russians, fascist theories nevertheless convinced as well as trained many millions of persons and left heavy deposits of influence upon other millions long after their political collapse.

It is the "democratic" cultures, however, in which we are mainly interested. That both philosophy and education have been of utmost importance to modern England, France, Norway, and other countries is shown by every cultural history that has been written about Western civilization. The same generalization applies to the United States. Philosophers have sought steadily to give distinctive expression to the beliefs, attitudes, and functions of the young nation from the earliest pre-Revolutionary days to our own. Education, too, has been regarded as one of our chief instruments of cultural solidarity and progress. The history of American *philosophy,* interpreted in the perspective of American *education,* is at the center of the adventure which is American *culture.* Yet the present volume cannot and should not isolate this triple relation wholly from still wider relations. They are wider, not only in the sense that our present and future are bound up with the present and future of the Soviet Union, of Asia, indeed of the world; they are also shaped

† See Paul Radin, *Primitive Man as a Philosopher.*

by cultures extending much deeper into the past than America's few short centuries of history.

The Role of Philosophy in Culture: A Point of View. Let us be perfectly clear. In approaching our study of the most influential philosophies of education of our day, we do so in terms of a particular point of view. Even in the two preceding chapters—though more conspicuously in this one—certain predilections have affected our exposition and our interpretation. To deny this would be to contend that these pages are immune to influences that are held to be universal everywhere else—a foolish contention indeed. This volume, no less than others on every conceivable subject, is conditioned by its cultural environment and the beliefs indigenous to that environment. The reader is urged to become as sensitive to them as possible, to criticize and compare them, not only with those of other writers and students in educational philosophy, but also with his own, and to decide for himself, as consciously as possible, which to reject, modify, or accept. There are two special reasons for this observation.

In the first place, the cultural interpretation is of utmost importance for the remaining chapters, for it constitutes *our most inflential instrument of critical appraisal.* Because of its centrality, we here summarize and supplement a few of the more important features of our key concept. Any culture is:

1. a product of the physical, biological, psychological, and social levels of the environment;
2. a distinctive level of nature, man-made, and not reducible to any of these other levels;
3. a complex unity of all animate and inanimate, physical and non-physical things or events that have been created or affected by man as a member of society;
4. a pattern or configuration of these things and events that possesses regularity in both time and space and is made possible by habit, custom, law, and other man-made processes or structures;
5. a continuity of human experience transmitted through learning and communicating that experience, rather than through biological heredity;
6. a way of life that profoundly conditions the attitudes and conduct of each individual member; and

7. a symbol encompassing all humanly built objects; all institutions —economic, religious, political, social; all arts, languages, philosophies; all mores, routines, practices; all beliefs, attitudes, faiths.

The last characterization deserves an additional comment. The position we shall take is that culture is to be regarded, not as a phenomenon of nature existing entirely by itself or generated out of itself, but rather as a *symbol* for important kinds of human experiences that are not sufficiently explained by any other symbol. In common with some, but by no means all, cultural theorists, we shall, in short, utilize culture as an abstraction—an idea through which to approach particularly the American culture of our day, with the hope that, by its use, we can more fruitfully clarify, explain, and act upon its meaning.

In the second place, it is only fair to state that a cultural interpretation of philosophy is by no means universally accepted. Although lip service is paid to it freely enough, the fact is that even the most recent histories of thought fail, with few exceptions, to project philosophy sharply upon the screen of specific cultures. This negligence is understandable. For one thing the knowledge and expertness in the social sciences that are indispensable to such an interpretation are relatively recent and limited. For another thing, much theory, especially philosophic theory, appears so specialized, so quarantined from experience, that there is a temptation to regard it as purely intellectual and completely self-contained.

Still, as we are able to expand our knowledge of economic and political forces, of anthropology and sociology, of class and racial influence upon psychological, esthetic, and religious experience, we find that more careful attention is paid to the near heresy that philosophers, also, are human beings. Like other human beings, they not only affect their cultural environments but are strongly affected by them. There is, in other words, a reciprocity of influence between philosophy and culture. Although it is surely true that such experts in culture as anthropologists are affected deeply by philosophic beliefs (sometimes called *metacultural* beliefs‡), it is at least as true that philosophers are affected by culture. Plato and Aristotle, for example, are occasionally treated less as geniuses spinning speculations out of the fecundity of their intellects than as Greek citizens and patriots brilliantly studying the upheavals that rocked

‡ See David Bidney, *Theoretical Anthropology,* pp. 156ff.

the Athenian life of their generation and offering grand-scale solutions in accordance with their aristocratic values. Others are similarly treated—the Englishman John Locke, for example, or the American philosopher-statesman whom he influenced, Thomas Jefferson.

It is unnecessary to argue that everyone who philosophizes does so only because of his interest in the culture. Although the philosopher who engages in "pure" thought is still, like the speculative mathematician or artist, inescapably a member of his culture, let us assume that he speculates for the sheer intellectual delight it affords. But let us also observe, as we study the biographies of influential thinkers, how often they were, or are, alive to the vital issues of their generation. Let us ask whether the moments of philosophy's highest creativity, richest originality, and greatest effect upon cultural life have not usually been moments when the challenge was keenest, the need for fresh analyses and syntheses most desperate.

After all, when we regard philosophy as essentially the attempt to express dependable beliefs—when, moreover, these no longer seem to coincide with realities, values, truths of a given time—surely it is plausible to anticipate that renewed questioning, balancing, and reconstructing are almost certain to occur. True, the most penetrating of these activities may not occur in academic halls. As in the instance of a Thomas Paine, they may emanate from men hardly regarded in their time as philosophers. Their role, nevertheless, continues to be played; and the more violent or tragic the drama of culture, the more conspicuous and powerful that role may prove to be.

From this viewpoint, the present culture, however strained, divided, or explosive it is in many ways, presents a magnificent opportunity. It calls upon philosophy to exercise the highest possible integrity in order that our institutions, habits, faiths may be scrutinized, reaffirmed, modified, or, if need be, reconstructed. Here is philosophy's prime obligation to our age of conflict and revolution.

The choices before us

Levels of Belief as Cultural-Educational Choices. A crisis-culture, typically, is not one for whose ills we find a single diagnosis or a single cure. The deeper and wider the crisis or the more complex the schemes of living that make up a given culture, the more numerous and difficult the choices that confront it.

Such a culture is our own. Individuals, groups, nations are by no means agreed on what is wrong, or right, with our basic patterns and choices of belief. As a matter of fact, the violent clashes of opposition and disagreement constitute one of the clearest symptoms of crisis itself.

Nevertheless, it is possible to organize the great choices before us and thus to observe how those patterns of belief that we considered, above, from the "inside" of philosophy grow in significance when they are viewed from the "outside," from the standpoint of culture. As a matter of fact, were we to continue to restrict these patterns to purely personal alternatives, we should be perpetuating a common fallacy of the philosophy textbooks. We should be assuming that patterns of belief are largely mind-made and subjective, whereas in fact they are also and more fundamentally social, economic, familial—in short, cultural and objective. This is what is meant by saying that the concepts and definitions considered above in abstract form can become fully meaningful only as they interpenetrate with experiences observable in concrete form.

We wish to recall, then, the several levels summarized in Chapter 2:

1. the *complacent* choice,
2. the *negative* choice,
3. the *skeptical* choice,
4. the *agnostic* choice,
5. the *eclectic* choice,
6. the *conservative* choice,
7. the *liberal* choice,
8. the *regressive* choice, and
9. the *radical* choice.

All of these choices, and perhaps others, have their coteries of contemporary spokesmen. Granting again that in actual experience they are never as sharp or distinct as they appear when isolated conceptually, nevertheless they do give us a kind of scale by which to view ourselves. All are couched in their own terms within the major institutions of our culture—within politics, religion, art, or education. We shall clarify this thesis with some educational examples.

Inadequate Levels of Choice. Let us consider, first, the complacent choice. While scarcely philosophic in any full sense, still it is not uncommon even in such a time of bewildering uncertainty as our own. Many schools refuse to face the issues between two such powerful cultures as those of Russia and America. Others yield to whatever pressures toward conformity happen to be dominant at a given time. Still others gloss over the disturbances created by shifting moral standards. In brief, they discourage the critical expression of beliefs by training young people to suppose that what *seems* on the surface to be real, true, or good about our culture *must be* real, true, or good.

The second and third levels—negativism and skepticism—are also widespread. When common opportunity, social harmony, or peace is rare, not only do negative reactions become exceptionally numerous but some skeptics cry that trustworthy patterns of belief are not possible at all. Here is one explanation for the avalanche of criticism falling upon current education. Doubt arises about the efficacy of most conventional activities. It extends to a demand for retrenchment "all along the line." It may even surreptitiously deny, as fascism openly denies, that most people can learn enough to rule themselves wisely, thus implying that *disbelief* in freedom or equality for the average individual is better than positive belief.

The next two levels of expression—agnosticism and eclecticism—are commonplace. In education, the latter is symbolized by a polyglot of courses that presents smatterings of many things without commitment or design; the former, by the extent to which, in the fraternity of scholars, impartiality becomes a badge of academic virtue and partiality becomes a vice. Yet, granting the case for diversified curriculums, granting also that to see "all sides of every question" is a worthy aim when it is not merely a smoke screen for timidity or hidden biases, we may also question whether these choices, too, do not mirror tensions in our culture. Could it be that the perplexing diversity of economic forms, the cross purposes of scientific research, the mutual hostility of political philosophies, the fierce oppositions between absolutism and experimentalism —could it be that such phenomena, rather than the reasons more frequently professed, are the reasons for the current fashion of neutrality and piecemeal education?

"Deeper" Levels of Choice. The levels of expression thus far glimpsed through the lens of our crisis-culture are by no means the most

adequate ones. Not that these choices are useless; from the Cynics of ancient Greece to the skeptics of the eighteenth century, and down to the "impartial spectators" and agnostics of our modern generation, periods of eruption have induced critiques that act as healthful purgatives. But these are still preliminary to the central task. Full expression of our patterns of belief must be organic and constructive. It must aim, not merely to unearth defects, but through examination to seek and estimate our strengths. It must aim also to weld truth, value, and reality into unified relations that overarch the various fields of nature and of man. Hence, if we wish to follow further, there are four chief routes remaining among which we must ultimately choose:

1. *We may, with the conservative, reaffirm consciously and clearly those habits of living and expressions of belief that have hitherto prevailed in modern culture.* In education, should we settle upon this choice, we would identify ourselves with the kind of theory and practice that we shall call the *essentialist* philosophy.

2. *Or we may, with the liberal, prefer to modify our beliefs and practices one step at a time.* Neither lagging too far behind nor moving too far ahead of the rate of change of the present culture, we would choose in education the program and doctrine of the *progressivist* philosophy.

3. *Or we may, with the regressivist, demand a reversion to the spirit and principles of an earlier and, for those of such persuasion, a nobler human order.* Convinced that the present culture is failing man, we would insist, educationally, upon a resurrection of the premises and proposals of the *perennialist* philosophy.

4. *Or, finally, we may, with the radical, choose to envision and assist in the birth of a new cultural design.* Convinced, too, that the present culture is no longer adequate, we would subscribe to the educational beliefs and actions of the *reconstructionist* philosophy.

We do not say that these are the only choices possible. We do not say that every educational philosophy of any consequence *must* fit into one of these categories. Some certainly do not. We do say that, for America at least, they are by far the most consequential and potent. Yet, we repeat, they must not be considered choices of a purely philosophic character. They *are* philosophic, of course. But more basically they are the choices that confront our "schizophrenic" and, in some ways, revolutionary culture. The choice that we make may well determine the structures and methods, not only of education, but also of virtually all our major institutions, habits, faiths, and practices.

Alternative philosophies of education: a thumbnail sketch

As a final step before turning to extended examination of alternative philosophies, and especially of the first three, we now state concisely, and *with minimum qualification,* what each one of these philosophies means. They are not treated impartially. As in the case of our conception of philosophy as the interpretation of culture, we have no wish to conceal the viewpoint from which we appraise them. But neither do we wish to conceal our intention to examine each pattern of belief and practice with as much care as space and competence permit. Each has its able and earnest devotees. Each must be listened to with patience and respect. Only when they have been given a fair hearing may we be able to decide fairly and confidently among them.

First: Essentialism. Essentialism is the philosophy of education that holds that the schools must be grounded, first of all, upon the *essentials,* that is, upon the tried and tested heritage of skills, facts, and laws of knowledge that have come down to us through modern civilization. The essentialist is, therefore, one who builds education largely upon the foundations of what we call the traditional curriculum. The mind of the student is conceived as a set of faculties, which the school provides with as much of the organized content of history and the objective world as it is able to contain.

The teacher serves chiefly as mediator between the store of knowledge possessed by the outside world and the mind of the student. Examinations are mainly devices by which schools measure the quantity and evaluate the quality of content held by the mind. Essentialism, we can readily understand, is extremely critical of any theories and practices in education that subordinate what it regards as the fundamental process of learning, a process that is primarily, though not exclusively, one of absorption.

Second: Progressivism. Essentialism is especially critical of the second major theory—progressivism. For this philosophy holds the primary purpose of education to be, not at all one of absorbing the maximum content of the outside world, but rather one of stimulating people to think with effectiveness. To think means to analyze, to criticize, to select among alternatives, and to venture solutions upon the basis of both analysis and selection—in short, to practice the scientific method. It is to carry on continuous, intelligent adjustments and readjustments with the natural and social environment of which everyone is a part. Only when this occurs can we properly say that we *progress.*

Schools, if properly organized, are media through which the child thus learns to live intelligently—that is to say, critically and responsibly. They are centers of democratic living, for they should provide endless opportunities to meet dynamic, timely problems by cooperative participation on the part of the largest possible number of student-citizens. In such an educational environment, teachers are also partners in the common enterprise of intelligent social experience; and learning takes place through active utilization of that experience.

Third: Perennialism. The third of our four constructive philosophies, perennialism, holds that the only hope for sound education, and indeed for a sound culture, lies in a restoration of the spirit that governed education during the Middle Ages. Hence, the perennialist is interested in emphasizing not so much the social heritage as the eternal principles of truth, goodness, and beauty, which are outside space and time—which are, in a profound sense, everlasting and therefore *perennial.* The medieval system of education was, in essence, dedicated to the search for "first principles" of this nature. The aim was to search out, by logical analysis, axioms so invulnerable and deductively certain that anyone possessing the necessary intellectual equipment would recognize them as self-evident.

It is the belief of perennialists today that education has become corrupted by its gradual departure from this medieval kind of certainty. Hence, the supreme aim of education should be to train intellectual leaders so brilliantly endowed with the intuitive capacity to recognize first principles that we may, for the first time in centuries, be led out of the darkness that threatens to engulf mankind and into the light of a rationally determined order.

Fourth: Reconstructionism. The fourth philosophy, reconstructionism, agrees on one point with perennialism: there is desperate need for clarity and certainty, for our civilization is fraught with confusion and bewilderment. It radically disagrees, however, with perennialism's solution. Instead of returning to the Middle Ages, it would attempt to build the widest possible consensus about the supreme aims that should govern man in the *reconstruction* of his environment.

These aims can be delineated through cooperative search. Indeed, the reconstructionist is convinced that already there is growing consensus or agreement about their basic characteristics. The world of the future should be a world that the common man rules not merely in theory but in fact. It should be a world in which the technological potentialities already clearly discernible are released for the creation of health, abundance, and security for the masses of people of every color, nationality, and creed. It should be a world in which national sovereignty is subordinated to international authority. In short, it should be a world in which the dreams of ancient Christianity and modern democracy are fused with modern technology and art into a culture that is controlled by the great majority of the people, who are the sovereign determiners of their own destiny.

A Word of Caution. To deal justly with these alternative philosophies we must recognize that they are by no means so concisely and discretely organized as our brief epitomizations might lead us to suppose. As we shall discover again and again in subsequent chapters, each position has something in common with the others. Essentialism and perennialism share a good deal of the same philosophic, educational, and cultural outlook, as do reconstructionism and progressivism. A diagram may help here if we bear in mind that it does not intend to measure the precise *extent* of overlappings either among the four positions regarded as wholes, or among individual advocates of these positions, who may differ in the degree to which they accept one or another of the several points of view.

There is a second need for caution. The concepts we have chosen to organize and interpret major educational theories are *only* concepts—that is to say, they are not to be regarded as objectively real systems that exist, as it were, independently of man's critical operations with and upon them. As in the case of the concept "culture," they are rather to be utilized as abstractions or intellectual tools that help us more clearly to organize, analyze, and evaluate interrelated, yet often quite heterogeneous, bodies of educational and cultural experience. In brief, they are working categories through which we hope to interpret more meaningfully the patterns of experience that they symbolize.

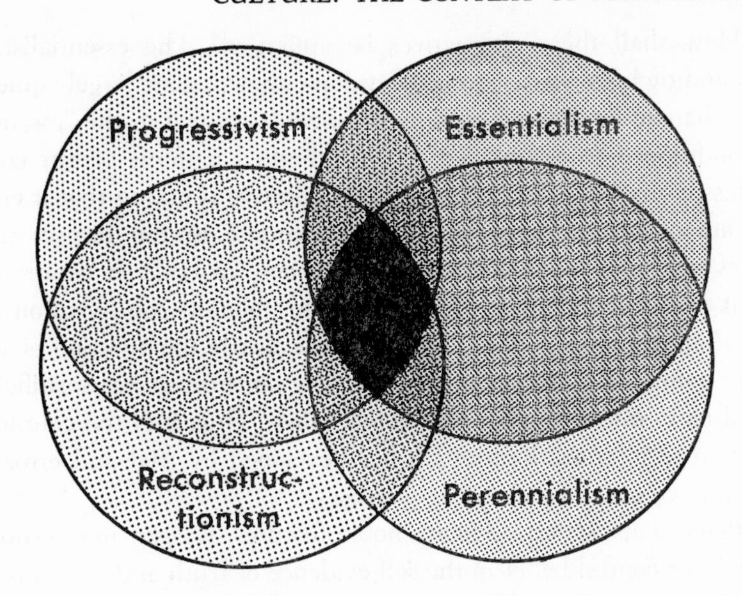

The Cultural Context in Perspective. Returning now to the cultural context of these working categories of educational belief, we see how they roughly parallel what many of us in America would call, respectively, the conservative, liberal, regressive, and radical levels of attitude and action in economics, religion, science, art, politics, and other fields. Recognizing that they overlap and that they are to be considered as organizing abstractions from diffused bodies of thinking and practice, let us nevertheless emphasize their broad differences of focus. The essentialist is the conservative because, however "liberal" his protestations, he would solve the problems of our time by developing behavior skilled mainly in conserving, rather than in changing, the essential content and structure of the pre-existent world. The progressivist is the genuine liberal because he would meet our crisis by developing minds and habits skilled as instruments in behalf of progressive, gradual, evolutionary change. The perennialist is the regressivist because he would deal with contemporary issues by reacting against them in favor of solutions extraordinarily similar to those of a culture long past—or even by escaping into an intellectual realm of timeless perfection. The reconstructionist is the radical because he would solve our problems not by conserving, or modifying, or retreating, but by future-looking. He would build a new order of civilization, under genuinely *public* control, dedicated to the fulfillment of the natural values for which humanity has been struggling, consciously or unconsciously, for many centuries.

How shall these alternatives be appraised? The essentialist, notwithstanding his sincerity, would develop minds that are largely quiescent rather than active—young citizens who, while trained in the "essentials," are conditioned to acceptance of the inherited patterns of our culture. Progressivism, while the techniques of reflective thinking that it emphasizes are of utmost importance, is inadequate in the respect that it focuses too much upon means at the expense of ends. It expresses the typical experimental spirit of open-minded, tolerant consideration of all sides of all questions, but it fails to answer clearly the question of where we are going. In this concern for *how* we *do* think it has insufficiently helped us to discover *what* we *should* think. Thus it is the counterpart of a culture in transition, which has developed by trial and error with minimum concern for clear-cut purposes.

Perennialism, despite many noble features, is open to question because, in its central belief in the self-evidence of truth and values beyond public and scientific verification, it sets up absolute and fixed standards. These, in the hands of corrupt leaders, could easily be utilized (as they have, historically, often been utilized) to justify arbitrary authority without sanction of the majority, who are always in a democracy the final judge of standards.

Reconstructionism, the remaining alternative, cannot claim the status of recognition or organized support that is enjoyed by the other three alternatives. It is probably fair to say that American culture and education are only now beginning to show serious concern for its implications. Also, it is unquestionably open to its own share of criticisms—for example, that it may encourage a brand of educational evangelism. Nevertheless, a number of educational thinkers and social scientists in various countries are converging toward this position. While repudiating no part of the constructive achievement of progressivism, while recognizing also the importance both of essential knowledge and rational analysis, this philosophy commits itself, first of all, to the renascence of culture. It is infused with the conviction that out of our period of crisis, struggle, and chronic frustration, out of the actual or potential revolutions occurring around us should emerge nothing less than control of the industrial system, of public services, and of human and natural resources by and for the common people, who, through the ages, have struggled for a life of security, decency, and peace for themselves and their children. We shall omit systematic consideration of reconstructionism in this volume, in order to focus upon the three positions that, thus far, are dominant in their influence upon American education.†

Philosophic Approaches to Education: Plan of Study

The Order of Treatment. We shall interpret the first three philosophies of education not in the sequence given above but as follows: (1) progressivism, (2) essentialism, and (3) perennialism. The reasons for this shift will become apparent as we proceed, but it is helpful to anticipate. Progressivism and its wider rationale, liberalism, have been in many ways the most articulate and influential schools of social, philosophical, and educational thought and action in the American culture of the past half-century. Even where they have not succeeded in bringing institutions and methods into complete harmony with their particular beliefs—and, of course, they frequently have not—they have received widespread and sincere verbal homage. Nor is this influence limited to America. Both through the international impact of our own leaders and through the emergence of theory and practice closer to the habits and structures of foreign lands, the movement called "progressive education" spreads far and wide.

But success never goes unchallenged. While it is true that both essentialism and perennialism are much older philosophies in the history of education, these levels of education-and-culture have in the past few years taken on fresh, even militant, vigor. Their recent formulations are conditioned, moreover, not merely by the explosive events and ideas of the present period of history, but by progressivism itself. Indeed, each of these positions (as well as reconstructionism, which, it should be remembered, we shall not develop in this volume for reasons already mentioned) may now be interpreted as a counteroffensive against progressivism. Still more broadly, they can be judged as the leading cultural alternatives, at least in America, to the liberal way of life.

† Readers who are interested in reconstructionism may consult Theodore Brameld, *Toward a Reconstructed Philosophy of Education.*

Although our attention must be focused upon the *educational* expression of these constructive levels, we should always remember, then, that the three philosophies are to be viewed in a broader perspective. The oppositions among them—sometimes subtle, sometimes crass, sometimes friendly, sometimes hostile—are at bottom *cultural* oppositions. Their manifestations through curriculum structures, psychologies of learning, and school administrations are all symptoms of beliefs, attitudes, habits, and institutions that permeate every strand of experience, whether it be economic, political, religious, scientific, esthetic, social, or personal. Those who accept one or another of these basic choices may not always be consistent about them; they may not always admit, either to themselves or to others, that the beliefs they hold about education are tied by a thousand knots to their beliefs about the culture. Nevertheless, it is our business to show that the knots are there, even if hidden, and that we need to examine them in order to see whether they are sufficiently secure.

It is our business to show these things for deeper reasons than simply because teachers and citizens are expected to have some knowledge of them as part of their intellectual equipment. Much more seriously, we are concerned to test our major educational patterns because America and the world are at a decisive juncture in their history. We have offered brief evidence to show that mankind is sickened with struggles, frustrations, and bewilderments, which are so epidemic as to endanger the survival of civilization. We have noted, too, how totalitarianism—either Fascist or Communist—has already overwhelmed large areas of the globe and now threatens other areas.

In America, the most persuasive choices before us are couched in less extreme forms than those that convince so many millions elsewhere. Our Communist movement is small; our Fascist movement is amorphous. Indeed, all the philosophies we are to examine profess devotion to the ideal of democracy. Each one sincerely holds that *it* is the most real, the truest, and the best exponent of that ideal. Yet, whether such claims can be sustained under inspection remains to be seen. We need to become supersensitive to the *meaning* of such words as democracy—to determine in what ways the perennialist's conception, say, differs from the progressivist's, to decide which of the two is the more defensible, and to ask whether either one is any longer wholly acceptable. Finally, we need to inquire whether, in view of America's strategic position as the leading world power, its chief philosophies of education-and-culture are not bound to affect deeply, and to be affected by, those of other powers, including either the Communist philosophy or the Fascist, or both.

The Practice of Educational Theories. If our concern with the crisis-culture that surrounds and infiltrates educational theories is unceasing, we should also be aware of the dramatization of these theories in practical teaching and learning. All three theories to be considered are in practical operation in the everyday programs of American education.

Without doubt the most widespread is the essentialist. The curriculums and methods of our typical urban and rural schools are probably still more heavily weighted by the institutions and habits conserved by this philosophy than by those of either the progressivist or the perennialist philosophy. To be sure, these curriculums and methods do not rest upon essentialist beliefs in any completely articulate way. They often exemplify a level of choice that is partly complacent or partly eclectic—perhaps both complacent and eclectic. Nevertheless, it is not difficult to discover a generous degree of compatibility between their implicit essentialism and the explicit philosophy that can be, and often is, brought to serve and improve upon their programs.

The prevalence of essentialist practices in education does not contradict our remarks above about the impact of progressivism on school practice as well as on theory. In terms of a consciously formulated philosophy of education, it remains true that progressivism thus far has been the most original, most prominent, and most alluring movement in American school history. Even if its influence continues to be theoretical more often than it is practical in its effects, eclectic more often than coherent, yet many schools and some colleges have been built upon its philosophic principles, while innumerable others have been influenced by them.

Perennialist schools, too, are easy to locate. All parochial education under control of the Roman Catholic Church, for example, is admittedly perennialist. In many public schools, also, the beliefs of this level of choice are to be found mingled with essentialist beliefs, since the latter are unusually hospitable to them. Perhaps most conspicuously, perennialism impinges strongly upon a number of leading colleges and universities whose leadership is secular.

It is not our main purpose to describe these varieties of educational experience. However, the reader should aim to become familiar with them and to appreciate that they are always the ultimate test of the philosophies that underlie practice. References in the Appendix describe examples. It is also a rewarding experiment to visit schools for the purpose of discovering their underlying philosophies. Do they consistently carry out any one of our major types? Do they merely provide, in eclectic fashion, a mixture of two or more types? Do any of the schools represent possibly a still different type of philosophy, or level of choice, from any of those we shall study?

Outline of Chapters. The three remaining parts of this book are organized in parallel fashion. The opening chapter of each part presents, in turn:

1. a preview of the entire level of choice, together with our evaluation of it;
2. an epitomization of its underlying philosophy;
3. the historic roots of that philosophy;
4. its beliefs about reality;
5. its beliefs about knowledge; and
6. its beliefs about value.

The middle chapter of each section is concerned with the educational theory that emerges from its philosophy:

1. its historic backgrounds;
2. its beliefs about learning;
3. its beliefs about the curriculum; and
4. its beliefs about the control of education.

The final chapter of each part is devoted to critical evaluation. Although the sequence of treatment is less systematic, the aim is, first, to determine the cultural matrix of the particular educational theory; second, to appraise its adequacy for our kind of culture. A special word should be offered here about the evaluation of progressivism in Chapter 6. Because this philosophy of education is viewed as standing at the center of current controversy, we propose to devote considerable attention to the nature of the counterattacks upon it and its own defense against them. The aim is to create a feeling of unusual conflict and tension. For if, as we shall contend, progressivism is a symbol of our unstable culture, then it is in this context that the other major positions, as alternatives to progressivism, must be presented and evaluated. Each part concludes with a summary of the respective philosophy.

It will be noted that, in terms of time, the organization of materials is backward rather than forward. We shall begin with the present-centered philosophy of progressivism, which emerged in the last half of the nineteenth century and reached its most mature expression sometime between the first and second quarters of the twentieth century.

Next is essentialism, which developed its main characteristics during the modern centuries, beginning with the Renaissance. This philosophy achieved its richest formulation about the middle of the nineteenth century, although it still continues to be powerful.

The third philosophy, perennialism, is by far the oldest in its direct origins. Its chief principles were shaped in ancient Greece several centuries before Christ, and it attained its widest sphere of influence—prior, at least, to our own period—in the thirteenth century after Christ.

When the reader has completed this volume, he may wish to look back sequentially upon the development of these three positions. He will discover many cases of perennialist influence upon essentialism and of essentialist influence upon progressivism. In the framework of this study, however, there is no advantage in arranging these positions in genetic order. It seems at least as logical to trace causes back from effects as, in the conventional history of any subject, to trace effects forward from causes. What we are most concerned with, in any case, is the cultural crisis *of our time*. Because this is the crux, we wish to view all three levels of choice as *present* choices, designed to appeal to us *now*. This is the wish, also, of their most important contemporary spokesmen.

Summary of Part One: Philosophy, Culture, and Education

The central challenge of Part I and of this entire work is, in essence, that education in our times is faced with the urgent obligation to assess its failures and successes honestly, relentlessly, and fearlessly. Reasons for such an obligation do not, however, become evident merely by the study of education as such. Rather, our first need is to analyze the deeply opposing views that beset theory and practice, by placing education in clear relation with two other spheres of human endeavor and creation:

the first, philosophy, the second, culture. Only as this is accomplished shall we be able to examine and select wisely among the major alternatives confronting the schools of America and the world.

The import of philosophy for education is, therefore, the theme of Chapter 2. Philosophy should be removed from its isolation as a rarefied academic discipline and brought into direct, intimate relation with everyday events. As a matter of fact, as Chapter 2 points out, "all of us philosophize whenever we try to express the things we believe about our lives and about our relations to the rest of life." The task becomes more difficult, of course, as we seek adequacy of expression when faced with conflicts of belief within ourselves, with other persons, or with other economic or cultural groups. Nor can we avoid making some kind of choice in the face of such conflicts. Even if we decide merely to yield to complacency, we are, in one sense, making a choice—just as we are doing so if, at another level, we decide that only a thoroughgoing refurbishment of our earlier patterns of belief and conduct can satisfy our intellectual, moral, and social aims and self-respect.

To engage in a conscientious effort at philosophic self-examination and articulation requires, further, that we consider our beliefs in terms of three important areas from which no human being can possibly escape: (1) the area of reality—studied by that branch of philosophy called *ontology*; (2) the area of knowledge—studied by *epistemology*; and (3) the area of value—studied by *axiology*. These areas and branches are concerned, respectively, with clarifying the premises and standards by which we believe some things are real, others illusory; some things true, others false; some things good, beautiful, or socially desirable, other things bad, ugly, or socially undesirable.

Philosophy is also concerned with the problem of relations: (1) relations that connect or fuse the subject matter within each of its three great areas or branches; (2) those that provide some principle of integration among its branches (naturalism and supernaturalism are influential samples); (3) those that relate philosophy to one or another field, such as religion, art, politics, and education; and (4) those that aim to bring all fields of knowledge and experience into an ordered outlook upon life and destiny. It goes without saying that philosophy's relational functions are difficult—at best, they can be achieved only in degree. Yet such achievement is not impossible. More than at any time in modern history, it now becomes imperative.

The reasons *why* it is imperative are the main concern of Chapter 3. In the conception of culture as the total environment fashioned by man, we find evidence for the diagnosis that ours is a culture caught in a maelstrom of strain, conflict, and frustration. However we may try to conceal our "schizophrenic" symptoms from ourselves, even defenders of American culture cannot deny such chronic oppositions as:

self-interest versus social-interest;
inequality versus equality;
planlessness versus planning;
nationalism versus internationalism;
absolutism versus experimentalism;
man-against-himself versus man-for-himself.

Already, moreover, some of these conflicts are bursting into revolutionary transformations—institutional, behavioral, attitudinal—which reach every corner of the globe:

the revolution in technology (notably communication, distribution, mass production);
the revolution in economics-politics (notably communism, fascism, democratic socialism, and the welfare state);
the revolution in potential or actual abundance (notably medicine, synthetics, food, and—most exciting of all—human abilities and self-directive powers).

It is in this kind of cultural context that both education and philosophy must now be reconsidered. Both are intrinsic to culture, simple or complex. On the one hand, philosophy can now be regarded as the effort of a culture to become conscious of and articulate to itself. On the other hand, education is the effort of a culture to reinforce and carry out the beliefs expressed through its philosophy.

This is not to say that beliefs and supporting practices are always of a single type. Particularly in a time of instability, beliefs crystallize on different levels of cultural as well as philosophic expression. In our American culture, they fall roughly into two main clusters: those levels of expression that seem inadequate because complacent, negative, skeptical, agnostic, or eclectic; and those that seem more adequate because, whether chiefly conservative, liberal, regressive, or radical, they are all rounded out as solidly constructive and integrated avenues of educational and cultural choice. It is these latter choices that, of course, deserve the bulk of our attention and respect. Let us reiterate that none is to be judged merely as a theory limited to schools. The schools, to be sure, are the pivot of our attention. But each way is also a choice—a decisive choice—which America needs to examine and evaluate as a therapeutic for the crisis-culture of our midcentury.

Notes

[1] Edward B. Tylor, *Primitive Culture,* p. 1.

[2] Franz Boas, "Anthropology," *Encyclopædia of the Social Sciences,* Vol. II, p. 79.

[3] A. L. Kroeber and Clyde Kluckhohn, *Culture: A Critical Review of Concepts and Definitions,* p. 145.

[4] Clyde Kluckhohn, *Mirror for Man,* pp. 228-261.

[5] Laura Thompson, *Culture in Crisis,* p. 161.

[6] David Bidney, *Theoretical Anthropology,* p. 349.

[7] H. G. Barnett, *Innovation: The Basis of Cultural Change,* p. 89. Copyright 1953 by McGraw-Hill Book Company and reprinted with their permission.

[8] Lewis Mumford, *The Condition of Man,* p. 14. Copyright 1944 by Harcourt, Brace and Company and reprinted with their permission.

[9] Hans Kohn, *The Twentieth Century, A Midway Account of the Western World,* p. 19. Copyright 1949 by Hans Kohn and reprinted with the permission of The Macmillan Company.

PART TWO

PROGRESSIVISM

Education as Cultural Transition

CHAPTER 4

Philosophic Beliefs of Progressivism

THE SINGLE MOST INFLUENTIAL PHILOSOPHY OF EDUCATION IN America for well over a quarter of a century has been progressivism. It has won the support of more outstanding theorists than any competing philosophy, and it has affected practice on every level, from nursery school to adult forum. It has also generated violent criticism as well as downright hostility among philosophers and scholars of differing orientations. Progressivism has been and still remains a vastly important point of view—enriching, exciting, controversial. No teacher and no citizen who is earnestly concerned with the schools of America or of the world can ignore or pass lightly over this philosophy and what it means for culture and education in the twentieth century.

Preview of Progressivism

Such immense influence derives not so much from its theoretical formulation, however, as from the modern milieu of which it is a sweeping and sensitive interpretation. This milieu has been of such a character as to encourage widespread acceptance and implementation of the very beliefs peculiar to progressivism. In Chapter 6 we shall pay further attention to the social, economic, and political conditions that have not only made progressivism a powerful movement but are now largely responsible for negative attacks upon it and for the present formulation of positive counterphilosophies. At this point, we wish merely to recall one salient emphasis from the picture of these conditions given above (see pp. 63-64): *the technological, experimental, this-worldly habits and accomplishments that have so powerfully shaped our modern culture.* Such habits and accomplishments, above all others, dominate the progressivist outlook. They have been reinterpreted and reworked into a theory and program of universal education.

"The Liberal Road to Culture." This outlook may be called "the liberal road to culture." It is the road considered by far the safest and most promising of all those open to us and along which we are, therefore, urged to continue traveling. By "liberal" used as an adjective we mean the flexible, curious, tolerant, and open-minded attitude. By "liberal" used as a noun we mean the kind of person who not only holds such an attitude but carries it over into adventurous, exploratory, continuously developing experience. He reminds one of the scientist who is experimentally engaged, day in and day out, in the controlled remaking of some part of his environment.

It follows that effective education is, above all else, the scientific method at work in every area of experience. Far from being limited to scientific laboratories, this method is equally applicable to personal and social life. It is more than a precise method, however—more than the exactitude with which personal and social problems are solved. It is the very quality with which humanity should approach all pressing problems. It is the spirit of open inquiry, of tireless investigation, of willingness to listen to opposing ideas and to give them an opportunity to prove their worth. Above all, it is the belief in man's ability to face the world with his own skills and powers and to solve his problems through his own active intelligence.

Good schools built on such a theory are potentially, though not always actually, culture's greatest single agency for genuine progress. Through them, the people can learn slowly how to act experimentally and so how to overcome the obstacles that always arise in the path of their onward march. Through them, the liberal way of life becomes synonymous with the democratic way. For democracy, to the progressivist, is the liberal way of thinking and behaving on a grand scale.

Persistent Doubts. Nevertheless, with all its strengths, with all its contributions both to education and to society at large, progressivism is open to certain stubbornly persistent doubts. These, too, spring from the soil of our culture, which now suffers from chronic instability, even revolutionary upheaval. In such a period, confidence in the methods of experimental change is sure to be less widespread than in a period of relative stability. Disturbing questions arise, in turn, as to the adequacy of liberalism when it is understood to be the cultural-philosophic expression of that kind of confidence. Furthermore, as critical voices challenge the sufficiency of the liberal outlook, they challenge also its educational counterpart.

This does not mean, of course, that all critics are agreed either on what is wrong with liberalism (and therefore progressivism) or what should be proposed in its place. As a matter of fact, their proposals are often at least as much in opposition to one another as to the theory that, in various respects, serves as their common foil. In Parts III and IV—in which we consider the essentialist and perennialist philosophies of education—we shall find the essentialist, for example, contending that the main underlying difficulty with progressivism is its failure to conserve those inherited beliefs about the culture that stem, presumably, from the law-abiding universe. We shall find the perennialist agreeing in part with his essentialist colleague but insisting more profoundly that the worst failure of the liberal-progressivist outlook is its disregard of self-evident, infallible principles of truth and value, principles serving as indispensable guides to the restoration of cultural order.

In contradistinction to both of these, our own critique centers on one thesis. *Progressivism is a philosophy of transition between two great cultural configurations.* It is the major rationale of a culture that is (1) shifting rapidly *away from* those ways of living that Western culture has achieved in the past and (2) shifting rapidly *toward* new ways of living that are still to be achieved in the future. In brief, progressivism is a transitional philosophy, standing between cultural patterns that are increasingly obsolescent and cultural patterns that still await an opportunity to prove their desirability and practicality.

Strengths and Weaknesses. In this perspective, progressivism is to be judged not as a philosophy deserving wholesale repudiation but as one to be supplemented and strengthened. Its priceless contributions to modern civilization and education should be incorporated within a larger framework. This framework should utilize progressivism's experimental approach to nature and man, should accept the evolutionary and technological beliefs as well as the achievements of recent decades, but should translate these into new, audacious conceptions of thought and programs of action.

Its liabilities as well as its assets should be assessed in the same spirit of frank inquiry and sharp criticism that progressivism itself has so freely applied to other positions. Accordingly, if we judge it in necessarily oversimplified terms, we may say that, in general, progressivism is: Strong in scientific method—weak in concern for the concrete and comprehensive outcomes of this method. Strong in teaching us how to think—weak in teaching us the goals toward which to think. Strong in characterizing as well as encouraging active intelligence—weak in estimating and counteracting the forces and restrictions that block its effective operation. Strong in encouraging individual self-expression and individual action—weak in integrating these successfully and powerfully with group self-expression and group action. Strong in tolerance of varying belief—weak in conviction or commitment to needed positive beliefs. Strong in the processes of ongoing, dynamic experience—weak in agreeing upon the products of such experience. Strong in believing that the present is important and real—weak in believing that the future is equally important and real. Strong in delineating the complexities and pluralities of experience—weak in fusing these into comprehensive, appealing, purposeful designs. In short, progressivism is strong in all the ways liberalism is strong and weak in the ways liberalism is weak.

Part II sketches the principal beliefs of progressivism, both as general philosophy and as educational theory, that point toward this evaluative balance. Utilizing the philosophic tools provided by Chapter 2, this chapter considers in succession certain dominant beliefs of progressivism: about reality, about knowledge, about values. Chapter 5 outlines its dominant educational beliefs, and Chapter 6 returns more specifically to evaluation of the entire theory.

First, however, it will further our understanding to note the general character of the progressivist philosophy and some of the historic influences that have contributed to it.

Ancestry and Background of Progressivism

THE GENERAL CHARACTER OF PROGRESSIVIST THOUGHT

Progressivist beliefs, formulated in philosophic terms, are characteristically of two classes: in some matters they are negative and diagnostic; in others they are positive and remedial. The former are expressive of opposition to authoritarianism and absolutism in all its forms, modern as well as ancient: religious, political, ethical, epistemological. The latter are expressive of man's confidence in his own natural powers, particularly his self-regenerative power to face continuously and to overcome satisfactorily the fears, superstitions, and bewilderments of an ever-threatening environment.

The philosophic term popularly used to characterize this outlook is *pragmatism*—a term made famous by a book of this title by William James. Today, although labeled by other terms, such as "instrumentalism" or "experimentalism," pragmatism is still widely held to be the single most original and most typically American of all the philosophies that have been formulated in our history.

Strictly speaking, pragmatism is a theory of logic. As Dewey says, the term "means only the rule of referring all thinking . . . to *consequences* for final meaning and test."[1] For our purposes, however, we shall use the term to connote an organized expression of beliefs about nature and man, with logic and epistemology its philosophic fulcrum. Indeed pragmatists themselves frankly recognize the cultural matrix within which their philosophy has grown to its present powerful stature.

Of all the sciences that employ this cultural matrix and have thus contributed to pragmatism—as it has contributed to them—we mention particularly biology, anthropology, psychology, and physics: Biology—because man is seen as an evolving, struggling organism interacting with his animate and inanimate environment. Anthropology—because man is also an organism with a very long history of interactions with his fellows living together in cultures. Psychology—because man is a behaving–thinking animal, subject, no less than other animals, to experimental understanding. And physics—because by means of this and allied sciences man has proved his astonishing capacity to come to grips with nature.

And yet this very capacity raises a problem of modern culture to which pragmatists never tire of returning. Can human beings, living together in societies, learn in time to transfer their genius in the natural sciences to the human and social sciences? Can they do for themselves what they have done for the soil, for the fluids and energies of matter and space? That they have the competence pragmatism does not doubt. That they will learn to use that competence is of considerable doubt. Yet, even on this question pragmatism is optimistic. Has not the culture of which it is the great liberal herald already shown that striking progress can be made in conquering man's *whole* environment, even including man himself?

The task before us, then, is to specify this competence as exactly as possible and at the same time to test it in actual practice. In the language common to pragmatism, what we must do if we are to move ahead is to put ideas to work. We must think not primarily for the sake of thinking but for the sake of doing. We must reject the spurious inheritance of pure intellectualism. First of all, we must apply our minds to the huge job of living. We must reject all doctrines that hold that we are helpless—that we can only submit to mysterious, overpowering forces. In this spirit of confidence education, far from being regarded as a passive conditioner of our existence, must be accepted as the greatest of all cultural instruments. It is the instrument by which we can become at last the masters, not the slaves, of cultural as well as all other kinds of natural change.

Philosophic threads

No philosophy springs full-blown from the soil of a single moment or locality. Although pragmatism is native to our recent American environment, it is also the descendant of a long line of ancestors—a line quite as long as written history.

Early Influences. Some of the philosophic threads woven into the developed pattern of pragmatism-progressivism can be traced as far back as ancient Greece.* Heraclitus, for example, expresses the belief that all reality is characterized by constant change, that nothing is permanent except the principle of change itself. In Socrates we find a noble attempt

* See standard histories of philosophy, cited in "What to Read" for Chapter 2. See also Hugh Miller, *An Historical Introduction to Modern Philosophy*, Part I, which contains good bibliographical suggestions.

to fuse epistemology and axiology in the principle that knowledge is the master key to virtue. The Sophist Protagoras sketches the theory that both truth and value are relative to time and place.

Even Plato and Aristotle, whose doctrines we shall find to be often in conflict with progressivism, provide it with elements that are by no means trivial. To consider but one example, the temperate spirit of the progressivist outlook is foreshadowed in Aristotle's frequent preference for moderation and compromise. Indeed, the direct influence of this immortal philosopher upon even the most sophisticated of contemporary pragmatists has been held to be tremendous.†

It is not always possible to trace the way by which such remote influences have entered into this philosophy. Certainly, they are more indirect that those of the earlier "modern" centuries beginning, perhaps, with the seventeenth.‡ No doubt such philosophers as the Englishmen Francis Bacon and John Locke and the Frenchman Jean Jacques Rousseau helped to generate the liberalism that is associated with pragmatic and, hence, progressivist attitudes. Bacon helped by his effort to refine the experimental method; Locke by his doctrine of political freedom; Rousseau by such beliefs as the goodness to be gained simply from being one's natural self. We must also mention the influence of such German thinkers as Immanuel Kant and Georg W. F. Hegel. The former attempted to ground a liberal glorification of the individual in the unassailable dignity of human personality; the latter insisted upon the dynamic, ever-readjusting processes of nature and society.

American Influences. The American philosophic influences flowing into progressivism are easier, though not too easy, to trace.* Benjamin Franklin, Thomas Paine, and Thomas Jefferson—the last strongly influenced by Locke—made important contributions. We may note their sophisticated attitude toward religious dogma, their belief in individuals, their vigorous democratic spirit. Such eloquent idealists as William T. Harris and Ralph Waldo Emerson, although closer to essentialism, must not be forgotten. Harris directly influenced John Dewey, the most influential of all progressivists. Emerson's "transcendentalism" is flavored with American practicality and common sense.

† See Paul A. Schilpp (ed.), *The Philosophy of John Dewey*, pp. 101ff.
‡ See histories of philosophy, especially Miller, *op. cit.*, Chaps. 11-16.
* See Herbert W. Schneider, *A History of American Philosophy*, Parts II. III; W. H. Werkmeister, *A History of Philosophical Ideas in America*.

Not until almost the beginning of the twentieth century, however, did a genuinely "native" outlook and interpretation of American culture begin to emerge. Through many media—through the arts, especially literature (Mark Twain is one example), through the psychological and social sciences, through education and even religion—the young nation began to break its European fetters and to reveal in philosophy an independence of imagination and creative power that it had revealed earlier in political revolution.

Two contributors to this declaration of cultural independence stand high above all others, prior to Dewey himself: Charles S. Peirce and William James. The stature of Peirce has grown steadily through the years. As his voluminous papers are posthumously published and interpreted, his originality and profundity become more and more conclusively demonstrated. It was from him that James gained and developed his central philosophic principle: that ideas are meaningless unless they make a difference in experience, unless they "work." Peirce is thoroughly scientific, naturalistic, and empirical in his thinking. The entire function of thinking, he says, is to habituate us to action.† Feeling, muscular effort—these are such typical manifestations of human activity that it is not only improper but impossible to separate them from the intellectual without being abstract and often misleading.

The influence of James has, of course, been very great throughout the twentieth century. His famous *Principles of Psychology* is still, in various respects, the greatest single achievement in this field by any American scholar-scientist. His works in philosophy have seemed like a fresh intellectual breeze blowing over the land. As in Peirce, the dominant point of view is one of living organisms that function through experience, action, flowing feelings, habit patterns. Concern is nearly always with the total self viewed in a range of overlapping perspectives —spiritual, emotional, physical.

Although Dewey alone has matched the genius of Peirce and James as philosophic emancipators, many philosophers, sociologists, and psychologists have absorbed and reworked their beliefs in various ways. One of the most brilliant, George Herbert Mead, strongly stimulated Dewey

† See Charles S. Peirce, *Chance, Love, and Logic,* pp. 43-48. For a summary of the relations of Peirce and James, see Schilpp, *op. cit.,* pp. 481ff. See also Charles Hartshorne and Paul Weiss (eds.), *Collected Papers of Charles Sanders Peirce;* Max H. Fisch (ed.), *Classic American Philosophers,* Chap. 1. Fisch also offers selections from James and Dewey.

as well as a number of able younger American philosophers, such as Charles Morris.* Mead's theory of the self, developing out of its active social relations with other selves in a process of continuous communication and role-playing, is growing in influence at a rate comparable, perhaps, only to that of Peirce's ideas.

We should mention at least one other philosopher in the pragmatic tradition, Max Carl Otto.† A great university teacher, Otto has devastatingly analyzed the paraphernalia of traditional philosophy and culture, including the shortcomings of supernatural religion. He has urged their replacement by scientific humanism, a faith in man's own power over the course of his evolutionary progress.

FOUR CULTURAL INFLUENCES

Other thinkers might readily be added to this list, but here we wish rather to emphasize important cultural influences upon progressivism. As its defenders would readily agree, at least four such influences, each closely interrelated with the others and with philosophy as such, are especially significant: the industrial revolution, modern science, the rise of democracy, and the American environment.‡ Each is here depicted as concisely as possible.

The Industrial Revolution. The familiar term "industrial revolution" is used broadly here to mean the era of modern economic change extending from the decline of feudalism to the rise and maturation of capitalism. Faint rumblings of this change were heard as far back as the fourteenth century, although it was not until the end of the nineteenth and the beginning of the twentieth that the revolution attained its greatest force. During these five or six centuries the transformations that have taken place throughout the Western and, more recently, the Eastern hemispheres are so breathtaking that even in our own generation we are still seeking to comprehend and adjust ourselves to them. To recall our characterization of philosophy as the expression of beliefs, we are still suffering from the shattering effects of the industrial revolution upon those beliefs that man had slowly learned to accept during the ancient

* See George H. Mead, *Mind, Self, and Society;* Charles Morris, *Paths of Life.*

† See Max C. Otto, *Things and Ideals;* and *The Human Enterprise.*

‡ Among historians especially sensitive to these wider influences are Charles A. Beard and Merle Curti, both of whom are in the liberal-progressivist tradition.

and medieval eras. Indeed, as we shall see in Part III, the essentialist philosophy—to cite the one that has perhaps been most influential—has been largely an effort to conserve as much of that old pattern as feasible while also accommodating itself to modern scientific and economic life.

The full impact of the industrial revolution upon men's attitudes and habits has been reflected with particular keenness, however, by pragmatists-progressivists—so much so that they are sometimes characterized as the interpreters, par excellence, of that revolution.* Whether this is so or not, it is they who have emphasized the new sense of power over natural forces that accompanied the exploration of the earth and the development of machines. They have stressed the consequent modern growth of vigorous self-confidence among men, as contrasted with the previous widespread sense of futility and weakness before these natural forces. They have been sensitive to the necessity of liberty and independence in an economic system based upon competition among profit-making individuals and, at the same time, they have recognized the relatedness of all phases of human life, especially through the factory system with its division of labor and concentration of populations.

Modern Science. Modern science has developed in close relation to the industrial revolution, as both effect and cause—effect, since science was supported and encouraged by the new economy; cause, since science was a chief instrument in the building of machines and the conquest of natural resources. Science has generously repaid the support and encouragement it received through invention, efficiency, and expansion of the whole productive process.

Perhaps the chief significance of science to such philosophies as progressivism lies in the powerful new method it provides for men to adjust themselves to their environments. It is a method that seeks to meet the difficulties continually arising in the course of such adjustments not by placating fearful and awesome powers, not by appeal to authority or dogma but by scrupulous examination, explanation, and control of the factors in each situation. Mathematics, measurement, laboratory precision come into prominence. Induction (the forming of generalizations from the comparison of particular data) becomes more central than deduction (the logical process of explaining particulars from prior generalizations).

* See Schilpp (ed.), *op. cit.*, p. 137.

True, the scientific method began to develop long before the modern era, but its achievements in the last two centuries have been far greater than in all preceding history. Indeed, before the Renaissance, the accomplishments of science were made with only the vaguest awareness that it provided the surest method of coping with the perplexities of nature and man. Among such achievements, none illustrates more fruitfully how the scientific method applies to the biological level of nature than the epoch-making *Origin of Species* by Charles Darwin. This is not to say that scientists today accept the evolutionary theory exactly as Darwin developed it. But its major axioms—namely, that plants and animals, including man himself, have a purely natural history, that all living things struggle to survive, and that change implies emergence of new forms from the old—are enormously important for modern philosophy in general and for pragmatism in particular.

The Rise of Democracy. Like both industry and science, modern democratic society is inextricably woven into the complex design of modern culture, of which all three are parts. Unquestionably, the first two developments speeded the advancing ascendancy of democracy. In order for the young competitive economy to succeed it had to be unbound from the chains of the medieval church and state; it needed political arrangements guaranteeing maximum freedom to the rising bourgeoisie (the young middle class), which carried the torch of the new power; and science had to be released from old restrictions, for without social freedom to inquire and explore it could not operate effectively.

The product of these joint influences was an explosive upsurge of confidence in the capacity and right of men to rule themselves, to direct their own lives toward whatever goals they might agree upon. Progressivism has encouraged this confidence without qualification, but it was expressed much earlier in the modern epoch in demands for universal education. To be sure, the roots of democracy extend deeper still—into the Judaic-Christian heritage of respect for personality and a faith in human brotherhood, and into the Greek heritage of devotion to rational capacities. But until men had learned how to implement these values through concrete economic, scientific, and social practices—which modern conditions had, for the first time, made widely possible—they could only dream, they could not actually test out democracy in the laboratories of wide social practice.

A Favorable Cultural Environment. None of these pervasive influences could fructify without a favorable environment. They required an environment that, on the one hand, could provide abundant industrial and other types of opportunity and, on the other hand, would not be too cluttered with the bric-a-brac of earlier beliefs, institutions, customs, habits, faiths.

Such an opportunity loomed from the moment of America's discovery. In its unbelievable fertility, its boundless territory, its rivers, minerals, forests—all of them opening before the awed gaze of its pioneers—the American continent provided ideal conditions for the firm establishment of an industrial order, for unhampered scientific work, and for the practice of democracy.

Naturally the impress of even earlier periods could not easily be dismissed. European culture, particularly in some halls of learning (and so well exemplified by modern philosophy itself) has continued to our own day to be influential in America. It was absorbed into education especially by way of essentialist theory. Even able thinkers like Emerson, responding as they did to the thrilling promise of the virgin continent, still seemed to be more under the influence of the old environment than emancipated by the new.

Nevertheless, a set of beliefs that was characteristically American began to emerge slowly and to find philosophic expression suitable to our culture. These beliefs, too, are partly the effect of European thought and practice, partly of still wider cultural influences. Yet, when Dewey, particularly, is called the leading American philosopher, this is a tribute not only to his technical brilliance but also to the fact that he has so sensitively and profoundly expressed that pattern of beliefs that, especially in the last hundred years, we have come to regard as most distinctively American.

For this reason, primarily, we shall confine our exposition of pragmatism-progressivism largely to Dewey's own interpretation,† but we shall not hesitate to include the views of fellow thinkers when these seem to contribute to our immediate aim. That aim is to understand this uniquely American philosophy because it constitutes the theoretical substructure of virtually every principle that has emerged, in practice, as progressive education.

† Dewey's major writings outside the field of education include *Experience and Nature, Art as Experience, The Quest for Certainty, Logic: Theory of Inquiry, Reconstruction in Philosophy, Human Nature and Conduct.* For an almost complete bibliography consult Schilpp, *op. cit.* See also Joseph Ratner (ed.), *Intelligence in the Modern World: John Dewey's Philosophy.*

Progressivist Beliefs about Reality

We may recall that by ontological beliefs we mean those expressing attitudes, convictions, and assumptions about existence itself, about what we believe to be fundamentally real as opposed to the unreal, the illusory.

The Progressivist Heresy. The question is sometimes raised whether the progressivist position is grounded in a genuine ontology at all. It repudiates any attempt to discover and describe what James called a "block universe"—a fixed, forever-the-same, pre-designed reality. It warns us that whenever we make such an attempt we invariably get lost in a hopeless tangle of arbitrary and meaningless speculations. The universe simply cannot be tied into a neat package and stamped "Inspected and Complete."

In fact, pragmatists question whether even the term "*uni*verse"—a term implying that existence is one vast, completed cosmos—is anything more than a mere verbalism. Many of their writings are severe critiques of all doctrines of absolute reality.‡ Throughout the centuries, they contend, these doctrines have allowed their advocates to play the pleasurable but futile game of escaping from practical life into a realm created by and existing largely within other-worldly imaginations. In their opposition to traditional cosmology and metaphysics pragmatists are philosophic heretics.

Experience as Reality. If, however, we search for an ontology that faces directly *toward* the here-and-now—that describes surroundings more modestly, less comprehensively, perhaps, but in the long run more fruitfully than absolutist doctrines—the key may be found in the titles of three of Dewey's famous works: *Experience and Nature, Art as Experience,* and *Experience and Education.* "Experience" is the key concept. What does Dewey mean by this oft-repeated term?

Ordinary usage gives us the cue. When we assert that a person is "experienced" in business we mean that he has learned how to perform his job by direct and frequent contact with the methods, materials, and

‡ Here, especially, the point of view of logical empiricism, or logical positivism, an important movement in recent philosophy, overlaps with pragmatism. Since, in this volume, logical posivitism is not given systematic attention, students are urged to read Chap. 25 in Miller, *op. cit.,* and to consult the bibliography given there. See also the journal *Philosophical Studies;* Herbert Feigl and Wilfrid Sellars (eds.), *Readings in Philosophical Analysis,* esp. pp. 3-26; National Society for the Study of Education, *Fifty-fourth Yearbook,* Part I, "Modern Philosophies and Education," Chap. 9.

people involved. We contrast him with another who has been isolated from such contact—who may be excellently trained but who has not yet put his training to practical tests. We get closest to reality, in short, when we are in the thick of things—when we are tilling the earth or running machines, when we are participating wholeheartedly in the events of our communities, when we are challenged by the never-ending curiosities, hazards, excitements of ordinary life.

To immerse ourselves thus in the empirical stream is not at all to conceal either the weaknesses in nature and society or their perfections and strengths. Human experience, with its terrible sufferings, its delights, sorrows, joys, beauties, uglinesses, hatreds, and loves—this is the reality into which, for better or for worse, all men are born and in which they perform their roles until they die. As Peirce expresses it, "Where hope is unchecked by any experience, it is likely that our optimism is extravagant." [2]

Ontological beliefs that are founded on experience may be said to possess a strong *evolutionary* quality. Experience is struggle. Life is action and change. Chance, the unexpected, the novel and unforeseen always play a major role. Men, like other animals, survive and advance as they, too, change, struggle, explore, dare, probe, and act.

Man's Most Unique Function—Mind. But, just as certain animals survive more successfully than others because they possess some such capacity as strength of jaw or speed of foot, so man survives because he too possesses a function that is more highly developed in him than in any other animal. This, says the pragmatist, is the power of intelligence —the power to remember, to imagine, to relate, to symbolize, to solve problems, and to communicate his thoughts to others of his kind.

Man's mind, accordingly, exists *within* the flow of experience—not at all *outside* of it. Mind is not some mysterious entity that defies scientific explanation in the natural realm. As a matter of fact, it is not an entity, a distinct organ or object, at all. On the contrary, mind behaves in organic relation with the body, the feelings, the habits, and the other responses of the total organism. It exists only in terms of its activities, of its ways of behaving, of what it does to give definite advantages to the organism of which it is a part. It *is,* indeed, what it *does*. But what it does is part and parcel of the tissue of that reality that is man living as a part of nature. Mind is, in essence, an especially important way of experiencing.

Typical Attributes of Experience. Since further attention is given elow to the way in which experience as "mind" operates, at this point e shall merely note four additional attributes of the progressivist ntology.*

1. *Experience is dynamic.* It moves at varying rates, pauses at emporary resting places, then once more is on its way. This characteris-c suggests that its dynamic action is also rhythmic—a kind of alternating, ut never merely repetitive, process of adjustment and readjustment, which ever continues because such is the way of nature. Life is never tatic. Change is everywhere, though rates of change vary immensely.

2. *Experience is temporal.* As planets, forests, animals, cultures merge and develop, they are never quite the same today as they were esterday. And it is certain that they will be different in the days and ears and centuries to come.

3. *Experience is spatial.* While experience pushes forward it pushes also outward, spreading fanwise ever more widely, yet never eaching the outermost limits of the universe because there are no outer-nost limits, at least so far as man's capacity to embrace their full mean-ng is concerned.

4. *Experience is pluralistic.* It is composed of a vast network of nultiple relations, which are just as real as the things related are real. At once spiritual and material, complex and simple, intellectual and emo-ional, experience enfolds all of the natural world within itself—the pebbles of the beach, the beasts of the forest, the simplest peasants and wisest statesmen of the human realm.

Progressivist Beliefs about Knowledge

Immediate and mediate experience

Although an empirical ontology is indispensable to the pragmatic outlook, we should point out that it becomes genuinely meaningful only as it falls within the range of man's observation, judgment, and con-trol.† This does not mean, as some classical philosophers believed, that

* See Schilpp, *op. cit.*, p. 529.
† See *ibid.*, p. 533.

man, by his power to perceive, literally *creates* objects in his surrounding world. Nature was *there* in that world aeons of time before the species *Homo sapiens* emerged upon the evolutionary scale. In remote areas of the heavens and even on our own earth, elements of nature exist that have never once come within the scope of human observation—and perhaps never will.

But, says the progressivist, having made clear this qualification, all of us distinguish between the *foreground* and the *background* of reality. The distinction is between experience that is in the focus of awareness and that which hovers on the dim periphery. Backgrounds shift to foregrounds as they become resources of reflective processes; foregrounds become backgrounds as they recede for the time being from the field of sharp attention and concern.

Immediate and Mediate Experience: An Illustration. A different way of describing our most distinctive human role—the operation of "knowing"—is to consider the relative distinction between two orders of experience: *immediate* and *mediate.*

Let us suppose, for example, that at this moment I am relaxing in my armchair so that, without at all expressing what I feel, I achieve a pattern of adjustment, unity, and balance, with both my surroundings and myself—with my study, books, pictures, the log fire, the landscape I glimpse outside; with my feelings of the moment, my fleeting thoughts, my quite unconscious breathing and posture.

Experience here is *immediate*. It is, one might easily suppose, so completely fused, so internally harmonious that, as I experience them, I and my environment are completely unified. This is what Dewey often calls the "undergoing" of an experience.

Let us suppose that now the telephone rings. I lift the receiver to hear a voice cry that an accident has occurred two miles from where I live. A friend is badly hurt, and I am wanted there at once.

I grab my hat, dash down the stairs and, reaching the corner, peer anxiously along the avenue. What shall I do next? Start walking rapidly? Call a taxicab? Try "thumbing" a ride? Or, though none is in sight, wait for a streetcar? Which has the best chance of getting me to the accident in the shortest time? Taxi service, I recall, is unreliable and slow. Streetcar service is just about as bad. Automobiles move with greater speed, and I've seen students getting rides from friendly passers-by. I'll try that, and then, if no one stops, I can count eventually on a streetcar anyway.

Now, this fairly common situation may be regarded as *mediate* experience for the simple reason that, to turn the adjective into a verb, "I mediate." I build a bridge between the starting point, where my sense of equilibrium was disturbed, and the ending point, where once again I shall hope to enjoy equilibrium. The entire episode exemplifies that rhythm of experience that may be epitomized as undergoing-doing-undergoing, where "doing" suggests a span of mediation.

Five Steps in Mediation: The Act of Thought. In this example we may observe thinking or intelligent behavior in its precise sense of reflection. The span of mediation is crossed by five familiar but fundamental steps, which taken together constitute an "act of thought."‡

The first is little more than a tendency to keep moving on the same even keel in the face of the blunt impact of some obstacle in the flow of immediate experience. In many instances we do exactly that; an obstacle may be so slight that we glide over it hardly aware that it is there.

Often, however, it stubbornly remains, and in such instances we take a second step. We stop, and we observe just what it is that interferes. We recall similar, though not identical, experiences. We weigh, measure, take apart. In short, we estimate the obstacle with whatever care its persistence and its size demand.

The more thoroughly we perform our task the more ready we now are for another step, the third. Here one or two or perhaps dozens of suggestions (taxis, streetcars, walking, automobiles) for conquering the measured obstacle flash across our minds. Such suggestions, when they have reached a point of quite definite specificity and clarity, eventually develop into what Dewey himself sometimes likes to call "ideas."

As we narrow down the possibilities we take still another step, the fourth. Here we imaginatively follow through, or anticipate, the consequences most likely to follow were we to act upon one or another of the likeliest proposals that have just occurred to us. We *infer* what would happen, without actually overtly testing our inference. This is a privilege that not only saves time but also avoids many of the "bumps and bruises" that other animals and some human beings suffer by more clumsy, less intelligent, trial and error.

When, however, we are tentatively satisfied that one proposal is promising enough to risk the trial, that it offers most assurance of leading

‡ The most influential statement of the "act of thought" is found in Dewey, *How We Think* (rev. ed.).

to a resolution of the difficulty that first induced our thought, we tak
the fifth and final step. In other words, we carry through. We test ou
inference overtly. We *do* in fact what hitherto we only imagined ou
selves doing. We discover by experiencing actual effects whether ou
choice of this rather than that idea was a judicious one.

Misconceptions to Be Avoided. The plausibility of this theory ir
vites a number of easy misconceptions. In the first place, we must nc
suppose that people think only when they are coerced by fears, di
comforts, or other maladjustments. To be sure, need is the prime in
pulse of reflection. Yet, it would be foolish to deny that some experts in
let us say, mathematics manipulate ideas mainly for the joy of sym
metry or the stimulation afforded by puzzling ideas.

In the second place, we must avoid the inference that wheneve
people think they inevitably proceed in the exact sequence of the fiv
steps outlined. Actually, a person may stop at any point. It may be argued
for example, that thinking ceases with step four whenever, as in th
case of more or less exclusively "intellectual" pursuits, a problem can b
solved without strictly overt action.

Third, reflection often zigzags back and forth. Consider our fre
quent need to regress from step three, where suggestions most ofte
occur, to step two, in order to examine and recall other factors that w
missed at first. The less sure we are of this or that suggestion the mor
we need to be sure that our analysis has been sufficiently thorough.

Fourth, in some situations we give greater attention to one phase o
thinking than we do to others (such as reasoning out, in step four, th
consequences of an intriguing possibility). Yet, in most problemati
situations each phase of thinking functions in relation to all other phases
each step is taken successfully only as we are sure of all the other steps

Finally, we need hardly emphasize that this whole dissection i
more artificial than is the actual process of thinking. For one thing, i
is not only at the fifth step that, in a strict sense, action first occurs. Thus
in step two analysis may require extensive physical manipulation. Fo
another thing, the time it takes to complete an act of thought varie
tremendously; in many instances, we meet the minor complications aris
ing in daily experience with greater speed than the time required t
recount them. Yet, in other instances, hours, days, months, years, o
decades are required to break through crucial obstacles. For example, ir
the case of a baffling disease (whether of the human body or of the body

olitic) whole generations may be required to meet the task successfully.

Mind: An Instrument. Whether simple or complex, the puzzles hat all men face and that all men must attempt to solve are common rist for the common mill of thought. No chasm divides primitive from ighly educated persons. No wall separates the child from the completely nature adult. The degree of care with which they think differs a great leal. The central process does not.

It is important to understand clearly why Dewey sometimes refers o mind as an instrument with which to operate upon nature and society. The use of mind is frequently crude, but mind is also capable of remarkble refinement and dexterity. When its operations are of this character, ve regard mind as truly *scientific* because of the method it employs—cientific whether utilized by a highly trained physician or by a skillful nechanic who has received no formal training. The point is that the ossession of this precious instrument is not the franchise solely of an ntellectual minority. Mind functions at some level whenever man, strugling to survive, tries to solve his daily problems by thinking and acting. Yet, even today it functions far less fruitfully and widely than it must f our culture is to achieve the status of which it is capable—a status in which it is governed by intelligence, by scientific method everywhere at work.

Knowledge and Truth

The Test of Ideas. We come now to the progressivist's conception of the character of knowledge and truth. "The workability of ideas" is, of course, the commonest way of stating this conception. For Peirce the test of truth is that an idea takes on meaning by giving significant relationship to things that previously lacked meaning. For James the test of truth (or at least *a* test of truth, for he offered several) is the satisfaction a person derives from having worked an idea through to harmonious conclusion and reward in terms of adjustment.*

Although James greatly refined this simple pragmatic notion and although the profundity and complexity of Peirce's philosophy have been more and more appreciated in recent years, it is Dewey who has given instrumentalist logic its most influential treatment. Such ancient terms as inquiry, meaning, judgment, inference, and verification take on a rich

*** See, for example, William James, *The Meaning of Truth.***

and fresh significance in his creative thinking. He and Mead have constructed a theory of language that regards communication as the most important of all media of social evolution.† Although we cannot venture here into these technical phases of philosophy, one thing should be emphasized: *the crucial test of whether an idea becomes true is its long-range effectiveness in the conquest of difficulties demanding that reflection shall mediate, thereby permitting us to resume our union with immediate experience.*

To say that an idea turns out to be true when it succeeds in reintegrating experience is to say that we may have innumerable ideas that turn out to be false because they fail to effect such reintegration. If, strictly speaking, ideas become for laymen what hypotheses are for scientists, then all ideas, like all hypotheses, must be weighed with caution, their weaknesses and strengths carefully balanced. They should rest upon rigorous analysis of the problematic situation out of which they emerge and which they are designed to correct. They should be "thought through" in terms of what would happen if we were to apply them. Finally, they should be tried out in action and rejected or revised if found to be inadequate.

But even ideas that produce the consequences desired never remain permanently true. Although some consequences are much more durable than others, each successive problematic situation in which ideas are employed will be different in some slight way from the preceding one. Thus, each new problematic situation will call for a reinterpretation of ideas that hitherto seemed fairly satisfactory.

Knowledge as "Passive." It is, therefore, plausible to contend (for analytic purposes and at the risk of a more artificial distinction than actual experience in thinking warrants) that we can differentiate between what is strictly "true" and what we merely "know." Although Dewey would perhaps not wholly approve of this differentiation, there seems to us a sense in which knowledge can be viewed as a kind of reservoir of information, facts, laws, habits, principles, and processes, which each person accumulates as he lives through the interworkings of experience. Further, knowledge is that vastly greater fund that other people have accumulated and from which an individual learns either by direct association with others or by indirect acquaintance through the records they have left. No problem a person confronts is ever so unique that he cannot draw

† See Mead, *op. cit.*; Dewey, *Experience and Nature,* Chap. 5.

pon his personal memory or the communal store, although some prob-
ems remain unsolved precisely because an individual's knowledge is too
mited to provide the cues needed for successful reflection on even the
implest plane.

Knowledge, we see, is social as well as individual. An individual's
hances of resolving life's recurring difficulties are greatly improved as
e becomes acquainted—at both first hand and second hand and on the
ridest possible scale—with other individuals, groups, nations, races,
nores, common practices.

Knowledge is also a product of definite activity. The more often we
ope directly with the demands of our environment or the richer our
xperience is in practice, the greater our preparation is for the inevitable
emands of the future.

Knowledge, therefore, grows. New experiences constantly enrich
nd change the import of whatever we already know. By these same
erms, however, knowledge always falls short of perfection. We cannot
uarantee that what by the test of its success yesterday turned out to be
rue will necessarily be true tomorrow by mere repetition of that test.
ituations change, and the knowledge we found suitable before may be
o longer suitable; it must be modified in the light of novel factors in the
volving milieu.

Truth as "Active." At this point the relation of truth and knowl-
dge begins to crystallize. Knowledge, we might say for purposes of
ogical classification, is comparatively *passive;* it is a cumulation of ex-
eriences and information waiting to be used again. Every truth, on the
ther hand, is comparatively *active*—the particular *result* of knowing, of
hoosing and directing some segment of knowledge through the hazards
f a rough terrain. It is the effect of a mediating process, which invariably
eshapes that segment so as to qualify, rearrange, and supplement the
ontent of the knowledge reservoir itself. To search for any particular
ruth would be utterly impossible without a general fund of knowledge.
But a general fund of knowledge is itself an accumulation of those products of active mediation that are designated truths. Moreover, the fund
would be forever sterile and inert except for new truths that continuously
upplement and modify that fund.

To make sure that this relationship is clear, let us consider the example above: my imperative need to reach the accident with utmost haste.
As I rehearsed various means in my imagination, I was recalling what-

ever "knowledge" I might already possess. In this case, knowledge h
been obtained mainly from actual experience in getting from one pla
to another rather than from reports of how others had done so. Yet t
idea that seemed most likely to succeed in this emergency—"thumbin
an automobile ride—was one that I had never tried. I had only seen st
dents utilize the idea, with enviable results. Here, therefore, was a simp
case of what might be termed *indirect* knowledge; I could not really clai
this particular experience as my own without having applied it to t
fresh problem I was now trying to meet.

Having once resolved to test out my preferred idea (or hypothes
the more formal term), it was essential that my store of *general* knowled
of travel in cities be applied to this *specific* case. I had to decide wheth
my best chance of stopping a car would be at this point on the avenu
or at the stop-and-go light a half-block ahead. I had also to deci
whether, imitating successful connoisseurs of this curious art of t
machine age, I should jerk my thumb in rhythmic intervals or wheth
I should step into the middle of the street and simply wave my arm
When, within a moment, I had decided upon the stop-and-go light f
my point of trial; when, within a minute, I had flagged a car and caug
my ride; when, within ten minutes, I had reached the accident; whe
accordingly, my idea was carried out and unified with action—then n
previous knowledge of transportation as a means of connecting two ge
graphically separated points had become definitely modified as "truth

I would probably remember this experience, then, and at the ne
relevant experience would be able to dip into a richer reservoir of know
edge than I had had before. I would be more confident. Yet, I wou
also find that my greater knowledge had undergone still further revisio
through the need to apply it to a situation not wholly like the previo
one. It would be a situation, therefore, in which once more my know
edge would be submitted to the means of thinking and testing, to t
criterion of whether such means could produce an anticipated end an
thus, still another truth.

Intelligence and Operationalism. Dewey has often emphasized h
preference for the term "intelligence" to such terms as "knowledge
"truth," or "mind," freighted as they are with historic connotations th
pragmatism rejects. Intelligence is, in essence, the experimental way
living, the central method of human interaction with environment. I

Dewey's technical but richly meaningful language it is "the product and expression of cumulative funding of the meanings reached" in "special inquiries (undertaken because of the presence of problems) . . ." [3] Here "product" implies the dependence of intelligence upon past experience, past knowledge; "expression" implies the active functioning of intelligence in the ongoing present; and "special inquiries" implies the particular difficulties of experience by which intelligent behavior is always motivated.

In still other words, intelligence is the habit of dealing with nature not by blind obedience or routine but by the relation of what we have previously known to what we do not yet know for certain. It is a habit that enables us to maintain continuity between the two by means of richer, more productive relations, interpreted and reinterpreted according to the consequences that they produce. Whether these consequences are more properly called "knowledge" or "truth" is of less importance than that they are dependable only to the degree that they meet the canons of experimental inquiry.‡

Finally, pragmatic epistemology is an accurate anticipation and expression of the theory called "operationalism." First stated by Peirce, it has been developed recently by such philosopher-scientists as P. W. Bridgman.* Operationalism regards even the most universal laws of nature as tools of scientific interpretation and control rather than as objective, fixed, eternal ordinances. Actually, science as a whole is treated as such a tool. By means of it man engages in the manipulation of the raw materials of the physical, biological, and other spheres, brings them within the compass of conceptual relations, formulates hypotheses, and tests them under laboratory conditions. As the surgeon *operates* upon a sick body after diagnosis and consideration of various possible cures and relevant laws of medicine, so the chemist or sociologist operates in comparable fashion upon bodies made up, respectively, of material compounds or human groups.

The operational method of utilizing ideas has already been implied in this book, both by the concept of culture and by the concepts of progressivism, essentialism, and perennialism. It will be recalled that all

‡ See Schilpp, *op. cit.*, p. 528.

* See Dewey, *The Quest for Certainty*, Chap. 7; P. W. Bridgman, *The Logic of Modern Physics.*

of these are to be regarded as *symbols* by which to organize and explain bodies of experience. They are not objective systems or existences but fruitful ways of approaching and interpreting human problems.

Progressivist Beliefs about Value

An empirical approach

Relations to Reality and Knowledge. We turn now to axiology, the third philosophic area underlying progressivism. The first and perhaps crucial point is that values are profoundly related both to beliefs about reality and to beliefs about knowledge. On the one hand, values arise out of the desires, urges, feelings, and habits of the human being—values that he possesses because he is at once a biological and a social animal. In this sense they are quite as real as any other facts, events, experiences. On the other hand, values are closely related to knowledge. If the test of ideas is the effectiveness with which they bring readjustments to immediate experience, then one may, indeed, contend that an idea is true when it is ultimately good and good when ultimately true. For values are, after all, "identical with goods that are the fruit of intelligently directed activity. . . ."[4]

This is not to say that values have no distinctive significance in themselves. It would be quite as hazardous to argue that beliefs about reality or about knowledge determine beliefs about value as it would be to argue that the latter determine the former. What, then, is the place of values in this potent philosophy?

Instrumental and Intrinsic Values. The answer to this question requires a further refining of terms. An operational distinction that is analogous to that made between mediate and immediate experience is to classify values as *instrumental* and *intrinsic*. Strictly speaking, instrumental values are those we attach to experiences that serve as a means to some desired end other than themselves. An operation for appendicitis has an instrumental value. An individual hardly cherishes the experience for its own sake; but he endures the pain, the inconvenience, and the expense because of the restoration of health that it offers as a reward. Health may be taken to exemplify an intrinsic value. A normal person cherishes good health because it is immediately satisfying. In this sense, we may speak of health as a kind of good in itself.

Progressivism is careful to warn, however, against any sharp distinction between these two classes of value.† In some contexts instrumental values themselves become intrinsic; in other contexts intrinsic values seem largely instrumental. Thus, an operation often gives to the surgeon who performs it a certain intrinsic satisfaction that he has done his work with precision and fine skill; at the moment, he may not think much beyond the operation to the beneficial effects that will follow for the patient. Health, on the other hand, is in some ways as much an instrumental as an intrinsic value. Even though almost all individuals regard this value as immediately good, it is also regarded as a necessary means to economic opportunity, leadership, successful education—indeed, to a variety of ends extending beyond itself.

Strictly speaking, all values—instrumental and intrinsic alike—are properly so labeled only as they emerge from the process of reflective deliberation. To feel a pleasurable sensation, let us say, is not even intrinsically good until it has become meaningful through its relationship with an experience involving the activities of mind. In this sense intrinsic values bear some analogy to knowledge. They are the cumulations of human experience that we continue to cherish as moral habits, traditions, symbols, immediacies. Instrumental values, by this analogy, are closer to truths, in the sense that they are the freshly created effects of intelligence as it operates in controlling the moral aspects of life. Like most analogies, however, this one is far from exact. The two kinds of value depend on each other, even as knowledge and truth do.

Social and Personal Values. Another helpful, if artificial, distinction is the distinction between *social* and *personal* values. In the first place, all values inevitably reveal a social quality. Individuals learn better to appreciate good health, let us say, as they associate with other healthy individuals. (Health is here taken to mean freedom from the many varieties of political and psychological disease as well as from contagious and organic physical diseases.) Certainly both the social and medical sciences become instruments of good health today because of the wide *sharing* of

† See Dewey, *Reconstruction in Philosophy*, pp. 170ff.

discoveries, diagnoses, and cures by countless experimenters through the centuries and across national boundaries.

The social character of values appears as still more fundamental when we analyze the nature of the self.‡ In order that the individual may become a self at all he must actively participate in a community of selves. Accurately speaking, the infant is not born a personality. He becomes one gradually as he is made conscious of his self by becoming conscious of other personalities. This occurs as the young child learns to communicate—a process that involves the anticipation of responses that others will make to his own vocal, written, overt gestures. Through these responses he discovers that there are other selves and that he, too, is a self with similar desires and capacities.

In the second place, values are personal. Pragmatic axiology disagrees emphatically with theories sometimes advanced by anthropologists that all doctrines of good and evil are little more than traditions, folkways, mores molded into individual life by streams of tribal evolution.* Not that it ignores the heavy residue these streams deposit upon all human experience, for pragmatism agrees that most ethical theories have woefully neglected their effects. But it does refute the simple equating of custom, let us say, with moral standards. Just as inherited bodies of knowledge are essential to but not identical with the truth-seeking process in its concern with current problems, so rules of right and wrong that each present generation inherits from past generations are essential to but not identical with what may be most distinctly valuable for individuals now. After all, societies exist only in so far as individual human beings exist. There can be no such thing as a society without individuals. Even though it be equally true that individuals apart from society have no meaning, either to themselves or to others, we must never forget that individuals do have the intelligence and the potential power to criticize, reject, or qualify whatever social standards of good and evil they find operating at a given time.

We conclude, therefore, that for the pragmatic philosophy values constantly develop in the interplay between fresh personal experiences

‡ See Mead, *op. cit.*; William H. Kilpatrick, *Selfhood and Civilization.* Kilpatrick provides the most thoughtful treatment of Mead's theory in an educational context.

* See John Dewey and James H. Tufts, *Ethics.* William Graham Sumner is a classic example of the sociological archdeterminist.

and cultural deposits—experiences that only real individuals, after all, can have, examine, direct. We conclude, also, that values that are not tested and retested by intelligence are scarcely worthy of being labeled values. They become little more than clichés or pious slogans on a very low plateau of social routine.

Such an axiology as that of pragmatism avoids dogmatic commandments and rigid moral axioms. Values, as an integral part of experience, are relative, temporal, dynamic. Just as in physics or biology laws should be defined as instruments of operation and control, which often need to be reshaped in the course of their use in achieving scientific truths, so laws that express convictions about values likewise need constant redefinition and reapplication in our striving world of morals.

Growth as Value. We can now understand why such a value as *growth* comes to be so strongly emphasized by the pragmatist-progressivist. When an organism grows it adds steadily to its life, both horizontally and vertically: horizontally by broadening and strengthening its connections with cross sections of the present cultural and natural environment; vertically by moving ever forward so that, as long as the organism lives, it explores the endless opportunities for adventurous experience that time so abundantly provides. Thus, it is not an exaggeration to say that growth affords its own sufficient criterion of value: growth is relative to itself and therefore intrinsically good, but it is also relative to further growth and therefore also instrumentally good.

Dewey finds in growth the nucleus of all pragmatic values:

> . . . the process of growth, of improvement and progress, rather than the static outcome and result, becomes the significant thing. Not health as an end fixed once and for all, but the needed improvement in health—a continual process—is the end and good. The end is no longer a terminus or limit to be reached. It is the active process of transforming the existing situation. Not perfection as a final goal, but the ever-enduring process of perfecting, maturing, refining is the aim of living. Honesty, industry, temperance, justice, like health, wealth and learning, are not goods to be possessed as they would be if they expressed fixed ends to be attained. They are directions of change in the quality of experience. Growth itself is the only moral "end." [5]

The pragmatic approach to art

It has been remarked by various students of Dewey that his great study of esthetics may eventually come to be regarded as his most enduring contribution to philosophy.† In any case, no achievement of any pragmatist more completely challenges traditional philosophies of life as well as of art or more richly expresses the healthful energy, the this-worldliness, and the breadth and depth of human experience. Here it is possible only to sample his brilliant work.

Esthetic Values. Values that are properly designated "esthetic" emphasize the *undergoing* phase of man's development—the having and enjoying of an experience. This is what Dewey often calls the "consummatory" moment in the rhythm of continuous interplay between individuals and their surroundings. Such values are, of course, related not only to values of other kinds but also to reality and knowledge. They are not to be pigeonholed according to some static formula of classification but are rather to be regarded as events within the vast time flow of nature.

One who loses oneself in the mood of fulfillment expressed in a symphony, a painting, or in such a humbler object as a flower garden is thereby attaining esthetic value. This is true whether the individual has himself given shape to the particular work of art or has simply shared it sympathetically with its creator. The important point is the wholeness, completeness, harmony that a composer or painter, listener or spectator achieves by identifying himself with whatever experience is designed—that is, carried through to a new balance of the forces and materials indigenous to it.

Thus it is that art emerges from "the live creature" of nature. Although it occurs only at the cost of tension, imbalance, and disequilibrium, its culmination is its own reward. In Dewey's characteristic terms: ". . . only when an organism shares in the ordered relations of its environment does it secure the stability essential to living. And when the participation comes after a phase of disruption and conflict, it bears within itself the germs of a consummation akin to the esthetic." [6] As art this consummation takes a multitude of forms: a pair of well-made shoes, a graceful dish, a bridge, a carefully planned street, a play, a dance. Great art, then, does not isolate itself from life. On the contrary, it strives, through countless media, to enrich the meaning of whatever in experience is most vital and significant.

† See Dewey, *Art as Experience.*

Science and Art. We should expect that the pragmatic philosophy would regard science and art not as separate but as complementary achievements of man.‡ Notwithstanding the strong emphasis placed upon the consummatory or intrinsic phase of creative experience, art also demands full utilization of the reflective, or, more precisely, the instrumental, phase. Such utilization is perhaps more apparent in some arts than in others; the so-called applied arts (for example, weaving, metalwork, ceramics) obviously require a wide range of practical and technological skills, processes and knowledge. But even the so-called fine arts (Dewey is skeptical of any rigid distinction between the fine arts and the applied arts) have similar requirements: music depends upon mathematically stated tempos; painting, upon spatial principles.

Indeed, any idea that art requires less exacting or active intelligence, strictly defined, than does science is completely spurious. The difference again is one of emphasis, not of kind. Both utilize essentially the same experiences of nature; both try to bring these experiences and man into a more meaningful relation. The artist, like the scientist, faces problems and tries to think them through and to *do* something about them. The need of readjustment because of maladjustment is just as real to him as it is to the scientist—often, perhaps, more real in the sense of being more directly and passionately felt.

The artist, however, tends to identify himself more immediately with the qualitative material of his particular medium of expression, and he is always intensely concerned to attain the fulfillment of form that that material (social events, stone, paint, steel, words, bodily rhythms, musical notes) challenges him to fulfill. The scientist, in contrast, is often less intimately identified with his material (the mathematical physicist works almost entirely with abstract symbols). Typically he regards the "doing" events of his experience as of more strategic importance than the "undergoing" events, which, we noted, highlight the esthetic mood.

Democracy as Value

The rise of modern democratic states, as we indicated above, has been one of the major sources of this American philosophy. Distinguished pragmatists do not, however, confine democracy to its political sense. It is political, to be sure. But it is much more—a pattern and program for

‡ See *ibid*, pp. 15f.

the whole range of life. Democracy is a challenging expression of fundamental values, attitudes, and practices. It is an ideal that we win in the very process of fulfilling it, an object worthy of religious faith, and, in a certain sense, a work of art.

Democracy: A Synthesis of Progressivist Beliefs. Democracy has already been encountered in this sketch of progressivist beliefs. Ontologically, the democratic way is that dynamic and interdependent *experience* that is living at its best. It is an outlet for some of the deepest drives of the individual—that is, for his need of dignity, respect, association, and responsibility, as he plays his particular role in the virile drama of the natural-social world.

Epistemologically, democracy is both seed and fruit of the widest practice of *intelligence*. It is that searching for truths that, in its most carefully delineated sense, is nothing less than science operating in and through the intermingling of men with their environments. In different words, it is the life of reflection applied to social intercourse. The issues that always exist in concrete group relationships are faced not merely by selfish interest and blind appeal to precedent or violence but by the same type of diagnosis, searching for hypotheses, and experimental programs that the individual relies upon when he applies his intelligence to difficulties that are more narrowly his own. If thinking, like communication, is essentially a phenomenon of the *social* self, then democracy, from the point of view of beliefs about knowledge and truth, is the institutionalization of that social self. In a broad sense, it is the five steps of the "act of thought," writ large in the efforts of people to meet effectively the recurring issues of their communal life.

Axiologically, the meaning of democracy has already been inferred. Its *values* are both instrumental and intrinsic. As a plausible ideal, it is "the *pursuit* of happiness," the steady effort to find mediating ways to the attainment of adequate ends, but it is also the immediate satisfactions enjoyed by such attainment. Democracy is both individual and social. *Each personality* requires the greatest opportunity and freedom to solve the problems that are distinctively his; but at the same time he so much needs the strength and experience of *other personalities* that, without them, his own freedom or equality is largely an illusion. Finally, democracy is symbolic of the supreme value of growth. It is not a fixed objective toward which we strive but that we can never hope to reach; it develops wherever and whenever men, within the flow of history, associate in mutual respect. If democracy has a moral meaning, as Dewey says, it is this: ". . . the supreme test of all political institutions and industrial arrangements shall be the contribution they make to the all-round growth of every member of society." [7]

We win democracy, in short, only as we *practice* it at every stage along the way—within our homes, clubs, trade unions, businesses, schools, states, and perhaps, eventually, within a family of nations.

Democracy: Critique and Norm. The winning of democracy by practicing it implies that democracy conceived as value should be regarded as both critique and norm of human experiences. Far from being merely a phenomenon to be described objectively and neutrally, it becomes, on the one hand, an instrument for criticizing both individual and social weaknesses and, on the other hand, a norm or standard toward which men should strive in order that the good life of democracy will exist. Let us briefly consider this key value from these two points of view.

As *critique,* democracy calls sharp attention to social obsolescences and failures of both the past and the present. Governments enforcing obedience to monarchical, autocratic, or theocratic power; economic systems exploiting many individuals by compelling them to toil for the benefit of a few other individuals; cultures stratifying and segregating races, classes, and creeds—all these, and many other failures, are condemned. Contemporary society is judged guilty on a long list of counts: too frequent blind acceptance of dogma or outworn custom; meek subjection of uncounted millions to religious, political, or economic hierarchies; widespread discrimination against minorities; lack of economic and other forms of opportunity, a lack that frustrates or destroys ambitions and abilities; absence of scientific planning by social institutions. It is little wonder that the pragmatist is hostile to all doctrines that are openly or surreptitiously totalitarian. He opposes fascism, religious authoritarianism, and Soviet communism alike because they are inimical to the value of democracy.

As *norm,* the democratic value is the closest approximation to any ultimate ideal that the pragmatist-progressivist is willing to accept.* We say closest *approximation* because his experimental temperament compels the pragmatist to admit that such a norm might conceivably be reshaped

* See Dewey, *Democracy and Education,* Chap. 7.

by the long course of events ahead of us, until even it no longer could be regarded as truly democratic. To consider such a contingency at the present stage of history is, however, to quibble over the improbable, to raise a merely academic question. To our own culture, and to all cultures as far as we can see, *democracy symbolizes that kind of growing life in which, first, each person consciously seeks and finds the fullest and the most varied satisfactions of his own capacities and in which, second, each group of persons seeks and finds comparable satisfactions through interplay with other groups.* Thus, the degree to which democracy can ever manifest itself is the degree to which such a measure can be adequately met. In this framework, men may rally round it as a religious symbol of "a common faith" in the capacity of man to rule over all nature, over all groups, and over himself and to do so in an ever more rational, more generous, more humane and cooperative way.†

Democracy as Art. Finally, democracy for the pragmatic philosophy may be regarded, in a profound sense, as a vast cultural work of art. If, as we have observed, art is at its core the free expression and consummation of creative human energies, then the democratic process becomes art at its very best. It is the privilege of each man to experience art by controlling, reshaping, earth and culture so that both he and other individuals will be invigorated and improved.

Like all values that we think of as esthetic, democracy is by no means, then, solely intellectual. The joy a person feels in freedom, in achievement and growth, in comradeship with others working with a sense of common aim, even in appreciation of the harmony and order of a culture that the majority of men themselves design and regulate for their own purposes—the joy inherent in these experiences points to the fact that democracy is warmed and colored by genuine creativity in its varied hues of feeling, change, rhythm, tension, struggle, balance, movement. The greatest art, the richest consummatory experience that human beings in modern life are capable of undergoing, is democracy itself.‡

Conclusion. These, then, are among the more basic beliefs undergirding progressive education. Our treatment has surely not been comprehensive, and our interpretation, conditioned by the frame of reference

† See Dewey, *A Common Faith.*

‡ See Dewey, *Experience and Nature,* Chap. 9; and *Art as Experience,* Chap. 14.

defined in Chapter 3, has inevitably colored what strives to be a friendly overview of this philosophy. Our main purpose has been to highlight general features that have come to be of particular importance to the progressivist program of the schools.

Our next task is to consider the beliefs about education that build directly upon this impressive groundwork of beliefs about natural-human experience.

Notes

[1] John Dewey, *Essays in Experimental Logic,* p. 330.

[2] Quoted from Max H. Fisch (ed.), *Classic American Philosophers,* p. 57.

[3] Quoted from Paul A. Schilpp (ed.), *The Philosophy of John Dewey,* p. 521.

[4] Dewey, *The Quest for Certainty,* p. 286.

[5] Dewey, *Reconstruction in Philosophy,* p. 177. Copyright 1920 by Henry Holt and Company, Inc. and reprinted with their permission.

[6] Dewey, *Art as Experience,* p. 15.

[7] Dewey, *Reconstruction in Philosophy,* p. 186.

CHAPTER 5

The Progressivist Pattern of Educational Beliefs

Progressivist Theory in Focus

THE TERM "PROGRESSIVISM" WILL NOW BE USED MORE STRICTLY to denote a cluster of harmonious and systematic beliefs about education, which rests upon another cluster of harmonious and systematic beliefs about philosophy—the American philosophy denoted by such terms as pragmatism, instrumentalism, and experimentalism. To change the metaphor, the beliefs outlined in the preceding chapter can be regarded as substructure and the beliefs outlined in this chapter as superstructure. If we were to carry this metaphor still further, we might imagine that the superstructure, in turn, consists of two stories: the first, educational theory; the second, concrete practice in school and community.

Actually, however, these ascending levels only roughly approximate the relationship between theory and practice. For one thing, progressivism as education and pragmatism as philosophy have been interwoven to an extraordinary extent through the work of Dewey. Far more insistently than any influential contemporary philosopher in America, if not in the world, he has maintained that the philosophy of education, properly understood, is also a philosophy of life.* His first great decade of influence (1894 to 1904 at the University of Chicago), during which many of his most fundamental views were formulated, was a period of fruitful educational as well as technical philosophizing. After that time, he de-

* See John Dewey, *Democracy and Education,* pp. 383ff.

voted much more of his attention to exploring the areas of ontology, epistemology, and axiology. But his vigorous interest in education never waned, and the channel between education and the wider philosophic areas was kept open by the support he received from a growing number of able disciples.

The free flow of ideas was not limited to philosophy and educational theory. Experimentation with pragmatism-progressivism as practice, which began toward the close of the nineteenth century and in which Dewey pioneered through his own laboratory school,† accelerated in the twentieth century. Pragmatism, which began with Peirce and was enriched by James and matured by Dewey, has now permeated to some degree almost every public school in America and has deeply affected the characters of more than a generation of young people. In addition, it has influenced uncounted teachers and pupils in other countries.‡

In this book we cannot be specifically concerned with the "second story" of day-by-day experimentation; but it is important at least to note that any effort to distinguish philosophy, educational theory, and educational practice by rigidly delimited categories does a certain violence to the facts. As much as any influential philosophy of our time, pragmatism-progressivism has insisted upon the interdependence, the continuity and interaction, of all kinds of experience, however theoretical at one extreme, however practical at the other. More than this, it has viewed all kinds of human experience, of thinking and of acting alike, as dynamic manifestations of the culture.*

We do not, of course, maintain that educational progressivists are all equally conscious of or consistent in their reliance upon the underlying philosophic principles. The fact is that certain very influential leaders sometimes go so far as to deny any logical relation between, let us say, pragmatic epistemology and progressivist methods of learning. Such attitudes are a reflection, however, not so much on the basic nature of pragmatist-progressivist thought as on the eclecticism or superficiality of some of their spokesmen. Certainly, as this position is symbolized by Dewey—and who, after all, is a better symbol?—progressivism should be viewed as one important inlay of a large cultural mosaic. It is a mosaic in which general philosophy, school practice, and wider institutional pat-

† See K. C. Mayhew and A. C. Edwards, *The Dewey School.*
‡ See Paul A. Schilpp (ed.), *The Philosophy of John Dewey,* Chap. 15.
* See Dewey, "Philosophy," *Encyclopædia of the Social Sciences.*

terns—especially liberal patterns—are equally significant parts. To an important degree, this same complex fusion will become apparent when we study in later pages the essentialist and perennialist interpretations of education.

Backgrounds of Progressive Education

European influences

Just as strands of influence, direct or indirect, on progressive education can be traced through the history of philosophy from ancient Greek thinking to American pragmatism, so strands of influence can be traced through the history of educational thought. To mention but one, there is the insistence of Plato that his leaders experience, as part of their long educational training, years of "learning by doing" in the rough-and-tumble environment of politics and war (see p. 316).

It is rather from the Renaissance world, however, with its revolts against medieval authoritarianism, than from the ancient world that "the new education" (as it is sometimes called) obtains more of its germinal ideas.† In Johann Comenius, for example, we discover a whole array of visionary proposals. Although we shall find that his views influenced essentialism as well as progressivism, nevertheless his beliefs in "work experience" and in fitting instruction to the child rather than the converse in early childhood education are astonishingly modern. We might go so far as to say that he anticipates by nearly three hundred years the "emerging curriculum" (see p. 142).

A philosopher-educator who is even closer to modern progressive education is Jean Jacques Rousseau. One of the greatest prophets of the French Revolution, he is concerned above all to establish a profound faith in the natural power of man. To be sure, it has been cogently argued, by

† See I. B. Berkson, *Education Faces the Future,* Chap. 6. The historic backgrounds of the educational theories discussed in this volume also rely heavily upon the following works: Robert Ulich, *History of Educational Thought;* Adolph Meyer, *The Development of Education in the Twentieth Century;* R. Freeman Butts, *A Cultural History of Education;* John S. Brubacher, *A History of the Problems of Education.*

Alexander Meiklejohn, that the immortal Frenchman is the forerunner of an educational and social philosophy that is more mature and more radical than progressivism.‡ It is also, however, true that Rousseau prepared the ground, as no one before him had, for what came to be known in our century as "the child-centered school"—one of progressivism's most fertile conceptions. He is concerned, above all, to encourage children to express their natural impulses; accordingly he is opposed to the stern discipline and forced "learning" that characterized the schools of his day. This is not to say that Rousseau's beliefs have been embodied in progressivism in the way he expressed them. Dewey himself has been critical of Rousseau for such inadequacies as his romantic and sentimental faith in the innate goodness of man.* Nevertheless, his has been one of the most powerful influences in behalf of an education that would be free from the strangle hold of fear and superstition or of domination by political and religious potentates—an education centering on man as a natural and social creature capable of mature, cooperative self-direction.†

As with Comenius, it would be difficult to say whether the great educational triumvirate of the Enlightenment—Johann Pestalozzi, Johann Herbart, and Friedrich Froebel—have had a greater influence on progressivism or on essentialism (see p. 316). As writers of their age, all three (but particularly Herbart) remained to some extent apologists for the dominant culture while, at the same time, they made innovations in education that are genuine and often startlingly modern. Pestalozzi, for example, often seems as strong a proponent of "self-activity" as Comenius or Rousseau. Direct observation rather than mere verbal learning, creative work, family life as educational experience—these are typically progressivist theories. Herbart anticipates the concept of the "whole child" by insisting upon a harmonious and justly proportioned development of all the learner's capacities, a development made possible educationally by building upon cumulative interests. Froebel, known as the founder of the kindergarten, insists, with Comenius and Rousseau, upon the right of the child to be free in the expression of his nature. Thus, he conceives the role of the teacher as guide, not as commander. He is one of the first to regard play and games as rich learning experience. As in Pestalozzi, discipline becomes more a matter of cooperation based upon

‡ See Alexander Meiklejohn, *Education between Two Worlds,* Chaps. 6, 16.
* See John Dewey, *Democracy and Education,* pp. 131-138.
† See Berkson, *op. cit.,* pp. 104f.

love for children than a military regulation enforced by threats of reprisal.‡

American influences

Earlier Leaders. Granting that the strongest influences upon progressivism in America were not primarily theoretical but were rather cultural in the sense discussed in Chapter 4, nevertheless, certain directly educational influences did lend added strength to progressivism's mature interpretation. William James, for example, influenced the profession widely by the publication of a series of lectures, *Talks to Teachers on Psychology,* which expound his characteristic belief that the strengthening of acquired habits by the individual—in order to develop his well-being—is the essence of good education.

More directly influential, however, was the monumental leadership of Horace Mann, Henry Barnard, and Francis Parker. Although none of these three educators was a first-rate theorist and although each could also be claimed to have been in some respects a forerunner of philosophies other than progressivism, nevertheless, all three are important precursors of this philosophy. In Mann we sense the deep faith of a pioneering democrat—an educator who actually believed, a century ago, that schools can become agents of social reform! In Barnard, although he was a more conservative leader, we find one of the first influential opponents of private schools as class-divisive and one of the first proponents of public schools as class-unifying.*

Among these great frontiersmen of the American public school system, it is Francis Parker who manifests most strikingly the early spirit of progressivism. Much of the revolutionary romanticism of Rousseau and Froebel is regenerated in Parker's brimming optimism, his faith in children, his love of nature. Probably more than any American educator before our own day he insists upon a central place in education for the creative arts and for creative work—an insistence that bore abundant fruit in his own experimental schools at Quincy, Massachusetts, and Chicago. Like James, he is strongly individualistic (he always makes the self supremely important); but, more than most progressivists before or since, Parker does not hesitate to criticize frankly our socio-economic

‡ See Ulich, *op. cit.*, pp. 258-291.
* See Merle Curti, *The Social Ideas of American Educators,* Chaps. 3, 4, 11.

system for its failure to provide sufficient security and opportunity for enough ordinary people.†

Many other American educators might be mentioned as early contributors. Felix Adler, founder of the Ethical Culture Society, remains a strong influence largely because of the excellent work the Society's progressive schools are still doing. Others, less theoretical, but nonetheless important because of their pioneering in laboratory schools, include Junius L. Meriam and Marietta Johnson.‡

Contemporary Leaders. While Dewey, of course, remains well into the midcentury the dominant intellectual force behind progressivism, he is the first to recognize the priceless contributions of a large number of other theorists and practitioners. Among these, two American philosophers of education stand above all others as devoted and able interpreters and as original supplementers of his work: William H. Kilpatrick and Boyd Bode.

Both scholars have successfully restated the original beliefs of pragmatism so as to make them as meaningful as possible to teachers, students, administrators, and parents. Both have been so articulately concerned with the psychology of learning that our section below on this subject draws often upon their formulations (see pp. 130-141). Both have deep positive convictions about the power of education to determine the course of history in an increasingly democratic direction.

Philosophers of education who hold somewhat less conspicuous, but nevertheless important, places in the progressivist camp include John L. Childs, Harold Taylor, R. Bruce Raup, George E. Axtelle, Gordon Hullfish, V. T. Thayer, William O. Stanley, Laurence G. Thomas, B. Othanel Smith, E. V. Sayers, Kenneth D. Benne, John P. Wynne, and Joseph K. Hart.*

We should also mention a number of distinguished American educators who, though not primarily philosophers, have made important contributions to the development of progressivist theory and practice: George S. Counts, educational sociologist; Goodwin Watson, educational psychologist; Harold Rugg, educational encyclopedist and esthetician; and, in the field of administration, such thoughtful leaders as Frank Baker,

† See Harold Rugg, *Foundations for American Education,* pp. 530-539.
‡ See Meyer, *op. cit.,* pp. 64-100; and Berkson, *op. cit.,* Chap. 7.
* Selections from many of these writers will be found in John S. Brubacher (ed.), *Eclectic Philosophy of Education.*

Ernest Melby, Harold Benjamin, Walter Anderson, Carleton Washburne, Willard Goslin, and Jesse H. Newlon.

Organized Progressivism. The theory and practice of progressivism have been supported by organizations that have made wide practical applications of the "new education." In America, the outstanding force for many years was the Progressive Education Association, founded in 1919 and for a time called the American Education Fellowship. Probably its most important achievement, among many worthy of note, was its development of the famous Eight-Year Study, in which thirty high schools across the country cooperated in evaluating the effects of progressivist as compared with traditional curriculums upon student success in high school and college.†

The New Education Fellowship is an international organization of progressivists with headquarters in London. Through it American educators have been able to communicate their experiences to teachers and students in Asia, Europe, and South America and have been enriched by the insights and experiences of progressivists abroad. International meetings have occurred in many countries under NEF auspices.

A much smaller American organization, the John Dewey Society, has made a strong impress on both theory and practice through its yearbooks, whose themes range from curriculum revision and teacher education to intercultural relations and spiritual values.

Finally, it should be noted that a number of other important groups, such as the Association for Childhood Education and the American Federation of Teachers, have recently given some impetus to experimentation with progressivist ideas that earlier in the century were often regarded as heretical and impractical. At the present time, the most influential, although sometimes an eclectic, promoter of progressivist methods is the Association for Supervision and Curriculum Development, a division of the National Education Association.

The remainder of this chapter selects from the immense literature of these organizations and of their leading spokesmen three general topics for discussion:

1. progressivist beliefs about learning;
2. the experimental curriculum: content and method; and
3. progressive education and social control.

† See W. M. Aikin, *The Story of the Eight-Year Study.*

Progressivist Beliefs about Learning

The child in his environment

The child is an experiencing organism, an integral part of the flow of events, relations, feelings, thoughts, things. To understand him we need to approach him as a natural being, associated with other natural beings and, like any other object of nature, subject to scientific analysis and individual development.

It follows that the child's behavior is wholly within the realm of his experience. In the most fundamental sense he is an animal more like than different from other animals. He, too, is engaged in the recurrent conflicts, the defeats and victories, of the struggle for existence. He, too, is immersed within the endless stream of emergent change.

Nevertheless, the child's powers are very different, in their potential refinement and complexity, from those of even the highest nonhuman animals. This is especially true of his intelligence, his ability to face and resolve problems. It is the practice of this ability that has enabled his species to achieve its mastery over all lower species as well as over inanimate nature. Accordingly, it is the practice and improvement of intelligence that is properly central to education.

By such practice and improvement the child will become a *better* child. That is to say, he will gain in self-mastery, he will attain fuller development, and he will become a happier adult for having learned how to utilize his intelligence effectively in adjusting and readjusting to his ever-shifting environment. To utilize his intelligence in such a way means, however, that he must also make full use of this environment. More exactly, he must have the opportunity to share freely, steadily, richly in the events of nature and culture immediately around him.

The school is "good" when it enables him to grow through such sharing, when it provides ways of expression for his total behavior pattern, when it permits him to act in relation to the actions of others. It is "bad" when it blocks expression of his feelings, when it denies satisfaction to his curiosity, when it turns him away from his own problems and interests, when it fails to provide opportunity for him to cope with them directly, overtly, experimentally.

Six Generalizations. The progressivist general psychological viewpoint may now be epitomized in six important generalizations.

1. *This psychology definitely and consistently applies the underlying pragmatic philosophy.* It is simply a way of looking through the triple lenses of reality, knowledge, and value as defined by such philosophers as Peirce, James, and, above all, Dewey. The more polished these lenses and the more expertly we learn how to adjust them, so that the image of the child in his environment is seen as a sharply outlined, integrated whole, the more clearly we shall have perceived the vibrant core of progressive education. Thus, for example, the ontological influence of organic evolution is strong in a psychology that asserts that all animal and therefore all human life is characterized by emerging natural processes requiring careful scientific explanations. Thus, too, the dynamic, re-creative qualities of reality are epitomized in the nature of the child: in his zestful enthusiasms, his eagerness, his amazing sensitivity and responsiveness, his endless questionings and discoveries—most important of all, perhaps, in the fact that the child repeatedly modifies and is modified by the experiences through which his behavior develops.

2. *As a direct inference from our first generalization, learning is itself a natural experience.* In a comprehensive sense it is simply the recurring effort of every organism to remove obstacles and reduce disturbances by building new responses into its pattern of development. The smallest child learns, as his own tendencies and responses become more and more organized, to select some stimuli from among the welter that impinge upon him and to assimilate and react to these more than to others. From this viewpoint learning is as functional to organic life as, let us say, nourishment. And, like the latter, it is most fully operative only when accompanied by appetite—appetite for the experiences that endlessly confront human beings as they explore their bewildering but intriguing world.

3. *Such a view of learning means that "the whole child" is necessarily involved in learning, not only his "mind."* Mind is, in any case, simply a term for relatively specialized behavior: it is the function that seeks to exercise deliberate control over one's relations by foreseeing consequences and meanings in events.* Hence, even the most intellectual processes are not cut off from feeling in some form, from habit, and from

* See Boyd H. Bode, *How We Learn,* Chap. 15.

bodily response. On the less refined levels of experience, learning is certain to embrace—at least as intimately as on more refined levels of experience—the muscular, glandular, emotional, and other constituents of any total structure of behavior.

4. *The child's surroundings are as fundamental to his nature as is his own body, which, in a way, is also part of his surroundings.* The self is always social and, as the child learns with his whole nature not with something separate called a "mind," his learning requires the steady aid of his environment. Each cooperates in changing the other.

5. *Learning functions on rising levels of complexity the highest of which is intelligence.* We should hardly say that the rabbit is able to reflect intelligently; we do say that he learns. Apes not only learn but apparently show considerable intelligence. Men often learn as lower animals do. They build responses into their behavior by sheer trial and error, impulsive acts, hasty choices, which involve, at most, one or two steps in the act of thought. The point is that reflection differs from other kinds of learning only in degree and not in kind. Reflection is more cautious, thorough, analytical, constructive, imaginative, and certainly more dependable than learning that is more overt, fumbling, and direct.

6. *Progressivism rejects several concepts concerning the nature of the child that are still held by widely influential traditional psychologies.* The child is not endowed with innate mental attributes; he conceals no chrysalises of intellect that at the proper time unfold their wings. The child is not a mechanism that responds to stimuli in the environment as a motor responds to drops of gasoline. He is neither a "soul-stuff" to which bodily activities have little immediate relationship nor mere atomic substance in which mental processes are altogether physical. In the older language of psychology, the child is not all mind or all matter for the excellent reason that he is clearly both.

By "both," however, the progressivist again must explain what he does *not* mean. He denies that the physical and the mental are parallel planes of human existence or that they are ultimately always separate, dualized, static, and discrete substances or elements. The older psychology's concept of "instincts," to consider one example, is replaced by a concept of plastic, overlapping tendencies, which are capable of being modified and directed in manifold ways. Likewise, progressivism discards the widely held theory that response follows stimulus in a one-two order of cause and effect, that behavior is merely the product of exercising and strengthening the sequences or bonds of stimulus-response (see pp. 224, 245). Agreeing that a given stimulus helps to determine the nature of the particular response, progressivism holds that the responses of which the child is capable (according to his capacities, interests, habits, environment) are themselves selectors and conditioners of particular stimuli. The child *invites* a certain stimulus because he has been conditioned to invite it. Response and stimulus are thus *interactive* because each is a function of the other.†

Living as Learning: An Illustration

In order to apply these generalizations more concretely to the progressivist theory of learning, we select for illustration a timely controversial problem—juvenile delinquency. That this problem is becoming dangerously chronic in many American communities, that perhaps its most dangerous aspect is the increase of promiscuity and general moral laxity among youth in their teens, few if any observers deny.

American educational leaders also recognize the existence of the problem. They may even admit, on occasion, that the maladjustments in family life induced by such factors as family migration and employment of both parents, by strains of insecurity and false allurements, create new tasks for public education. Yet, these leaders have too infrequently undertaken to deal directly with the problem of juvenile delinquency. Even when they have not been wholly preoccupied with teacher shortages, budgets, and curriculum routines, they have hesitated to examine carefully the students' family disturbances, sex practices, and personal and social values. Some hesitate because they regard the curriculum as already over-filled with more important subject matter—others because they fear reprisals from community groups which consider such delicate and personal areas of experience to be beyond the proper boundaries of education.

Does this mean, then, that young people are not learning about the mores and morals of sexual relations? The question is rhetorical. Of course, they are learning. They are learning when conflicts or tensions occur at home. They are learning from their classmates, in neighborhood gangs, in dance halls, from "comic" magazines and movies, down the

† See Dewey, *Human Nature and Conduct,* Part I; Rugg, *op. cit.,* Chap. 4; Bode, *op. cit.,* Chaps. 14-15.

alley, behind the barn, in the "cola" parlor. They are learning afternoons and week ends, when school is "out." They are often learning when they least recognize that they are learning.

The progressivist does not ask us to choose, then, between learning-in-school and nonlearning-out-of-school. Rather, the issue is between *two kinds of learning*. One is expertly directed toward constructive consequences and evaluated according to a clear conception of the good life, a desirable culture; the other is nondirected, determined by unexamined, static, conflicting values. The difference, in other words, is between what Dewey calls genuinely *educative* as against *miseducative* learning.‡ One stimulates growth and steadily enriches personal and social relations; the other weakens or destroys the individual's capacity to grow.

If education is to deal with such problems as juvenile delinquency, then, it must shift radically away from the traditional pattern of fixed courses, fixed hours, fixed rules, and fixed objectives and toward a widening pattern whose subject matter encompasses nothing less than the entire, complex environment. If sex is important to young people, then it is important to the school. If family stability is important to them, then that is important to the school. If after-class play and relaxation are important to them, then the school program should reach out into the late afternoons and evenings, into week ends and summers, and should extend through the whole neighborhood in which the child carries on his daily activities.

In short, a public education that walls itself off from the most deeply felt aspects of living and concerns itself with courses and academic requirements that are the least deeply felt aspects of the child's experience is an irresponsible education. At its door must be laid no small part of the blame for juvenile delinquency.

We are now better prepared to rephrase and supplement in terms of progressivist learning some of the general statements made above about the child and his environment. Implicit or explicit in the illustration are the following concepts, which are especially relevant to the progressivist theory of learning: (1) interest, (2) effort, (3) purpose, (4) intelligence, (5) habit, (6) growth, (7) organism, and (8) culture. We shall try to dissect the core of each concept as it is interpreted by this theory.

Interest. To say that a child is "interested" in a particular experience is to say that he is responding to it because it "clicks." It arouses a

‡ See Dewey, *Experience and Education*, pp. 12ff.

eling or a whole cluster of feelings, emotions, and impulses. It has eaning for him to the degree that it can be associated with meanings e has already derived from previous experiences. But its meaning is not lentical with those previously learned meanings. There is in this new xperience an element of novelty, of the uncertain, which excites him try to find out how it may be brought into harmony with older experinces so that it, too, will become more meaningful.

To return to our illustration, it is obvious that the affairs of family fe or of boy-girl associations are keenly "interesting" in this sense. No xperiences are closer to the feelings and relations of normal persons, hatever their age. Yet few experiences generate more uncertainty, perlexity, explosive emotion—or more eagerness to find certainty, order, armony of feeling. If, as the Progressive Education Association declared its very first statement of policy, interest is the motive of all work and ould be "satisfied and developed through . . . direct and indirect conct with the world and its activities,"[1] then the personal needs and ifficulties that underlie the problem of juvenile delinquency constitute a ost proper subject matter for education.*

Effort. Dewey's *Interest and Effort in Education,* an early and relavely little-known book, is one of his richest contributions to education. n it he argues that a correctly organized effort in learning—prolonged ntellectual concentration or hard practice in developing a manual skill— vill not be separate from but must be fused throughout with interest.

This is merely to say that all of us work most intensively at tasks in which we are motivated by our impulses, desires, talents. To force effort pon children when they are not in the least interested, when they do ot feel or see any significance in what they are compelled to do, can only nean that they will probably learn far better to dislike that kind of effort han they will learn the content or skill that is the ostensible educational bjective.

The total effort involved in learning to understand family life in a iven community may be greater than that involved in grammar-drilling r fact-memorizing. It may, for example, require firsthand investigations f social agencies or tenement districts, as well as prolonged sociological tudy. Yet it is problematic, meaningful, and vital to most young people.

Purpose. Interest and effort combine with a third important factor, urpose. Although progressivist theory seems to certain of its critics to

* See William H. Kilpatrick, *Philosophy of Education,* Chap. 20.

have inadequately analyzed this concept, nevertheless progressivists insist that purpose, in some sense, is essential to all effective learning.

By "purpose," in the present context, Dewey and his disciples mean the foreseen consequences of a particular interest and its related effort, both being biologically derived. Educationally speaking, learners need to see where a given experience may lead and why it is important for them to clarify it and so to satisfy the impulse that motivated them in the beginning. Kilpatrick, in an excellent discussion entitled "Purpose: Its Place in the Life of Learning," epitomizes the progressivist view: ". . . purpose . . . permits a higher degree of efficiency of action than otherwise would be possible; but it also means that desirable results will be effected in the degree that purposes are critically chosen and intelligently directed." [2]

Thus, the chief purpose of learning about sex under expert guidance would be to help discover a stable but dynamic pattern for marriage and the family so as to assure minimum conflict and maximum satisfaction. Here is a very real purpose for boys and girls who are approaching adulthood; it stems from a deep interest in themselves and in one another. So real and so interesting is it that they will inevitably deal with it in primary experience, whether the schools do or not.

Intelligence. Between motivating interest and achieved purpose is the all-important phase of learning we have called "intelligence." This is the careful, sustained effort to think through and reorganize a disorganized situation. When we act immediately, spontaneously, on impulse, the end result is likely to be far less satisfactory than when we stop to consider what will happen *if* we act. By *observing* carefully as many relevant elements in the situation as possible, by *recalling* past observations and past experiences somewhat similar to the present one, and by *judging* the significance of the latter in terms of the former, we are able to reformulate and carry out our purpose, confident that its attainment is most likely to be the best possible under the circumstances.

This crucial phase of learning is, of course, what is termed above "mediate experience" (see pp. 103-107). In this relation we may say that "knowledge" stands to "recollection" as "truth" stands to tried-out "purpose."

Again the illustration of juvenile delinquency is apt. One of the major reasons why sex conduct becomes destructive is that it is so often ıerely impulsive. Its consequences are not sufficiently thought through. 'o bring intelligence to bear upon it, therefore, is to delay response in rder to examine as many facets of the experience as possible. Such an xamination requires all the care of observation, recollection, and judgıent that can be mustered. Educationally this involves the difficult reponsibility of studying the history of sex mores and standards, of seeing heir changing patterns in perspective, and of noting the effects of sexual ıxity today upon disease, illegitimacy, and family disintegration. It inolves the careful weighing of modifications that might be desirable in he traditional role of women as mothers and homemakers. It involves the levelopment of a conception of love and marriage that conforms to our cientific knowledge, to twentieth-century moral standards, and to the deals of young people increasingly emancipated from the forbidding uthoritarianism of earlier generations.

Habit. "The basic characteristic of habit," says Dewey, "is that very experience enacted and undergone modifies the one who acts and ındergoes, while this modification affects, whether we wish it or not, he quality of subsequent experiences." [3] The importance of this progresivist conception of learning is threefold.‡

First, habit is often an obstacle to effective learning. To the degree hat we are tempted to fall back upon routine reactions, we too often fail o bring intelligence to bear upon new situations, following instead ıabitual behavior patterns regardless of whether they are appropriate or ıot. Nevertheless, we thereby modify both ourselves and our ongoing xperience.

Second, habits are indispensable aids to learning because they help ıs to perform a great many actions automatically or reflexively, thus nabling us to give our primary attention to consciously reflective action.

Third, we can, if we are encouraged to do so, acquire the habit of eflective behavior, just as we can acquire habits on routine or motor evels of action. We can become *habitually* intelligent.

Progressivist learning of habits is properly concerned with decreasng the negative effects and with increasing the positive effects. Habits ıre "bad" when they become flabby excuses for avoiding reflection, 'good" when they become the ally of reflection.

‡ See Dewey, *Human Nature and Conduct,* Part I; Rugg, *op. cit.,* pp. 112-16; Curti, *op. cit.,* pp. 515-517.

Today our most imperative intellectual need in education is to de vote attention and practice especially to the third kind of habit—that is to controlled, experimental reactions to the problems we meet in our en vironment. Just as the scientist learns to analyze, infer, and test hi hypotheses with habitual expertness, so the average citizen can learn t meet his everyday problems far more reflectively than he now does. I such a problem as juvenile delinquency is to be coped with successfully both young people and adults will have to face it much more often wit habits that encourage reflection, much less often with habits that dis courage reflection.

They will also, of course, resort to habits of the second kind. Fo example, they will employ the skills of written and spoken communica tion as they investigate scientifically the causes of delinquency in a par ticular community. Such habitual skills as these, however, are not an tithetical to the habit of intelligence. Rather they are complementary Contrary to distorted views of the meanings of progressive education for example, that it fails to teach the three R's—progressivism recognize the importance of the habits of skills as well as of the habits of reflection

Growth. Learning is also an axiological experience. That is to say it tends either to improve or to damage the child's physiological, psycho logical, and social values. Only when it strengthens the whole learner b enabling him, bodily and spiritually, to pursue his deepest interest wit sustained and efficient effort, only when it efficiently and continuousl strengthens his habits of motor skill and his habits of reflection, does i help the child to grow.

Juvenile delinquency signifies, by the same measures, just the op posite of the value of growth. If our public schools are to be appraised by this value, they will become good in so far as they help to create a socia environment in which youth can develop normal, wholesome attitude toward the psychology of sex, boy-girl friendships, and love and marriage They will provide an abundance of learning experiences in which the same intelligent process of reflective thinking and action is applied t family and other human-relations problems that is more frequently ap plied to other kinds of problems. Frustration, conflict, superstition, ortho doxy, silence, taboos, rote learning of moral rules—these are widesprea evils that must be uprooted from education. Only as young people gai in critical self-awareness, self-confidence, positiveness, and articulatenes bout the learnings that are at the very core of their experience will they eally grow.

Organism. The child's responses are a function of the unity of he organism. He learns, therefore, with his body as well as with his mind. Aore strictly, he never learns with merely the one *or* the other because either ever exists without the other; neither functions except in some egree for the other. The familiar term "organismic" denotes the comlete interrelatedness that characterizes progressivist psychology, as do lso two other terms of recent popularity—"Gestalt" and "field." Both f these connote the flexible unities and patterned configurations that are ndigenous to the fusion of all individual and social life. Even more ecent is the psychology termed "transactionalism"—a term derived from Dewey and connoting the dynamic wholeness of man's inner and outer xperience as it centers in phenomena of perception.*

One helpful way to bring out the significance of organism for learnng is to note once more the import of "immediate" and "mediate" experience. We recall that by the former, as distinguished from the roblem-solving quality of the latter, is meant the "undergoing" or "conummatory" phase of behavior. It is on that phase that, as James might ave put it, we "perch" for the time being, rather than "flit." We enjoy sense of full communion with ourselves and our surroundings, as an rtist enjoys identification with the designs and symmetries of a concerto r a mural.

Learning, then, is most completely organic when it is both immeliate, in the way of esthetic appreciation, and mediate, in the way of cientific analysis. Each phase of learning is complementary, not antagnistic, to the other.† Just as the student of painting may become quite cientific, so the student of chemistry may sometimes become quite artistic. The important point in this regard is that the continuum of *immediacynediacy-immediacy,* which we noted in discussing pragmatic beliefs bout reality and knowledge, is not only, in another context, the coninuum of *intrinsic-instrumental-intrinsic* values but is also the continuum f *undergoing-doing-undergoing,* which seems especially apropos to prag-

* See Bode, *op. cit.,* Chap. 14; and Hadley Cantril, *The "Why" of Man's Experience.*

† See Rugg, *op. cit.,* Chap. 7. Rugg believes Dewey has overstressed the actor of mediation in learning.

matic beliefs about art (see pp. 101-104, 112-113, 116-117). All thre
hyphenated phrases simply suggest, in different perspectives, the rhyth
mic, emerging wholeness of learning. They suggest also that feelings o
the body and ideas of the mind function as partners in one organic ente
prise.

This psychological doctrine has a direct relevance to our key illus
tration. That love and family life reveal spiritual and physical, intellectua
and emotional, scientific and esthetic qualities is evident from the vas
store of physiological and sociological treatises, and from the poetry an
music devoted to these themes. If education is to treat these themes wit
even nearly the same richness, then it must be just as honestly concerne
with, let us say, the esthetics and morals of sex experience as with it
hygiene and biology. Any more limited treatment again involves a kin
of truncated and haphazard learning that only guarantees that youn
people will receive their sex education elsewhere than in the publi
schools.

Culture. Although the concepts we have thus far defined impl
the sociality of learning, it is important to make sure that this final aspec
becomes sufficiently explicit. That the child never learns in isolation fro
others is a truism progressivists never tire of affirming. The "self" tha
the child acquires is, in great measure, the product of communicatio
with other "selves"; it is the blending of responses that develop into per
sonality "roles" as he slowly learns to anticipate how others expect hi
to respond (see pp. 113-114).

Our conception of culture, as stated in Chapter 3, includes, howeve
much more than a socio-psychological recognition of human interdepend
ence.‡ Kilpatrick expresses this conception when he says that cultur
means: ". . . all those transmitted results of prior human experience an
contrivance through which the group now carries on its life. This in
cludes, especially, language, customs, tools, institutions, knowledge, dis
tinctions, ideals, and standards."[4]

In this context we may say that schools are set up by a culture pri
marily to *guarantee its continuity*. The institutions and practices erecte
by the long, arduous trials and struggles of earlier generations must b

‡ See Dewey, *Freedom and Culture,* Chap. 2; and *Democracy and Educa
tion,* p. 3; Kilpatrick, *op. cit.,* Chap. 6; John L. Childs, *Education and Moral*
pp. 141-143.

aintained by later generations. This is not merely because men cherish
em for their own sakes but because without them each successive gen-
ation would have the impossible task of "starting from scratch" to
evelop controls over its hazardous surroundings.

Such a view of the cultural necessity of controlled learning is preg-
ant with implications regarding the development of the culture. On the
ebit side, it tempts us to consider learning as a mere device to reinforce
adition, a mirror of historical events. On the credit side, the progressivist
careful to point out that, although certain societies have cultivated an
lucation chiefly to preserve the past, every culture, no matter how static
appears, is continuously evolving. Education does not operate in its
ll sense, accordingly, unless it recognizes and relates to this evolution
accepting the *bequests* of the culture, certainly, but also recognizing
eir *pertinence and usefulness* to contemporary practices and problems
ongoing communal experience.

We again dramatize the progressivist learning concept, now in terms
culture, by the example of the obligation of public schools to face
riously the problem of juvenile delinquency. When schools explore
onestly and thoroughly the problems, customs, and ideals of family life
d sex relationships, they must conclude that the achievements that
ave slowly matured through the ages are worthy of profound respect;
ithout them we would be thrown into a state of moral chaos. But this
nservative conclusion is not inconsistent with the recognition that the
eaning of such problems, customs, and ideals must be reinterpreted to
eet the changed conditions of each successive generation.

It is common knowledge that the attitude of many young people
ward sexual experience is increasingly in conflict with that of older
ople. Education, as a central agent of cultural continuity, thus con-
onts a critical alternative. *Either* it will continue to ignore the interests
d perplexities of our younger people and so be compelled to share
sponsibility for the decline of moral standards. *Or* it will try to investi-
te the issues involved and to help boys and girls advance toward new
oral formulations that they can conscientiously accept—formulations
at rest firmly upon habits and knowledge accumulated by the culture,
it shaped to agree with the social and personal needs of contemporary
perience. The breach between learning and living will begin to be
osed when public education selects the latter of these options.

The Experimental Curriculum: Content and Method

The subject matter of progressive education

The proper subject matter of a curriculum, say such progressivists
Rugg, is any experience that is educative.* This is to say, with Dewe
that the good school is concerned with every kind of learning that hel
students, young and old, to grow. There is no single body of content,
system of courses, no universal method of teaching that is appropriate
every kind of school. For, like experience itself, the needs and intere
of individuals and groups vary from place to place, from time to tim
from culture to culture.

The well-constructed curriculum is not unlike a laboratory. It is u
ceasingly experimental, and all its participants—teachers and studen
alike—are, in some fashion, staff scientists. Hence, it is necessary to avo
rigidity in school requirements, absolute boundaries, mechanical stan
ards, preconceived solutions. Just as the experimental method is flexib
exploratory, tolerant of the novel, curious to try the hitherto untried,
too is its educational symbol. The progressivist curriculum travels u
hesitatingly down the "liberal road to culture."

At the same time, advocates of progressive education are qui
willing to recognize that certain learning areas, to which traditional su
ject-matter labels may be attached, are proper organizational devic
They are equally willing to try various forms of curriculum structu
Belying the caricatures of progressive education, which depict it as d
organized, atomistic, and planless, Dewey and his followers have nev
denied the need of careful structuring and planning. What they do i
sist upon is a curriculum that grows through cooperative interests, thin
ing, and action. It is in this sense that Kilpatrick calls the term "emergi
curriculum" his ideal—an ideal that includes, but extends beyond, h
famous theory of the "project method." †

Five Types of Curriculum Structure. In assessing the accomplis

* See Rugg, *op. cit.*, p. 701.

† See National Society for the Study of Education, *Forty-first Yearboo*
Part I, "Philosophies of Education," p. 77; Kilpatrick, *Philosophy of Educatio*
Chap. 23; Samuel Tenenbaum, *William Heard Kilpatrick*, Chaps. 15-22.

ments of progressivism during the last half-century, Rugg finds five major types of effort to rebuild the curriculum, of which the first four are greater or lesser compromises with the traditional curriculum pattern:‡

1. reorganization within a particular subject: juggling items about with little actual redesigning;
2. correlation of two or more bodies of subject matter: for example, between English and the social studies;
3. grouping together and integrating related subjects within broad fields of knowledge: for example, "general education" in the natural sciences or arts;
4. "core curriculum": a loosely used term to suggest blocks of learning experiences around common needs;
5. "experience-centered curriculum": dissolving subject-matter lines and emphasizing "units."

The "units" of the "experience-centered curriculum," which cut across fields and clusters of needs, are generated and shaped by the questions and experiences of the learners themselves—are directed toward the total personality development of each learner by exposing him to a wide range of emotional, motor, intellectual, and social experiences.

In the order of these five, we can observe increasing degrees of emancipation from traditional curriculums, with the core curriculum by far the most progressive of the subject-matter types and therefore closest to the full-fledged experience-centered pattern. As the Eight-Year Study reveals, moreover, not only may two or more types overlap even within a single school system but there may be still other variations, ranging from almost conservative plans to close approximations of Kilpatrick's ideal.

The Study of History: An Example. The way in which a particular subject matter becomes a creative learning experience might be illustrated by many examples. History, however, is a particularly apt one because of the familiar criticism that progressive education too often neglects intensive study of the past. As we shall find in the next two parts, both essentialists and perennialists repeatedly make this attack.

It is true that progressivists rebel against the conventional teaching of history. They deny that a study of the social heritage that is divorced

‡ See Rugg, *op. cit.*, Chap. 22.

from present impulses, problems, and purposes can be fully educative learning. They are devastating, therefore, in their critique of segregated courses in ancient, medieval, or modern history as these have usually been taught in our public schools and colleges.

At the same time, progressivists are insistent that history is an indispensable educative tool if properly utilized. Indispensable because the scientific method always requires knowledge of what has already happened in order to anticipate what may happen. Indispensable because the continuity of culture, which education helps so powerfully to reinforce, requires the deepest possible understanding of habits and institutions evolving from the past into the present and toward the future. Indispensable, finally, because the flow of temporal events is always from immediacies that have already been, through mediacies that are now, into new immediacies that become fresh consummations and syntheses of those events.

For history to be learned on these premises, two guiding rules must constantly be implemented. One is that the ongoing *present* is always the fulcrum of interest; hence if history is to be significant it must necessarily be drawn upon whenever learners see its significance *for* the present. Once they do see it, however (as students of a crucial problem such as marriage and family life come to recognize a need to understand the roots of these basic cultural institutions), then a motivation for historical study is provided. As Dewey points out:

> Just as the individual has to draw in memory upon his own past to understand the conditions in which he individually finds himself, so the issues and problems of present *social* life are in such intimate and direct connection with the past that students cannot be prepared to understand either these problems or the best way of dealing with them without delving into their roots in the past.[5]

The second rule, which applies especially to the primary and secondary school, is that history should be taught not as a separate subject but as an organic phase of every larger unit of learning. This rule is implemented by the most advanced curriculum structures listed above. In the experience-centered curriculum, especially, history becomes so natural to each designed unit that its subject-matter character completely disappears. Rather, it becomes one basic experience within the total process of living as learning.

PROGRESSIVIST METHOD: SOME CENTRAL ISSUES

We now consider a number of issues that elucidate the curriculum principles of progressivist theory in terms of educational method.†

The Nature of Real Problems. Teachers and administrators in charge of conventional curriculums often remark that they are already practicing "sane" progressive education. Look at the "problem approach," they say, which has become increasingly popular. Such skills as mathematics deal with problems, do they not? And do not science courses too? And is it not becoming a common approach in the social studies, arts, and other areas as well?

As with other issues, the best method of appraising such a contention is to square it against relevant philosophic beliefs. When we do, we find that what is *called* "progressivist" is too often not at all in accord with progressivist beliefs. The problem approach is not in accord when "problems" are artificially contrived without careful consideration of whether they bear upon situations that are meaningful to students. A large proportion of the ordinary exercises in, let us say, arithmetic have no such bearing. They are, in fact, counterfeit problems—textbook stereotypes divorced from economic occupations and other cultural interests.

The problem approach fails again when the problems are merely "recipes," which, when the ingredients are mixed and stirred according to direction, are guaranteed to turn out dishes quite identical with those of previously successful cooks. To change the analogy, such problems resemble puzzles in a magazine with solutions given on a back page. The student's job is to ferret out answers, which the teacher carefully conceals. This type of learning exemplifies the method of *deduction*—the application of a given formula to prove, or illustrate, some specific case.

Progressive education does not deny the need for practice in the form of exercises or deductions at the proper time and in the proper place. It does deny that they should occupy a central position in the curriculum. The experimental method cannot function *merely* by drawing upon a reservoir of knowledge—upon rules, laws, given facts—or upon repetitive skills. The evolutionary quality of all experience imparts

† Most issues here lean heavily on Dewey, *Democracy and Education.* See also Kilpatrick, *Foundations of Method* and *Philosophy of Education;* National Society for the Study of Education, *Fifty-fourth Yearbook,* Part I, "Modern Philosophies and Education," Chap. 5.

to every genuinely problematic situation a similar quality—a quality of the temporal, the unique, and the particular. Speaking again in terms of logic, such situations demand a technique that is in essence *inductive:* the examination of all factors that are relevant and the seeking out of relationships, the process guided throughout by tentatively maintained ends-in-view which, when tried out, may eliminate the initiating quandary.

The Use of Drill. How, then, can progressivists justify a place for drill? If they do are they not inconsistent? If they do not are they not guilty of failure to produce well-trained, highly skilled worker-citizens?

Their reply rests upon the now familiar psychological position that memorizing and rote practice rarely succeed in stimulating interest, much less any strong impulse to carry on intelligent activity. But interest geared to intelligent activity very often leads to recognition of the need for those dexterities that demand concentrated practice, for memorizing of appropriate material, and for the logical and manual abilities that will help to carry out the deductions required by the more inductive task.

The best way to perfect a given skill is by its constant use in whatever vital projects students may pursue. The effective use of language, for example, is not taught so well by formal grammar and vocabulary lessons, or similar techniques, as it is by permeating the curriculum at every point with language opportunities—above all, by providing many opportunities for communication among students, teachers, and resource people of the community. Words, say instrumentalists, are man's chief tool of meaning and control. But as with any tool, he becomes expert in their use only by applying them as a means to obtain worthwhile ends. Repetitious exercise is justified, therefore, only if it is commonly perceived by all participants as such a means.

Work versus *Play or Work* and *Play?* A partly related issue is raised by the contention of critics that progressivist methods often confuse work and play. Education, if it is sound, is hard work, they say, and "sugar-coating" of courses or skills by reducing them to "easy fun" merely encourages laxity of standards.

The progressivist replies that to identify schooling with work and much outside activity with play means again that the former is divorced from ongoing experience while the latter remains an intimate part of such experience. Only when work is cut off from the drives, enthusiasms, and talents of the growing individual does it become a necessary evil—an onerous task to be completed as quickly as possible. Labor, under these conditions, is considered antithetical to leisure-time activity.

Work that is meaningful and creative, however, is not a burden to be avoided. In the joy and satisfaction it affords, one might properly contend that it is similar to play. The latter, on the other hand, has many of the qualities of work; children's games and adult diversions often require reflection, imaginative planning, and extraordinary energy. Recreation as learning provides a good illustration of Kilpatrick's fruitful concept of "concomitant learning"—learning that occurs not so much by deliberate or formal instruction as by the fact that the human organism functions as a unified whole and hence that every experience he has affects the learner's personality.

Progressivists also recognize relative distinctions between the two activities. They call attention to the fact that work of any kind, in school or not, requires periods of relaxation. They perceive dangers in types of work that cause people to react to monotony or drudgery by indulging in unhealthful, falsely stimulating pleasures—a danger especially common in our industrial culture. But even work that permits the individual's capacities to function on a high plane of intelligent activity—even this calls for respite, recreation, especially when, in the course of such activity, the worker attains temporary goals or resting places. In this sense we may say, perhaps, that play is one form of what has been termed "immediate experience." In esthetic terms, it is a more consummatory, undergoing phase of human life.

But we should also recall that immediate experience is not totally disjoined from preceding and succeeding activities that require conscious effort and control. The activities of mediate experience at once arise out of immediate experience and continuously regenerate and recondition it. Play, then, must be removed from the fringes of school programs, where it is inaccurately termed *extra*curricular. Children learn equally from work *and* play when both are functional to their fields of meaning.

The Issue of Indoctrination. Still another issue arising from the educational method typical of experimental schools is that of indoctrination. If that method is, at heart, inductive in the way that science is inductive, if it is tolerant of various kinds of evidence and alternative points of view, will it not necessarily oppose all programs of education that seek to impose some single doctrine—religious, political, moral, or of any other category? The answer is unequivocal: it will, of course, oppose them.

But this answer is too negative. No education, say progressivists, is strictly impartial or objective. All teachers are influenced by values, attitudes, customs—the entire philosophic equipment of culture—and these saturate content as well as practice throughout. Hence, educators should not be deluded by the superficial rationalization that they can immunize themselves from these influences. Their task is rather to bring them all as closely as possible within the range of conscious scrutiny, to ensure that teachers and students be frank and critical about their beliefs.

Several inferences follow. One is the necessity of academic freedom as the right of children or adults to confront any controversial issue of importance. It implies unrestricted opportunity to examine facts and test hypotheses. But the choices that result from intelligent activity are still not to be indoctrinated—that is, they must not be taught in such a way as to preclude questioning or possible alternatives. A second inference is that choices are true for a limited time, subject always to the probability that they will need to be revised. Finally, this philosophy reveals an underlying conviction that the method of intelligence is in all respects the best method that men have found by which they are able to advance. This conviction is as close to "indoctrination" as progressivism ever approaches in theory. Nevertheless, even this conviction, which it would like all of us to share, is open to rigorous inspection and debate.‡

Child-Centered or Community-Centered Schools? A further issue, which will be particularly significant to our cultural evaluation in the next chapter, is whether the center of a good school is the individual child, his interests and growth, or the problems and development of the community of which the school is part.

Stated so baldly, the distinction between child-centered and community-centered schools is, of course, sharper than either the theory or practice of progressivism warrants. All advocates would insist that no school can or should be exclusively either. Nevertheless, strong differences of emphasis may be discerned, differences extending deep beneath the surface of the culture that nourishes this provocative philosophy of life and education.

‡ See Kilpatrick (ed.), *The Educational Frontier*, Chaps. 4, 9; Childs, *Education and Morals*.

The child-centered emphasis is revealed in the characteristic concern of the progressivist curriculum for rounded, organismic learning—the curriculum that encourages individual initiative, release of feelings, spontaneity of ideas, creative expression. Such a curriculum requires that the teacher know every student as thoroughly as possible—not by class grades alone (in fact, these are held to be of minor consequence) but by his family relationships, his emotional and physical health, his special abilities and limitations. Thus, the teacher's abundant use of tests and records is intended to produce a comprehensive profile of the student—his knowledge, social sensitivity, appreciations, interests, progress, skill in problem solving, and adjustment as a total personality. The pupil is allowed wide deviations in terms of his individuality and in the pace and ingredients of class study. Lock-step courses are utterly taboo. A comprehensive view of the moderately child-centered school, in which the social content is given considerable emphasis but in which the child is still *a,* if not *the,* center of attention, is portrayed in "The American Elementary School," a work sponsored by the John Dewey Society and published as its *Thirteenth Yearbook.**

The community-centered school, which is more rare in its best curriculum expressions, is still most graphically represented by Elsie Clapp's *Community Schools in Action*—a description and interpretation of an actual experiment of the 'thirties, which employed the surrounding natural-social environment as a learning laboratory. The premise from which this kind of education proceeds is, of course, entirely sound progressivism: if learning everywhere builds into the lives of individuals, then it follows that the school should constantly utilize and mold into its curriculum the widest possible resources of living. Such a curriculum includes nothing less than the resources of the entire human community—from the school block to the farthest reaches of our planet. Children should spend a lage part of their time in direct contact with every feature of their surroundings that might become material to be analyzed, reworked, assimilated into their own personal behavior.

The application of this principle may be illustrated almost endlessly. Students discover *art* everywhere around them: in trips to museums, in plays, movies, symphonies, in everyday materials and incidents (land-

* See also Harold Rugg and Ann Shumaker, *The Child-Centered School,* which is the classic study.

scapes, clays, metals, folklore, the small tragedies and comedies of their neighborhoods). In their *social studies* they may have a direct acquaintance with tenement conditions, factories, markets, farms, courts, mines. The *natural sciences,* too, may be related to their immediate environment. Chemistry analyzes drinking water as a project in consumer education; physics studies the efficiency of the local power station; botany investigates a plant disease that has been plaguing nearby farms.†

Why Adult Education? Ideally, the community school becomes a vibrant center of neighborhood life—a center from which the activities of students and teachers radiate in all possible directions and also toward which other members of the community gravitate. It is no wonder that adult education becomes a corollary of this wider approach to education of children.

Indeed, the learning of mature men and women has a special importance for progressivists. Their position regarding adult education rises from the belief that men *may* continue to grow throughout their lives but that there is no certainty that they *must* do so. Stated otherwise, if children learn everywhere, beyond as well as within the rigid boundaries of the public school—and much too often to their detriment—then parents may learn also, and nevertheless be victimized by crosscurrents of belief, propaganda, superstition, and outright falsehood. As a matter of fact, the average adult is perhaps even more susceptible than children to learning that inhibits rather than stimulates growth. Children, at least, have the benefit of some kind of organized educational direction, whereas adults, bound by the prejudice that education ceases at the age of leaving school, usually lack even that direction.

Education through the years after formal graduation is not, then, merely a comfortable leisure-time activity. It is mandatory for healthy community living among adults for the same reason that it is mandatory for their more youthful years. It is an empirical education, never limited merely to books and lectures. It enables citizens to face the grim issues of our unstable time not with prejudice, ignorance, or whim, nor with mere classroom knowledge soon made obsolete by changing community circumstances but with an alert capacity to analyze these issues clearly and to implement analyses with intelligent self-confidence.

† See S. E. T. Lund, *The School-Centered Community;* Joseph K. Hart, *Education in the Humane Community.*

Progressive Education and Social Control

THE DEMOCRATIC SCHOOL

Freedom and Order. Progressivist thinkers find themselves returning again and again to the problem of freedom. Characteristically, Dewey regards it as soluble *educationally* only as it is examined and interpreted *culturally*.‡ Thus, the classroom teacher who is perplexed over how much and what kinds of freedom to encourage among his students, how much discipline and guidance to exercise, what kinds of initiative and latitude to allow must first ask himself: "What does freedom mean in society at large? What does order mean? How can freedom be related to order so as to become its ally rather than its enemy?"

As liberals, the most generalized answer progressivists offer to such questions is that freedom means positive opportunity for individuals living interdependently together to use their powers for individual and community growth. Politically, freedom is more than a merely negative absence of restraint—the doctrine that characterizes the schools of *laissez faire* and minimum government. Freedom is a positive potential which is realized only through social arrangements that at once protect and encourage every person to deal forthrightly and cooperatively with all his problems. Democracy is the living symbol of organized freedom because it alone among cultural ideals provides that every normal person shall share fully and publicly in the interplay of events *and* the making of decisions. Peirce's anticipation of this view is succinctly stated: ". . . the problem becomes how to fix belief, not in the individual merely, but in the community." [6]

This doctrine of *shared* experience must be underscored as central to progressivist theory. It is the normative principle that freedom is genuine only when individuals, working and living in groups, are together able to discuss and express their interests fully and continuously. Any social institution that in any way blocks such interplay, that prohibits members of a race or religion from joining at *every* point in the activities of the community, that subordinates women, that denies working people

‡ This problem is discussed in many of Dewey's writings. See *Freedom and Culture; Experience and Education; Democracy and Education*, Chap. 7; *Human Nature and Conduct; Liberalism and Social Action; Problems of Men.*

complete participation in economic affairs, is so far *un*free and therefore *un*democratic.*

The order resulting from maximum sharing is *man-made* order in the most unqualified sense. It is not order superimposed by some supreme ruler, individual or collective, divine or mundane. It is therefore less final, more modifiable and pluralistic, than the metaphysical, religious, or political order that rests upon a foundation of unchallengeable authority. Because it has been fashioned from the dynamic stuff of practice, from the needs and impulses, the actions and purposes, of real human beings, it is more substantial and satisfying in the long run. It will grow as democracy grows; its means ever reshape its ends; and its ends change into new means. The key to order, finally, must be intelligence; for it is chiefly the freedom of intelligence that enables individuals, and therefore the democracy individuals create, to deal with their natural and social environment constructively, unifiedly, developmentally.

Thus freedom and order are reciprocal, not antithetical, concepts. Without the institutions, habits, organized methods provided by the culture, freedom would degenerate into sheer anarchy. Without the right to question, to probe, to tolerate, to try, order would degenerate into sheer rigidity.

Democratic Discipline. This thumbnail summary of major pragmatic beliefs about freedom and order applies at every point to the truly democratic school. Freedom in education means freedom to achieve. It is, therefore, an encompassing synonym for all the constituent and integrated aspects of learning: interest, effort, purpose, intelligence, habit, growth, organism, culture. It is opportunity for pursuit of his interests by every child. But it is also opportunity for pursuit of interests by the group to which the child belongs. It thrives in the kind of school in which experiences are shared fully by *all* children of the community.

Freedom, then, does *not* mean uninhibited license—destructive, antisocial, lawless behavior. On the contrary, as Dewey puts it:

> . . . freedom from restriction, the negative side, is to be prized only as a means to a freedom which is power: power to frame purposes, to judge wisely, to evaluate desires by the consequences which will result from acting upon them; power to select and order means to carry chosen ends into operation.[7]

* See R. Bruce Raup and others, *Improvement of Practical Intelligence;* William O. Stanley, *Education and Social Integration.*

Progressivism repudiates the traditional adage that to spare the rod spoils the child. It denies that teachers must exercise stern, military-like discipline in order that students will not "get out of hand." It insists that dire threats of punishment and artificial inducements of reward are pedagogically improper devices—devices resting upon a pleasure-pain psychology no more defensible than the obsolete hedonistic ethics from which it originally springs.

Discipline assumes quite different meanings, therefore, for the tradition-harnessed teacher and for the progressivist. Recognizing that order in education is desirable and necessary, the latter holds that the surest and best order develops out of the joint experience of those involved. When students help to make their own rules because they come to see that regularity of procedure is necessary to attain their own purposes, there is seldom any problem of discipline. Controls are established by their beneficiaries, and although not as refined or exacting as if determined "from above," they may be for that very reason all the more stable.

It follows that the progressivist teacher is more a guide and fellow explorer in the educative adventure than a taskmaster and iron-handed ruler. This by no means implies that his function thereby becomes less useful; on the contrary, his role is more important and difficult, more painstaking and energy-consuming, than in the formal school where his own and his students' duties are carefully routinized and preplanned by superior officers. He must know each child as intimately as possible. He must encourage maximum give-and-take in and out of the classroom and be willing to accept criticism of himself. He must, with the cooperation of his students and colleagues, constantly modify each plan of study; therefore he must ever resist the temptation to fall back upon a repetitious and mechanized program. He must, in short, practice as well as preach democracy—and this is hard work.

Democratic Administration. As thoroughgoing progressivists in the field of school administration have argued,† the kind of freedom and order that applies to democratic society at large should apply to classrooms and to school systems. Such an application would involve a radical modification of inherited practices on the administrative level and on the teaching level.

† See John Dewey Society, *Tenth Yearbook,* "Democracy in the Administration of Higher Education"; G. Robert Koopman, Alice Miel, and Paul J. Misner, *Democracy in School Administration;* Kilpatrick, *Philosophy of Education,* Chap. 24.

Perhaps the severest indictment made against typical administrative practices is that they tend to exaggerate such values as efficiency in business at the expense of values, such as growth, that are more educationally rewarding. Thus, schools are too often governed by strict lines of authority running from the superintendent at the top down through the descending levels of principals, supervisors, teachers to the students themselves at the bottom level. The progressivist principle of continuous interplay among all individuals and groups, which is the highest test of any democratic community, is violated by this kind of system. Students take orders from teachers, teachers from principals, principals from the superintendent. He, in turn, is responsible to the board of education, which, although nominally democratic, frequently represents only that small segment of the population that is willing to endorse "efficient" school administration.

The progressivist administrator, on the contrary, encourages faculty participation in all important matters affecting the welfare of the school. Curriculum plans, budgets, tenure rules are subjects of thorough discussion and sometimes faculty decision. Students may have their own councils in which problems relevant to discipline, recreation, and courses of study are considered with a minimum of faculty control. Parents, too, are urged to concern themselves with the school program; parent-teacher associations, advisory committees of citizens, and adult forums are all commonly influential in the best types of progressivist systems.

The school as agent of democratic planning

The progressivist belief that schools are established by a culture to guarantee its continuity—a belief to which we have already alluded and shall allude still further below (see pp. 140-141, 162-167)—gives us a clue to the position of this philosophy on the thorny issue of education and social change. Few, if any, progressivists would defend the familiar view of essentialism that education is inevitably and chiefly not the refashioner but the reflector of cultural tradition and habit (see pp. 203-205, 270-273). Those who urge community-centered schools would strongly agree that, while education must always recognize and respect the milieu within which it operates, it can and should criticize social weaknesses, make clear-cut proposals, and act strategically to bring about improvements.

The familiar concept of "interaction" should clarify this position. The effective school works *with*, not *against*, its environment. It tries to assess obstacles and resistances that stand in the way of evolution and then to utilize these experimentally and cooperatively. It neither sits back and rationalizes its feebleness by professing a philosophy of fatalism, nor does it overestimate its own strength and impatiently try to effect immediate and radical progress.‡ Again the central belief is in the scientific method, now crystallized in terms of *social* intelligence. Education *could* become a gigantic force for democratic evolution if it would only free itself from false psychologies of learning, from false philosophies of historic change—if it would face and solve problems of culture with the same productive brilliance that physics and other laboratory sciences have demonstrated in dealing with the problems of nature.

How Shall Teachers Act? To "spell out" the progressivist approach to social problems by applying abstract formulas to concrete problems is not, however, so simple. Even within the ranks of leading theorists, astonishing differences are to be found on such practical questions as how teachers should act together to exert influence not only within the public school but also upon the wider environment. While again there is broad agreement that teachers should be active in community life, there is no general agreement on the extent to which this implies aggressive participation in and loyal identification with economic or political movements. Kilpatrick and Hullfish, for example, strongly oppose affiliation with organized labor. Such affiliation, they insist, too often results in teachers' losing their freedom to think independently, because they become propagandists for and servants of a special interest group. On the other hand, such leaders as Childs, Axtelle, and Dewey take a different view. Dewey asks:

> If teachers are workers who are bound in common ties with other workers, what action do they need to take? The answer is short and conclusive. Ally themselves with their friends against their common foe, the privileged class, and in the alliance develop the character, skill, and intelligence that are necessary to make a democratic social order a fact.[8]

The assumption in this striking statement is that social intelligence means social action and that social action is never possible in a vacuum.

‡ See Bode, *Democracy as a Way of Life*, Chap. 7.

Teachers must themselves choose whether or not to associate with those organized forces in our democracy that strive to improve opportunities for men and women to live more fully and richly. In this conviction, as much, perhaps, as in any other in all his educational writings, Dewey repudiates the more innocuous and "safe" interpretation of which some of his followers have been accused.*

"The Planning Society." Nevertheless, it is possible to find in Dewey's writings a strong note of warning against what he would regard as too extreme or militant an approach to social action and social control. An archenemy of the Soviet Union, he believes it substitutes a tyrannical authoritarianism for genuine self-government and free intelligence. On several occasions he has painstakingly analyzed Marxism, the official philosophy of that country and of the Communist movement, and has rejected it on several grounds: that it substitutes violence for intelligence; that it sets up a philosophy of history which, despite its materialistic basis, is seldom less absolutistic than old-fashioned theology; and that it predetermines its own development by predicting a planned society.†

Now, it is especially against the doctrine of a "planned society" that Dewey and virtually all leading progressivists warn teachers and citizens generally to be on their guard. For in a planned society we have a monstrous counterpart of ancient and medieval faiths in fixed and final ends. In it, we detect the notion that we can foretell the future of society and lay down "blueprints" of its structure. In it, worst of all, we find lurking an insidious ethic of the ends *justifying* the means: of believing that because the end of a planned society is presumably moral, therefore any means, however cruel or violent, that may be necessary to attain it are also moral. In this ethical context, the goal of a planned society conflicts with the scientific method which, we remember, constructs ends only *in the process* of meeting the serious problems of *present* society, which views ends as emerging from the means we utilize.

How then *should* education approach these problems? First of all, honest analysis will reveal certain facts about the dangers and failures of what we have called our free-enterprise era. Dewey, more forcefully than most other progressivists, severely criticizes capitalist economic practices. He shows how mis-educative are the effects of a system that

* See Berkson, *op. cit.*, pp. 216ff., 288-293.

† See Dewey, *Freedom and Culture; Liberalism and Social Action;* and *Philosophy and Civilization.*

exaggerates pecuniary gain to the extent that it becomes the supreme aim of life, the final criterion of success. He indicts this system for failing to assure security against the ravages of unemployment, old age, war. He points to the fact that millions perform jobs for which they are unsuited or which are so routine and atomized as to arouse in the worker no feeling of significance, no sense of social aim.‡

Education, meanwhile, has too often added to the confusion. Where it has concerned itself with the economy at all, it has often taught young people to be acquiescent and uncritical. To the extent that it has ignored economic problems, wishing to be left in peace, it has allowed cultural confusion to be reinforced by learning-living situations outside of school that are frequently purposeless, chaotic, and destructive.

This kind of analysis leads to testable programs of action. On the one hand, schools must endeavor to become much more democratic within their own walls. On the other hand, as social institutions, they must teach the average citizen why and how to improve the democratic structure outside their walls. Such a tremendous task points, above all, to *the need for a fresh patterning of order*. It must be an order in which cultural affinity with the heritage of freedom is firmly maintained, but which recognizes that the anarchy of ruthless, competitive individualism can no longer be tolerated in a closely knit world. Hence it must be an order which would substitute, in the place of planless economic practice, varying degrees of planning. It would be an order which we may term "planning society."

Let us not, however, imply that this task is at all inconsistent with the basic theory of progressivism. By means of it, rather, schools become channels through which pass a myriad of the most exciting, pressing issues, practices, events, proposals of the local, national, and international community. The planning society is, in fact, but a graphic demonstration of wide-scale democratic learning. It is an hypothesis that, like all hypotheses, must be shaped and reshaped as it evolves from specific stage to specific stage, from present plan to present plan, from means to ends, and that, in turn, becomes means to still further ends.

And since the most crucial of such means is the universal practice—in school and out—of free intelligence, we find here the most compelling reason why art, broadly understood, should be encouraged by progressive education. As we have seen, art is the artists' freedom to express by iden-

‡ See Kilpatrick (ed.), *The Educational Frontier*, Chap. 2.

tifying themselves with and transforming the materials of nature and society. Hence, it becomes the very essence of democratic and educational endeavor blended into one. And scientific method, which too often we identify only with cold and impersonal specialization, becomes also a full working partner of esthetic creativity—the master instrument by which men everywhere can share in planning and cultivating their lives in the ever-growing garden of experience.

Notes

[1] Quoted from I. B. Berkson, *Education Faces the Future,* p. 129.

[2] William H. Kilpatrick, *Philosophy of Education,* p. 254.

[3] John Dewey, *Experience and Education,* pp. 26-27.

[4] Quoted from National Society for the Study of Education, *Forty-first Yearbook,* Part I, "Philosophies of Education," p. 61. Published 1942 and reprinted with the permission of the Society.

[5] Dewey, *Experience and Education,* p. 93. Published 1938 by The Macmillan Company and reprinted with the permission of Kappa Delta Pi.

[6] From Max H. Fisch (ed.), *Classic American Philosophers,* p. 63.

[7] Dewey, *Experience and Education,* p. 74.

[8] Dewey, *Education Today,* p. 307. Copyright 1940 by G. P. Putnam's Sons and reprinted with their permission.

CHAPTER 6

A Cultural Evaluation of Progressivism

THE BELIEF OF DEWEY THAT THE HISTORY OF PHILOSOPHY IS A critical portrait of the history of culture applies not only to patterns of belief with which he is unsympathetic but equally to his own pattern.* If, then, we are successfully to evaluate his position and that of his associates we shall have to observe pragmatic-progressivist behavior in its natural setting of economic, social, political, and similar trends. We shall have to study its character not as an erudite system of thought immunized *against* experience but, taking it at its own word, as a product *of* experience. Thus far pragmatism-progressivism is in accord with the frame of reference through which each major position is viewed within this book, namely, that all philosophies of education are in essence interpretations of the cultures within which they find expression.

Indeed, the constant cross-fertilization of cultural events with beliefs about those events is so central to progressivism that, in the two preceding chapters, we have found it essential to record many instances of such cross-fertilization. Particularly, we underscored four influences without which Dewey, or Peirce and James before him, would scarcely have been able to formulate their mature doctrines, without which, there-

* See John Dewey, "Philosophy," *Encyclopædia of the Social Sciences.*

fore, a Bode or a Kilpatrick could not have formulated his. These influences are the industrial revolution, modern science, the rise of democracy, and a generous environment. Although it might be cogently argued that the first of these four is most fundamental, we are more concerned at the moment to re-emphasize their interdependence. Modern science, for example, has been indispensable to the development of industrialism; yet the latter has provided frequent opportunities for science to refine its method and to deepen its probings. Equally important is the fact that democracy, especially in America, has attained its phenomenal growth in no small measure because of a fertile and rich environment; yet the development of this environment has been nourished by political and social institutions, which—in quite imperfect ways, to be sure—have translated such traditional American ideals as equality and freedom into the realities of everyday practice.

The chief value judgment we shall place upon pragmatism-progressivism has also been stated in a preliminary way. Pragmatism-progressivism is the highest philosophical and educational embodiment of what we like to call the *liberal way of life*. Therefore, like liberalism itself, it is in some ways a powerful and adequate interpretation of contemporary culture; in other ways, it is a feeble and inadequate interpretation. Its success in exposing and criticizing the beliefs of earlier cultures has been striking, and its success in articulating and justifying the motives, habits, and aims of our younger American culture—especially of the past century—is of the highest order. Its success, however, in providing a sufficient rationale and program for a mature, designed culture is far less substantial. The most charitable judgment that can be placed upon progressivism is that, like liberalism, it is *transitional* to that kind of culture.

We develop this appraisal by means of the following three main topics:

1. education in a liberal culture;
2. progressivism on the firing-line; and
3. the transitional character of progressivism.

The reader should bear in mind that a number of issues that are touched lightly in this chapter are considered more fully in Parts III and IV.

Education in a Liberal Culture

The Impact of Industrialism

The emphasis that progressivism gives to culture is revealed by its characteristic assumption that education is an institution established by organized groups of people to guarantee the continuity from generation to generation of their habits, structures, customs, attitudes. By this is meant, to quote Dewey: "It is the function of education to see to it that individuals are so trained as to be capable of entering into the heritage of these values which already exist, trained also in sensitiveness to the defects of what already exists and in ability to recreate and improve." [1]

From Agrarianism to Industrialism. If, in good pragmatic fashion, we apply Dewey's statement operationally—that is, if we go below it to the deeper meaning of the development of our culture and our education—we note a trend with far-reaching consequences. The key to this trend, the progressivist would agree, lies in the shift from agrarianism to industrialism.* The industrial revolution, which had begun to transform Europe even before the thirteen colonies had joined to form a federal union, soon began to transform America as well. The cherished dream of Jefferson—that the population of the new country should be composed chiefly of small, self-sufficient, but independent farmers—was fading rapidly by the time the nineteenth century had reached its midway mark. Before the century's end many American cities had become huge, machines had become more intricate and efficient than had ever been imagined, and businessmen had obtained ever larger shares of political as well as economic power. Industrialism became the most powerful of all the forces shaping the course of American history.

What has been the effect of this trend on the nation's schools? The story of how they were established by the young nation as public, tax-supported institutions having the purpose of teaching all the children of all the people is perhaps the most glorious story in the history of education.

* See William H. Kilpatrick, in National Society for the Study of Education, *Forty-first Yearbook,* Part I, "Philosophies of Education," pp. 63-65; John Dewey, in Kilpatrick (ed.), *The Educational Frontier,* Chap. 2; Newton Edwards and Herman G. Richey, *The School in the American Social Order;* George S. Counts, *Education and American Civilization.*

From the progressivist viewpoint, however, the way in which the schools have carried out this purpose is considerably less glorious. Some, perpetuating the customs of the European heritage, have, from earliest times, reflected the belief that the main purpose of education is to prepare young people to become "ladies and gentlemen" by veneering them with the classical tradition—a belief for which we find imposing philosophic support even today. Many other schools, from the beginning of American history until the Civil War, reflected the impact of the agrarian period. Although industrialism was already on the march, this was a period when most young people took part in cultivating the fields, caring for livestock, making their own clothes, and helping with the many tasks connected with living in a hardy, pioneer environment. Thus they acquired skills and facts that were important to their culture by sharing immediately and directly in it. Their other educational needs—reading, 'riting, 'rithmetic and a smattering of "wisdom"—were provided by the school.

If, during this agrarian period, the educational distinction made between what children learned informally through intimate acquaintance with their surroundings and what they learned formally within their classrooms was not wholly justifiable in terms of all we now know about good education, it was at least a plausible dualism. It made sense in the period of direct and significant participation by children in the simple, isolated, self-sufficient community of the typical rural family. From the two spheres of home and school children learned much of what was really essential to their experience.

For the same reason, however, that the dualism made some sense for our earlier agricultural society it makes no sense for our later industrial society. As industrialism has grown toward its present giant stature children have shared less and less directly in their parents' occupations. Division of labor has extended so far that now these occupations rarely have any direct connection with family experience. Farmers today almost never make their own clothes or produce all their own food, and many consume only a minor part of what their lands ordinarily produce. The home, moreover, is far less typically the center of family activity and interest not only for the father, who is probably the wage earner, but often also for the children and the mother. Outside amusements, rapid transportation, stuffy apartments, commercialized excitements, and group affiliations—all produce a fundamental challenge to education itself.

Schools for an Industrial Order. This challenge, insists the pro-

gressivist, is that an industrial order and an agrarian order demand differ-
nt kinds of schools. If we place the psychological principle of "living as
earning" (see pp. 130-141) within such a historic setting and if we recall
hat the primary purpose of education, according to this principle, is to
rovide learning that meets the needs and interests of living, we may
ay that a three-R's curriculum merely combined with family experience
annot possibly meet contemporary needs and interests. For this reason
he school's obligation becomes much greater—to ensure that the concerns
of culture created by an industrial age will be met educatively. This is
the first responsibility of good public education.

Thus, we see why, for Dewey and for others of his persuasion, this responsibility has at least three aspects: (1) to ensure that the school helps individuals to enter fully into the existing industrial and technological order; (2) to teach them to be critical of such cultural weaknesses and failures as family instability and unemployment; and (3) to help them to correct these wherever and whenever possible. Any less comprehensive a program can only assure that a great gap will continue to separate curriculums and methods of learning from our turbulent economic, political, and moral culture. Rote learning, sterile subject matters, and authoritarian discipline are tragic instances of cultural lag. Functional learning, vital subject matters, self-discipline are educational efforts to catch up with the culture.

Industrialism and liberalism

Thus far our sketch of progressivism in its cultural context has been derived largely from its own theorists; it demonstrates our contention that they are themselves culturally oriented. From this point on, however, our analysis derives less from the progressivists themselves and more from our own interpretation.

We need now to build a wider perspective for the value judgment that progressivism is an educational expression of liberalism—a term embracing a cluster of political, ethical, and social attitudes as well as correlative practices, all peculiarly suited to the civilization that emerged with the Renaissance and reached the peak of its vitality early in the present century. While the industrial revolution generated many of these attitudes and practices, liberalism, in turn, gave intellectual and moral sanction to industrialism.

To etch the present picture as sharply as possible, let us imagine modern culture as having three mutually supporting levels of experience: first, the "bottom" or foundation level, of industrial life with its network of socio-economic relations typified by the factory system, division of labor, technology, and business control; second, the "middle" level, of liberal attitudes and practices that articulate, reflect, and reinforce the industrial level; and third, the "top" level, of organized education resting upon both liberalism and industrialism while helping to give meaning and strength to both. Imagined in this way, each level supports the other two, with industrialism still the most basic and with liberalism operating somewhere in between it and organized education.

The picture fails, however, in one serious respect. Like many oversimplifications, it does not take account of the factor of time. Actually, all three levels—liberalism, the educational level above, and the industrial level below—have undergone historic evolution. All three have together experienced at least two major, although *overlapping,* periods. The first, which we shall call "early liberalism," extended from the seventeenth to perhaps the first third of the nineteenth century; the second, which we shall call "later liberalism," has extended from the latter time to our own generation, reaching its widest range of influence in the past five or six decades.

Early Liberalism. Early liberalism was a pattern of attitudes and practices designed to bolster a "new" culture that was partly agrarian, partly industrial, and increasingly anti-feudal. Therefore it was, above all, a symbol of the kind of liberty required by men who were in revolt against a decadent and outmoded medieval order. As an ideal it epitomized what men increasingly sought in practice, namely, the right to inquire about and engage in commercial, industrial, and agricultural activity unrestricted by inherited privilege or by monarchical or theocratic power. In essence, this was *laissez faire* liberty—freedom from restraint. It was exactly what was needed by the new, high-spirited, competitive economy manned by groups of individuals struggling ruthlessly against other individuals for markets and profits.

Moreover, while early liberalism was providing a theoretical justification for the habits and values of the emerging industrial era, it was also supporting the kind of education that would enhance these habits and values. This was the education, proposed by such early liberals as Locke, that was designed especially for those who were taking over political as well as economic control of the new system. We shall find in it an anticipation of what much later came to be called "essentialism."

Later Liberalism. In the later period we note not so much a rejection as a modification and widening of the earlier liberalism.‡ While it continues to oppose the medieval order and while it stresses with unremitting vigor such values as independence and freedom of inquiry, it criticizes the narrowness, negativeness, and remnants of absolutism that still lurked in earlier liberal doctrine. Early liberalism really cared little about liberty for everyone. It was much more interested in guaranteeing that the virile, young middle classes have the right to oppose restrictions upon their power than it was in guaranteeing that the lower working classes, who depended on the middle classes for employment, should also enjoy certain rights, especially the right to a job. Educationally, too, early liberalism was concerned to teach young people that their first duty and their best chance of success lay in accepting wholeheartedly the major tenets of the industrial system. Thus, it provided its own justification for subservience to an order that, although different from the ancient and medieval orders, could be no less domineering over the lives of ordinary men.*

Later liberalism not only called attention to these limitations of its precursor but also sought to correct them. Early in the nineteenth century a number of critics had begun to speak out—some, such as Robert Owen, were already advocates of a more radical philosophy; others, such as John Stuart Mill, were eloquent advocates of a liberalism that guaranteed liberty not merely to the middle-class citizen but to *all* citizens. By the time of the American Civil War the beliefs for which Mill was probably the most brilliant European spokesman began to find ready response in "the land of opportunity."

Such a widened liberalism was especially plausible in the generous natural environment of America, to which we refer above, and it was strengthened and widened by the unique spirit of the American frontier. True, as Frederick Jackson Turner and other historians have shown, such a spirit could not be captured by any simple formula, nor could it be said to have influenced only those who experienced the life of the frontier directly. Its qualities included assertiveness, shrewdness, optimism, tough-

‡ See Dewey, *Individualism, Old and New;* and *Characters and Events.*
* See Harold Laski, *The Rise of Liberalism;* L. T. Hobhouse, *Liberalism,* Chap. 6.

mindedness, restlessness, ingenuity, adventuresomeness, self-respect. Such qualities, as they developed in the generations of pioneers who pushed back the boundaries of a vast and rich territory, seemed to be reflected in the habits and attitudes of the more settled populations in the East.† Counts sums up both the liabilities and the assets of the pioneer influence:

> If there was much in this early society that we would be happy to leave to history—the bitter toil, the lack of refinement, and the crudeness of manners—there was also much that we would like to preserve as the essence of American character. The life on the frontier and on the farm bred in our people a sturdy and self-reliant quality, an inventive and resourceful mind, a sense of individual worth and integrity, an abhorrence of show and pretense, a fierce assertion of human equality, a deep love of personal freedom.[2]

We can understand, then, why some interpreters of liberalism wished to imply much more than the unhampered freedom of a minority to engage in exploitation of the majority. It still meant this to some, of course. But it meant to others the freedom of every individual to pursue his own ends by exercising his fullest nature, powers, and capacities. It meant, finally, *public* education—an education not limited to those who could afford to pay, not open merely to the few who expected to domineer over the many, but an education for rich and poor, black and white, high and low alike.

The development of later liberalism and of related theories in education was not completed, however, in the nineteenth century. The environment's capacity to provide such a magnificent opportunity for enterprising individuals could not indefinitely remain the same. As we have seen, the agrarian culture was increasingly supplanted by an industrial culture. Successful conquest of geographical frontiers—lands, forests, river power, minerals—meant that eventually no such frontiers would remain to be conquered. As we approached and entered the twentieth century, the rise of economic empires within the nation, the spread of rapid communication, transportation, and interstate commerce persistently called attention to the fact that *the individualistic period of*

† See Frederick Jackson Turner, *The Frontier in American History;* Counts, *op. cit.*, Part II.

r history was waning. Even the deep-rooted American faith that the ajority of our problems could be solved locally or at most at the state vel came to be questioned as evidence accumulated that they were not ing solved on these levels. In short, technology and industrialism were ssolving our provincialism. They were compelling the nation to unify ıd direct ever larger segments of its economic and political experience ıd even to consider joining cooperatively with other nations.

Such educational leaders as Dewey responded to these changes. hey urged schools to join hands with the culture, to take industrial life to account, to emphasize social and interdependent as well as individual ıd independent aspects of experience.

The Swinging Pendulum. Let us summarize our discussion of beralism to this point. Early liberalism—with its counterparts, on the ıltural level below, of individualistic capitalism, small-scale enterprise ıd agriculture, and, on the level above, of an education reflecting that der—has been waning for at least a century. Later liberalism, meanhile, has gradually come into prominence. It is a liberalism still charterized by strong regard for such frontier and agrarian virtues as selfliance and self-assertiveness; therefore, in important respects, it is *ontinuous with* earlier liberalism. In fact, many values of our early Meran heritage remain vital and should be perpetuated. But later liberalism also characterized much more strongly and self-consciously by such irtues as cooperation, community participation, and collective responbility.

Now, the important point for our understanding of progressivism that the education and, indeed, the culture for which it stands are rofoundly saturated with *both kinds of virtue*—individual *and* social, ersonal *and* communal. Although, as we have seen, progressivism rejects he three-R's school of the agrarian period, it does not reject the indiidualistic values that were hidden corollaries of that kind of school. lthough it rejects quite as strongly any kind of "totalitarian" education hat threatens to submerge the individual, it nevertheless insists that nodern education must give much greater attention to the problems and eeds created by the larger whole of an interlocking political and inlustrial order.

Swinging pendulum fashion between these two poles of value, proressivism as educational theory and practice reflects and reinforces the wo great levels of culture below it. It reflects the industrial level because,

in America certainly, economic life remains individualistic at son
points (witness the small farmer and shopkeeper) collective and centra
ized at other points (witness industrial monopoly and growing feder
authority). It reflects and reinforces the liberal level because, as the lat
period clearly reveals, that level is also concerned to preserve and respe
the same two poles of value.

Liberalism Epitomized. Here is a conception of liberalism whic
constructed out of the history of modern culture, prepares us to unde
stand more clearly why progressivism plays the role that it does in ou
own day. Opposed to all "either-or" philosophies, it tries to become, an
largely succeeds as, a philosophy of "both-and." Although sensitivel
opposed to any "extreme view," any "absolute choice," any "blueprinte
future," it accepts from its inheritance the positive worth of liberty a
the right to speak, think, worship, act, live as far as possible according t
one's deepest personal needs. At the same time it stresses, especially i
recent decades, the increasing importance of the community and the pu
pose of increasing unity and cohesiveness among groups. It strives, there
fore, to give a fair hearing to economic, political, and ethical proposal
that might further liberate man, that might help him to find better way
of living together and growing with his fellows.

But it is also very important to bear in mind that the liberal tempe
is essentially cautious. The liberal approach is tolerant, sympathetic, open
minded, curious about novel suggestions and new ways of acting and plan
ning. But it is unsympathetic to dogmatic proposals, rigid tradition
arrogant authority, stubborn prejudice. The liberal is on his guard agains
"recklessness." Granting that ours is a period of inevitable change, o
unique social demands, he never strays too far from the path along whic
our culture has been patiently moving for so long. Progress must occur i
many areas, step by step, gradually. To edge forward a little at a time
from where we were, to where we are, toward where we might later be—
testing, trying, planning, replanning, modifying, experimenting carefull
—this is as essential to the liberal's mood and strategy as it is to the scientis
whom, above all others, he seeks to emulate.

The success of liberalism-progressivism

That later liberalism succeeded during the past half-century or more ı profoundly influencing and in giving voice to a large proportion of merican institutions, practices, habits, and attitudes is a matter of record. ı politics, it grew in power and prestige through such Presidents as 'heodore Roosevelt, Woodrow Wilson, and, above all, Franklin Roose- elt. In the world of economics, supported by the world of politics, the orking people were increasingly protected in their right to organize; olitical experiments in a "mixed economy" and in new federal responsi- ilities were encouraged. In law, both political and economic experimenta- on was supported by the Constitutional interpretations of such liberal ustices as Oliver Wendell Holmes. In education, progressivist schools ere established in many parts of the country as well as abroad; they not nly attracted wide attention but also influenced countless others on very level and in every locality.

It is unnecessary and would be unsound to contend that the liberal oad to culture has been the only road along which our people have raveled in recent decades. We have been too diversified, too fluid, too usy "succeeding" to know or care very much whether we have always een unified in our efforts, consistent in our direction, or harmonious in he beliefs that serve as our guides. Nonetheless, after all reversals, con- radictions, and vacillations have been taken into account (we may cite he conservatism of the Coolidge-Hoover period of the 'twenties, the wars nd depressions, the conservative decisions of the Supreme Court, opposi- ion by big business to labor's growth and to federal controls, the trend o states' rights and private industrial control during the Eisenhower dministration, widespread and bitter resistance to progressive educa- ion), it is still impossible to deny that liberalism-progressivism has been nd remains today an attractive and impelling choice. It has seemed to uit, as no other choice has suited, a culture at once individual and social, ndependent and interdependent, private and public in its orientation. Above all, it has seemed to fit a culture much more preoccupied with the ery process of expansion and growth than with their possible boundaries nd goals. Even when it has not succeeded in capturing the whole of a particular institution—as experimental education has failed to capture the public schools of America—the confidence and optimism of leading ad- vocates, such as Kilpatrick, that it will eventually succeed are indeed exuberant.‡

‡ See Samuel Tenenbaum, *William Heard Kilpatrick.*

Progressive Education: Attack and Defense

Nevertheless, liberalism-progressivism is by no means as secure or dom
nant as we might suppose from the confidence and optimism of its su
porters. The fact is that the theory and practice of progressive educatio
are now on the defensive in many places. The spokesmen for education
tradition and for classical learning, against whom Dewey and his lieuten
ants took the offensive in the early years of our century, have themselv
begun a counteroffensive. At the same time, critical voices of a mo
radical inflection are beginning to be heard.

We shall postpone examination of the cultural background of th
counteroffensive until we have observed some of its more overt expre
sions. For classificatory purposes let us group these into three main camp
each of which can be viewed both from *outside* and from *inside* the edu
cational profession. The objections from outside the profession are con
sidered first.

THE COUNTEROFFENSIVE FROM OUTSIDE THE PROFESSION

Objections from Cultural Conservatism. Sharp objections to pro
gressivism come from those groups in the culture which do not wish th
schools to become instruments of social inquiry and liberal action. The
view is that education is established to reinforce and conserve those in
herited structures, rituals, and routines which they themselves suppor
and in which they hold a special, often powerful, interest. One of thei
most vocal, persistent organizational spokesman has been the Nationa
Association of Manufacturers. In the past quarter-century or more th
Association has spent many millions of dollars propagandizing *for* a sys
tem of education designed to strengthen the economic-political *status qu*
and *against* any type of education that might help students to question it
righteousness and supremacy.

Often, however, objections to progressive education come from in
dividuals or organizations who may not be fully aware of the motives o
the powerful pressure groups for whom they are, in fact, acting as agents
American educational history is filled with instances in which popula
newspaper columnists, patriotic organizations, business clubs, and loca
school boards have joined the attack on progressive education. The year

the Cold War multiplied these expressions of hostility. Mass-circula-
on magazines and newspapers, and such organizations as the National
ouncil for American Education, with large funds derived from unre-
ealed sources—these and many other influences have sought to discredit
rogressivism by implicating it in social evils ranging from "juvenile
elinquency" to "communism." *

We must, of course, recognize that organized efforts to protect school
hildren against modern ways of learning were made long before the
eriod of "progressive education." And, although such efforts, of the past
nd the present, have often failed, they have sometimes succeeded—in-
reasingly so in recent years. We may note that many attacks have been
rong enough to remove progressively oriented textbooks and magazines
om library shelves and even to eliminate whole plans of study from
cal or state programs. On occasion, as in Pasadena, California, they
ave managed to disrupt an entire school system and to dismiss its super-
ntendent.†

But the negative effects of conservative counterattacks have been even
nore widespread than these victories. With their power to intimidate the
ducational world *they have prevented from being tried at all* innumer-
ble liberal projects, controversial learning materials, reorganized curricu-
ums, or faculty programs built upon those progressive principles that
e have been discussing throughout this Part. Today many educational
eaders scrupulously avoid even the term "progressive education." Or, if
hey use the term at all, they use it in reference to the past, as though
rogressive education were an outmoded educational fad to be viewed
with tolerant amusement but as no longer an active force in the schools.

Objections from Cultural Absolutism. Another group in the cul-
ure objects to progressivism as a way of learning and living just because
t involves an attempt to substitute experimentalism for absolutism in one
way or another of its cultural forms. This type of objection is expressed
y persons or groups who are often allied with the first type discussed
bove, but this is not always so. Organized religious bodies (particularly
ut not only the Roman Catholics) have become distressed over what they
onsider the heretical influence of progressive education. Often, of

* See Theodore Brameld (ed.), *The Battle for Free Schools;* Ernest O. Melby
nd Morton Puner (eds.), *Freedom and Public Education;* V. T. Thayer, *Public
Education and Its Critics;* C. Winfield Scott and Clyde M. Hill (eds.), *Public Education Under Criticism.*

† See David Hulburd, *This Happened in Pasadena.*

course, it is not specifically progressivism that they are attacking b
rather secular, nonabsolutistic learning in general, with Dewey and h
followers acting as scapegoats for a much more diffused hostility. /
Thayer shows in his *Public Education and Its Critics,* this hostility is ve
deep-seated and is probably becoming more intense and more wid
spread.†

Moreover, political absolutism, typified by such regressive advocat
of racial inequality as the "white supremacy" clique in the South,
deeply hostile to progressivism's support of nonsegregated schools and c
complete intermingling of cultural groups. We may also observe that th
Soviet Union, as it has moved closer to a nationalist policy and to a Con
munist form of absolutism, has increasingly and sometimes insultingl
opposed Dewey's views and the kind of education that he represents.

Objection from "Left of Center." The third general type of crit
cism emanating from nonprofessional groups may be called "left o
center" criticism. This type is not so clearly crystallized as are the critica
opinions of the first two groups, and it differs from them in its concer
with those weaknesses of progressivism that might be overcome b
strengthening already attained achievements.

This concern is exemplified by the fact that our outstanding experi
mental schools have been supported, almost without exception, by th
liberal segments of middle-class and upper-class communities. The cur
riculums of these schools seem, accordingly, to avoid penetrating study o
economic maladjustments that might derive from economic control
largely vested in their own class. To state the objection in other terms
progressivist practitioners have been and remain influenced more strongl
by a psychological than by a sociological approach to the problems of lif
because this approach is generally "safer." It is an approach concerned s
much more with individual children and their "felt needs" than with th
social forces that impinge upon them that its curriculum need not jeop
ardize the sources of financial support upon which both private an
public progressive education has, thus far, largely relied.

† As an example of the bitterness of the hostility, we may note that Judg
John A. Mathews, speaking at a Roman Catholic communion breakfast, calle
Dewey's philosophy of progressive education "un-American and an 'open sesame
to secularism which is communism in embryo" (quoted in the New York *Times*
October 18, 1954).

‡ The Soviet press attacked Dewey on the occasion of his ninetieth birthday
October 20, 1949.

HE COUNTEROFFENSIVE FROM WITHIN THE PROFESSION

Each of the general types of criticism outlined above has its loose quivalent within the educational profession. By equivalent we do not ean that critical educators necessarily associate themselves with one or nother of the cultural pressures that oppose progressivism. Nevertheless, e intentional or unintentional reciprocity of support between educators nd wider organizations is striking in its practical effects.

The Essentialist Counteroffensive. Let us consider the kind of bjections to progressivism symbolized by the position of the National ssociation of Manufacturers. Its opposition to the spirit of inquiry encouraged by the "new education," its continuous effort to build in the minds of the young an acceptance of and even reverence for its own conomic philosophy—such reactions to progressivism are startlingly simi-r to the constant, if more generalized, reiterations of such essentialists as e late Michael Demiashkevich that experimental schools fail to teach dequate respect for the social heritage (see pp. 244, 249).

Conservative organizations and essentialist educators both tend, in ther words, to stress the value of "what has been" as a test for "what is" nd "what should be," however often they profess their devotion to liberty," "truth," or the "good." And although it is important to emphaize that essentialist philosophers would repudiate an affinity to any such ltrareactionary a group as the National Council for American Educaon, their objection that progressivism overstresses learning by doing and nderstresses learning as absorption of subject matter lends considerable upport to conservative cultural forces. For learning as absorption cultivates mental habits of acquiescence in, rather than experimentation with, the cultural environment. Such habits are also encouraged by many college presidents and professors who object that schools of education have been captured by progressivist leaders and thus train teachers n faulty methods at the expense of subject matters and mental discipline. Likewise, the frequent disapproval by the essentialist of what he considers oo much activity and freedom, too little discipline and respect for those n authority, finds sympathy among those economic groups who wish every child to grow up to be an obedient and loyal worker-citizen—obedient and loyal to *them.*

It is not surprising, when we consider postwar trends toward conservativism, that, like attacks from the outside against progressivism, attacks from within the profession have become more frequent and mo vehement. A number of books addressed to lay audiences have be widely publicized and praised—most conspicuously, Arthur Bestor's *Ed cational Wastelands* and Gordon K. Chalmers' *The Republic and t Person,* both aimed mainly at the target of progressivism.

The Perennialist Counteroffensive. Let us consider, next, the pr fessional counteroffensive from the absolutists. Here cooperation betwe cultural institutions and practicing educators is unusually frank. This especially true of the Catholic Church, whose parochial schools, whi rest upon perennialism in one major form, are themselves directly co trolled by the ecclesiastic hierarchy. Both the Church and its schools a vigorous and unceasing in their repudiation of an educational theo which would prevent children from being indoctrinated in the dogm of the "one true faith." While they do not deny that some progressiv methods have a certain usefulness, they hold that these are subordinat indeed inferior, to the supreme purpose of education: to prepare mortals for the afterlife.

If, however, religious absolutists and parochial educators are solid united through the Church in their opposition to progressivism, the uni between absolutists in the wider culture and those in secular educati is not always so clear. We are thinking here of such lay perennialists Robert M. Hutchins, who finds in the philosophy of Dewey not only a undue emphasis on experimentalism but also an obsession with voc tionalism and usefulness (see pp. 332-335). The inductive metho which pragmatism stresses in its epistemology, means, say perennialist that not even the teacher can be certain of the conclusions to which study will lead. Worst of all, young people so educated enter adult li untrained either as leaders or as followers, with the consequence that o rampant political confusion becomes still more confused.

In Hutchins' critique, which has attracted nationwide attention, w see another example of how educators tend to support organization forces outside the profession, whether they recognize the alliance or no The views of lay perennialists have been so welcome to other absoluti groups, such as the Church, that they have frequently been quoted an paraphrased by the latter. They have also been drawn upon in th propaganda materials of economic pressure groups who find in peren nialism's arguments still further ammunition for their costly, but appa ently rewarding, attacks upon progressive education.

The Reconstructionist Counteroffensive. Educators whom we term 'econstructionist' share the essentialists' and the perennialists' feeling of issatisfaction with progressivism. But, unlike the other two groups of itics, their dissatisfaction stems from the fear that the magnificent chievements of progressivism will not be consolidated with enough vigor nd rapidity.

We should expect that reconstructionist educators would ally themselves with social, political, and other nonprofessional groups who share heir implied cultural attitudes Their support of radically democratic novements, such as world government, is by no means insignificant, s we may observe from the records of G. D. H. Cole in England and ewis Mumford in America.† It is, however, more difficult in the case f reconstructionism to point out clear-cut alliances between educators nd community forces than in the case of essentialism or perennialism. In he first place, reconstructionism, as we have said, is still a less wellrticulated movement. And, in the second place, the prevailing political emper in America today discourages such alliances much more than it oes the other two.

HE ACCOMPLISHMENTS OF PROGRESSIVISM

Before evaluating further the present status of progressivism, it is air to record not only some of the strengths and accomplishments to which its proponents call attention but also their replies to the types of riticism noted above.

Self-Criticism. As a theory that encourages scientific analysis, rogressivism expects analysis of itself. Not the least of its accomplishments is the willingness of some of its leaders to examine progressivism nd, finding shortcomings, to offer improvements. Bode, for example, has een severe in his indictment of what he regards as real or apparent innsistencies: method versus content, individualism versus cooperation, ntellectualism versus overt experience, and others. He pleads for a new nd clearer sense of direction for education and finds this in democracy as he nonabsolutist, experimental way of life.* Dewey, too, has recognized

† See G. D. H. Cole, *Europe, Russia, and the Future;* Lewis Mumford, *n the Name of Sanity.*

* See Boyd H. Bode, *Modern Educational Theories;* and *Progressive Education at the Crossroads.*

how easily progressivist schools may pervert his philosophy. Therefor
he vigorously warns against anarchy as a spurious substitute for genuir
freedom in education, against lack of careful curriculum planning, an
against the tendency to other faulty educational practices of which ove
zealous but inadequately trained teachers and administrators have som
times been guilty.†

Meeting the Counteroffensive. While progressivism has recent
been examining itself, it has also been replying to critics from oth
camps. Dewey and his allies have challenged the validity, for example,
the perennialist and essentialist counteroffensives.‡ They have demo
strated again and again that their theory of dynamic experience is su
ported by the accumulating testimony of science and scholarship—hi
torical, physical, biological, psychological, sociological. They insist th
the decline of absolutism in religion and the increase of political an
economic experimentation illustrate the gradual acceptance by the peop
of the belief that scientific naturalism provides a more trustworthy an
rewarding ontology than do inherited metaphysical or mechanistic sy
tems.* They suggest that the record of technological progress and scie
tific discovery of the last several centuries evidences the superiority
instrumentalism as a technique of inquiry over other epistemologie
They contend that the continuing flexibility of their axiology is far mo
in harmony with the phenomena of our swiftly flowing culture than
the kind of moral authoritarianism or social traditionalism which, in th
face of all cultural change, upholds static, pre-established ethical pri
ciples.§

Progressivists do not remain silent before the intimations of th
counteroffensive from "left of center." They cite the attention given b
such experimental institutions as Sarah Lawrence College and Ne
Lincoln School to controversial economic-political issues and to grou
centered as well as child-centered learning. They recall the appreciatio

† See Dewey, *Experience and Education,* a defense of progressivism again
its own archenthusiasts.

‡ See series "The New Failure of Nerve," *Partisan Review,* January-Februar
March-April 1943; John Dewey Society, *Twelfth Yearbook,* "Educational Freedo
in an Age of Anxiety."

* See Y. H. Krikorian (ed.), *Naturalism and the Human Spirit.*

§ See Dewey's reply to his critics in Paul A. Schilpp (ed.), *The Philosop
of John Dewey.*

ıown by progressivists, and especially by Dewey, for the cultural and ›ciological as well as the psychological phases of human experience. At ıe same time, they do not hesitate to question certain of the beliefs of ıeir more radical critics quite as vigorously as the latter question certain f theirs. Thus, their response to such concepts as "future-centered eduation" is antagonistic or at least dubious. They are so apprehensive that ıch education would lead to static-mindedness, even to fanaticism, that ıey much prefer to emphasize fluid, ever-changing experiences.‡ On the /hole, however, they seem less ready to engage in controversy with critics rom this side than they are with those from the other side, employing ften a "silent treatment" of reconstructionist types of criticism, as though ıey were hardly worth noting. Whether more fundamental reasons for his tactic might be adduced—such as an uneasy conscience that they are erhaps most vulnerable here—is at least an interesting conjecture.

The Record of Educational Progress. As their most relevant defense, rogressivists call attention to the concrete achievements of experimental chools. Granting mistakes and conceding weaknesses, the record is imressive. Voluminous evidence supports the conclusion not only that the verage child learns as well by progressivist methods as by the essentialist nethod, let us say, but that he frequently learns much better.* Some ompetent psychologists, to be sure, are convinced from their researches hat there is a greater need for formal exercise in certain skills than is ften claimed by functional and organismic theory. But in acquiring and tilizing the knowledge of society, art, and, to a large degree, natural cience, in developing critical attitudes, initiative, and individuality, and n participating cooperatively and happily both in school and community ffairs—in ways such as these there is little doubt that progressivist learnng is more effective than that based on older principles.†

The progressivist also reminds us that many of his basic ideas, which nly he and his associates advocated a few years ago, are now accepted by nany who do not classify themselves as progressivists at all. Indeed, they re accepted by some of the very leaders who like to ridicule the label

‡ See E. V. Sayers, "Social Patterns and Educational Goals," *School and Society*, July 3, 1948.

* See Melby and Puner, *op. cit.*, esp. pp. 227-247; Scott and Hill, *op. cit.*, sp. pp. 271-293.

† See W. M. Aikin, *The Story of the Eight-Year Study;* I. B. Berkson, *Eduation Faces the Future*, Chap. 11.

"progressive education." Accordingly, he seeks further opportunity to te
his hypotheses. Is it not absurd, he asks, to condemn wholesale the weal
nesses of public education and even of democracy by calling these institu
tions over-progressivized when, as a matter of fact, the majority of schoo
are only now beginning to respond sympathetically to his viewpoint-
when they are only now beginning to emerge from their agrarian trad
tion and to become full-fledged partners of an industrial age?

The Transitional Character of Progressivism

Thus far, we have taken two of the three steps toward our cultural evalu
tion of progressivism. The first step carried us to the judgment that pro
gressivism, along with its philosophic core of pragmatism, is the educa
tional corollary of later liberalism. Therefore, it seeks to encourage school
that are, both in theory and practice, genuinely liberal. Like the scientifi
method, which is their most frequently applied guiding belief, they ar
mobile and inductive. Also, at their best they are strongly individualize
in their approach to learning at the same time that they aim to becom
strongly socialized.

The second step in our evaluation led to the generalization that pro
gressivism, especially in the last several years, has been the storm cente
of a vigorous and frequently bitter educational controversy. In this con
troversy progressivism's earlier aggressive and often victorious attack
upon traditional types of education have partially shifted to a defensiv
position in the face of a strong counteroffensive from three sides: from
cultural conservatives more or less consciously allied with essentialists
from cultural absolutists allied with perennialists; and from cultura
radicals aligned with reconstructionists. From their defensive position
progressivists have not remained silent but have often replied convinc
ingly to their critics both inside and outside the profession. At many
points they have maintained their influence in practice as well as theory

Nevertheless, the counteroffensive continues, waxing and waning
according to the shifting public mood created by particular educationa
and cultural issues. Our third and final step remains to be taken. We
shall inquire into some of the *causes* of this stormy climate of opinion

specially into the causes discernible in the industrial and liberal milieu within which progressivism operates.

LIBERALISM IN A CRISIS-CULTURE

A Period of Instability. To inquire into the causes of this controversy it may be helpful to recall a few of the characteristics of our crisis-culture. In Chapter 3 we discussed some of the shocks to which contemporary institutions, habits, and beliefs are being subjected. Alternating periods of stimulating prosperity and enervating depression, of precarious peace and ruinous war, of revolution and counterrevolution have made the twentieth century one of the most fearful and most violent in recorded history. In summary, ours has been a century of pervasive and deep-cutting conflicts within and among nations—conflicts that, not unique to this period, are nevertheless insidious in their diversity of manifestations.

It is in this climate of fluctuations, confusions, and cross purposes that we may detect the deepest causes of much of the present skepticism and hostility toward liberalism in general and toward progressivism in particular. For if it is true, as we have asserted, that liberalism more than any other outlook has implemented and verbalized the meanings and intentions of recent American culture (indeed, of the wider Western culture), then it is liberalism that is certain to be most severely attacked when that culture suffers from such painful and chronic tensions and disturbances as we have described.

Look once more at the record of events. The outstanding liberal apostle of internationalism in our time, Woodrow Wilson, not only failed to prevent World War I but failed also to establish a workable League of Nations. And not only did his great liberal successor, Franklin Roosevelt, fail to prevent World War II but the social measures taken under his leadership, as "cures" for the worst depression in American history, were largely discarded the moment postwar prosperity had lulled the people into a sense of dubious security. Even such liberal interpretations of the Constitution as those of Justice Holmes have not been firmly established as legal precedents; on the contrary, decisions of the Supreme Court fluctuate so curiously that we can only predict that the philosophy of law most likely to govern any particular case is seldom, if ever, predictable.

Let us grant that Presidents Wilson and Roosevelt could no more be held wholly responsible for the tragedies in which they played such prominent roles than could the jurist Holmes or the philosopher Dewe be held responsible for the failures of their culture. Nevertheless, i the spirit of fairness for which liberals are themselves notable, we mus insist that if these men deserve a share of credit for the assets of ou period then they also deserve a share of responsibility for its debits. Th plain truth is that, when inventories are taken, the proud achievement of our liberal culture are reduced by the grim liabilities of fear, depriva tion, and blood.

It is to be expected, then, that thinking people should ask persisten and plaguing questions. Can America any longer rely so buoyantly upo its zestful ingenuity, its energetic capacity to extricate itself from difficul situations, its haughty self-sufficiency, its rich natural resources, its eager ness to try proposed schemes and to venture along whatever path th moment offers? Can we expect to solve the problems that now beset u by continuing to resort to pseudo-optimistic beliefs in compromise, i growth for the sake of further growth, in cautious progress? Can we rel so confidently and so exclusively upon the reasonableness of the scientifi method and the experimental mode of thinking to direct our cultura development? Can we afford to gaze so intently upon the flow of *presen* experience that we must regard the future as intangible? Is the liberal' typically slow and tentative approach to the problems of depression exploitation, and global war adequate to cope with pressures and faith that are daring and uncompromising?

The Strengths of Liberalism. That the liberal's answer to suc questions is earnest and persuasive has been made evident in our presenta tion of his educational theories and cultural accomplishments. Further his own criticisms and proposals regarding the cultural crisis are far fron vacillating or feeble.

The progressivist may contend, for example (and we should agre with his contention), that the counteroffensive against experimenta schools by forces outside as well as inside the profession may arise largel not so much from asserted *educational* objections as from unasserted *cu tural* premises. Thus, he may argue that the opposition of conservative and regressivists in business and in organized religion is often traceable t a fear that progressivism, if it became widely influential in public educa tion, might encourage widespread criticism of the system of private ente prise, or that it might educate the peoples of the earth to believe that *the* e the sole "absolute" determiners of their ultimate fate. Still more :assly, conservative hostility stems, so progressivism might also assert, om a fear that progressivism implies an educational standard that would reatly increase the costs of public schooling and, consequently, the tax ite.

On a broader plane, we should remember that, because liberalism is n experimental rather than absolutist outlook, it *tends* often to lend its ifluence toward the more or less experimental side of the chief conflicts f our crisis-culture: toward social-interest rather than self-interest, to-ard equality rather than inequality, toward planning rather than lanlessness, toward internationalism rather than nationalism, toward ian-for-himself rather than man-against-himself (see pp. 53-62). Simi-irly, it has often inclined to support extensive changes in behalf of reater technological achievement, greater economic-political libertarian-sm, greater abundance. Finally, it would probably point out that the ffort of conservative or regressive groups to combat liberalism in various orms, educational or otherwise, derives, in large part, from their lack of onfidence in or fear of its liberating, democratic spirit.

On the whole, however, liberalism, as the supreme rationale of re-ent institutional and behavioral experience, has as conspicuously demon-trated a skill in reconciling or accommodating itself to cultural conflicts s it has a militant or confirmed commitment to one as against another ide of most of those conflicts. And, after all, is not this conciliatory mood ntirely in keeping with the liberal's typical beliefs? Despite all the im-erfections of recent history, he holds that, by his methods, cultural ;ains have clearly outrun cultural losses. By free speech and fair play, y experimentation, by moderate evolutionary change he has helped to entilate the minds of men with the breezes of conflicting doctrine. He ias encouraged them to make decisions on basic issues only after they iave considered all sides and to recognize the danger of regarding any ne answer to a question as *the* right answer. Moreover, his conviction hat progress can best be made slowly and experimentally discourages iasty actions and impetuous decisions. True, his approach to problems lemands consummate patience. Yet he is confident that in the long run uch an approach better ensures progress. So many thousands of reforms iave been effected in economics, politics, education—indeed, in every hase of cultural experience—that we may expect still more reforms if we will but trust the liberal road along which we have already traveled so far.

A Forward Look. What, then, is our appraisal of both the over-all critique and the defense of liberalism as these are variously expressed? That liberalism's methods deserve high commendation is clear. That it often has been a capable and devoted servant of American civilization is indisputable. But the primary issue before us is not whether it *has been* capable and devoted but whether it *can continue to be* capable in the period of extreme stress that we have already entered.

Judging by this criterion we are at once faced with a disturbing question. *Is later liberalism, like early liberalism a century ago, becoming defective in its capacity to interpret and direct the course of dominant events?* Just as later liberalism, however, did not so much reject the early liberalism as it supplemented and strengthened it, so the need today may be to supplement and strengthen later liberalism in crucial areas.

Perhaps the most familiar and the most persistent objection to later liberalism centers on its tendency to fluctuate in its policies in accordance with the demands of the particular occasion. Always eager to take into account variable factors, it seems often to waver from position to position, from strategy to strategy. The ease with which liberals allow the pendulum to swing back and forth from ends to means—or from the individual to the group—leads to the question of whether they do not too often select the one or the other depending upon the immediate opportunity of choice rather than upon any clearly defined or defensible principles. That liberals do on occasion take strong and definite stands and that flexibility of attitude and practice is more commendable than dogmatic rigidity are fully appreciated. But the charge of vacillation remains.

Let us turn our attention, therefore, to two related and comprehensive areas in which it is pertinent to inquire whether or not later liberalism and, so, both pragmatism and progressivism have responded adequately to the crisis of our time. Each area may be conceptualized as an area of chronic tension between pairs of theoretical but also thoroughly practical terms: the first, tension between means and ends; the second, tension between individuality and sociality. Our considered judgment is that, with all its energy and competence, this philosophy of education-and-culture in its characteristic formulations is incapable of satisfactorily releasing either state of tension. On the contrary, it adds much to their severity.

THE TENSION BETWEEN MEANS AND ENDS

Hypothesis and Commitment. As our first illustration of an area of conflict let us recall the key methodological principle that has been defined above as an "act of thought." This principle is the problem-solving technique also stressed in progressivist learning (see pp. 105-107, 145-146).

Although we in no way minimize the logical clarity as well as the usefulness of this technique, the practical and frequently repeated question that we raise here is whether the centrality of problem solving does not offer a philosophic justification for lack of strong commitment to anything so much as the method itself.† Emphasis, in other words, is more often upon "how we think"—upon analyzing, setting up, and testing hypotheses—than upon the clear-cut conclusions, objectives, or commitments that should be sought as results of thinking.

True, many passages in the writings of progressivists, and especially of Dewey, recognize the need for defined and positive conclusions. Not only does his fruitful concept of immediate experience as capable of becoming an intrinsically valued end provide an ontological basis for the view that intelligence mediates *in behalf of* such experience but, we should recall, he holds that the test of truth lies in the *consequence* of thinking. Thus, it would be an absurd distortion to argue that ends are not important along with means.

Nevertheless, when ends are attained, they are always subject to such incessant modification that they often seem to evade our grasp. When we ask the progressivist to specify to *what* ends we should be committed, one of his favorite answers is the ambiguous one of a warning against rigidity and dogma. In short, if we obtain sufficient perspective toward pragmatism-progressivism taken as a whole, we must conclude

† See Berkson, *op. cit.*, pp. 29ff.; Paul A. Schilpp (ed.), *The Philosophy of John Dewey,* pp. 362ff. Mead himself has said that Dewey's philosophy insists "upon the statement of the end in terms of the means. . . ." As such, it is an expression of the American belief that "the ideal phase of politics and business has been found in the process rather than in their objectives" (quoted from George H. Mead, "The Philosophies of Royce, James, and Dewey in Their American Setting," *International Journal of Ethics,* January 1930). The same attitude is expressed by Dewey, in a metaphor: "If it is better to travel than to arrive, it is because traveling is a constant arriving, while the arrival that precludes further traveling is most easily attained by going to sleep or dying." (quoted from Tenenbaum, *op. cit.*, p. 169).

that no single feature is as prominent as its brilliant delineation of the *process* of inquiry.‡

Now, the main point to be noted is that such an *emphasis* upon process is strikingly congenial to the culture that has offered it such generous support. If any aggregate of characteristics has dominated this culture, it is precisely those of movement, development, action, change. Just as liberalism—notably in its later form—has aimed to liberate men from the constrictions of exploitation, of limited privileges and rights, so pragmatism-progressivism has aimed to liberate men from fixed categories, static routines, and absolute dominations and to provide in their place a common faith in the growing, ongoing, continuous, and evolutionary aspects of culture.

Progressive education, plausibly and typically, has accented much the same kind of methodological concern. In its rebellion against the rigidities of authoritarian schooling, it tends to uphold the *solving* of problems as supremely important. But it has not as persistently upheld the need for commitment to solutions that should result *from* problem solving—especially not if such solutions take the form of encompassing cultural goals. Just as capitalism and technology opened up vast resources of nature to investigation and exploited these resources with minor concern for eventualities, so schools geared to our industrial era may encourage the investigation of novel, ever-expanding frontiers of experience and yet subordinate the inclusive achievements that might be desired as the results of such investigation.

We reiterate that the choice—strictly speaking—is never between mutually exclusive alternatives, and defenders of the progressivist position correctly claim that an artificial issue is created by critics who attempt to distinguish too rigidly between ends and means. What is not artificial is the point of stress. The *stress* of the progressivist is upon "how" rather than "what," upon process rather than product, upon hypotheses rather than commitments. Or, to state the difficulty less severely, let us say that the "what" is always somehow *contained in* the "how," the product *in* the process, commitments *in* hypotheses.

Certainly such subordination of positive and explicit ends may be clearly observed in the careful pronouncements of organized progressivists. Even assuming that Dewey himself pays equally meticulous attention to both factors of the equation of means and ends, it still remains

‡ See Dewey, *Logic, Theory of Inquiry.*

rue that many of his most influential followers have chosen to read him otherwise. As an especially relevant example, we may note that such an astute disciple as Bode concludes an impassioned plea for fresh cultural direction and purpose with little more than a restatement of experimental method as the ideal democratic end.*

Tolerance and Conviction. A state of tension may also be observed in the use of pragmatism by some progressivists in such a way as to discourage strong and forthright convictions. The teacher, especially, is tempted to suppose that convictions are incompatible with democratic education. Hence, a correct opposition to indoctrination becomes, on occasion, a much more doubtful opposition to programs of learning that seek and attain expression of systematic and positive beliefs.†

Granting that progressivists, again, are not always unified or explicit in this matter, the degree to which even Dewey sometimes discourages clear-cut convictions among teachers and students is astonishing. He and his disciples disapprove of the careful study of religion by public education, for example, apparently because they question whether the curriculum could deal critically enough with doctrines or practices antithetical to those with which they are themselves in sympathy. For somewhat similar reasons, most progressivists would not allow Communists to teach, even when they are professionally fully qualified.‡ In short, many seem curiously reluctant to risk giving to a teacher whose own beliefs are attained by methods or principles contrary to theirs the privilege of holding and defending them in the open forum that every democratic classroom should aim to provide. Some seem reluctant, also, to provide abundant opportunities, in institutions where they are influential, for a thorough study of positions toward which they are hostile—especially if

* See Bode, *Progressive Education at the Crossroads;* Brameld, "Absolutism and Democracy," *Educational Forum,* March 1939; Berkson, *op. cit.,* p. 288; John Dewey Society, *Fifth Yearbook,* "Workers' Education in the United States," pp. 292-302.

† See Kilpatrick (ed.), *op. cit.,* pp. 146-150.

‡ See John L. Childs, "Communists and the Right to Teach," *Nation,* February 26, 1949. Since this statement was written, the cultural climate, worsened mainly by Soviet-American tensions, has generated many other statements of similar intent by progressivists who earlier were much less equivocal in their defense of the rights of an unpopular minority. By comparison with these progressivists the position of Harold Taylor in *On Education and Freedom* is remarkably forthright. It is also significant that Dewey, in one of his last public statements before his death, strongly opposed loyalty oaths for teachers; see the New York *Times,* June 12, 1951.

such study is conducted by persons deeply convinced of those positions. Moreover, the argument is not persuasive that teachers of strong conviction (including Catholic or Communist teachers) would not submit their own beliefs to thorough and objective scrutiny. Before proposing to exclude their views from democratic schools, one would suppose that the progressivist, to be consistent with his inductive and cooperative methods, would first experiment with policies and programs offering such teachers the opportunity to *demonstrate* their capacity or incapacity for objective analysis—the opportunity, also, to share their convictions with others, and to subject them to the comparison and criticism of students and fellow teachers. Since, typically, the progressivist is unwilling to follow such a practice, it is ironic that he would still no doubt generally approve this statement by Childs: ". . . any group which seeks to get its views adopted by suppressing the views of others is breaking with the morality of the democratic process and is therefore to be condemned and its views held suspect."[3] On these terms, must we not here hold many progressivists themselves somewhat suspect?

In the light of such difficulties, one wonders, indeed, whether progressivists are always as tolerant as they earnestly profess. No doubt they are tolerant enough of tolerance in the abstract—that is to say, of scientific inquiry and of open-mindedness up to a point. Sometimes individual progressivists go further (again, Dewey is usually the best proof) by taking fairly radical stands on political and economic issues. But many other progressivists, such as administrators in well-to-do suburban schools, easily disclose convictions that prove to be pleasantly inoffensive to the controlling groups of their communities.†

It is therefore difficult to generalize on the issue of tolerance and conviction. Perhaps a fair statement is that, as with liberalism, the extent to which convictions are encouraged by progressive education depends upon the extent to which they are congenial to the prevailing climate of habit and opinion. For this reason, the most congenial—and surely the safest—conviction is sometimes lack of conviction except in behalf of the cautious and tentative means by which ends should be attained.

Present and Future. A final example of the tension between means and ends is the liberal-progressivist view of time. Past, present, and future

† See Lester B. Ball and Harold G. Shane, "The New AEF Policy in Review," *Progressive Education,* April 1948.

are all conceded to be objective events. Not only is the study of past history, for example, indispensable to progressive education but also, as in his concern with ends, the progressivist teacher does not disregard the importance of the future.‡

Again, however, the question to be answered is not whether the philosophy of the pragmatist includes the future in its ontology but where he focuses his attention. Here the answer is clear. Seldom if ever do Dewey and other liberals formulate the definite characteristics of a future order toward which we might because of the formulation be better prepared to take confident steps. More strongly, they usually dismiss all such formulations as "utopian"—a term that, to them, is repugnant.

The rapidity of present social change and the conviction that conflict and uncertainty are ultimate traits of existence* even provide a rationalization for minimizing attention to the future. As Kilpatrick expresses it:

> The world of affairs is clearly changing more rapidly in our day than ever before, and the stream of events always develops in novel fashion. The future becomes thus even more uncertain than hitherto. Some things we can, to be sure, in reason foretell: Seasons will recur; children will be born, grow up, live out their time, and die. . . . But who can foretell what specific significant events will happen, what new problems will arise? . . . Who can now foretell what Europe, or the world, will be like in another twenty years? [4]

This remarkable quotation helps us to understand how progressivism, again like liberalism, derives its beliefs not primarily from philosophy but from its cultural environment. Especially the American environment has been one of process and movement and, correspondingly, one of short-range vision and of strong preoccupation with the present. Such preoccupation is not surprising. A youthful country brimming with opportunity and enticement, with untapped wealth, with unbounded optimism, with problems needing to be settled quickly should not be too worried about what lies far ahead—or, accordingly, with mature cultural designs.

‡ See Dewey, *Reconstruction in Philosophy*, pp. 96, 183.
* See Dewey, *Human Nature and Conduct*, p. 12.

We can well understand that this kind of interest is reflected in progressive education. Of course, the present is never conceived as a mere moment, and learning always involves some stretching back into the past and forward into the future. But when we ask *"How far?"* the answer usually given is that we cannot reach too far ahead without jeopardizing our dependence upon passing experience. In a culture hitherto fairly content with its immediate resources and exuberant abilities the correct statement that we cannot clairvoyantly "foretell" what the future *will* be easily comes to imply that we must not try to foresee too concretely what the future *could* or *should* be. Thus, the sound insight that good schools cannot merely prepare for later adult life † is subtly, perhaps unconsciously, transformed into the far less defensible belief that education should be so centrally concerned with current events of living as to neglect sustained attention to an aggressive program and comprehensive purpose for the crucial cultural period looming before us.

The tension between individuality and sociality

The analysis of later liberalism made above suggests that it is a philosophy expressed distinctively through individuality and sociality, through both the personal and the communal. Perhaps its greatest appeal lies in this interactive principle—a principle that Dewey stated with great impact as far back as 1897 in *My Pedagogic Creed*. We quote in part here:

> This educational process has two sides—one psychological and one sociological—and . . . neither can be subordinated to the other, or neglected, without evil results following. Of these two sides, the psychological is the basis. The child's own instincts and powers furnish the material and give the starting-point for all education. . . . Knowledge of social conditions . . . is necessary in order properly to interpret the child's powers. The child has his own instincts and tendencies, but we do not know what these mean until we can translate them into their social equivalents. . . . In sum, I believe that the individual who is to be educated is a social individual, and that society is an organic union of individuals.[5]

† See Dewey, *Democracy and Education,* Chap. 5

Now the problem posed by this relation lies not in its almost too obvious plausibility but in its meaning for a period of history increasingly and pervasively different from that in which it was first expressed. We have already met this problem in various forms—all of them forms of severe cultural conflict. Its most disturbing features may, however, be restated in two questions: (1) How can the individual hope to develop his "powers" and "tendencies" in the midst of and in active relation to cultural patterns and institutions that are constantly becoming more gigantic, more powerful, more impersonal, and more collective? (2) If there is still hope that the individual can achieve this development, what kinds of cultural institutions and practices should he help to build and apply so that they, in turn, will lend support to his development? Let us consider these questions in turn.

The Individual Emphasis. Despite many qualifications, liberal-progressivists have often led us to believe that the best way for an individual to develop himself, and thereby society, is to utilize fully his capacities, especially his intelligence. This belief is supported by the potent individualistic influence of William James. It is supported still more strongly by the insistence of Dewey that the powers of the child are the "starting-point" of all education, by his intensive analysis of the reflective capacities of the individual, by the psychology and logic of an "act of thought," and by the progressivist view of the behavioral patterns of human nature. Further, we should not forget that the individualistic stress in progressivism, even today unacceptable to many conventional schools, was a legitimate protest against the stern formalism of traditional education a half-century or more ago.

Whatever the causes of their concern with the individual, it is interesting to observe how many of Dewey's disciples have persisted in emphasizing the biopsychological aspects of experience. To be sure, at times they consider the sociological aspect as carefully as does Dewey himself. Yet it would be difficult to deny, for example, that Bode's most characteristic contribution is his brilliant psychological study, *How We Learn,* or that the same type of psychological concern likewise overshadows all others in the creative writings of Kilpatrick.‡

We can well understand when we consider this emphasis on the

‡ See Merle Curti, *The Social Ideas of American Educators,* Chap. 13; Bode, *How We Learn;* Kilpatrick, *Selfhood and Civilization* and *Philosophy of Education;* National Society for the Study of Education, *Forty-first Yearbook,* Part I, Chap. 2.

individual why the child-centered school, referred to above (see pp. 148-149), has played so prominent a role in the history of progressive education. Despite the tireless insistence of all exponents that the good school is *both* individual and social, despite the progressivist enthusiasm for "shared interests" and "community life," the child-centered program is still conspicuous for its frequency and popularity. We find the major premise of the individualist emphasis, which may reflect the spirit of Rousseau more genuinely than that of Dewey, to be this: the most fruitful way to deal with the problems of our culture is, above all, for each individual to be conditioned and encouraged to study the culture primarily from the point of view of an *individual* living with *other individuals*. Help the child to live richly and intelligently, release him from the bondage of traditional authority and passive learning, and the good society will most surely emerge.

The Social Emphasis. Although it may be shown that the child-centered school continues to be more influential in practice than the community-centered school (even on the college level the "individual interests" and "felt needs" of Sarah Lawrence or Bennington students, for example, often become the pivot of learning activities), nevertheless, it is important to recognize that the community-centered approach to education has not been entirely neglected. We have seen how Dewey himself has manifested a marked social concern both in his educational experiments and in his political, social, and educational theory. Recent experiments in community-centered education have also been noted. And we should not overlook the sociocultural aspects of Kilpatrick's summation of a lifetime: his *Philosophy of Education*.

By their social emphasis progressivists appear to recognize the weakness of their individualistic emphasis. Some of them are ready to agree that the overconcern for the individual in education is a more or less subtle reflection of a competitive economic order and of the values of pecuniary success attained by self-interest at the expense of social-interest. When influenced by such a mood as was induced by the depression of the 'thirties they even seem willing to declare that the harsh power of industrial monopoly, race hatred, and national strife cannot be met by the gentle optimism or the abortive anarchism that an exaggerated faith in the cult of "child development" sometimes invites. They would no doubt agree that such a faith is symptomatic of cultural lag—an aftermath of the earlier liberalism that later liberalism inherited but failed to integrate fully into its own beliefs concerning the importance of society and culture.

Remaining Doubts. To summarize the argument up to this point, we see that progressivism is characterized by both a strong individual and strong social emphasis. The two emphases create a state of tension which is epitomized in our first question: How can individuals develop their capacities in the face of such impersonal social configurations and power structures as now prevail in the culture? Our doubts about the progressivist's capacity to answer this question satisfactorily are expressed as briefly as possible.

1. *The continued influence of the psychological, individual-centered phase of the liberal-progressivist movement is too dominant to permit it to unite solidly around a straightforward social orientation.* This results partly from Dewey's keen interest in the process of intelligence, probably more directly from the views of his psychology-minded followers, but most of all from the culture that supports the movement. This culture is still individual-centered in various ways, still vacillating and uncertain, for example, as to the extent to which it should relinquish private enterprise for social enterprise, local authority for federal authority, national rights for international rights. It is a culture in which the motivation of individualism prevails in many communities that have supported our outstanding examples of progressivism as educational practice.‡

We have noted that these communities are largely middle-class, well-to-do, and well educated and that they pride themselves on their hospitality to liberal trends. But their school systems are unlikely to challenge seriously the heritage of individualism so long as this heritage remains a convenient apologia for the status and dominance of their controlling citizen groups. Even if, in some cases, students participate actively in economic-political controversy or deal realistically with social weaknesses and failures, the gap between what they do *in school* and what they accept and desire from their privileged position *out of school* is hardly likely to generate the social strategies or commitments required by an age of crisis. On the contrary, it is more than likely to add to the frustrations and confusions from which few of even these fortunate children can hope to escape.*

‡ Note the list of thirty schools in the Eight-Year Study; many are either private schools or well-to-do suburban public schools.

* See Berkson, *op. cit.*, pp. 216ff.

2. *Doubt about the social emphasis is further enhanced by the reluctance of liberal-progressivists to deal relentlessly with the stubborn, often irrationally maintained cultural obstacles that stand in the way of the intelligent action that they endorse.* It is true, of course, that they do not ignore these obstacles. Such pragmatists as Otto have devoted many years to exposing absolutism—especially the authoritarian, antidemocratic qualities inherent in traditional religion. They have recognized, from the psychological point of view, the importance of the Freudian and neo-Freudian theories of unconscious drives behind conscious effort and, from the sociological point of view, the power of nationalism, racialism, and profit-hungry aggrandizement. On these issues, also, Dewey is conspicuous in the forthrightness of his social and economic analyses.

It is, however, not at all certain that liberalism-progressivism is sufficiently persistent or aggressively realistic to provide the social diagnoses and therapies necessary to cope with such obstacles. It would not be difficult to show, for example, that the emphatic psychological concern of a Bode or a Kilpatrick has largely ignored the psychoanalytic and psychiatric aspects of human behavior and, hence, some of the hidden springs of learning experience. Still more seriously, relatively little attention has been given by pragmatic philosophers and sociologists (notably, since the great depression of the 'thirties) to realistic understanding of socio-economic classes, to the power structures built by these classes, to pressure-group tactics, or to the monstrous influence of the newer techniques of mass communication in shaping public opinion.

It is true that certain exponents of the liberal position continue to criticize organized religion for its authoritarianism. It is true, further, that, especially in recent years, others have devoted their exceptional talents and energies to indictments of communism and the Soviet Union. But it is also true that they have devoted these same talents and energies far less persistently to aggressive attacks upon industrial monopoly, superpatriotism, "Red baiting," or similar forces and practices, all of which they also ostensibly oppose. Hence, to the degree that most intellectual leaders of progressivism temper *their* concern for sharp negative analyses of such obstacles in the path of democratic progress may we not expect the administrator or teacher who looks to these leaders for guidance to temper *his* ostensible concern?

3. *The uncertainty, shallowness, or direct avoidance of sharp negative analyses of cultural obstacles invites a judgment of insufficiency as to*

positive social strategies for coping with these obstacles. The general character of the progressivist method—centered in scientific problem solving—is of vast importance and needs to be used much more universally than it has been used thus far. The pragmatist's contention that the social sciences lag behind the natural sciences and that we have not yet approached many economic, national, and similar issues in an experimental manner is equally valid. Nevertheless, the question persists whether we have been offered a workable model of the way we should approach these issues. The liberal-progressivist's typical confidence in gradualism, his caution against undue haste, his warning that we must never be drastic or impatient cause us to wonder whether "the failure of reasonable man" does not lie in his reluctance to understand the unreasonableness of his enemies—especially of his enemies' ruthless economic and national power.

Dewey's somewhat belated concern with the problem of social struggle against such enemies illustrates the grounds for our judgment. His legitimate opposition to the Marxian theory of dialectical materialism on the ground that it is absolutist and even metaphysical seems to deter him from asking directly whether other aspects of this theory might not strengthen his own methodology in dealing with, let us say, economic conflict. In one or two books he somewhat uncertainly considers this question. But he does not answer it; he does not admit that the concept of "class struggle," operationally interpreted and adjusted to a culture differing greatly from that of Marx himself, might be utilized for both fruitful diagnosis and vigorous democratic action.‡ And although it is true that at least one leading disciple has recognized that the concept might possibly be applied to educational practice, it is not certain, judging by a later definitive treatment of his philosophy, to what degree even he continues to maintain this earlier view.* Meanwhile, the great majority of progressivists have flatly rejected this view if they have considered it at all. They have resorted to the more comfortable, more congenial way of multiple means and social compromises. Some of them, as we have seen, have even gone so far as to oppose affiliation of teachers with organized labor on the ground that this is incompatible with the liberal spirit of tolerance toward all.

Indeed, we may dispute that any of the leading liberal-progressivists

‡ See Dewey, *Liberalism and Social Action;* and *Freedom and Culture.*
* See Childs, "Democracy, Education, and the Class Struggle," *Social Frontier,* June 1936; and compare his *Education and Morals.*

have in the last decade deepened their concern with social techniques, including those of a less controversial character. Only superficial attention has been paid to the bearing upon school programs of the revolution in communication. Progressivists recognize that audio-visual learning is immensely important. Yet the meaning of this revolution for radically improved ways of teaching, for adult education, for world understanding has not challenged any leading educational theory, *including* the one presumably most eager to encourage growth and novelty.

Also relevant to our judgment is the paucity of contributions by progressivists to the philosophy and psychology of *group* behavior and *group* dynamics. Despite the pioneering of Mead and Dewey in developing the concept of the social self, the collective world that has risen like a giant since their formulations were matured has had little noticeable effect in broadening the concept. That it should be extended has now been brilliantly recognized by Raup and his associates, by Stanley, and by a few leaders of intercultural education.† Yet, with the exception of Thorstein Veblen, who was not primarily a liberal but a democratic radical, perhaps the two modern thinkers who have most strongly influenced American social science and experimental education in shifting toward social-centered and away from individual-centered action have been European-trained: Karl Mannheim and Kurt Lewin. It is doubtful, moreover, whether any American has sharpened our thinking about political strategies suitable to our crisis-culture more than has the English interpreter of our democracy Harold Laski.‡

What, then, is the common denominator of the several points we have tried to make in centering upon progressivism's social emphasis? In brief, it is that liberal-progressivism has not convincingly answered our first question above: how can the individual hope to develop his "powers" and "tendencies" in active relation to cultural patterns, institutions, and groupings that are constantly becoming more gigantic, more powerful, more impersonal, and more collective? The personal-psychological emphasis that continues to infect the sociological and cultural areas of analysis, plus the faltering analyses of inimical social forces and correc-

† See R. Bruce Raup and others, *The Improvement of Practical Intelligence;* publications of the Center for Human Relations Studies, New York University; William O. Stanley, *Education and Social Integration.*

‡ See Thorstein Veblen, *The Theory of the Leisure Class;* Karl Mannheim, *Diagnosis of Our Time;* Kurt Lewin, *Resolving Social Conflicts;* Harold Laski, *The American Democracy.*

tive strategies, combine to produce a state of tension in which average individuals cannot find aggressive, systematic, or dedicated ways of acting in concert with their fellows.

The Need for a Cultural Norm. We turn now to our second question: If there is still hope that the individual can achieve a full personal development, what cultural institutions and practices should he help to build so that they, in turn, will lend support to this development? The implication of our question is that individual and social processes need to be guided by norms if they are to have clear intent and expectation. Does the philosophy with which we are now concerned provide such norms or standards?

In a degree, of course, it does. Our exposition of its axiology has disclosed the devotion of progressivism to the ideal of democracy—an ideal that has been defined sometimes in terms of maximum interaction among growing individuals and groups, sometimes as the experimental method in personal and social operation. Nevertheless, as is true in the other areas of tension, a certain quality of ambiguous hesitation haunts the quest for certainty. We have felt this quality throughout our examination of the means-ends relation. In the appreciation of commitment, there is a stress on hypothesis; in the recognition of the future, a stress on the present; in the admiration of conviction, a stress on tolerance. The same hesitation, in another context, has appeared in the tension of individuality and sociality. The liberal's commendable concern, on the one hand, to keep both aspects in dynamic balance prevents him from providing, on the other hand, culturally designed objectives that are sufficiently concrete or unequivocal to include both individuality and sociality.

This generalization might be illustrated in many concrete ways. Progressivist administrators, for example, are among those who speak out clearly for federal aid to education while at the same time usually opposing the principle that democratic federal aid should be accompanied, in our interfused culture, by democratic federal controls. Again, progressivist high school or college curriculums are seldom geared to a future-centered exploration of the types of cultural institutions citizens should choose.

Let us consider a more basic illustration. Dewey and his colleagues insist that individuals should enjoy the right to growth, to equal opportunity and participation—in short, to all values of democracy. But they do not outline graphically the normative contours of a culture by which we could measure our failures and successes in attaining individual satisfaction of these democratic values. Indeed, we may ask whether we are even provided with an adequate conception of the good individual; for so long as we fear a definite conception of the good society how can we conceive of the good individual when, on the progressivist's own premises, he becomes meaningful only in the context of society?

The "Planning" and the "Planned" Society. We conclude with a still more dramatic example of hesitation in answering our second question: progressivism's strong opposition to a "planned" society and its equally strong support of a "planning" society (see pp. 155-158). Progressivist reasons for this position have been sufficiently provided so that it is necessary only to ask whether these reasons are convincing.

Does the liberal-progressivist philosophy, which offers such persuasive objections to religious and political absolutism, offer comparably persuasive expectations of individual and social achievement? In its legitimate opposition to totalitarianism does it not fail to envisage alternative arrangements for an increasingly collective but also democratic world? In its dislike of cultural uniformity does it not shy away from the tangible objective of cultural pluralities that are joined by the challenging ideal of "one human race"? In its key belief that education is an agent of cultural continuity does it not hesitate to agree upon a direction for that continuity? In its resentment against traditional individualism and the motives of self-interest does it not also discourage us from fashioning modifiable blueprints by which we might construct a cultural order based much more fully upon cooperation and motives of social-interest—a system by which we might channel the revolutions in technology, politics-economics, and abundance toward world-wide democratic goals? In objecting to blueprints on the ground that we cannot know in advance what should be *planned* does it not divert us from deciding for what people should be *planning*? In correctly warning us against the fanaticism and bigotry that sometimes accompany commitment to social purposes does not liberalism-progressivism disavow also that esthetic fervor or religious dynamic without which men never create greatly or hope boldly?

We do not imply that the answers to these questions are clearly negative or positive. Rather, as we have suggested, this impelling philosophy frequently provides abundant materials *for* the answers. But it is clear that, when the balance is struck, the fashioning is by no means yet accomplished. Like the rapidly shifting industrial and political structures upon which it rests, pragmatism is a philosophy in transition between the fixed universe against which it rebels and the designed culture which needs now to be created. Liberalism is the rationale of this pendulous state—of this unrelieved tension between means and ends, between individuality and sociality.

And so progressivism, as the philosopher-administrator Harold Taylor states it revealingly, "will accept as true the fact that *education is an instrument of social transition*. It will thus be a liberal philosophy, taking as its goal the development of free men in a changing social order." [6] In short, progressivism is the educational effort of an adolescent culture, suffering from the pleasant agonies of growing up, from preoccupation with the excitement of present events, from the cultural period of trying and erring when the protections of infancy have been left behind but the planned autonomies of maturity await future delineation and fulfillment.

Summary of Beliefs about Progressivism

Progressivism is the educational expression of the "liberal road to culture." Influenced deeply by the fertile and eager American environment, it is grounded philosophically in pragmatism-instrumentalism-experimentalism as developed primarily by three emancipating thinkers: Peirce, James, and Dewey. Its beliefs about reality focus on the concept that natural experience is dynamic, temporal, spatial, pluralistic. Its beliefs about knowledge revolve around intelligence as the scientific method operating in every area of experience. (Thus, the act of thought—awareness of obstacles, analysis, suggestions, inference, and active testing—becomes central to logic as a theory of inquiry into problems significant for living.) Pragmatic beliefs about value, related always to nature and intelligence, crystallize in: (1) such interactive principles of conduct as intrinsic and instrumental and personal and social values; (2) a philosophy of art that stresses the rhythm of esthetic expression between the doing or mediate phase of experience and the undergoing or immediate phase; (3) the supreme value of democracy both as critique of the shortcomings of our culture and as norm of the possibilities for growing and sharing richly in the creative opportunities of natural and cultural life.

As educational theory and practice, progressivism, like pragmatism, derives from many thinkers and cultural influences and commands great prestige through organizations as well as experimental schools. Its doctrine of learning rests upon its ontology, epistemology, and axiology. Therefore, it stresses the fullness of experience and the "whole child" as the proper subject matter of education, and it refines its psychology through such operational concepts as interest, effort, habit, growth, organism, culture, and, above all, intelligence. Its curriculum proposals, typically experimental, are perhaps most advanced in the "experience-centered curriculum," which discards fixed contents and routines in favor of units built cooperatively upon needs and interests of the learners. In developing its educational methodology, progressivism aims to substitute "real problems" for the "cookbook problems" of traditional courses; it admits drill only as a subordinate technique; it rejects indoctrination and the dichotomy between work and play; it supports both child-centered and community-centered schools but would prefer that one school should be both; and it favors greatly widened adult education. In its approach to the problem of education and social control, progressivism insists that freedom is a positive correlate of order. Hence, it approves the kind of discipline that emerges from freely associated living and participating, just as it disapproves line-staff school administrations. Progressivists are not equally agreed, however, in translating into concrete practice their generalizations about social control. For example, some favor and some disfavor affiliation of teachers with organized labor. They are also not agreed or clear on how much or what kinds of social controls they favor in the "planning society," which they endorse in opposition to both *laissez faire* individualism and a "planned society."

In evaluating progressivism it is necessary to bear in mind that its strengths and weaknesses are those of Western culture, in general, and American culture, in particular. It is from these cultures that progressivism emerges and to which it renders loyal service. In essence, Western culture developed to its present stage of acute instability after breaking away from medievalism and evolving through two overlapping stages, which we have called early and later liberalism. Early liberalism was characterized by the virtues of private competition, agrarian self-sufficiency, and frontier independence. Later liberalism, while incorporating strong qualities of its precursor, is much more fully industrialized, integrated, and dynamic. Progressivism is the epitome of later liberalism in that it attempts to maintain a steady growth of relations between individual-social responsibilities and activities. In contradistinction to the three-R's school of agrarian culture, it wishes to widen the sphere of learning interests so as to embrace the entire communal experience of children and adults while at the same time always paying close attention to the interests of the individual. Its greater concern with the continuous *process* of interaction between self and society than with the determination of the normative and descriptive *products* of that interaction gives it a peculiarly pendulum-like quality.

In recent years the flexibility and cultural continuity that characterize liberalism, although extremely popular in progressive education and in liberal politics, law, and economics, have faced determined opposition. Progressive education has become a term of repugnance to great numbers of educators and laymen who have been influenced by well-organized, widely publicized, heavily financed attacks. Although progressivism meets many of its critics effectively, they continue to be articulate and often influential.

Ultimate reasons for the strength of the attackers, however, are not to be discovered merely in critical evaluation of educational beliefs and practices. And they are not to be found only in the fact that some progressivist leaders fail, because of their own eclectic tendencies, to recognize the actual unity between their educational methods and the philosophic principles that underlie these methods. They are found still more fundamentally in the roots of a culture that suffers acutely from crisis—from the fears and intimidations spawned by the Cold War and other insecurities—a culture that tends, therefore, to become restless, dissatisfied with the optimistic and compromising spirit of gradual progress so excellently typified by later liberalism.

If we are not to turn back from liberalism-progressivism to either the conservative-essentialist or the regressivist-perennialist alternative (both of which have strong appeal for some individuals and some powerful groups, both of which deserve to be heard with the care and respect we shall try to apply to them in the next two parts), our task is not to reject but to re-examine, correct, and supplement liberalism-progressivism as fully and forthrightly as possible. Basic to our task is the diagnosis of two spheres of tension that are, we believe, chronic to this theory and program: one, the tension between means and ends; the other, the tension between individuality and sociality. The great opportunity that now rises before citizens and teachers in search of a philosophy of life and education appropriate to our revolutionary age is to consider how each of these tensions can be at once utilized and constructively released: the tension between means and ends, through courageous commitments, convictions, and future-centered purposes, which, in the course of their attainment, strengthen and refine scientific methodology; the tension between individuality and sociality, through relentless analysis of cultural obstacles, through aggressive social strategies, and through enhancement of the values of the individual in the normative matrix of a designed world order and a *planned* democratic culture.

The task is supremely difficult, and we may fail. But it must be undertaken if we are to maintain and advance the richest single contribution thus far made by American philosophy and education to the welfare of mankind.

Notes

[1] Quoted from William H. Kilpatrick (ed.), *The Educational Frontier,* p. 292.

[2] George S. Counts, *Education and American Civilization,* p. 103. Copyright 1952 by Teachers College, Columbia University, and reprinted with their permission.

[3] John L. Childs, *Education and Morals,* p. 196.

[4] Quoted from National Society for the Study of Education, *Forty-first Yearbook,* Part I, "Philosophies of Education," p. 65. Published 1942 and reprinted with the permission of the Society.

[5] John Dewey, *My Pedagogic Creed,* Personal Growth Leaflet 19, pp. 6-10.

[6] Harold Taylor, "Education as Experiment," *Antioch Review,* Summer 1949 (italics supplied). See also Taylor (ed.), *Essays in Teaching.*

PART THREE

ESSENTIALISM

Education as Cultural Conservation

CHAPTER 7

The Essentialist Pattern of Philosophic Beliefs

Preview of Essentialism

The "Conservative Road to Culture." OF THE ROADS ALONG which a culture may choose to travel when confronted with the imperative of choice, none is more appealing to a certain type of citizen than that which bears the signpost "Conservative Road." For various reasons—perhaps the habit of ultra-caution or a stake in inherited economic arrangements—he finds himself supporting the preservation of practices and beliefs that characterized the institutional patterns of the period preceding the uncertain and unstable present. The error of the present culture, according to the conservative, is that it has strayed too far from the road laid out for it by the past. The surest solution for its difficulties is to return to the road. Then, and only then, can it hope to regain confidence in itself; then, and only then, can it move forward with certainty and stability.

In this analogy is to be found the cultural key to essentialism, whether as critic of an educational philosophy such as progressivism or as advocate, in its own right, of an alternative philosophy. As critic, it finds in progressivism, which it regards as its chief opponent, an embodiment of all the precarious fluctuations of our time—a way of life and education that reflects only too accurately the desperate gropings of rootless and restless persons and therefore glorifies the very cultural characteristics most congenial to its own spirit: activity, tentativeness, flexibility, self-direction, trial and error. As advocate, essentialism recognizes certain values in these cultural characteristics, but it values more highly others, which it thinks are much more needed as stabilizers: time-tested content, orderly sequence, inherited principles, guided discipline. These valued characteristics it derives from the highly complex culture and correlative philosophies of at least four centuries. Their origins are often dated from the Renaissance; their endings, at their highest maturation, were clearly discernible by the latter half of the nineteenth century.

The aim of Part III, to sketch essentialism in necessarily broad strokes and to evaluate it in terms of the characteristic beliefs of the long era of postmedieval civilization (hereafter referred to as the "modern era"), is faced, perhaps, by greater difficulties of achievement than the aims of either Part II or Part IV. For both progressivism and perennialism, notwithstanding their own inadequacies, are more systematic and coherent than a philosophy of education that weaves into its own pattern so great a variety of diverse strands. Indeed, one basic characteristic of essentialism is a wide *eclecticism,* typified by the presence within its camp of both professed idealists and professed realists. We shall see, however, that even this curious and sometimes uncomfortable fellowship is quite understandable when judged not primarily in technical philosophic terms but rather by the culture that they both help to justify and in behalf of which they both would muster education's arsenal of resources.

Our Modern Heritage: The Source of Dependable Belief. Allowing for many differences of emphasis and sometimes outright contradictions, what, then, is the central doctrine of essentialism? In briefest compass, it views the established beliefs and institutions of our modern heritage as not only real but true, and not only true but good. It recognizes, of course, that this heritage is marred by flaws—by war, disease, and poverty—but it insists that these are usually, if not always, the results of mistakes in human judgment not evils inherent in the universe or in man. "Ignorance," in other words, is simply a term for misjudging the underlying rightness and order of the universe and "understanding" a term for accurately judging its rightness and order.

Thus, this philosophy, however erudite its varying formulations and however earnestly some of its representatives may protest their "liberal" spirit, has been and is being used skillfully and subtly to maintain inherited cultural patterns. Its import becomes clearer, moreover, as the internal conflicts of our age become sharper. No previous era has undergone radical transformation without eloquent and loyal resistance from those who believed they had little to gain by change and, perhaps, much to lose. Our own is no exception. It may be asserted without exaggeration that the conservative mood, as reflected by popular books and scholarly works of historians, literary critics, and economists, is today more fashionable, certainly in some intellectual circles, than any other mood. The essentialist in education also reflects this mood. The very character of his doctrine (although sometimes contradicted by his *professed* intent) would utilize schools to strengthen and refine rather than to alter the complex structure of attitudes, beliefs, and institutions so patiently and expensively erected by the predecessors of our own period of culture.

Preliminary Evaluation. Having provided this general setting, we propose now to interpret essentialism under three large headings which parallel those employed in the preceding three chapters. Chapter 7 considers beliefs of a general philosophic quality; Chapter 8 considers beliefs concerning education specifically; and Chapter 9 provides a cultural evaluation of essentialism.

As in the treatment of progressivism, all three topics are interwoven. Hence, even our more descriptive approach to the first and second is by no means unaffected by our opinion that, despite great lasting contributions, essentialism is no longer a satisfactory philosophy of education either in its wider connotations or in its direct, practical applications.

It is no longer satisfactory for one overwhelming reason. However attractive the conservative mind and attitude may be even in this period, an age of sweeping reconstruction, such as our own, cannot establish a stable yet dynamic culture by perpetuating or restoring beliefs and habits that were much more suitable for an age now well beyond its crest of maximum achievement. In the respect that the preponderant influence of essentialism is directed toward such an objective it may be regarded as the supreme example for our day of a "cultural lag" in educational philosophy. Yet it is important that we conscientiously try to respect and to understand essentialism, for otherwise we shall be in no position to see why it must now be supplanted by a different theory and practice.

Paralleling the development of Chapter 4, the remainder of this chapter considers:

1. essentialism in the history of thought;
2. essentialist beliefs about reality;
3. essentialist beliefs about knowledge; and
4. essentialist beliefs about value.

Essentialism in the History of Thought

Patterns and objectives of modern thought

Like many important philosophies of our time, essentialism has a long and honorable ancestry. We should therefore expect its most typical contemporary feature—an articulate, sophisticated concern with the conservation of inherited culture patterns—to derive in certain respects from the very earliest Western philosophers.* Plato particularly should be mentioned, for he is often regarded as the founder of *objective idealism*—one of two dominant forms of contemporary essentialist theory. Equally important from the point of view of what we shall call *objective realism* is Democritus, who developed the first systematic theory that the whole world, including man, is composed of atoms—particles of matter differing from one another only by such quantitative relations as size and shape. Aristotle, too, was fascinated by the structures of objective reality; although a disciple of Plato, he tried to provide a philosophy as realistic, in some ways, as the Democritean.

But such thinkers, including those of medieval civilization, are only precursors to essentialism. We shall observe below that the thought of Plato and Aristotle provides the pattern not so much for essentialism as for perennialism. Essentialism † is above all a *modern* theory—a product of the Renaissance centuries. *In place of an ancient and medieval absolutism symbolized by the unchallengeable, dogmatic authority of the Church, modern essentialist philosophy aims to provide a systematized, unified conception of man and the universe that will be as appropriate as possible to modern needs and institutions.* Sometimes this conception is developed in almost if not entirely natural and material terms. In this case, we tend to view it as does the modern *realist*.

It is not, however, easy to define realism concisely, for different exponents of the position tend to stress different facets of the over-all posi-

* See Hugh Miller, *An Historical Introduction to Modern Philosophy*, Chaps. 4-7.

† It is important to note that the term itself is not used commonly by academic philosophers; rather, it has been largely pre-empted by educational philosophers. One recent book by an academic philosopher, Frederick Mayer, entitled *Essentialism*, is a well-argued statement of a position quite hostile to that of the educational essentialist as well as to his philosophic allies.

tion. It may help to quote a synthesis of its meanings as expressed by several great philosophers, compiled by one of our ablest educational essentialists:

> Nature is a primary self-evident reality, a starting point in philosophizing. . . . The primary qualities of experience exist in the physical world. . . . There is something which produces my sensations and perceptions . . . which cannot be known to be mental in character. . . . Mind is *like* a mirror receiving images from the physical world. . . . The mind of a child is similar to a blank sheet of paper upon which the world proceeds to write its impressions.[1]

At other times essentialism is developed from more spiritual or mentalist premises, in which case we tend to view it as does the modern *idealist*. We may be helped to obtain a preliminary notion of idealism, too, by considering some of its meanings as expressed at different times by historic representatives:

> Ultimate reality is of the same substance as ideas. . . . Behind the phenomenal world is an infinite Spirit which is both substructure and creator of the cosmos. . . . The existence of God is made necessary by certain factors in selfhood. . . . The self is the prime reality. . . . Man as a thinking being is a part of God. . . . By examining his own ideas and testing their consistency, man can achieve truth . . . The self reads meaning and unity into the objective world.[2]

It will be noted that in both the realist and idealist positions the stress may be either on the universe as a whole or on the self and its ideas or perceptions. Both positions, in other words, attempt to take into consideration the world *and* the individual, with a concern for their interrelations.

Finally, essentialism may be depicted as an adroit *combination* of realism and idealism in one system of philosophic thought. Indeed, we shall find that in educational theory this combination tends to become more significant and useful than the attempt to divide realism and idealism into two completely antithetical positions.

Regardless of such differences, which may become extremely involved, the leading thinkers of the era beginning in about the fifteenth century are, with such exceptions as we observed in Chapter 4 or shal note below, concerned with two objectives. The first is to build a set of beliefs by which men can live in a culture increasingly secular, increasingly scientific, increasingly industrial. The second is to ensure that this set of beliefs continues in some way to provide a foundation of certainty to which men can subscribe and in which they can trust. Essentialism's task is to translate these objectives into workable educational practice—a task in which it succeeded so well that it captured virtually all secular schools from the time of the Renaissance until the period of the rise of progressivism.

Modern thinkers contributing to essentialist beliefs

European Thinkers. Since essentialism has matured during several centuries of our modern era, perhaps the best way to try to understand it is to make the acquaintance of some of its historic contributors. In Europe, the most influential thinkers may be roughly classified, though under a variety of labels, as *idealists* or *realists*. The aim here (as in parallel Chapters 4 and 10) is to provide only a sampling of modern thinkers, preparatory to considering their influence upon contemporary essentialism. Readers who lack a background in the history of philosophy may wish to consult suggestions for reading offered in the footnotes and Bibliography.†

The greatest period in the history of modern idealism is centered in the Germany of the seventeenth and eighteenth centuries—in such intellectual giants as G. W. Leibnitz, Immanuel Kant, G. W. F. Hegel, and Arthur Schopenhauer. All four are excellent representatives of the two great objectives mentioned above. Leibnitz, a brilliant mathematician and man of affairs, constructed a theory of the universe in which all events and facts are related in a system of perfect "pre-established harmony." Kant endeavored to preserve the venerable beliefs in "God, freedom, and immortality" by arguing that, though they cannot be established by the canons of "pure reason," they remain necessary assumptions of the moral

† See footnotes and "What to Read" for Chapters 2, 4, 5. See also Miller, *op. cit.*, Chaps. 11-20; N. P. Stallknecht and R. S. Brumbaugh, *The Spirit of Western Philosophy*, Chaps. 8-13; Robert F. Davidson, *Philosophies Men Live By*, Chaps. 3, 6, and 13. This chapter is most indebted to John H. Randall, Jr., *The Making of the Modern Mind.*

life, of "practical reason." Hegel attempted to reconcile the scientific and spiritual approaches to life in one breath-taking speculation: all nature and all society are arranged with such exact logical order that they express necessarily the perfect "reason" of a Supreme Being. The sensitivity shown by Hegel to dynamic qualities in the emerging civilization also appears in Schopenhauer's sorrowful speculation that human life, in essence, is an insatiable longing for satisfactions that are never to be achieved through experience. Such longing can be overcome only by being obliterated in that eternal and absolute Nothingness to which age-old Oriental philosophies have beckoned us.

These idealists differ from the earlier type of philosopher and churchman in their tireless efforts to build a philosophy that might withstand the rigid scrutiny of rational analysis and allow room for new developments in science and culture. Hegel's solution is typical of this objective. He embraces every fact and every event in a sweeping conception of spiritual reality. The meaning of the term *objective* is thus especially unequivocal in the Hegelian system: the spiritual or ideal (here synonymous terms) is by no means an inner, private phenomenon; it is not equivalent to one's own soul or subjective mind; rather it is the core of the universe itself, in which all individuals and all physical things perceived by our senses are members.

Somewhat prior to but overlapping the German idealist movement is "British empiricism"—the forerunner of contemporary realism. The greatest thinkers in this movement include Thomas Hobbes, John Locke, George Berkeley, and David Hume. Hobbes's greatest fame rests, perhaps, on his contributions to political philosophy. He endeavored to justify absolute monarchy by proving that men are materialistic, egoistic beings who need to set up an all-powerful authority to protect themselves against their own predatory and cruel impulses.

Locke's empiricism had a different political purpose. As the most influential philosophy of "early liberalism" (see pp. 164-165) and as support for the Revolution of 1688, it seeks to prove that, since ideas are derived solely from man's own perceptions and reflections, he may be properly subjected to no other political or ecclesiastical authority than himself. There are, for example, no "innate ideas" to which tyrants can resort as authority for their acts. Yet Locke succeeded not so much in rejecting all forms of absolutism as in substituting a more modern, middle-class variety for the old-fashioned monarchical absolutism to which Hobbes remained loyal. Moreover, as Berkeley showed, Locke's kind of empiricism logically requires a spiritual base—a Supreme Being who is Himself the ultimate *cause* of the very sense perceptions that Locke emphasizes.

It was left, then, for Hume to follow the argument to its logical outcome by demonstrating the superfluity of the cumbersome apparatus of metaphysical absolutism that his British colleagues tried to construct on either a material or a spiritual substructure. But this was an outcome so distasteful to the culture that even Hume qualified it. Modern philosophy has devoted itself, in considerable measure, to "refuting" his heresy.

That such idealists and realists (with the partial exception of Hume) could still, despite all their differences, aim toward ultimate objectives that are astonishingly akin is revealed by Baruch Spinoza. A philosopher of Jewish background who spent many years in Holland, Spinoza brilliantly conceived of the geometrically exact and uniform world of nature as, at the same time, a world of the spirit. For him "the intellectual love of God" is identical with scientific understanding of the universe. Even human action and appetite are treated as if they were "lines, planes or bodies"; and freedom may be attained only by understanding the complete, predetermined regularity of a world operating according to God's decrees. Thus, Spinoza sought, without making compromises between them, to *identify* what we call the idealist with the realist patterns of belief.

American Thinkers. Until the recent development of pragmatism and instrumentalism, the course of philosophy in America followed closely the European pattern. Such an emulation may be explained by the fact that the new land was settled almost exclusively by people educated in the literature, art, and politics of the Old World—in fact formed mainly by Old World culture. Thus, it might have been expected that both idealism and realism should have been imported to our shores, to be developed further in the young nation.‡

Idealism in America is frequently dated from Jonathan Edwards.

‡ See Herbert W. Schneider, *A History of American Philosophy*. For recent broad interpretations of realism, see R. W. Sellars, V. J. McGill, and Marvin Farber (eds.), *Philosophy for the Future*. For a recent interpretation of idealism, see W. E. Hocking, *Science and the Idea of God*.

Strongly influenced by Berkeley, among others, this outstanding thinker of the Puritan period tried to prove the unqualified supremacy of God but to leave a place for the exercise of free will—a reconciliation congenial to an infant culture already given to encouraging individualism and self-reliance. Although idealism has continued to be extremely influential since Edwards' time, we shall mention here but three other figures: Josiah Royce, often regarded as the most original American idealist down to the present day; Ralph Waldo Emerson, the great "transcendentalist"; and W. E. Hocking. The cultural significance of these and other idealists is perhaps as well revealed by Emerson as by any other. Influenced by German thought, he was fascinated by the vision of "the One," which embraces animals, trees, moons, and men. He was nevertheless already sufficiently a man of his time and country to emphasize the need for individual assertion and control over environment.

The attempt of American realism to break away from idealist-religious philosophies began early in our history. But it was not until William James, whom we recall as primarily a pragmatist (see p. 96), that the outlines of a realist position with a native coloration could be clearly discerned. Since James, two Englishmen who for many years resided in America have been among those who have especially deepened the realist philosophy: Alfred North Whitehead and Bertrand Russell.* George Santayana, part European and part American, is a third important contributor. The range of thinking among recent realist writers is a wide one, and it would be difficult to determine whether many realists (Whitehead is one example) belong more to progressivism or to essentialism so far as their educational and social ideas are concerned. Yet one may note that much of their interest in realism, in the structures of external nature and especially in the connections of individual minds with those structures, follows closely the work of its early forerunners—Hobbes, Locke, and others. It has been the consuming preoccupation of many American realists to prove that *objects exist prior to and are independent of the operations of the mind.*† Although at first glance such a concern seems remote from the practical affairs of education, we shall find that

* See Alfred N. Whitehead, *The Aims of Education and Other Essays;* Bertrand Russell, *Education and the Good Life.*

† See William P. Montague, *The Ways of Things,* pp. 230ff.; and *The Ways of Knowing.*

it has considerable significance for the public schools of our time.

To say, however, that contemporary realists are concerned only with the problem of knowledge would be a serious distortion. Not only have Russell, Whitehead, and Santayana turned their thinking to many aspects of human existence but other realists, too, such as Ralph Barton Perry, Roy Wood Sellars, and Wilbur M. Urban, have been concerned with profound ontological and axiological as well as epistemological problems. The remarkable synthesis of both realism and idealism that we found in Spinoza has even been emulated in our own day, though in quite different terms, by Urban. His position, sometimes called "idealistic realism," again highlights the paradoxical affinity of the two positions. Influenced strongly by classical European philosophy, Urban insists that much of the controversy between idealism and realism has been futile—that any adequate system must of course recognize the complementary needs of mind and body, spirit and things. His culminating work, *Beyond Realism and Idealism,* endeavors to demonstrate this thesis.

Meanwhile, the influence of modern realism upon American political beliefs is easy to establish, even in this prefatory sketch. The American Revolution reveals many evidences of the stubborn effort to reconcile the demands of freedom with age-old habits of compliance with pre-established cosmic order. We may note, for example, how heavily the Declaration of Independence relies philosophically upon the realist Locke—especially upon the doctrine of natural rights, which holds that laws of nature give men certain inalienable rights, which, by the very fact that they are so given and hence are prior to any fluctuations of experience, cannot rightfully be abrogated.

Today the essentialist point of view in social philosophy continues to be influential. Just as the hand of Puritanism, exemplified by Jonathan Edwards, still weighs heavily upon our religious and moral habits, so the historic beliefs associated with thinkers such as Locke still weigh heavily upon our political and economic habits. One instance is the widespread American reception that was given, especially by business groups, to Friedrich A. Hayek's *The Road to Serfdom* and similar books.* A European theorist, he deals with burning issues of our day, but his typical economic premises are the familiar ones of such conservative statesmen as former President Herbert Hoover. Hayek pleads for "belief in the tradi-

* See also F. A. Hayek, *Individualism and Economic Order;* and *The Counter-Revolution of Science;* Herbert Hoover, *The Challenge to Liberty.*

ional values for which we have stood in the past" and compliance with a kind of absolute "rule of law."

Perhaps the most forthright and scholarly American advocate of this type of cultural outlook is Russell Kirk. In *The Conservative Mind* and *A Program for Conservatives* he is scathing in his denunciation of progressivism and liberalism ("No thinker's work, during the past century," he declares, "has become more thoroughly obsolete than that of John Dewey. . . ."), and energetically declares a point of view resting upon

> A belief in an order that is more than human, which [is] . . . susceptible of improvement only by an inner working, not by mundane schemes of perfectibility. This conviction lies at the heart of American respect for the past, as the record of Providential purpose. The conservative mind is suffused with veneration. Men and nations . . . are governed by moral laws. . . . An eternal chain of duty links the generations that are dead, and the generation that is living now, and the generations yet to be born. We have no right, in this brief existence of ours, to alter irrevocably the shape of things, in contempt of our ancestors and of the rights of posterity. . . .

Accordingly, Kirk pleads for a "reaffirmation of the truth that lies in tradition." He wishes to defend "the classes and regions in which tradition still is a living force . . ." and to assure a "returning to family and church and voluntary association of their old responsibilities as transmitters of tradition." [3]

In many respects the assumptions of Kirk's and Hayek's works are similar to those of perhaps the greatest political essentialist of modern history—Edmund Burke, the archexponent of the contention that perpetuation of a given value over a long period of time is the strongest possible argument in favor of its permanent worth. His reverence for established institutions led him to the judgment that "The place of every man determines his duty. . . ." [4]—a place presumably fixed by historically prescribed patterns of order.

With this brief background, we should be ready to appreciate the great scope of essentialism as a general point of view. Let us fill in some of the more important gaps in this background by considering, in turn, the three philosophic areas: reality, knowledge, and value.

Essentialist Beliefs about Reality

The common denominator of the essentialist ontology—its beliefs about reality—is the conception of a world governed by unimpeachable and predetermined order, a world conceived, both by idealists and realists, as ruling over or through man according to its inviolable dictates. It is a conception in which, therefore, whatever meaning man possesses must be reconciled as far as possible with that kind of world.

It will become evident that in only a few major respects have there been any far-reaching modifications of the inherited framework sketched above. For, we must remember, it is just this framework that essentialism is primarily concerned to accept and conserve.

Objective realism as world system

If by the term "objective realism" is meant a systematic view of the physical, natural world and of man's place in that world, we may say that two major scientific fields have dominated all others in shaping objective realism. The first is the field of physics, including such sciences as astronomy and chemistry, which entered its first great period of influence with Sir Isaac Newton. The second is biology, especially as interpreted through the theory of evolution with which we associate the name of Charles Darwin. Both these fields have, of course, influenced philosophies other than essentialism, but in other ways (see pp. 93, 98-99).

The World as Machine. To consider first the physical sciences, we may recall that it was Newton's supreme achievement to carry the researches of his predecessors, such as Copernicus and Galileo, to a logical and apparently ultimate conclusion by proving that every aspect of the physical world can be brought within the compass of all-inclusive order. With nothing in nature determined by chance, the simplest incident can be explained by physical laws, such as the law of gravitation. All nature operates with the efficiency and regularity of a clock. From the time of Newton until our own day this theory, which we may call *mechanism,* has continued to exert immense influence—the theory, in brief, that the world itself operates by the causes and effects, the pushes and pulls, of a monstrous machine.

Mathematics is central to the theory of mechanism. All motions and relations in physical nature are reducible to quantitative terms which, expressed in abstract equations, aim to encompass and explain every event in nature. It is as if the whole universe had become a magnificent system of geometry. So it was with essentialist philosophers as far back as Spinoza; so it remains for many scientists, philosophers, and laymen today.

Now, the point to which we must pay strict attention is that the world as a machine is simply there, moving perpetually under its own power. The method of science consists primarily in reducing all observed processes to a mathematical account, to an expression of law and of universal order, which exist in nature itself. It is true that to build this awe-inspiring structure, Newton and his scientific descendants carried on many important experiments and thus foreshadowed the meaning of the experimental method as it is understood, for example, by the instrumentalist. It is also true, however, that the emphasis in traditional mechanism has been strongly *deductive*. That is, it has been in large measure concerned with postulating, extending, and applying general mathematical laws of nature to an ever-widening range of particular phenomena. The *inductive* method, the building up of generalizations from particular observations and experiments, is not by any means ignored; indeed, it is regarded as indispensable. Nevertheless, the essentially deductive character of much mechanistic science was well expressed, a century after Newton, by the Frenchman P. H. D. Holbach:

> Man . . . is the work of Nature. He exists in Nature. He is submitted to her laws. He cannot deliver himself from them. . . . The universe, that vast assemblage of everything that exists, presents only matter and motion . . . an immense, an uninterrupted succession of causes and effects.[5]

This simple and comprehensive picture of the world has now been amended, for nature has been found to be far more complicated than Newtonian physics assumed. First molecular physics and then atomic physics, which led to the most devastating scientific discovery in history (atomic fission), accelerated a shift in thought that had already begun a hundred years before. To the new physicists the universe appears to be an expanding field of explosive *energies* rather than a body of mobile *matter*. But such changes in recent science have not fundamentally modified the beliefs about the universe that we associate with the realist and especially the mechanist position. These beliefs, we reiterate, are stil geared to the acceptance of a physical world governed chiefly, if no wholly, by mechanical processes and physical elements. The order of nature, even if recognized today to be far more intricate and manifold than previously supposed, is *still there waiting to be revealed to man* in all its awesome regularity.*

Evolution in Objective Realism. The second great scientific contribution to modern realism—evolution—holds that every organism, from the simplest plant to the most complex animal, may be brought within the compass of natural explanation. Although the particular laws that Darwin formulated are no longer universally accepted by the scientific world, the realist approach to evolution and biology is often analogous to its approach to physics. Our task, the realist maintains, is to observe causes, effects, and other temporal events in the organic sphere and to explain them in terms of uniformities with a prior existence in nature.

Although Darwin himself was not a mechanist in certain respects, it is interesting to note how, long before his time, scientists were reducing organic structures and processes to biochemical compounds and reactions. In terms of such analyses, living things became as mechanical as, let us say, chunks of earth or burning gasoline. Life itself, many biologists now believe, will be produced in the laboratory as soon as we learn more of its chemical relations. Moreover, the science of genetics is now able to effect such radical changes in plants and animals that it can literally produce new species and thus demonstrate the laws of heredity within the laboratory.

The evolutionary theory has also been applied to astronomy, geology, and sociology. Not only was our earth, for example, "born" from the sun in some remote era but it has slowly developed through different stages to its present stage. Cultures, too, have evolved systematically: the founder of modern sociology, Auguste Comte, and the great philosopher of evolution, Herbert Spencer, both tried to show how group life is subject to forces that carry men along in a current of inevitable and regular change. In anthropology the realist position is today strongly maintained in America by Leslie White, who conceives of culture as a self-existent, autonomous level of nature, which operates under its own laws and whose members are totally without "free will." This is the thesis of his book *The Science of Culture.*

* See E. A. Burtt, *The Metaphysical Foundations of Modern Science.*

OBJECTIVE IDEALISM AS WORLD SYSTEM

The central point to be made about *objective idealism* is that, al-hough it is distinguished from realism by a greater "cosmic optimism" nd in other ways, its basic formulation in modern philosophy is gov-erned by a concern to come to terms with modern science and modern ulture.

The "Spiritual Interpretation of History." We refer above to Hegel's daring synthesis of science and religion within a single cosmology. Perhaps the most influential application of this synthesis is the Hegelian heory of history, which attempts to determine the laws governing every tage of civilization, to demonstrate why each stage followed its predeces-or as it did, and to account for the powerful forces of social change that eem to deny fixity to any one period of history.

Hegel's answer to these difficult questions is still accepted in essence by many thinkers of our generation. This answer, briefly, is that *history is God thinking*—thinking His way through, and thus expressing, the eter-nal dynamic shiftings of the world, which is itself spiritually real. It is clear that this interpretation of history, far from denying the facts of movement and conflict, regards them as fundamental. It has been well said that Hegel's God is a "man of war." * Although Hegel lived before Darwin, it is significant that he anticipates the struggling, restless quali-ties of reality upon which evolution, as a scientific theory, rests. But counterbalancing his stress upon *becoming,* upon endless movement, he emphasizes equally the *being,* the necessity, of each event in history. No war, no government, no social achievement is accidental; each step in the march of civilization is spiritually ordained.†

Microcosm and Macrocosm. We now introduce two philosophic terms not previously used in this volume—*macrocosm* and *microcosm.* Macrocosm refers to the entire universe and usually connotes a cosmic design and unity, that is, a cosmology. Microcosm refers to the single part, the separate fact, or, on the human level, the individual man or institu-tion, each of which in design and unity minutely reproduces the uni-verse. Thus, for example, analogies are drawn between the vast solar sys-tem and the tiny atom: the nucleus of the atom resembles the sun and the electrons, revolving around the nucleus, resemble the planets. Hence, we

* See Josiah Royce, *The Spirit of Modern Philosophy,* p. 216.

† See Theodore Brameld, *A Philosophic Approach to Communism,* pp. 49-53.

see that the macrocosm-microcosm concept may be fruitfully utilized even by objective realism. It is, however, more often utilized by idealism to clarify the spiritual affinity between God and man.

The theory of God as macrocosm has already been suggested in our reference to the Hegelian doctrine of history. According to this doctrine God, far from being apart from the human world or directing it from "on high," is *immanent,* that is, He is a manifestation of and existing within history itself. The macrocosmic God of today is—much as it was for Hegel—a universal Mind, which includes within itself all things, all energies, all time and space, all individual minds. Every law of science—physical and physiological alike—is an equally marvelous expression of the harmony and reliability of God's own handiwork. Hence, it is unnecessary to deny the multiplicity of events that lead many contemporary thinkers to regard the world as pluralistic. However numerous they may be, these events are ultimately joined in one unified and spiritual whole, of which God is the supreme source. He is the Thinker thinking His thoughts and thereby creating everything real.

In fact, the literature of objective idealism is rich with ingenious logical devices, often borrowed from science, to prove God's existence. The famous "argument from design," for example, attempts to demonstrate that the mechanistic perfection of nature requires a Maker, a Supervisor, just as any clock requires someone to construct and wind it. Closely related to this argument is the equally familiar "cosmological argument," an adaptation of the law of causality: if, as science itself holds, every natural effect without exception is caused, then so too must the whole world have a Cause. (For the treatment of comparable "arguments" by perennialism, see p. 304.) Although many philosophers have raised doubts about the validity of such arguments, they continue to be expressed and widely accepted by those holding generally essentialist attitudes.

The traditionally religious tone of objective idealism might lead to the belief that the theory of organic evolution would have a disturbing effect upon it. It is true that if one identifies religion with Christian fundamentalism, with a literal acceptance of the Biblical story of creation, one cannot, of course, believe that man emerged from lower species of animals. The sophisticated philosophy we are now considering, however, finds little trouble in accepting evolution. As might be expected, we need only include the objective uniformities observed in the development of species along with any other given uniformity of nature and to assert that they too are ordinances of a macrocosmic God. Just as civilizations pass through logically ordered stages, so do plants, lower animals, and human beings.

Meanwhile, if man still finds difficulty in comprehending the spiritual macrocosm in any complete sense,‡ he is able at least to comprehend in some measure the most perfect earthly microcosm of that reality—himself. Even the human body is an amazing demonstration of symmetry and order (consider, for example, such complicated but efficient organs as the eye). Still more revealing is the human mind. Its capacity for logical reasoning, for proceeding logically from step to step to a finally valid conclusion, is a microcosmic demonstration of the systematic process that we find in the macrocosmic steps of historic development.

Recent idealism develops this microcosmic concern with the individual by its concentrated attention on the "self" and the "person." (One of the most influential contemporary religious philosophies is called *personalism.**) The aim of this attention is to reveal the spiritual uniqueness of the self, which is, indeed, a phenomenon of nature but also more than natural—more than a fact capable of scientific analysis. It is aware both of itself, directly, and of other selves in a community of selves who are attuned with one another. In his recognition of the individual's awareness of other individuals we find an anticipation of the idealist's social philosophy (developed so beautifully by Royce in his *Philosophy of Loyalty* and other works) as well as another device for bringing the self back into relation with the macrocosm. For, since a community of selves is already a more inclusive spiritual reality than a single self, it partakes more fully of the universal Self. It is, we might say, intermediate between God Himself and the human person, who is, as Hocking expresses it, "an imperfect image of the whole cosmos. . . ."[6]

Man thinking, then, is but a simple expression of God thinking. This is not to say, of course, that, as *subjective idealism* holds, man himself is the *source* of reality, but that, although he may first come in contact with God through intimate awareness of his own spiritual self, the fact is that God's Self, as universal, is prior to and the Cause of man's self. You and I, in short, are basically real because we are the personal representa-

‡ See F. H. Bradley, *Appearance and Reality.*

* Probably the outstanding American personalist is Edgar S. Brightman. See his *A Philosophy of Religion.*

tives of an ideal cosmic Being. We approach Him only as we reflect Hi
in our own spiritual life, or, more exactly, as we develop our own divin
quality by closer approximation of God.

Essentialist Beliefs about Knowledge

The theory of man as a reflection of God is a direct bridge to an unde
standing of essentialist beliefs about knowledge. For if man, at his mos
real, is a microcosm of the universe, then *he knows* in the degree to whic
his mind is able to *reflect* that universe—to reproduce accurately an
adjust to the historical and contemporary contents of the physical, bic
logical, social, esthetic, religious spheres. This generalization agai
applies, on the whole, both to the idealist *and* the realist.

The body-mind controversy

One cannot say, of course, that differences between the realist an
the idealist types of essentialist thought are not far-reaching. Indeed
much modern philosophic writing has been devoted to a continuou
battle between these two schools within the very area we are now enter
ing—namely, epistemology, or the theory of knowledge.

Idealists take the position that, since the spiritual is the key to reality
we know within and through the mind; the body, like all physical objects
is ultimately subject to and embraced by the mind. Realists take just the
opposite position: since the material is the key to reality, we know withi
and through the body. For many of them the mind is itself ultimatel
physical and obedient to the same rules as govern all other physical ob
jects. Considerable highly technical discussion has been devoted to the
effort of recent realists to disprove the case for idealism, especially in it
epistemological emphases. Perry is among the more eminent of these
thinkers. He has demonstrated with great cogency that idealists commi
a fallacy when they premise that, because human beings know object
only through their ideas, therefore ideas and mind are *responsible fo*
objects. The fallacy derives from attributing causal efficacy to the "egocen-

ric predicament" that we perceive things only if we are present to perceive them.†

A third position, also militantly defended by epistemologists from the Frenchman René Descartes to the American Arthur O. Lovejoy, is that mind and body cannot actually be united and, hence, a *dualism* is inescapable.‡ The old religious belief of the separateness of the "soul" is often, although not necessarily, implied in this third position.

The mind-body controversy likewise permeates modern psychology —so deeply, indeed, that it illustrates perfectly how philosophic assumptions must underlie all scientific work, the protests of some scientists notwithstanding. As a matter of fact, the psychological dispute over the *primacy* of mind or body or the *parallelism** of mind and body has often been scientifically fruitful. It has produced many excellent techniques of experimentation, the results of which, in turn, have enriched our understanding of human behavior. The main point, however, is that either the "body" approach or the "mind" approach, if followed far enough, supports modern essentialism in its approach to knowledge. We shall find that both approaches develop attitudes and habits that have serious practical consequences for education and for the culture it serves.

The idealist approach to knowledge

We know most truly, say the idealists, as we understand our own spiritual selves, but such understanding is enhanced as we come to recognize that the marvelous rationality of which our minds are capable is but a small part of the perfect rationality of an Infinite Mind. The various ways in which this general position is elaborated by idealism are so astute that to develop them comprehensively we should have to devote volumes to mere exposition. For example, it is possible to speak of at least four main types of idealism in the history of American philosophy—personal, speculative, dynamic, and absolute §—all of which try, in one way or another, to take into account scientific knowledge and thus to reflect the experimental mood of the young culture. As Royce expresses it, "The very existence of natural science, then, is an illustration of our thesis that

† See Ralph B. Perry, *Present Philosophical Tendencies.*
‡ See Arthur O. Lovejoy, *The Revolt against Dualism.*
* See Edna Heidbreder, *Seven Psychologies,* Chap. 4.
§ See Schneider, *op. cit.,* p. 466.

the universe is endlessly engaged in the spiritual task of interpreting its own life." [7]

It would be difficult to find an American who is as convincing in his analysis of the psychology of idealism and thus of the process by which knowledge is obtained as the British idealist T. H. Green. Men approach their own spiritual selves most closely, says Green, by *introspection.* Thus we discover that the unique feature of mind is a consciousness that cannot possibly be identified with sensation, for every mental experience involves *relations among* sensations. The element of redness, for example, would be meaningless as redness; it becomes meaningful only as the power of consciousness organizes it into a related whole, as in a red sunset. And since this power is not itself reducible to a sensation, it must be, strictly speaking, an "extra-natural" principle.‡ Mind itself becomes a *substance* *—not a material substance, to be sure, but one possessing its own spiritual autonomy and uniqueness.

For many idealists, and especially for those in the Hegelian tradition, this spiritual, mentalistic substance expresses its own laws of logic, which, in turn, offer the main cue to the laws of the universe. The *dialectical* process of thinking from step to step in an irreversible sequence is found, for example, to be strictly comparable to the process by which cultures evolve from stage to stage according to God's laws of history. In the language of modern religious philosophy, the inspiration which enables me, as a *finite* being, to know that I have found a universal truth is the realization that my mind is attuned to God's *infinite* mind, that I am in complete, rational harmony with Him. By the same criterion, I err, I am victimized by falsehood, when this harmony is incomplete, when communication between me and the cosmic Self is clouded by the welter of my feelings or distorted by my sense perceptions.

The realist approach to knowledge

Realists in psychology and epistemology are, largely, within the great tradition heralded by Newton in the physical sciences. One of the main aims of realism has been to observe human beings as it does any other material objects and to explain mind and its operations in terms that are applicable to the explanation of a machine. Although this aim has

‡ See T. H. Green, *Prolegomena to Ethics.*
* See Boyd H. Bode, *How We Learn,* Chaps. 2, 3.

been beset by great obstacles, nevertheless, for nearly a century realism has prevailed over idealism in psychology precisely because it has utilized much more fully the methods and canons of the physical sciences. We discuss briefly three realist movements in psychology—*associationism, behaviorism,* and *connectionism*—all of which have greater epistemological and cultural implications than their scientific proponents usually appreciate.†

Associationism. The first realist movement in psychology, associationism, stems from British philosophy, especially from Locke. The ideas or contents of the mind are an association of elements—"atoms" of sensation and perception. The associationist studies them chiefly by introspection—the method employed by the idealist—but he does so without preconceptions about the "soul" or other spiritual substances which presumably glue them together.

Despite the exclusion of such preconceptions, associationism faces many theoretical difficulties. As in the case of the idealist Green, the associationist is constantly forced to resort to some "extra-natural" principle to perform the *associating* of mental atoms. And he is never sure that the ideas each of us holds is a reliable, a "true," mental image of the object we perceive outside ourselves. We are, as it were, prisoners of our own subjectivity.

Behaviorism. The second realist movement in psychology, behaviorism, arose largely as a protest against just such difficulties. The term "behavior" is preferred to "mental life" because the total organism, in its neurological, physiological, and biological experience, is the psychologist's concern. In the behaviorist's most orthodox formulation such terms as "mind" and "consciousness" are only confusing relics of a prescientific approach. Purely objective methods of observation and measurement replace such methods as introspection, the chief psychological process being that of *conditioning* the organism to respond to stimuli and thereby to form habits. The body is the fundamental fact. Even "thinking" is regarded as a complex of neuromuscular habits centered in the larynx, by which we respond with and to silent or spoken language. Personality is the name we give to the individual's pattern of conditioned reactions.

† This interpretation relies heavily upon Heidbreder, *op. cit.,* Chaps. 4, 7, 8. For a more inclusive cultural interpretation, see F. S. C. Northrop, *The Meeting of East and West,* esp. Chap. 3

Although behaviorism as it was originally conceived has been modified, its guiding assumption is still that the individual is essentially explainable in mechanical terms. It substitutes the postulate of materialism—that human beings are subject entirely to physical laws—for the postulate of idealism—that they are subject entirely to spiritual laws.

Connectionism. Behaviorism has influenced a number of psychologies of our day (the progressivist, for one), but probably its greatest impact has been upon the third and recently most conspicuous realist approach to knowing and knowledge, namely, connectionism. Although difficult to characterize in few words (its leading exponents are at times rather eclectic), the term "connectionism" itself is simple enough. It suggests that all animals, including human beings, build patterns of response by "stamping in" and "stamping out" *connections between* stimulus (S) and response (R). In this way bonds of connection are built up or broken down. The chief "laws" governing this process include "the law of exercise" and "the law of effect." The first suggests that frequency and recency of stamping will strengthen connections; the second that the individual tends to retain responses that are satisfying (*i.e.*, pleasurable) and to eliminate those that are annoying (*i.e.*, painful). Since the S-R-bond process can be measured with a high degree of precision, psychological experiences can be subjected to highly precise quantitative experimentation.

Connectionism modifies orthodox behaviorism in at least three ways. First, it tends to stress heredity rather than environment as an explanation of behavior. Although recognizing the influence of environment, it emphasizes the individual's native equipment, including his reflexes, ability, and intelligence. Second, connectionism emphasizes the importance of the feelings of pleasure and pain, regarding these also as hereditary equipment that governs the selection or rejection of stimuli and responses. Third, it makes no fetish—as the orthodox behaviorists seem to do—of avoiding such terms as "thinking," "consciousness," or "mind." On the contrary, it regards these as useful terms, which, however, require careful redefinition. "Thinking," for example, is explained as reacting to situations by selecting the elements that are necessary to satisfactory responses and by employing analysis and abstraction to break down complex situations into their details. "Mind" is regarded as a measurable object of nature.

The correspondence theory of knowledge

In discussing the realist *approach* to knowledge, we have not yet indicated how genuine knowledge, as contrasted with error or falsehood, is actually *attained*. We should note carefully that the correspondence theory of knowledge, as the characteristic realist statement of this process is known, holds that, in general, what we know to be true is the product of an agreement obtaining *between* the facts, relations, processes, and laws of the objective world *and* our individual judgments about these phenomena.

Types of Realists in Epistemology. But all realists are not satisfied with any single generalization. Among them one finds varying expressions of the common epistemological point of view. In America two main types, *neorealists* and *critical realists,* have been most influential. Both types are philosophic allies of related psychological movements.

The neorealists are psychologically close to behaviorism. Knowledge is presented to the mind directly from the world. It is therefore interpreted as a body of specific responses to external stimuli with little or no reference to intervening intellectual processes.

Critical realists are more in the tradition of Locke and the associationists, who, we recall, premise intellectual mediators or substances which fuse clusters of sensations. Knowledge is *re*-presented through these mediators. Perhaps the most famous critical realist of our day is Santayana, whose theory of the "realm of essence" holds that a kind of bridge connects the outside object and the inside idea of the object, partaking of the essence of both object and idea without being either one.* Hence, he speaks of a realm not of existence but of "subsistence." In Santayana's theory the strange alliance of realists and idealists again begins to appear, for the realm of "subsistence" is characterized by numbers and shapes that are "real" yet cannot be perceived in the material world. Recent realism revivifies in this theory a much older form, which we are to study in Part IV, that of scholastic realism, which is itself a grandparent of objective idealism.

Three Inferences from the Correspondence Theory. The arguments of these schools of thought and the various terms they attach to their respective theories of truth often become so complicated that it is

* See George Santayana, *The Realm of Essence.*

fortunate that, for our purposes, we need not analyze them in depth.* Three main inferences to be drawn from them are, however, relevant to our interest.

The first inference is that realist psychologies and philosophies are inclined to accept a more or less completely mechanistic world, within which human beings exist and function. It is a world governed primarily by the cause-effect determinations of physical and chemical processes and most accurately conveyed to the mind through mathematically formulated laws.

The second inference is the basic assumption underlying the correspondence theory—namely, that the "stamping in" of responses to stimuli (as stressed particularly by connectionism) provides reliable knowledge. Without such an assumption there would be no need to encourage techniques of stamping. Hence, stimuli that emanate from the given environment—both of nature and society—are the source of the truth-process; human responses are the product. The "mind," or whatever the organ of response formation may be called, is exposed to this environment in much the same way as a camera plate is exposed to light. And while the apparatus of exposure, timing, and position is often complex (especially in critical realism), the net effect is in essence similar.

The third inference is that the correspondence theory of knowledge, allowing for some substitution of terms, is usually *equally appropriate to the theories of idealists and realists.* For both, the universe of antecedent order is the source and criterion of everything we know. True, idealism insists upon a correspondence between the finite self and the infinite Self, while realists speak of the mind's dependence upon "nature" or "matter." Realists are also more neutral and "objective" about what they perceive as cold facts and uniformities than their more optimistic idealist allies, who, in contrast, find the universe to be radiating rosy hues of hope and purpose. But both the realists and the idealists assume a pre-existent and cosmic source of truth with which it is the business of the mind to correspond.

* It should be recognized that the term "correspondence" would not be acceptable to all realists or idealists. For example, the term "coherence" is preferred by some, with resulting qualifications. See William P. Montague, *The Ways of Knowing;* Miller, *op. cit.,* Chap. 23. For a clear exposition of the issues raised by neo-realism and critical realism, see Joseph Blau, *Men and Movements in American Philosophy,* Chap. 8.

Essentialist Beliefs about Value

That essentialism's beliefs about reality and knowledge strongly condition its beliefs about value is revealed by the common denominator of its axiology: values, like truths, are rooted in and derived from an objective source. The character of this source and of the values deriving from it depends upon whether the view is that of the idealist or of the realist.

Nevertheless, it is not impossible again to discover striking similarities between the realist and the idealist wings of this momentous educational philosophy, especially when they are appraised from a point of reference beyond themselves—namely, the culture. From this point of reference we find that both wings of essentialism strongly tend to substantiate and transmit inherited principles and practices of morality, art, and social conduct. Further, these principles and practices so often color essentialism's attitudes about all aspects of the culture, including education, that we must inquire whether its beliefs about value are not even more impelling determinants of its outlook than are its beliefs about reality or truth.

The idealist theory of value

Idealists have usually assumed that ethical laws are themselves cosmic laws. Hence, you and I, as selves, succeed in becoming good only as we share actively in them. The practical effect of this position is obvious. In less philosophic language, organized religion, for example, teaches the same doctrine: God's commandments can solve all problems of moral conduct for those who are ready to accept and practice them. While upholding this authoritarian doctrine of values, idealists are, nevertheless, eager to convey the impression that the individual person is himself an active determinant of values. They do so, in general, by interpreting the self as becoming more and more fully a self in its unity with other selves and so, finally, with the supreme Self. Nevertheless, it is this supreme Self who is always the source as well as the goal of the values for which you and I strive.

The Modern Character of Idealist Axiology. The way in which idealists develop this position is a striking illustration of how modern philosophy differs from its medieval forebear. Wishing to adapt themselves to the "this-worldliness" of modern civilization—a wish shared by idealists as well as by realists—objective idealists, especially those of the Hegelian strain, do not deny the existence of evil. On the contrary, they regard evil as a real human experience. But since their universe is warmly toned with the qualities of inherent goodness, some of them (Royce is one) try to prove that evil is always subordinate or, at least, that it is meaningful only when contrasted with its exact opposite.

Emphasis on logical argument rather than on mere dogma is another example of the spirit of modern idealism. As an example, we may consider the brilliant ethics of Kant, a philosopher who still commands many distinguished followers. Deeply disturbed by the threat to traditional faiths—a threat to which he himself lends support in his philosophy of science—Kant seeks to ground standards of conduct in unimpeachable moral law. Therefore, he sets up a "categorical imperative" of obligation to duty, which, he insists, is completely consistent and unconditional whether it is ever obeyed or not. Paraphrased, the law states that each of us should always act as we would want such acts to be performed by all of us everywhere and at all times. For example, it is our duty to be strictly honest because honesty is a good that we universally approve; hence, even if we violate our duty in respect to honesty, we could not possibly wish to see acts of stealing become the general rule.

A final example of the influence of modern attitudes upon idealist ethics is its tendency to stress the freedom of the individual. Kant is again a dominant figure, for he argues in behalf of moral freedom and other axiological principles that are threatened by the strict cause-effect determinations of modern science. The moral self is free precisely because it has emancipated itself from these determinations and has joined hands with other selves in a spiritual union that is ultimately supernatural. The law of duty, in other words, requires the assumption of sufficient freedom to carry out its commands. This assumption, in turn, requires that we hold membership in an order of reality in which freedom is possible—a reality above and beyond our world of necessity and ruled by a Being able to grant immortal membership to mortal beings and reward them for their obedience to the categorical imperative.

Since the time of Kant many thinkers have tried to strengthen or modify his original formulation to accord with contemporary conditions. For example, Ernst Cassirer, an able and influential neo-Kantian, develops a doctrine culminating in the ideal of "progressive self-liberation." [8]

Today few theories of ethics of any school exert greater influence than Kant's. Shorn of its complications it reveals to men how they may seek personal goodness regardless of how overpowering the pressures of heredity and environment or how strong the temptations of a lustful and competing world.†

Idealist Social Theory. Idealism's approach to ethical values is paralleled by a similar approach to social and political thought. Hegel, for example, finds an increasing spiritual quality in every social institution from the family to the nation—a spirituality that, in turn, justifies an ardent nationalism and patriotism. Under the terms of this spirituality, the state becomes sacred—becomes, indeed, the expression of God Himself—a point of view adapted with telling success over a century later by the idealist philosophers of totalitarian Italy and Germany.

The spiritual totalitarianism of Hegel and his disciples is by no means the only social consequence of objective idealism. The strong individualistic spirit of postmedieval culture is reflected frequently in thinkers such as Kant, and even to some extent in Hegel. Green, Royce, and Croce are among the recent idealists who have insisted upon the great value of liberty for the self and in relations among selves. Nevertheless, whether the emphasis is upon microcosm or macrocosm, modern idealists tend to agree that the social and political life of man is a manifestation of his membership in a community of spiritual persons, the supreme ruler of whom is God.

The erudite and frequently conservative implications of this social philosophy are epitomized by the contemporary idealist Hocking, who states:

> . . . the authority of Society is derived . . . Society can expect every man to do his duty, on one condition: that it speaks for a divine Will, which expects every man to do his duty. It is this being beyond Society which provides the staying power for a flagging conscience and a flagging love . . . God is the law of a normal social life.[9]

Idealist Esthetics. Let us briefly sample the esthetic flavor of idealism.‡ Virtually all of its great representatives have been fascinated

† One of the important distinctions not developed explicitly in this chapter is suggested by Kant's position: the distinction between "theism" and "deism." See Randall, *op. cit.*, pp. 294ff.

‡ See selections by idealists in Melvin Rader, *A Modern Book of Esthetics.*

by the philosophy of art, but again none more profoundly than Kant. Men enjoy a "disinterested pleasure" in objects of beauty, says Kant, which enables them to forget their limited and warped perceptions; thus they glimpse together, momentarily, their common and eternal unity. Hegel's esthetic theory partakes of the same tone: a work of art, whether in architecture, poetry, music, or any other medium, is an expression of the spirituality of life. Men grasp the universals of reality through the feelings and sensations induced by a natural object, such as a piece of wood or the sound of a bell. Other idealists—Benedetto Croce, for example—have particularly stressed this feeling tone in their theories of art, and so have tended to ally themselves with an esthetics that is reminiscent of modern naturalism.

On the whole, however, idealists judge the beauty of an object by the extent to which it penetrates through the crudity and ugliness of everyday experience to those symmetrical, harmonious patterns of nature that resemble the workings of the logical mind. The idealist sculptor Saint-Gaudens removes the blemishes and uncouthness of the individual, physical Abraham Lincoln in order to "idealize" him—to reveal his spiritual universality and perfection as we have come to conceive them in our spiritual imaginations. Here, he says, is the "true" Lincoln. Here, also, is the meaning of the immortal dictum of the poet John Keats that "beauty is truth, truth beauty."

The realist theory of value

The simplest introduction to realist ethics is through its ontological belief that the source of all human experience lies in the regularities of the material environment. Therefore, we must try to approach values as we approach knowledge, namely, by "objective" understanding of facts and events to which people happen to attach judgments of worth and for which they express desire, admiration, dislike, disapproval. Sometimes the consequence of this objective approach is to discount values entirely, as purely arbitrary concepts beneath the dignity of "scientific" investigation—an attitude prevalent today in some university departments of social science. We shall see, however, that not all social realists are quite so naïve as to suppose that they can ignore the problem of values. Certainly they cannot escape the problem even though they may *try* to ignore it.

Ethical Determinism. One of realism's most influential theories, for example, may be called *ethical determinism.* Since all elements of nature, including man, are linked together in an endless chain of causes and effects, therefore, whether the individual is good or bad depends entirely upon the past causes that have shaped his present conduct. Similarly, what he will be in the future will be largely determined by the causal chain now being forged.

It is not impossible for this point of view to be held by essentialists of either hereditarian or environmentalist leanings. The former assume that conduct is chiefly the product of inherited biopsychological equipment: wars, for example, may be caused ultimately by the fact that men have an instinct to be brutish (see discussion of Hobbes, p. 209). The environmentalists deny the existence of such instincts: men may be conditioned to be peace-loving as well as to be warlike. But the important inference of either position is that they have very little if any *free choice* in the matter. What men are morally is determined by the patterns of response that have been indelibly stamped upon them by the equipment of their heredity or the stimuli of their environment.*

The rigid and difficult implications of ethical determinism have led some philosophers of realist preference to discuss ethical principles in rather different ways. Thus the utilitarians of the nineteenth century prefer to approach human conduct by analyzing psychological motivations and consequences in purely natural terms, thus approaching, in some respects, the position of progressivism. In general, however, they reflect the individualism and mechanism of their own age, attempting to measure values by a kind of "calculus" of pleasures from which they may determine "the greatest happiness of the greatest number." † In their pleasure-pain principle they again demonstrate the dependence of psychology upon philosophy; it will be recalled how connectionists predicate the importance of the pleasure-pain principle in the learning process.

It is impossible to embrace realism's beliefs about values in a single harmonious interpretation. Perry, for example, regards value as any object of *interest*—a theory suggestive of progressivism.‡ More influential, perhaps, is the famous realist Russell, who, although not always harmonious

* It is of course possible for idealists also to be "determinists" in the sense that God determines the course of things. This is especially true of such theologians as Calvin, but also in more subtle ways of such philosophers as Hegel.

† See A. K. Rogers, *A Student's History of Philosophy,* pp. 443ff.

‡ See Perry, ***Realms of Value.***

even with himself, reveals in his famous essay "A Free Man's Worship," a favorite mood of many realists. Man, he says, must be understood in "the world which Science presents for our belief . . . a world of cold causality in which one's hopes and fears are the product of the accidental collocations of atoms"; a world in which facts, not goods, are supreme; a world where "omnipotent matter rolls on its relentless way"; yet a world in which men do somehow manage to fashion ideals and a "passion for eternal things. . . ."[10]

Realist Social Theory. The transition from the realist position on individual ethics to the realist social philosophy is a logical one, for realism approaches political and economic values and practices with the same scientific "neutrality" with which Russell approaches the "free man." Much of the social science of our day is realistic in this sense: economics seeks to discover and objectify the inviolable laws of the market or of the business cycle; sociology, the structures of social organizations; political science, the behavior of pressure groups or political parties. Vilfredo Pareto may be mentioned here as one of the most influential social realists of the past half-century.

This approach is by no means new, however. Adam Smith was but one of many classical economists who attempted to universalize the laws of capitalism. Before him, Niccolò Machiavelli formulated what he was certain were objective principles of politics by showing how "the Prince" behaves in "real life." Machiavelli's influence, more than four hundred years after he wrote, remains astonishingly widespread.

The theory of evolution, a more recent basis of the realist's social beliefs, illustrates especially well how the cultural milieu may color ostensibly impartial findings. Thus, Spencer attempts to prove that the biological doctrine of the struggle for existence, being a fundamental law of all animate beings, imposes upon sociology the conception of a competitive culture rooted in self-interest and self-aggrandizement—a convenient doctrine, widely approved to this day, for justifying the profit system. The general attempt to prove that the struggle for existence applies also to society and culture is referred to as "social Darwinism."

William Graham Sumner is another conservative apologist for the competitive culture: in the name of science he argues that attempts to ameliorate the inhumane social effects of economic competition are strictly contrary to natural law. He goes so far as to assert that in the struggle for existence, "Nothing but might has ever made right" and "nothing but might makes right now." [11] He regards folkways, the cultural habits of peoples, as the effects of natural forces that men unconsciously set in operation and that allow little or no exception because they lack the power of intellectual reflection and intent. For Sumner the study of folkways has much the same importance to sociology as the study of cells has to physiology—a good example of the way in which the social realist emulates the natural scientist.*

We do not mean to imply that Spencer and Sumner are typical of all social realists; and even their own extreme determinism and conformism are on occasion qualified by more liberal tendencies. Their attempts to ground moral conduct upon presumably objective descriptions of group behavior, however, illustrate one of the most common logical devices of the realist: to hold that what has been and is characteristic of man and society (*descriptively*) is by this very fact what ought to be (*normatively*), because such conduct is natural, orderly, and inevitable (see pp. 41-42). This inference, however cautiously or unconsciously made, brings the social values of some realists into a strange alliance with those of some idealists. For, like the idealist, the realist may contend—and now with the prestige of science to support him—that "whatever is, is right."

Realist Esthetics. We discuss briefly, in conclusion, realist theories of art. Although even more difficult to categorize than realist beliefs about conduct and society, realist theories of art all concentrate largely on expressing life "as it is" and, therefore, on its complex pleasures and pains, its alternating harmonies and disharmonies.

In their crudest form these theories are examples of the timeworn belief that art is *imitation* of nature. Few realists, however, would interpret imitation as mere reproduction in mirror-like fashion, but rather as honest *expression* that conveys some aspect of the world clearly and significantly through the chosen medium of the artist. The emphasis of realist art is not upon "beauty" in the idealist's sense of a pattern of spiritual perfection behind the façade of appearances but upon both beauty and ugliness—in fact, upon all elements of reality—as legitimate values of art.

As we have found to be the case in other philosophic areas, realists and pragmatists have common tendencies with regard to art: both are "down to earth"; both reflect the influence of science. But the tone of the realist esthetics of Santayana, for example, is again different from that of

* See Schneider, *op. cit.*, pp. 382, 396-400.

the pragmatist esthetics of Dewey. Santayana stresses more strongly the hedonic—that is, pleasurable—factor in art, just as other realists stress still more strongly the factors of emotion and will.

We may illustrate realist esthetics in its more social and determinist mood through the works of the American novelist Theodore Dreiser and the American painter John Steuart Curry.† Running through Dreiser's novels is always the relentless power of cause and effect upon the fate of individual human beings—a power analogous to the "pull" of the sun upon the planets. The viewer of Curry's paintings feels the vigorous honesty of his effort to portray the regions of America as a great pageant of tragedies and joys. But he may also sense in these paintings an effort to disclose more than the eye perceives. As one critic expresses it, Curry fixes upon detailed facts that somehow have the capacity to expand into universal experiences.‡ Curiously, it is just this universality that is present in the artist-scientist-philosopher Spinoza. Both are trying to give us, as it were, a picture of the *real* world. Both aim to depict it as exactly as possible. But both aim also to reveal a profound and determined order running through the storms and stresses, the fluctuations and discords, of nature and life.

Notes

[1] J. Donald Butler, *Four Philosophies and Their Practice in Education and Religion,* pp. 299-300. Copyright 1951 by Harper and Brothers and reprinted with their permission.

[2] *Ibid.,* p. 161.

[3] Russell Kirk, *A Program for Conservatives,* pp. 62, 41-42, 308, 310. Copyright 1954 by Henry Regnery Company and reprinted with their permission.

[4] Quoted from J. H. Randall, Jr., *The Making of the Modern Mind,* p. 435.

[5] *Ibid.,* p. 274.

[6] W. E. Hocking, *Types of Philosophy,* p. 409.

[7] Quoted from Max Fisch (ed.), *Classic American Philosophers,* p. 240.

[8] Ernst Cassirer, *An Essay on Man,* p. 228.

[9] W. E. Hocking, *Science and the Idea of God,* p. 83. Copyright 1944 by the University of North Carolina Press and reprinted with their permission.

[10] *Selected Papers of Bertrand Russell,* pp. 2ff.

[11] William Graham Sumner, *Folkways,* p. 62.

† See Theodore Dreiser, *Jennie Gerhardt;* and *American Tragedy.* Reproductions of Curry's paintings may be found in many volumes on modern American art. See also *Catalogue of a Loan Exhibition of Drawings and Paintings by John Steuart Curry,* Lakeside Press, Chicago, 1939.

‡ See Laurence Schmeckebier, *John Steuart Curry's Pageant of America;* selections by realists in Rader, *op. cit.*

CHAPTER 8

The Essentialist Pattern of Educational Beliefs

WE NOW ASCEND FROM THE PHILOSOPHIC FOUNDATIONS OF essentialism to its theory of education. In following this analysis and interpretation, the reader should guard against four misconceptions.

First, it is not our purpose to demonstrate that essentialist educa-ional theory invariably rises directly and logically from essentialist philo-ophic beliefs. Although in general the fundamental philosophy and the ducational theory are consistent, essentialist beliefs about education ometimes modify, supplement, or even deviate from the beliefs of such minent philosophers as Berkeley, Kant, or Santayana. Not all idealists r realists are necessarily systematic educational essentialists, but it is robably correct to say that almost all if not all educational essentialists re realists, idealists, or a combination of the two.

Second, the reader should observe that our presentation of essentialist ducation will be no more detailed than was our presentation of its hilosophy. Both are so selective that, as in Chapter 7, the reader of this hapter should be prepared for certain simplifications that can be elabo-ated only by additional acquaintance with the literature.*

* Important bibliographical references regarding essentialist education are noted in the footnotes to this chapter and in "What to Read." As a further uide to the issues raised, see John S. Brubacher, *Modern Philosophies of Educa-tion* (2nd ed.); J. Donald Butler, *Four Philosophies and Their Practice in Edu-cation and Religion;* Harry S. Broudy, *Building a Philosophy of Education.*

Third, this chapter is concerned primarily with basic educational theory; hence, the day-to-day practices of essentialist schools can be considered only incidentally.

Fourth, we are interested in broad lines and dominant characteristics and shall not draw the fine distinctions among various essentialist philosophies of education that would be found in a more elaborate or exhaustive interpretation.

The Rise of Essentialist Education

Historic backgrounds

The educational theory of essentialism, although more eclectic than most other leading theories, has both a negative and a positive purpose. Negatively, essentialists struggle to emancipate themselves, as do modern philosophers in general, from the world-view of the Middle Ages. Positively, they struggle to substitute for it another world-view that is appropriate to a more secular, scientific, industrial civilization. We find, therefore, that the great educational thinkers of essentialism extend over a long period of history. Although ancient and medieval beliefs contribute to the total pattern, its distinctive features emerge with Renaissance educators such as Erasmus and reach fruition in such twentieth-century Americans as William C. Bagley.

Erasmus, Comenius, and Locke. The spirit of the early revolt against medieval other-worldliness and dogma is nowhere more courageously exemplified than in Erasmus, who lived in the late fifteenth and early sixteenth centuries. In urging curriculums devoted to a "humanism" of classical learning and an international outlook he was bitterly opposed in his own time. But it was a time of increasing susceptibility to new ideas, and his influence in behalf of well-trained teachers and schools for the middle class as well as for the aristocracy could not be totally suppressed.†

Comenius is one of the first Renaissance educators who sought to

† This historic section is especially indebted to Robert Ulich, *History of Educational Thought.*

systematize the teaching process. He foreshadowed modern realism in his insistence that "everything be taught through the senses"—a belief he carried into practice by including pictures in his famous textbook on foreign languages. Like so many leaders of his era, however, he was also deeply absolutist: he believed that the world is at once dynamic and purposeful and that education's chief task is to shape the human creature into an image of the divine.

Among the academic philosophers mentioned in the preceding chapter none is more representative or educationally influential than the realist Locke. As the archadvocate of the seventeenth-century middle-class revolution, Locke, we recall, substituted a new social theory, of adjustment to external nature and social order, for the theory inherited from preceding ages, of adjustment to supernatural and monarchical authority. This substitution has great, if not always obvious, significance for the kind of school he advocated. A "this-worldly" thinker (though making some provision for deity), he wished to gear education more closely to practical situations. He was, however, greatly interested in the education of "gentlemen" who are "set right"—that is, are taught the proper rules and habits of the economic and political order that they are assigned to govern—and who "once set right . . . will quickly bring all the rest to order." [1] Needless to say, "the rest" could only mean the lower classes of working people who, for another three centuries at least, were to remain subservient to these same "gentlemen." It is no wonder that, along with more humane proposals, Locke also favored "working schools" for pauper children, who would be trained for industry in order to repay what the community had spent to keep them alive.

Pestalozzi, Froebel, and Herbart. Of the very many other historic figures who might be chosen to illustrate the development of essentialist ideas some also influenced other educational movements. We noted in Chapter 5, for example, that Pestalozzi, Froebel, and Herbart might be claimed by progressivism as well as by essentialism, depending upon which aspects of their thought are emphasized. Perhaps the most accurate generalization that can be made about all three is that, although they sought valiantly to break through the historic philosophies and cultural habits that tied them so securely to their age, they could not fully succeed. Thus, Pestalozzi believed deeply in "Nature" (indeed, he is often close to Rousseau), and in this mood he anticipated the naturalism of such thinkers as Dewey. But he is, at the same time, essentialist in that he is unwilling to deny the transcendental. "God," he says, "is the nearest relationship of man." [2]

Froebel sought the same difficult synthesis. Deeply devoted to the education of little children and eager for them to express themselves creatively, he nevertheless saw a metaphysical quality in such expression. Indeed, no statement by any essentialist educator of the idealist wing is more clearly metaphysical than this: "Education consists in leading man as a thinking, intelligent being, growing into self-consciousness, to a pure and unsullied, conscious and free representation of the inner law of Divine Unity, and in teaching him means thereto. . . . This Unity is God." [3]

Of the three, however, Herbart is perhaps most articulately essentialist. A critical disciple of Kant, he insisted that the goal of education is to attune one's soul to a "vision of the Absolute," from which one may derive one's faith "in the ultimate victory of the good." [4] Also deeply influenced by the theory of associationism, which he derived especially from Locke, he is sometimes regarded as the first systematic educational psychologist. His famous laws of instruction were reframed so convincingly by his followers that even today some "lesson plans" follow the five mechanical steps of "preparation, presentation, association, systematization, application." Herbart was a believer in "mental states," which are linked together somewhat as chemical elements are linked to form a compound.

Harris. The influence of these and other theories upon American essentialism is so powerful that whatever educational philosophy developed in the first two centuries of American history was strongly imitative of them. True, a Franklin or an Emerson might flavor his beliefs with the ingredients of a new culture. Our first professional philosopher-educator, William T. Harris, who became a United States Commissioner of Education, is much more typically European, however, than native American in outlook.

Harris, a devout follower of Hegel, applied objective idealism with relentless consistency to the emerging public school system. Believing that reality unfolds according to an inevitable design of spiritual unity, he insisted that education's chief task is to acquiesce in this process. He even defended the rise of industrial capitalism as both necessary and desirable and thus implied that opposition or criticism by the worker is nothing short of traitorous. Like Sumner, who argued from the premises of "scientific" realism, Harris, the idealist, concluded that on the whole "whatever is, is right." The school, in short, is an agent for preserving inherited values and adjusting man to society. For this is in accord with absolute ontological law.‡

TWENTIETH-CENTURY ESSENTIALISTS

During the first quarter of the twentieth century the essentialist philosophy of education, although it dominated the practice of most schools, failed—with one exception—to add much to educational theory. But this one exception is of great importance. We refer to the "scientific" or "measurement" movement, which, although it claims to repudiate philosophy, actually functions more or less consistently upon the premises of realism. We mention this movement again below.

Until the 1930's essentialism continued to be overshadowed by progressivism in any explicit philosophic formulation. Then, in the depression years, a well-organized counterattack upon progressivism was launched, spearheaded by the Essentialist Committee for the Advancement of Education. The commander of the counterattack, William C. Bagley, although not regarded as a professional philosopher, considered himself a realist and appreciated the importance of a philosophic grounding for education. It is significant to note that he found himself identified with other thinkers who were educational idealists, outstanding among them Michael Demiashkevich, who coined the label "essentialist" and who cooperated closely with Bagley in the Committee.

Certain others who have contributed to the revival of the position prefer to avoid the essentialist label. One of these is the educational realist, Frederick S. Breed, whose formulation is in general endorsed by the student of comparative education Isaac L. Kandel.* Ross L. Finney should be mentioned as another influential social-educational realist. Among the educational idealists, besides Demiashkevich, two are outstanding: H. H. Horne and Robert Ulich. The latter, like Demiashkevich, was born in Europe and received a thorough philosophic training there before coming to America. All of these essentialist leaders have been influential professors of education.

‡ See Merle Curti, *The Social Ideas of American Educators,* Chap. 9.

* The author values personal letters on their philosophic positions from Breed and Kandel, as well as from Bagley.

The Essentialist Committee has been inactive since the death of Bagley in 1946, but, indirectly, its influence continues to be more vigorous, perhaps, than ever before.‡ Meanwhile, a number of other theoretical formulations strongly resembling essentialism, without so identifying themselves, have received justified attention—among them, that of J. Donald Butler, professor of the history and philosophy of education in a theological seminary, and Gordon K. Chalmers, college president and philosopher. Other books of essentialist tone, which we shall not discuss here because they are too inadequate as philosophic analyses, have appeared in connection with the attack on progressivism.*

Our roster would be incomplete without mention of at least four other educators who, although not primarily theorists, have contributed to the essentialist position: Charles H. Judd, psychologist and administrator; Henry C. Morrison, curriculum expert; George Strayer, administration expert; and Franklin Bobbitt, curriculum expert. Like all the others mentioned above, these leaders are sometimes difficult to characterize accurately because their dominantly essentialist outlook is qualified by eclectic elements of progressivist, perennialist, and other attitudes and practices.

Essentialist Concepts of Learning

The correspondence theory as presupposition

Although learning is studied as a psychological process, it also presupposes, more or less explicitly, an ontology, an epistemology, and an axiology; that is to say, it presupposes a body of beliefs about the nature of the reality we study, about the reliability of the knowledge we presumably derive from study, and about the values related both to reality and knowledge. The essentialist, especially if he is a realist, may refuse

‡ See William W. Brickman, "Essentialism Ten Years After," *School and Society*, May 15, 1948. This article contains footnote references to several periodical discussions of essentialism.

* The reader may wish to consult the "What to Read" items for Chapter 8 by such critics of progressivism as Bernard I. Bell, Mortimer Smith, Albert Lynd and Arthur Bestor, the last of whom is the most scholarly.

to acknowledge such presuppositions, but their presence is nicely illustrated in the fact that all varieties of essentialist learning rest more or less directly upon the correspondence theory of knowledge. This theory, we recall, seeks to establish the truth of an idea by the accuracy with which it presents or, more popularly, *re*-presents an object to the mind (see pp. 225-226).

The idealist and the realist, to be sure, differ in their interpretations of the nature of the object. The idealist will usually characterize the object as spiritual, immaterial, or ideal; the realist, as physical, material, or mechanical. In either case and despite a variety of refinements, the central device for testing ideas is the same, namely, by correspondence, or representation. Learning is then measured by the degree of skill, exactitude, and permanence with which such correspondence is effected.

Explicit support for this interpretation may be found in the essentialist camp itself, as illustrated by this statement of Horne, one of its most ardent representatives:

> . . . true ideas *represent* the situation correctly. The proposition, the sun shines, is true because the sun does shine. A true proposition states what is so. It is only a question of fact. There is no question of making the sun shine, or controlling the shining of the sun, but only of the fact whether the sun shines. Truth is the agreement of statement with fact . . . *This view is held by realists and idealists alike.* Realists and idealists differ, not in their theory of truth, but in their theory of reality.[5]

Educationally the significance of this approach to knowledge is to place students in a position of being receptive to and spectators of the contents of the universe. Whether the universe be conceived as primarily physical or spiritual and whether the particular course of study be concerned with history, art, geography, economics, biology, or any other segment of the whole body of knowledge—the aim of learning is receptive. Teachers are agents of that whole, selecting relevant elements from the vast welter of historical and contemporary facts, laws, practices, customs, achievements that compose its contents. They then organize learning situations that seem to them most conducive to conveying the elements selected.

In accordance with these theoretical premises it is practicable to determine by objective measures whether a particular student is entitled to promotion, graduation, or other honors. So far as he is able to *re*-present the world to which he has been exposed he is educated; so far as he is incapable of doing so he is uneducated. In this sense the correspondence theory of knowledge governs the construction and application of essentialist types of examinations. Strictly speaking, to examine means to determine the fullness and accuracy of the mind's agreement with reality.

In this preliminary statement we have sought to epitomize only the common core of essentialist learning. Even within these limits we are painfully aware that almost every theorist within the essentialist movement would insist upon further qualifications—qualifications governed to some extent by the divergent emphases of the idealists and realists within the movement.

The idealist theory of learning

Microcosm as Cue. Idealism as a philosophy of life tends, oftener than realism, to begin with the individual person, the much-emphasized "self," and to move outward from understanding of self toward understanding of the objective world. To apply the ontological terminology used in Chapter 7 to learning theory, the microcosm supplies the cue to the macrocosm. As the self learns about its own thought processes and gradually formulates laws of the mind it simultaneously acquires insight into the processes and laws of other selves and eventually of the universe. As conceived by Kant, time and space, for example, are really creations of the mind, even though they must be projected in external events before men can grasp their meaning.

It follows that idealism often tends to respect and to stress subjective psychological ideas and processes. Introspection and intuition, for example, are more congenial to it than to realism. Moreover, the capacity of the mind—in idealist theory—to combine related parts into qualitative wholes of meaning suggests that idealism thus far anticipates the Gestalt approach to learning.

On this subjective and personal premise, learning may be defined as the self-development of mind as spiritual substance. In this sense *mind creates itself*. And the kind of education that emphasizes the training of faculties—the ability to remember, to reason logically, to comprehend the unity among things, to know the "permanent" values and truths of our heritage—is usually supported even by essentialists of the idealist school who accept some of the newer findings of experimental psychology.

Despite considerable ambiguity in his exposition, this concept of learning appears to be generally accepted by Chalmers. He writes repeatedly of the individual as "valuable and subject to law within himself." Chalmers contrasts a "responsible liberalism," which is reminiscent of "early liberalism" as described in Chapter 6, with what he terms the "disintegrated liberalism" of Dewey and the progressivists, who, he claims, have too long diverted their followers from the truth that "the performance peculiar to the liberally educated man" is "writing and speaking and calculating. . . ."[6]

Macrocosm as Ground. But we have also found in our brief review of idealism that, when viewed in the great perspective of modern culture, it cannot be interpreted too exclusively in subjective, or individualist, terms. Although such an emphasis is inevitably strong, especially in democratic countries like England (recall the idealist Green) and America (recall Royce), the idealist's need to ground the individual in cosmic order is almost invariably stronger and cannot be suppressed. The idealist movement is ultimately an *objective* movement. As the potent tradition of Hegelianism reveals, it is a theory of the macrocosm, of the world, which the individual mirrors in himself (see pp. 217-220).†

Thus we return to the central feature of idealist learning. The individual learns as he gradually acquiesces in the spirituality of total Being, that is, of God. He may, to be sure, *begin* with himself in this process, for we must not disregard the idealist's stress upon *self-creation;* indeed, we feel a strong esthetic quality, reminiscent of Plato, in this spiritual outreaching. Nevertheless, except in the case of a reversion to subjective idealism, the idealists hold that the individual always comes to know himself better by having grasped his relationship to the cosmic ground. Learning does not usually *end* with the self.

The phraseologies with which this position is developed by con-

† It is doubtful whether most conventional textbooks in educational philosophy give anything approaching sufficient emphasis to the macrocosmic, objective side of idealism—an emphasis crucial to understanding its significance as a rationale for modern culture. For a more adequate interpretation, see the educational theory of the academic philosopher and objective idealist Theodore M. Greene in "Modern Philosophies and Education," *Fifty-fourth Yearbook,* Part I, National Society for the Study of Education.

temporary essentialists, of course, vary greatly. Horne speaks of the learner "as a finite personality growing into the likeness of an infinite ideal." He repeatedly calls attention to the purposeful nature of the cosmos, which one increasingly appreciates as one develops "reverence for the spiritual realities of existence." [7] Demiashkevich stresses divine laws and eternal truths, which all individuals should learn, and derives from this concept the need "to educate children for the respect and preservation of fundamental social values"—for the "ultimate certainty" of "metaphysical faith." [8] Chalmers refers frequently to an ontological "norm," which, although never precisely defined, carries overtones of objective idealism. At one point in his writing he goes so far as to predicate "the existence of a fixed and absolute God, no matter what our changing ideas of Him may be, and of a definite and abiding truth, no matter how liable to error may be the man-made concepts by which . . . we try more perfectly to express it." [9]

By comparison with these theorists, Ulich is more ready to include scientific and naturalistic ideas within his theory of learning, even though, as a disciple of the idealist Kant, he builds his outlook upon a firm belief in "transpersonal" spheres of reality, a "deeper dimension of Being," and "the immanent laws of the universe." While often radiant with ideas that would be applauded by progressivists, he states that "the mind of man . . . participates in a higher rational order which represents the unity of principles and laws. . . ." Hence, after all possible concessions, Ulich's over-all educational position rests upon belief in a spiritual universe that governs all learning and serves as a final judge of what is and is not good education. In a book called (by the idealist Hocking) his "magnum opus," Ulich pleads for "common participation in the world of the mind . . . ," for the hope "that we may arrange our lives according to universal laws . . . ," for a "feeling of unity with the All-Embracing . . ." and "the divine ground. . . ." ‡

A younger idealist-educator, Butler, summarizes well the general position: "there is that . . . harmony of relation between individual man and the cosmos which is necessary to the basic well-being of selves as selves." Man and cosmos are "ultimately united in one Creative Person who *is* all that ultimately is. . . ." [10]

‡ See Ulich, *Crisis and Hope in American Education,* p. 168; *Fundamentals of Democratic Education,* pp. 97, 151, 143; *The Human Career—A Philosophy of Self-Transcendence,* pp. 232, 235, 245.

THE REALIST THEORY OF LEARNING

The Influence of Thorndike. Despite the continued influence of idealist theories of learning on school theory and practice, realist views have undoubtedly received far greater attention from recent educational psychology. For example, the widely read *Forty-first Yearbook* (Part II) of the National Society for the Study of Education, "The Psychology of Learning," scarcely recognizes idealism (at best, it is slightly implied by the Gestaltists) but gives preponderant space to the two realist positions, behaviorism and connectionism.

The outstanding American realist in educational psychology is Edward L. Thorndike, to whose theory of connectionism we have above referred and to which we shall refer below (see pp. 224, 247, 250).† Here we merely recall that, despite significant contributions to the science of learning, Thorndike is not at all as immune to philosophic assumptions as he and his followers sometimes wish us to believe. Not only does connectionism seek to reduce the study of the human being largely to mechanistic, quantitative explanations analagous to, if not identical with, those of the physical world ("whatever exists, exists in some amount," Thorndike insists [11]) but it also tends strongly to encourage learning through adjustment to "the given." By "stamping in" and "stamping out" responses to stimuli, the teacher acts as the agent of reinforcement for habits and beliefs congenial to the dominant institutions of the inherited culture (see pp. 272-273). The S-R-bond psychology, as a derivation of this theory, is still possibly the most influential one in teacher-training programs.

Examples of Realist Learning Theory. Although not all realists in educational philosophy subscribe formally to connectionism, most realist beliefs about learning are similar to connectionist views. The key argument of Breed, for example, is that "the criterion of truth is regarded as conformity or consistency" with "objective facts"; that "knowledge is not a process of creation, but of disclosure" of reality; that "the constitution of the external world finally determines" the validity of ideas; that this "concurrence" is properly called the "correspondence test of truth"; and that the "realist accepts scientific facts and laws as part of the relatively unchangeable foundation upon which he builds his enterprises."

† See Edward L. Thorndike, *Selected Writings from a Connectionist's Psychology.*

Breed's efforts to reconcile his theories of functional learning with his realist predilections only confuse his thinking. Despite numerous amendments and contradictions, the total effect is one of response to the externally prior, thus giving practical support to Thorndikian views of learning in an epistemological rather than a psychological framework.‡

Bagley's realism reflects the influence of the biological more than the physical sciences. For him emergent evolution is probably the central ontological principle of the modern world, and in this respect he is sometimes close to progressivism. His eclectic tendencies, moreover, make it quite impossible to associate him consistently with connectionism or any other one psychological school. Nevertheless, the Essentialist Platform, which he was largely instrumental in formulating, lends support to the correspondence theory; its planks on learning include: familiarity with man's past as a basis for interpretation of the present, recognition of permanent moral values, and the authority of plain facts.* In *Education and Emergent Man,* which he regarded as his most representative book, his main theme supports mental discipline, definite and stable values, knowledge of backgrounds, in short, "the conservation of well established fact and principle. . . ."[12] All of these beliefs, it should be noted, are congenial to idealists as well as to realists.

The realist on whom we shall draw for a final illustration of essentialist learning theory is the sociologist-philosopher Finney. As in our treatment of Bagley and others, we can do no more than select the main threads of his thought, possibly at some cost to its occasional complexity. Finney's greatest interest is in "the social nature of mental life," which he finds to be primarily "passive mentation." By this key term he means that the great multitude of men normally and uncritically accept what the culture provides them and that this is entirely in accord with what "nature has decreed." "Education is therefore the reproductive process of the social life; by it the social heritage is reproduced into each rising generation."

Conservative anthropologists and sociologists, such as Sumner, thus apparently have a greater direct or indirect influence upon Finney than do

‡ See Frederick S. Breed, *Education and the New Realism,* pp. 35f., 49, 54, 96f., 165. See also his chapter in "Philosophies of Education," *Forty-first Yearbook,* Part I, National Society for the Study of Education.

* See William C. Bagley, "An Essentialist's Platform for the Advancement of American Education," *Educational Administration and Supervision,* April 1938.

the psychologists, such as Thorndike. Nevertheless, his educational theory is surprisingly similar to that of Thorndike, for although he recognizes the importance of problem solving and other kinds of "active mentation," as Thorndike does, he gives much greater weight to *re*-presenting the acceptable in the learning situation—and in this case the *culturally* acceptable. The fact that, although he is a sociologist, he never disputes the hereditary nature of intelligence also offers support to the Thorndikian position. His educational doctrine, which rests upon the major premise that the masses of the people have rather low intelligence and are best taught by a kind of "passive mentation," is perfectly congenial to the view that learning consists chiefly of building S-R bonds.†

The Essentialist Curriculum

The Study of Common Denominators as Semantic Exercise. It should be clear from the discussion above that the essentialist curriculum is a miniature of the world that teachers, administrators, and their supporters wish young people to regard as the real, true, and valuable world. This does not, of course, mean that essentialism advocates only one curriculum pattern for all types of schools; many different patterns have been proposed at different times and places.

Despite this variety, if we search for common denominators, we can find them revealed in the Essentialist Platform. It advocates, for example, "a rich, sequential, and systematic curriculum based on an irreducible body of knowledge, skills, and attitudes common to a democratic culture." It is a curriculum, moreover, in which there is "Stress upon adequate mastery of the content . . ." and "Presentation of this material as economically as possible . . ." according to "rigorous standards of scholastic attainment as a condition of promotion." It is the right of the child "to be guided, disciplined, and instructed." [13]

Such phrases as these invite profitable exercise in semantic analysis,

† See Ross L. Finney, *A Sociological Philosophy of Education,* pp. 46-71. Compare the more liberal-toned socio-cultural theory of learning by an academic realist, James K. Feibleman, in "Modern Philosophies and Education," *op. cit.*

for their precise meanings depend upon philosophic reference points. Thus, the phrase "irreducible body of knowledge, skills, and attitudes" raises the question of how we can determine what is "irreducible," a question that cannot be answered without searching into essentialism's foundational beliefs. There we discover the presumed existence of absolute laws and pre-existent processes and facts. Every individual must know these in order to adjust to the universe and, hence, to the culture of which they are the very fiber. Again, the implications of such phrases as "mastery of the content" or "rigorous standards" require us to attune our minds to these laws, processes, facts—and to do so with the utmost thoroughness, persistence, and exactitude.

On such terms the role of the teacher becomes that of a liaison officer between the world, as it is portrayed through the curriculum, and the receptive student. Hence, to the essentialist it is highly desirable that maximum receptivity be controlled by means of strict scholastic records, penalties, rewards, attentiveness, obedience.

The Idealist Curriculum. Common denominators, however, do not lay bare the variations from type that one finds among both idealists and realists. For example, such idealists as Ulich would undoubtedly insist upon a more flexible, more individualized program of study than the Essentialist Platform seems to recommend. In some of his writings, indeed, Ulich reveals close affinity with the progressivist "core curriculum" and similar proposals.‡ But even Ulich, perhaps the most cosmopolitan and forward looking of living American essentialists, accommodates in his curriculum proposals considerable traditional subject matter and method. Training in foreign languages is particularly stressed for its "thoroughness and exactness," and he insists, of course, upon religious understanding of the spiritual universe. It is, however, only fair to mention that Ulich is himself unhappy with the label, essentialism, as he is with "isms" of every kind.*

Horne, too, reveals the influence of progressivist thought in the curriculum area. He urges us to consider the needs and abilities of children; and his "essential studies" include the scientific method, the inorganic and organic physical world, the human environment, and appreciation of as well as skill in the arts. But Horne's language affords

‡ See Ulich, *Crisis and Hope in American Education,* Chap. 3; and *Fundamentals of Democratic Education,* pp. 207, 210.

* See Ulich, *The Human Career,* pp. 240ff.

equally good semantic practice; indeed, such a sentence as the following is quite meaningless unless judged in the context of his guiding beliefs:

> The chosen subject-matter should teach pupils to know the facts and opinions they need to know in order to feel and act as they need to feel and act; to feel as they should feel about the values of living in order to think and act as they should; and to do the useful, proper, and right things in order that they may think and feel as they should.[14]

What does he mean by "need to know," by "should feel," by the "useful, proper, and right things"? The answer is that these concepts and commandments are derived from "a sense of cosmic adjustment"—from the "mutual fitness of man and his environment" [15]—a position wholly congenial to those habits of conservation to which even the liberal-tempered Horne thus lends his heaviest support.

Butler, who is probably the ablest disciple of Horne, adds little to such formulations. He strongly believes that "each oncoming generation should be given opportunity for appreciative acquaintance with the Bible, that its Author may have the occasion to communicate Himself." [16] Like Horne, Butler gladly concedes the value of some progressivist practices.

Cultural conservation by means of the idealist curriculum is supported most unequivocally by Demiashkevich. Although he, too, sometimes pays compliments, albeit begrudgingly, to the influence of progressivism, the weight of his thought is emphatically on the side of the "residual functions" of the school, such as "intellectual training" and "character building"—functions that require heavy doses of formal discipline through memory, examinations, book learning, repetition, perseverance, "reasonable punishment," and reverence for the unchanging "constants" of morality.*

Chalmers' curriculum proposals on the college level are, as a whole consistent with Demiashkevich's on the school level. In stressing the humanities much more than the sciences he seeks to highlight his belief in "the person"—especially the creative, imaginative person, as symbolized by the poet. He has very little admiration for the types of curriculum favored by progressivists.†

* See Michael Demiashkevich, *Introduction to the Philosophy of Education*, pp. 165ff., 309, 351.

† See Gordon Chalmers, *The Republic and the Person*, Chaps. 6, 9, 14, 15.

The Realist Curriculum. Like idealists, realist philosophers of education vary among themselves in their views on the curriculum. Bagley, for example, is more ready than many of his associates to favor a modified activity program for elementary students. Breed often pays tribute to similar curriculum practices, even though his application of the "disclosure" theory of knowledge, with its concomitants of passive and receptive learning, would negate the effects of such practices. Finney sees in the study of such subjects as Latin an appalling waste of time.

Despite these minor concessions to progressivism, realist essentialists are generally opposed to both the spirit and substance of the progressivist curriculum. Their theory rests upon the broad belief that the curriculum consists of a series of blocks built one upon the other, from simple beginnings in numbers and language to very complex structures. Also, with Bagley once again their most vociferous spokesman, they insist that old views of "transfer of training" still have validity. Even though some of the connectionists tried to prove, under Thorndike's leadership, that we do not transfer what we have learned in one specific response to another specific response, Bagley argues that we still transfer general "traits," such as "persistence, neatness, ability to concentrate on difficult tasks" and "self-confidence." Most essentialists argue that the transfer of general traits justifies the inclusion in the curriculum of rigorous courses in Latin, mathematics, and natural science, all of which—according to the essentialist view—develop habits of intellectual discipline that are themselves transferable even if the contents of courses are not.‡

The Thorndikian concern for specificity of response as essential to learning is better exemplified by Bobbitt and others who have tried to apply mechanistic techniques to determining the major objectives of education. By analyzing the precise activities and purposes of adults, they have attempted to determine exactly the desirable contents of a curriculum. While this "job analysis" approach has potential merit for a philosophy of education of fairly radical intent, its primary effect has been thus far to reinforce the *status quo*. Bobbitt, particularly, premises that the aims of adults are determined by customary purposes. This is an assumption that so far fails to penetrate the surface of tradition and convention that it allows him to set as an educational objective the cultivation of a religious "attitude and desire of obedience to the immutable

‡ See Bagley, *Education and Emergent Man,* pp. 82-93; Harold Rugg, *Foundations for American Education,* pp. 134f.

and eternal laws which appear to exist in the nature of things" and of confidence "in the beneficence of these laws." The characteristic essentialist flavor of this statement is to tempt individuals to accept uncritically "immutable and eternal laws," thus reinforcing the culture's propensity to conform with pre-established authority derived from the past.*

Morrison's theory is another interesting sample of the realist approach to curriculum building. Although he is himself impatient with formal philosophy, his writings contain many beliefs that seriously require philosophic inspection. He holds that the supreme purpose of education is "adjustment," interpreting the term, according to a central postulate of realism, as adjustment to "natural law"—to "conformity with the general trend of all evolution" and "to the conditions of civilized existence." Like many essentialists, Morrison never questions whether this trend and these conditions are generally satisfactory, simply implying that they are.† Judd shares Morrison's governing beliefs and overall position with, however, some qualification.‡

General Education in a Free Society. The continued vitality of the essentialist curriculum is no more graphically revealed than by the wide reception given to the Harvard Report, *General Education in a Free Society,* a book that continues to be praised by Chalmers and other essentialist leaders. Its varied roster of authors includes academicians ranging from two biologists to two philosophers. Since one of the latter is Ulich, we may assume that his own thinking is embodied in this report, although he has since conceded that the report deserves some criticism. The introduction by President James B. Conant states that "the document represents a unanimity of opinion not based on compromise between divergent views." [17] If, as we may rightly suspect, a realist position is held by some of the twelve writers, this unanimity again illustrates that a working partnership with idealists is practicable and justifies our re-emphasizing similarities rather than differences between these two wings of essentialism.

Ulich's beliefs, or at least beliefs with which he has hitherto been in accord, are illustrated by the attempt of the authors to maintain a balanced consideration of both "heritage and change." Although they acknowledge the significance of some of the industrial and other cul-

* See Franklin Bobbitt, *How to Make a Curriculum,* page 24.
† See Henry C. Morrison, *Basic Principles in Education,* pp. 345, 365-384.
‡ See I. B. Berkson, *Education Faces the Future,* pp. 280-287.

tural events of the past century—events that impose new requirements on the curriculum and that demand a program of both general and specialized education—the authors have such a deep regard for the cultural heritage that they believe "a received idea of the good . . . is in fact necessary to education." The Report does not make clear the meaning of "received" in this context, but it does make clear its tenet that one major task of education is to perpetuate "common beliefs." Viewed in the total context of the statement these "common beliefs" may be variously identified as: "an appeal to things as they are"; values "rooted in facts"; "human ideals . . . somehow a part of nature"; or "stable truths."[18]

Supported by such essentialist premises, the Report endorses many traditional subject matters and methods. Although it makes a number of curriculum proposals that its authors regard as innovations, it offers in general merely a recombining of conventional subject matters that largely retains traditional high school and college courses of study and makes relatively few additions of new kinds of material. The Report expresses mildly the schools' need to face the great controversial issues of our time but does not emphasize that to deal with these is a central obligation of contemporary education. Much greater concern is expressed for such honorable and safe traits as the ability to think effectively, to communicate clearly, to make relevant judgments, to discriminate among values. Memorization of passages of literature, study of foreign languages, including Latin, a study of American history that is "strongly factual in nature," courses in mathematics and science to be taught by *re*-presentation (thus presupposing the correspondence theory of knowledge)—these are typical of the Report's curriculum proposals.[19]

It is to be noted that many concessions are made to beliefs found in other philosophies and practices. These are not, however, woven into an organic, unified statement of the authors' position. Thus, although they recognize, for example, the pragmatic conception of truth, the authors have little regard for established psychological principles of functional learning. In sum, the tone of the Report is essentialist also in its strong eclectic tendencies.

Appraised in the kind of cultural framework that is fundamental to educational understanding, but which its authors largely disregard, *General Education in a Free Society* emerges as the most important educational apologia for cultural conservation presented in the name of "middle-of-the-road" liberalism that has appeared since the Essentialist Platform of 1938.

Essentialist Views of the School's Role in Society

The general position

American essentialists without exception believe in democracy. Some of them have been ardent defenders of the Bill of Rights and other cherished foundations of our government, and it is even possible to find among them educators who, on specific political issues, have assumed moderately radical positions.*

At the same time *as a group* they tend to interpret democracy in terms more closely related to the "early liberalism" of Locke than to the "later liberalism" of Dewey (see pp. 163-168). Democracy is likely to be conceived less as an experimental process of interaction between individual and society, between means and ends, than as a corpus of inherited principles with their concomitant institutions, which education has the duty to convey and citizens the duty to revere and respect. The student may detect, therefore, a strong note of historic individualism in many essentialists—and an equally strong resistance to the welfare state or other developments that seek to modify democracy in a more socialized direction.†

There are, however, some realist and idealist educators who support, on philosophic grounds, a more contemporary, progressivist-tempered view. Idealists, influenced perhaps by Rousseau, may conceive of democracy as a spiritual fusion of selves—a kind of super-person.‡ Realists may regard the trend away from *laissez faire* individualism as a progressive symbol of organic evolution. §

* This was true especially of Bagley during his lifetime. Kandel and Ulich have often shown "later liberal" attitudes on specific issues.

† Breed and Chalmers (one a realist, the other an idealist) are outstanding examples.

‡ Meiklejohn is the best exponent—indeed, more than any other idealist educator he projects his thinking in a radical direction. For this reason it is not possible to include him among the essentialists as a group. Ulich, too, as we have seen, is frequently atypical.

§ Bagley is an example.

On the whole, however, perhaps because so many essentialists tend to take for granted that schools fulfill their primary obligation when they transmit cultural habits and practices from generation to generation, they have a less penetrating and persistent interest in the school's role in society than in learning and the curriculum. Some essentialists, such as Butler, almost never express any views on the subject of school-and-society. In those writings in which the subject is discussed at all, the essentialist position sometimes lacks consistency—among the statements of different essentialists or within the statements of any one.

The essays of the realist Kandel are probably representative of the predominant tone as well as the inconsistencies of the essentialist position on the school's role in society. He has frequently repeated that the primary and proper responsibility of education is to "reproduce the type, to transmit the social heritage, and to adjust the individual to the society" by inculcating facts, skills, knowledge.[20] He has on occasion, however, respected a less acquiescent and more creative cultural role for the school.

A similar observation might be made of the position of such idealists as Ulich and Horne, whose discussion of school and society also swings back and forth from the pole of education as cultural reinforcement to the pole of education as a guide to social change. Actually, they explicitly attempt to accommodate both aims within their theory. They might assert, for example, that the aim of education is both to reinforce established essentials (principles and practices drawn from the cultural heritage) and to change the culture progressively toward perfection, so as to include further essentials (not yet discovered but awaiting discovery) in the all-inclusive reality. Nevertheless, one cannot find any single treatment of the subject by these writers that does not convey a sense of eclecticism, or at least of ambiguity.†

A common character of the essentialist position may, however, be adduced from the literature: since society is integral with reality as a whole, it is also integral with and subject to the same spiritual or physical universalities as other aspects of reality are—universalities of law, order, custom, which it is the primary duty of education to disclose and to perpetuate. Although variously formulated and amended, this is the explicit or implicit major premise of all leading essentialists.

Let us now consider some practical social applications of this

† See Ulich, *Crisis and Hope in American Education;* Herman H. Horne, in "Philosophies of Education," *op. cit.*

premise. What, for example, does essentialism contribute to the question of how and by whom education should be controlled?

How essentialists control education

As agents of the inherited culture, essentialism holds, schools should be planned and directed by those who most authoritatively represent the economic, political, and other institutions of the culture. Indeed, such institutions should provide the model for educational structures and practices.

The "Line-Staff" Pattern of Control. In this deep-rooted traditional belief of the essentialists we may observe the intellectual foundation for the widespread acceptance of the "line-staff" administrative structure, in accordance with which the direction and operation of schools is modeled closely upon efficient methods of modern business. Superintendents and other officials are vested with authority by boards of education presumably representing the community. These officials delegate their power to principals and other lower staff officials through descending levels of authority; thereby, the policies and programs established by the governing school boards are correctly administered by staff members down the line. If the administrators are realists, they probably often utilize "objective" fact finding, testing, and measuring in settling such problems as class size, grade placement, promotion, and homogeneous grouping. School board members, standing at the top of the hierarchy of power, tend to be sympathetic to this kind of administration because they typically accept such arrangements and procedures in their own business and professional lives.

As some essentialists have modified their beliefs about the curriculum, some have also begun to modify this pattern of school administration. Thus, such influential experts among them as Strayer now advocate a more democratic administrative procedure, including the participation of teachers *within* the line-staff framework.‡ Broadly considered, however, essentialism has scarcely modified the basic position that the school not only should serve those who have become or are to become leaders of our economic and political institutions but should follow the orders of present leaders.

‡ See National Education Association, Educational Policies Commission, *The Structure and Administration of Education in American Democracy.*

This does not mean that essentialism would limit education's services to the select few; all children and youth are to be educated. To be sure, the high school curriculum ought to provide adequate subject matter for those who are preparing for college and thereby for an eventual place in the upper stratum of community life. (Here, indeed, is one of the central, if not always explicit, cultural causes of the curriculum principles we have noted above; for the good college is itself assumed to be essentialist in structure and aim.) But the school must also provide industrial or other kinds of training for millions of future workers—workers who must be sufficiently skilled to serve the economic order and hence the dominant group that shapes and administers the school's policies, workers who learn that it is to their own advantage to be loyal to those upon whom they are financially dependent. Essentialism's entire position on school administration is implicitly or explicitly premised on the fact that the capitalist-industrialist economic society is itself line-staff—with the lines of authority running from the top echelons of managers to the lowest ranks of workers.*

Essentialist Discipline in the Context of Control. Essentialist acquiescence in capitalist-industrialist society may help us to understand why the essentialist conception of discipline also extends far beyond the school and into the culture. Such thinkers as Bagley and Ulich are primarily interested in the *intellectual* discipline they consider necessary to learning. But the cultivation of such learning habits as memorization and acquisition of facts in sequential order are educationally suited to building the cultural habits needed by efficient, obedient workers. Even distasteful and uninviting work sometimes becomes in this setting a desirable educational objective.†

Although some essentialists only imply their support of such "transfer of training," others very directly express their support. Finney is particularly frank. He endorses a program of "habituation," which "precedes thinking" and is determined by the child's "elders." Since great masses of people are incapable of serious thinking, what is needed is

> . . . a system of school discipline as inflexible and final as that which obtains in the army. It should be kept out of sight for the most part, to be sure. On the surface of things the school should

* See Curti, *op. cit.,* Chap. 6.
† See Demiashkevich, *op. cit.,* p. 313.

> present the appearance of voluntary self-government by the students themselves . . . But the student body should understand perfectly that absolutely irresistible compulsion is closeted with the faculty and board, to be used to the uttermost if necessary. And it should be brought to bear upon the lessons as well as upon school decorum and ordinary morals.[21]

The opening chapters of Finney's extraordinary volume do not so clearly express this theme. But the heart of his argument is that the "duller half of the school population" must inevitably depend upon "memoriter training and sheer drill" which will enable them to follow their leaders as they grow into working adults.

The Importance of Leadership. The essentialist position on the relation of leadership to control and discipline may easily be inferred from its general position on administration. To most essentialists the director of the school is comparable to the director of society: the former is the best judge of the teacher's or the student's interests, just as the latter is the best judge of the citizen's interests.

In certain essentialist writings the language in which the role of leadership is described seems almost identical with that of perennialism (see pp. 339-340). Both Demiashkevich and Finney, for example, plead for the cultivation of an intellectual and moral elite that would conceive, formulate, and direct the general policies of society. It seems clear, therefore, that some essentialists—their protestations to the contrary notwithstanding—are in disagreement with conceptions of democracy that place ultimate responsibility for policy shaping in the hands of the majority of ordinary people.‡

Although others, such as Bagley, have more confidence in popular capacity, the essentialist group as a whole holds that the leader is qualified by his superiority to determine generally the education and activities of those in his charge. From this position we may derive the import of another important plank in the Essentialist Platform: "Protection of the child in his right to be guided, disciplined, and instructed"—the responsibility of the mature for the control of the immature.[22] In the context of the whole position, the "mature" are to be identified with those who, because of intellect, authority, or prestige, are able to grasp the truest

‡ See Demiashkevich, *op. cit.*, pp. 402ff.; Finney, *op. cit.*, p. 341. Compare Russell Kirk, *A Program for Conservatives.*

and most valuable characteristics of reality—a reality conceived as ordered and governed by pre-existent spiritual or natural laws happily congenial to the inherited culture.

OTHER TYPICAL SOCIAL BELIEFS

Although individual exponents of the essentialist philosophy touch upon many other social beliefs, we cite merely a few samples.

On the issue of federal aid to the schools, it is difficult to generalize about the essentialist position. Some essentialists favor federal aid, but many are critical of any trend that might weaken the tradition of local school autonomy. Hence they are almost sure to be vehemently opposed, as a group, to any kind of federal control. Also, they strongly support the heritage of separation of church and state. Although many idealist educators would favor nonsectarian religious instruction in the public schools, even they are skeptical of any encroachments by organized religion upon the "autonomy" of education.

How, then, may the schools become a more powerful social force? The essentialist's central answer is likely to be that they must, above all, repudiate the "weaknesses" of progressivism in favor of the "strengths" that can be derived only from implementing the beliefs about learning, the curriculum, and control that stem from the philosophic roots of idealism and/or realism. If we consider that these essentialist beliefs are also, in various ways, the roots of modern culture with its array of established economic, political, and social arrangements, it is not surprising that one finds little careful analysis of such issues as the organization of the profession for economic and political action. Such disregard is, indeed, eloquent testimony that most essentialists do not consider the subject worth much if any attention, because they find it difficult to consider education in such a social context. Rather, they tend to dismiss teachers' unions affiliated with labor and other forms of bold participation in cultural change as "radical" and "extreme."

We may cite as representative and revealing of their common orientation Judd's encompassing belief that it "is not proper for the educational system to attempt to control the policies of the state and the nation." [23] It is not proper for the reason, explicit or not, that "the state and the nation" (more correctly, the culture) control education. The conception that the public schools might possibly be the *ally* of other cultural institutions in a democracy—that they should interact with and even help to direct economic and social events or to effect political change—is foreign to the attitudes and habits underlying the essentialist's typical codification of his responsibilities and tasks.

Notes

[1] Quoted from Robert Ulich, *History of Educational Thought,* p. 204.
[2] *Ibid.,* p. 261.
[3] *Ibid.,* pp. 286f.
[4] *Ibid.,* pp. 281, 283.
[5] Herman H. Horne, *The Democratic Philosophy of Education,* pp. 500f. Copyright 1932 by The Macmillan Company and reprinted with their permission (italics supplied).
[6] Gordon K. Chalmers, *The Republic and the Person,* pp. 5, 9-43, 149.
[7] National Society for the Study of Education, *Forty-first Yearbook,* Part I, "Philosophies of Education," pp. 154-156.
[8] Michael Demiashkevich, *Introduction to the Philosophy of Education,* pp. 348, 143, 358.
[9] Chalmers, *op. cit.,* pp. 248, 23.
[10] J. Donald Butler, *Four Philosophies and Their Practice in Education and Religion,* pp. 490, 492.
[11] Quoted from Harold Rugg, *Foundations for American Education,* pp. 125f.
[12] William C. Bagley, *Education and Emergent Man,* pp. 154-163.
[13] Essentialist Committee, "Summary of Theses" (mimeographed).
[14] Quoted from National Society for the Study of Education, *Forty-first Yearbook,* Part I, "Philosophies of Education," p. 160. Published 1942 and reprinted with the permission of the Society.
[15] *Ibid.,* pp. 162f.
[16] Butler, *op. cit.,* p. 519.
[17] Harvard Committee, *General Education in a Free Society,* p. vi.
[18] *Ibid.,* pp. 46, 151, 73, 106.
[19] *Ibid.,* pp. 65, 113, 141.
[20] Isaac L. Kandel, *Conflicting Theories of Education,* p. 32.
[21] Ross L. Finney, *A Sociological Philosophy of Education,* p. 480. See also pp. 395, 467-479.
[22] Essentialist Committee, *op. cit.*
[23] Charles H. Judd, *Education and Social Progress,* p. 268.

CHAPTER 9

A Cultural Evaluation of Essentialism

ESSENTIALISM AS A PHILOSOPHIC AND EDUCATIONAL MOVEMENT seems less willing to investigate its own cultural motivations than, for example, progressivism is. This unwillingness may derive from the fact that essentialism has been so strongly identified with the inherited characteristics of modern culture that it has failed to achieve the perspective on itself that more dissident movements are able to achieve. An individual whose strongest motive is to "adjust" by complying with the demands of his environment is unlikely to probe deeply into the cultural forces that affect him. Likewise, a philosophy of education-and-culture primarily dedicated to conserving hitherto dominant patterns of belief and conduct is unlikely to examine too critically the complex milieu surrounding it.

This does not mean, of course, that essentialists are oblivious of social change. All of them, whether educators like Bagley, academic philosophers like Hocking, or conservative essayists like Kirk, make many comments upon the instabilities, the failures and successes of our culture. Bagley, for example, has attempted to attribute the weaknesses of public education—as epitomized by progressivism—to the tidal waves of increasing school population and thus to the expediency of the low academic standards that have accompanied this huge increase.* More insightful observations have been made by Ulich; indeed, he has expressed such concern with the cultural crises of our time that, on this score even more than in his regard for functional learning and other features of progressivism, his position cannot be classified as essentialist without considerable qualification.†

Let us grant, however, that all genuine essentialists, as philosophers who operate on a constructive and not a complacent level of belief, are more or less willing to recognize the strains and conflicts in our culture. Let us grant, also, that all of them are earnestly concerned to defend their own concepts of the "democratic way of life." Even so, our major evaluative judgment is that the position they represent is not, for our age, an adequate position. Their critique of our inherited culture, when they offer one, is unable sufficiently to release its ties to that culture. Constructed primarily to sanction the hopes and ambitions of modern industrial civilization, essentialism can no more severely challenge the major assumptions of its own intellectual and educational system than it can repudiate the culture that has sired those beliefs. Essentialism, as the child of the postmedieval world, is its devoted heir.

In the history of cultures, however, the service performed by the conservation of beliefs is not always equally defensible. It is less and less defensible in our culture. An age sickened by crisis—racked by revolutions in technology, politics, economics, even human nature—is not to be cured by sophisticated apologias for time-honored structures and habits. It is primarily for this reason that essentialism, despite all its contributions to our modern past, is now an unsatisfactory philosophy. We develop this contention through these topics:

1. modern idealism and realism: underpinnings of modern culture;
2. the conserving role of essentialist education; and
3. the obsolescence of essentialism.

* See William C. Bagley, "The Significance of the Essentialist Movement in Educational Theory," *Classical Journal,* March 1939.

† See Robert Ulich, *Conditions of Civilized Living; Crisis and Hope in American Education;* and *The Human Career—A Philosophy of Self-Transcendence.*

Modern Idealism and Realism: Underpinnings of Modern Culture

Philosophy outside the context of culture

Philosophy, as we observed above (see pp. 20-25, 70-74), is an indispensable tool for any mature person—certainly for any professional worker in education—who seeks to be clear about his basic beliefs and, hence, about the actions that should follow from them. But any attempt at philosophy that fails, for example, to appraise beliefs in the living context of culture, and fails thereby to perform adequately its function of clarification, performs only a disservice better not even attempted.

That too much of the so-called philosophy taught in our teacher-training institutions fails in this way is well illustrated by several textbooks used widely in educational courses. Many such books classify educational theories into three conventional types—idealism, realism, and pragmatism—with the ocasional inclusion of two or three others, such as naturalism or scholasticism. But none of these expositions ever clearly poses the question of how far conventional philosophies are the product and rationale of the institutions, habits, attitudes, and customs that compose the man-made environment called modern culture. Instead, the reader is asked to assume that every philosophy is primarily an intellectual creation that somehow generates itself by its own logic, that each incubates its own self-contained system of beliefs, as though the culture scarcely existed. In effect, the student is left to choose arbitrarily among these philosophies, perhaps solely on the basis of his temperamental preferences. Lacking any other legitimate criterion of choice, he comes to the dangerous conclusion that one philosophy can hardly be determined, except by personal preference, to be more valid or defensible than any of the others. Such half-finished, irresponsible philosophizing heavily contributes to the superficiality, confusion, and frustration so chronic today among people in general and among teachers in particular.

Our position, in contradistinction to this overintellectualized approach, is that thinkers who build profound conceptions of the world are also real human beings living in real cultures. However sophisticated their interpretations may be, they cannot escape the cultural impact. This is no less true, moreover, of philosophies that choose to exclude explicit awareness of the social or psychological roots of their central beliefs than of other philosophies that deliberately and consciously include such awareness within their total conceptions. It is so apparent, for example, that pragmatism is one of the latter types of philosophy that even such textbooks as are described above cannot altogether ignore its cultural motivations. But that idealism and realism also reflect as well as support an important era in cultural evolution—even support it by providing an underpinning—seldom if ever seems to occur to the authors of these textbooks. Hence, the reader is never directly confronted with the question of why, if idealism and realism are so completely different, the same educational-cultural outlook should be sufficiently congenial to representatives of both as to invite common membership in, let us say, the Essentialist Committee. Such textbooks also fail to provide the reader with any sharp judgmental tools by which to analyze both philosophies in broad historical perspective and thereby to determine what their significance may be for a time such as our own.

Philosophy within the context of culture

The reader who follows the main road of modern philosophy in the context of culture achieves a very different perspective upon the relative values of alternative philosophies. Acknowledging that many bypaths, short-cuts, and blind alleys have lured minor philosophers, the student may, nevertheless, observe that the main road has been traveled by the most influential philosophers in an audacious effort to accomplish one objective: to supplant the static and closed world-view of feudal culture with one that would be more congenial to the economic, scientific, and political events that, beginning with the Renaissance, transformed the character of Europe and America.

Science and the Industrial Order. The cultural relations of modern philosophy may be clarified by another reference to the rise of modern physical science and the industrial order. Since Copernicus, as we pointed out in Chapter 7, science has sought to explain the phenomena of physical nature by objective, quantitative canons—canons that exclude caprice, revelation, magic, or mere dogmatic authority. During the modern period, too, philosophers have sought to produce an organized and consistent system of beliefs that would be in harmony with the parallel scientific study of the universe, society, and man. Descartes, Hobbes, Spinoza, Locke, Kant—all of these and many others dedicated themselves to this tremendous task.

What we have not sufficiently emphasized in our discussions above is that modern science itself arose because of the occurrence of cultural events that encouraged and supported the revolutionary departures that it symbolizes. These events include the exploration of uncharted seas and continents, the construction of great cities, and the rapid growth of a new type of industrial system called capitalism.

Capitalism, as a profit-making economy, utilizes very different productive techniques from those utilized by the feudal economy, techniques that require the continuous collaboration of science. For, whereas feudalism was based largely on handcraftsmanship—on the production of single commodities by single individuals—the industrial economy is based upon mass methods of production, which are made possible only by the vastly greater speed and efficiency of machine *technology* (a term by which we denote the "marriage" of science and economics). Indeed, despite the great contributions that have been made by "pure science" divorced from practical interests, and despite the influence of other factors, such as climate or nationalism, we tend to agree with those cultural historians who assert that the insatiable appetite of the industrial system for better instruments of production has probably given greater impetus to the development of science than any other single factor.‡

At the same time that the processes of nature were being subjected to scientific explanation thinkers were hard at work exploring social and individual processes and attempting to explain them by comparable principles. Thus, Adam Smith and his associates sought to formulate economic and political laws with the same finality and regularity that they ascribed to activity in the natural world. Hume and others prepared the ground for an equally inclusive science of mental processes—a psychology that would explain the phenomena of the mind in terms as objective as those of modern chemistry or physics. Pervading many such efforts (for example, Berkeley's) was a deep religious concern to show that the elements and events of both inanimate and animate nature are the ordi-

‡ The generalizations in this paragraph, while crucial to our interpretation of essentialism and, indeed, of all philosophies of education, need to be qualified and elaborated at many points in order to interpret adequately the complex patterns of modern history. It would be extremely helpful, therefore, for the student to consult such references as are provided in "What to Read" in the Appendix.

nances of a spiritual being Who is Himself the supreme Maker of law the Author of nature, and the Cause of all we perceive. In short, it was held to be possible to find natural, political, economic, psychological, *and* religious laws that could stand, each in its respective area, as coordinate manifestations of the same orderly universe. Each would thereby have the effect of supporting the others.*

Scope and Success of the Modern World-View. In the perspective of four hundred years of social evolution, we can well understand why the modern world-view came to serve as a solid foundation for the industrializing culture, which, by the eighteenth and nineteenth centuries, already dominated most of the European and American continents. This world-view offered a rationale for industrial enterprises by demonstrating how they are governed by undeviating economic law. It accounted for religious belief, when that was desired, by demonstrating that spiritual law is harmonious with scientific and social law. It even justified political revolts by demonstrating that men must sometimes fight to protect the inalienable rights established by the laws of nature.

In many ways this great world-view succeeded in providing the needed rationale. The industrial-scientific culture was a releasing force of vast power, proving its superiority over earlier cultural systems by establishing, among other advances, a higher standard of living and greater opportunities for millions of people. The philosophies that it produced not only probed more deeply into man's inner being, giving him a renewed sense of his significance, but projected their findings upon nature, history, art, religion—upon every important segment of reality. The idealist, for example, found cosmic support for his strong belief in individual spiritual freedom. Further, the beliefs propounded by modern thinkers were, in *their own time,* often radical—at once thoroughgoing and future-looking. They helped, on the one hand, to speed revolt against monarchical, papal, manorial authority by puncturing and collapsing the flimsy pretensions upon which so much of that authority depended. They anticipated and sanctioned, on the other hand, such institutions as political democracy and a profit-making economy—institutions that in an earlier age were heretical or immoral but for men of the new age were both daring and desirable.

Qualifications and Limitations. As is true of all efforts at general-

* See John H. Randall, Jr., *The Making of the Modern Mind,* Books II, III, esp. Chap. 7.

zed interpretation, qualifications and limitations could now be stated at length. We shall confine ourselves to three that are especially pertinent to our cultural evaluation of essentialist thought.

1. *Despite their contributions to a common cultural cause, realist and idealist views are in many ways dissimilar*. We have recorded above a few such differences. The idealist, for example, tends to look upon man and the world more optimistically and warmly than does the colder, material-minded realist and, hence, to view progress as inherent in a purposeful reality. It can also be argued cogently that idealism tends to emphasize the "selfhood" and subjectivity of the individual more strongly than realism, thus allowing more room for personal freedom and autonomous action. The "soul" seems to be striving, even emotionally, toward spiritual perfection. Again, idealism often favors a monistic conception of the world, which contrasts with the more pluralistic conceptions of realism. More basic than all of these, at least to their exponents, is the "stuff" with which each builds its system of reality: idealism, a spiritual substance identified with mind; realism, a material substance identified with body.

Such differences between idealists and realists are not, however, always so sharp as is implied by conventional historians of thought or by philosophers of education. One may observe, for example, an undercurrent of cosmic optimism expressed by some modern philosophers of realist sympathies, such as Spencer, or an emphasis on individual freedom expressed by other realists, especially by friends of *laissez faire,* such as Locke. In regard to the old philosophic argument of monism versus pluralism, some mechanistic materialists (Holbach is one) seem quite as monistic as most objective idealists are, while some idealists (Green is one) are as pluralistic as most realists.

Despite these similarities and overlappings, we wish to emphasize that we are not predicating any logical or otherwise technical identification of realism and idealism. Despite the philosophy of a Spinoza or an Urban, such an identification would be absurd in view of the fact that the history of modern thought is so largely devoted to disputes between them. For many reasons (temperamental as well as more precisely philosophic) the two schools are in genuine opposition at many more points than we have suggested.†

† It is obvious to any student of modern philosophy that our discussion of dissimilarities could be extended much further. Also, it is apparent that various move-

But the question that should disturb the ease with which idealists and realists have regarded themselves as implacable foes is why, if this is so, they can so often join hands congenially in a *practical, socially consequential* movement such as education. Is their congeniality *merely* a coincidence, occurring despite lack of common ground? The answer to this question is strongly negative. The distinctions among particular thinkers and schools, although interesting, legitimate, and subject to endless ramifications, are not at all subject to the easy compartmentalizing that one finds in the rootless and artificial classifications of so many textbooks. *For, despite all their differences, modern realism and modern idealism belong to a united front; they are engaged in a task so momentous as to require the talents and interests of both: the task of constructing the intellectual and moral foundations for a modern culture common to both.*‡

The realist's great contribution is a world-view that is largely, if not always entirely, physical, orderly, and subject to precise examination and understanding by men who are themselves subject to exactly the same precisions because they are parts of the same universe. The idealist's great contribution is a world-view that is largely, if not entirely, spiritual, orderly, and subject to understanding by persons who are themselves spiritual and thereby possessed of some of the qualities of the cosmic Person. Our two remaining qualifications and limitations are devoted mainly to further support for this pivotal contention.

2. *Renaissance and post-Renaissance thought do not at all relinquish the full spirit or substance of the absolutism that was central to ancient and medieval thought.* Absolutism has been retained because the industrial era has demanded its own type of absolutism as sanction for its own type of domination over the lives of ordinary men. What modern thought usually does succeed in accomplishing is to substitute scientifically expressed, sophisticated absolutist formulations for the out-

---

ments in philosophy that overlap with realism and idealism and yet are somewhat distinctive might have been considered in a more elaborate study. One of these movements is existentialism, which has influenced Ulich and has been interpreted as an educational theory by Ralph Harper in "Modern Philosophies and Education," *Fifty-fourth Yearbook,* Part I, National Society for the Study of Education. Readers are also urged to investigate the histories of philosophy listed in "What to Read" for Chapter 2. The generalizations here stated will be sustained, we believe, after such investigation.

‡ See F. S. C. Northrop, *The Meeting of East and West,* Chaps. 3-5.

moded formulations of an earlier era. Whether in the form of Hegelian "dialectic idealism" or of Newtonian "mechanistic materialism," these absolutisms hold that the order and design of the universe are completely pre-established and increasingly known. Thus, the idealist regards the individual self as ultimately "free" only in so far as it abides by the laws of "freedom" established by the cosmic Self. In all influential expressions, however, both realism and idealism provide sanction for the kinds of microcosmic freedom congenial to a new kind of macrocosmic order—an order often characterized, no less than the one it supplanted, by overarching authority and ruthless power.

3. *The institutions and practices of the modern world, far from being hostile to such a sanction for freedom, welcome and encourage it in every possible way.* For what we must not forget is that this era has been structured so as to place great responsibilities upon certain groups—notably, the rising middle classes, which, from their beginnings, have been eager to promote industrial enterprise, trade, experimentation, and exploration. Sometimes very subtly (as in Spinoza), sometimes more obtusely (as in Spencer), philosophy comes again and again to the service of these middle classes. With differing arguments—cosmological, ethical, logical—philosophy provides an intellectual bulwark that, on the one hand, supports the right of emerging groups to criticize and act against the hitherto dominant groups of a feudal and theocratic culture and, on the other hand, defends their equal right to endeavor to establish a new pattern of authority for an industrial, secular culture in which they themselves would rule.*

In this double task we have found modern idealism and modern realism to be generous allies. The former pictures a spiritual universe in which man is good when he expresses his own spiritual self and thereby strives to embrace God by revering His benevolent mandates. The latter pictures a material universe in which man is good so long as he understands and abides by its orderly natural and social processes. To be sure, no two philosophic systems highlight the same vistas or color their canvases with the same pigments. Since each possesses its own esthetic uniqueness, the picture created by idealists tends to be warmer and more emotionally toned than that created by realists. The focus, moreover, may be on the individual in his search for independence of expression and movement, on the state, on religion, or on a science, such as physics,

* See Randall, *op. cit.*, p. 440.

biology, or sociology. Seldom, however, does any philosophy of the modern era become influential if it fails to provide support in some form for the middle-class pattern of civilization, which by the eighteenth century had already pervaded most of the Western world.

It is in this third qualification that we detect the main import of essentialist education as conservator of modern culture.

•

The Conserving Role of Essentialist Education

The Pre-existent as the Real, the True, and the Good

Essentialism, as a theory of education-and-culture, is much too sophisticated to deny that contemporary institutions and practices have failed in many ways to meet contemporary needs. Nevertheless, it steadfastly maintains that the supreme educational task is to develop in men sufficient acuteness and skill to enable them to penetrate the clouds of ignorance that conceal from them the underlying unity, order, and rightness that are indigenous to and pre-existent in the culture and await disclosure. Such an educational task is, of course, great and endless. Not only do men differ greatly in capacity but even the exceptionally able may easily misinterpret the world. They may mistake some part for the whole; or the processes of nature and society may themselves be undergoing changes that, although they, too, are expressions of the basic unity and order, are elusive because dynamic and evolving.

Two Emphases: Institutions and Axioms. The conscious, ulterior aim of essentialist education, to conserve the inherited culture as wisely as possible, is effected by two related means. The first is to rely on the *practices, habits, and institutions* that have been discovered, established, and tested. The other is to be increasingly aware of the *axioms, rights, laws, and principles* that, existing beneath practices, habits, and institutions, may or may not have been discovered and revealed. To illustrate: the Constitution of the United States may be revered by the essentialist for its authorship and accepted as a verbalized actuality (his concern for learning via the printed page reinforces such acceptance); or the essentialist may stress "natural rights" and other axioms whose significance lies in universal, pre-existent principles more real and more valuable than the Constitution itself.

Although the essentialist might stress both *institutions* and *principles,* a difference in emphasis is important enough to reveal some disagreement among essentialists over the chief service to be rendered by their doctrine. The educator who stresses the heritage of such institutional arrangements as "private enterpise" may seem more conservative than the one who devotes primary attention to rights and axioms; thus the latter may argue that certain institutional changes are needed in order to fulfill such rights and axioms. The second type of emphasis, nevertheless, may produce an even more profound and more long-term conserving effect.

The Conserving Function of Rights and Axioms. Emphasis upon rights and axioms exercises such a conserving effect in two ways. In the first place, the frame of mind cultivated by this emphasis is one of respect for and conformity to laws and rights that man finds existing within an already designed cosmos, whether such laws and rights have been previously discovered or are waiting to be discovered. The student trained under essentialism thus learns to accept what the world presents to him—whether as institutions and practices, or as laws, axioms, and principles not yet fully understood, perhaps, but awaiting recognition and acceptance.

In the second place, emphasis upon rights and axioms performs a conserving function because abstract laws, axioms, and principles are, after all, derived from institutions and practices—that is, from social, political, economic, religious, and other contexts. They are *abstract* only in the sense of being *abstracted from* such contexts of the culture. Upon close inspection the essentialist's universal axioms prove to have a cultural history of their own: they were created to support definite institutions and practices of very definite periods.

The doctrine of "natural rights" is an excellent example of the abstraction of "universal" laws from elements in the culture. It was developed by such thinkers as Hobbes, Locke, and Rousseau for political purposes at a time of great social and economic upheaval. Devised, first of all, to give moral support to the economic struggles of the rising middle classes, it provided justification both for their right to rebel against older authority and for their right to establish themselves as the new authority.

The question of how essentialism operates as an agent of cultural re-enforcement may now be given one answer: in urging the primacy of already existent principles it thereby exerts its influence in behalf of some institution or practice for which these principles were devised and which they loyally support. In this way essentialists help to strengthen whatever vitality and meaning the institution or practice may still possess.

Acquiescent learning

The conserving import of essentialist education is revealed also by the essentialist conception of the learning process. For, granting again many psychological distinctions between them and many concessions to progressivist learning, we may observe that idealists and realists, nevertheless, agree on one presupposition of learning: they both tend to interpret the mind as receptor and reflector of the antecedently given world of natural or spiritual realities, truths, and values. Such a theory of receptivity is, of course, congenial to the theory of pre-existent principles and/or institutions. In this respect essentialist learning serves to cultivate acceptance of these principles and/or institutions.

There is another related way in which, especially in our own time, learning as receptivity is helpful to cultural conservation. Through the process that Finney so aptly termed "passive mentation" the "immature" learner not only absorbs the facts, practices, beliefs, rules, and responses selected by those who, being "mature," believe it is their duty to select them but, of even greater consequence, acquires the *habit* of absorption. With continuous practice as he grows into adulthood the individual will almost certainly so firmly acquire the attitudes and responses of "passive mentation" that he is unlikely ever to change them. Whether the essentialist derives his theory from hereditarian or from environmentalist preferences the practical effect remains the same. In either case learning consists largely of stocking the mind-substance, of enriching mental states, of strengthening S-R bonds, as the case may be, with contents and skills derived from the storehouse of the given culture.

Now the potent conserving effect of this kind of learning is clear. In relegating critical thinking, the questioning attitude, cooperative planning, and other characteristics of progressivist learning to a secondary place (if he seriously includes them at all) the essentialist helps to form the kind of citizen who most readily absorbs what those in authority teach him to absorb.† The pupil will, of course, acquire beliefs about "individual initiative" and "freedom of speech" as well as about other American traditions that presumably encourage an active, critical response to his own environment. Indeed, his teacher will doubtless believe sincerely in such traditions. But, because he has little experimental opportunity to translate generalities into classroom or community experience, his belief in them becomes largely a verbal substitute for concrete practice.

The Obsolescence of Essentialism

"Conservation," past and present

Essentialist inculcation of the traditions of the culture is directly relevant to the final question of our evaluation: How far is essentialism an adequate and defensible theory of education for our present culture-in-flux? Certainly, it should not be denied that this theory performed a valuable service (for example, by providing training in industrial skills and in cultivating middle-class virtues, such as thrift) throughout the long era during which the power of the middle classes grew to a position of dominance. The momentous influence of Locke, Harris, Bagley, Thorndike, and numerous other thinkers testifies to this service. It also performed the service of placing education on more scientific grounds, by insisting upon exactitude of data and precision of measurement.

But culture changes—sometimes at breathless speed. Beliefs that were once forward looking or that may have strongly supported the advance of relatively efficient and productive institutions may gradually come to retard them. When this occurs, as it has often in history, older patterns of belief—whether or not philosophically formulated—may become *opponents* of novel, emerging cultural arrangements and *proponents* of patterns with which men have long been comfortably familiar and to which they easily render habitual allegiance.

With this historical perspective we may appreciate more and more

† Let it be reiterated that progressivist learning is *not* thereby ignored. Indeed, some essentialists—Ulich, for example—give it a prominent place within their own larger framework.

clearly the stellar conserving role of essentialism, particularly for the present period. As the political, religious, and other lieutenants of the middle classes solidified their control over institutions; as the recurring periods of war and depression and the exploitation of millions proved the inability of those middle classes to assure a stable and satisfactory life for the multitudes; as criticisms of "early liberalism" by Mill, Marx, Dewey, Owen, and others became more devastating and bitter (see pp. 164-167); as the later "measurement movement" initiated by realists in education and the social sciences often proved to be even more apologetic for the rightness of "whatever is" than had objective idealism—as such trends and realizations crystallized simultaneously throughout the nineteenth and twentieth centuries, the permanent value of inherited arrangements no longer seemed so easy to condone.

Indeed, "conservation" as the supreme objective of education took on a different, a far more defensive connotation, which reveals the *contemporary* role of the essentialist. Despite many apologies, qualifications, and even intents that ally essentialism with "later liberalism," its role is one of preserving—by justification and revivification—the cultural habits and correlative beliefs that have prevailed over the long era of modern culture. It is no wonder when we consider how deep the impress of that era that its protagonists continue to be vociferous and many.

•

Essentialism as cultural lag

Notwithstanding the earnestness of those protagonists of essentialism who work in the social sciences, religion, education, and other fields, their efforts reveal the presence of cultural lag. It is a lag, moreover, of gravest consequence for the future of our culture.

Our Revolutionary Period. The cultural period through which man is now passing is properly characterized as a period of revolution (see pp. 62-66). It is revolutionary in the sense that abnormally rapid and fundamental innovations are occurring in every area of human experience—in morals, science, art, certainly in economics and politics. These innovations call for a twofold reaction by every thinking man: on the one hand, maximum awareness of their causes and characteristics; on the other hand, fullest consideration of every important proposal to direct and shape the culture toward ends that seem desirable as alternatives to or supplements of earlier patterns of belief and practice.

Essentialists have themselves sometimes sensed certain revolutionary symptoms in the present period.* Indeed, it is because of a profound feeling of disturbance that they have recently, even if only momentarily, taken the counteroffensive and attacked what they regard as a major cause of the current confusion of cultural aims—namely, progressive education. They fail to meet the demands of our time, however, in respect of the twofold reaction described above. They do not analyze adequately the significance of such movements as progressivism in its cultural matrix of "later liberalism"; hence, they cannot successfully evaluate its significance for our revolutionary period. And they do not consider objectively to what extent their own proposals would resolve the present confusions and conflicts of our culture or to what extent these proposals would perpetuate the very patterns of belief, habits, and associated institutions that are so heavily responsible for such confusions and conflicts.

Let us consider again what is perhaps the single most graphic example of essentialist support of traditional patterns of belief—namely, belief in freedom of competition and profit making founded upon the traditional system of economic relations. Notwithstanding doubts raised by deviants among essentialists and even occasional activity by a few of them in "Liberal Parties" and "Teachers' Guilds," the greatest part of their philosophic apparatus operates uncritically in behalf of that system's perpetuation. To observe how this occurs we may consider three interconnected cogs in that apparatus: (1) the continuous glorification of our social heritage; (2) the correspondence theory of knowledge, with its corollary of acquiescent learning; (3) the central belief in an antecedently ordered world that applies as well to the laws and principles of cultural life. All three cogs, we submit, conceal such serious flaws in the essentialist structure as to invite the conclusion that it is now largely, indeed precariously, an obsolete structure.

"Social Heritage" as Concealment. The central difficulty caused by essentialism's support of cultural tradition is not that it glorifies the social heritage but that it does so in uncritical terms. That is to say, it does not help students to distinguish between past achievements that are decidedly worth understanding, even worth preserving, and those that, having served their original purpose, are no longer worth preserving.

* See Ulich, *Conditions of Civilized Living;* and *Crisis and Hope in American Education;* Gordon K. Chalmers, *The Republic and the Person,* Chap. 3; Alan Valentine, *The Age of Conformity.*

Many esentialist thinkers thus tend to commit the common logical fallacy of identifying parts with the whole—of implying that because modern culture records great accomplishments in *some* areas therefore it does so in virtually *all* areas.

Some interpreters of essentialism, it is true, attempt to distinguish between the "essentials" of the social heritage and the mere "traditions" of custom and habit. The "essentials," they say, are the permanent and indispensable features of that heritage; it is these they wish to preserve. So long as no clear judgments of cultural appraisal are provided, however, the distinction is difficult to maintain: "essentials" and "traditions" are easily confused with each other by one who wishes to find in the latter convenient examples of the former.

The confusion of "essentials" with "traditions" may be illustrated by reference to the "essential" virtues—honesty, respect, duty, devotion, and many others—which this type of education selects for inculcation in the young. Seldom does it question whether they are meaningful in the abstract; almost never does it seem to be aware that *these virtues are meaningful only when delineated within the experience of a particular culture*. Seldom, accordingly, does it either ask or answer the question: How shall we decide *which* elements of the heritage are to be retained and perpetuated? This is a question that should embarrass the several authors of the Harvard Report almost as much as it should such essentialists as Demiashkevich or Chalmers. For again and again essentialists of all types tempt us to suppose that the heritage is itself a sufficient criterion —that it is, in and of itself, a norm, a primary source of goodness and truth.

Returning specifically to the traditional economic system, we wish to stress the point that *generalities* about the past tend to conceal *specificities* that probably do not apply to all of the past and certainly not to the present and future. We may consider, as an example, the value of freedom. It is undoubtedly true that, with the rise of a new industrial order, freedom was achieved in newly significant ways by *some* individuals—and especially by individuals of the middle classes. But it is inaccurate to conclude therefrom that freedom was achieved by all or most of the people—especially of the working classes. Groups of people are not free in any sense that is empirically meaningful so long as they are subjected to domination by others—so long as they are denied the opportunity to satisfy a large part of their wants or to participate, by means of political and economic authority, to a degree commensurate with their numbers in determining the policies under which these wants are to be satisfied.*

Such subjection and such denial have been very widespread throughout modern economic society. In some areas, indeed, they have become even more widespread, as the earlier period of modern history, with its relatively open, competitive system of small business capitalism, has been strongly modified by the relatively closed, noncompetitive system of monopoly, corporate capitalism. For in the latter fewer and fewer individuals are "free" to work or earn as they please or to make their own independent plans. In a century of world-wide wars, fewer are free even to *exist*. Nevertheless, whenever they are taught to accept "freedom" in some absolute, abstract, undifferentiated sense—whenever they are taught that "freedom" is somehow grounded in a pre-existent, orderly system of nature or in a universal God—they thereupon fasten still further strands to the heavy bonds of acquiescent, uncritical response.

The "Correspondence Theory of Knowledge" as Concealment. The correspondence theory of knowledge, assumed alike by this kind of realist bond building and by idealist learning, becomes then a second main device of concealment geared closely to the first. Although the idealist concept of "correspondence" may suggest an active meeting of mind with Mind, the practical effect of the idealist theory of learning is often not too different from that of the realist. So long as the learner is placed in the role of "understanding" the given culture by corresponding with (that is, presenting or *re*-presenting) whatever content is chosen for him to assimilate he is ill equipped to analyze the reliability of the content. He is ill equipped to determine in what ways it is incomplete, distorted, or unobjectively selected by his teachers, many of whom have identified what should be learned with what controlling groups in the culture (school boards, for example) most want him to learn. His primary duty is to incorporate that content into his mind-substance and then to reflect it as faithfully as possible in his own knowledge, habits, and behavior.

We may thus understand why it is that essentialist education so often receives the wholehearted support of those who benefit by retention of inherited social institutions. Conservative newspaper columnists and pressure groups composed of manufacturers and "patriots" welcome the

* See Robert A. Dahl and Charles E. Lindblom, *Politics, Economics, and Welfare,* Chap. 5.

kinds of theory and practice that cultivate "passive mentation," the shrewdest of them fully recognizing its usefulness in developing citizens at once amenable to and uncritical of their own authority. In this cultural context we may recognize the motivational source of the attacks on progressivism discussed in Chapter 6 as a fear that progressivism will challenge established controls; we may likewise recognize the source of essentialism's reluctance to challenge these attacks. Thus, *even if we assume that some essentialists do not consciously intend that their doctrine shall be utilized to serve conservative economic or political interests, the program they endorse has the effect of making them, more often than not, useful partners of these interests.*

Let us epitomize our analysis of how essentialist learning serves as a barrier against cultural change. In a culture suffering as ours does from actual as well as potential instability, one of the ways by which men seek to restore stability, or at least to protect whatever shreds of stability remain, is by teaching people to accept and to revere the given order. Whether the given order is in reality what it is pictured to be (a culture in which men are "free," for example) is of less importance than that, in the interests of those who control that order, the accepted picture be firmly impressed upon the receptive mentalities and nervous systems of the largest possible number of citizens, young and old.

"Antecedently Uniform Reality" as Concealment. The final important cog in essentialism's apparatus of concealment is the key belief that the reality that is to be assimilated and adjusted to is one of already established uniformity—a reality governed by physical and/or spiritual laws which are themselves cosmically and permanently established. This belief, an absolutist carry-over from medieval culture and philosophy, expresses itself in two major practical consequences. Either it is a way of inviting conformity with already existing institutions, or it is a way of inviting conformity with the axioms and principles that underlie institutions whether or not the latter currently exist. How can this kind of ontology operate as still another device to conceal the real character of contemporary economic, social, and moral experience?

Such an ontology leads to acceptance of the premise of classical economic theory that the laws governing our traditional economic system (the law of supply and demand, for example) are so inviolable, so universal that we must respond to them with the same abject humility with which we respond to the law of gravity. Habituation to this kind of response serves both forms of concealment noted above: the first, the "social heritage," by identifying a *particular* economic order with the *general* order, which, embodied in the social heritage, is assumed to be the fountainhead of all important knowledge and value; the second, the "correspondence theory of knowledge," by disclosing to us the laws of economic life through acquiescent learning, with its concomitant effect of undiscriminating adjustment to traditional practices.

The theory of an antecedently uniform reality in so far as it is taught as the exclusive theory serves as concealment in other ways. It fails, for example, to consider the challenge of a radically different approach to reality, namely, the operational theory of scientific discovery, outlined in Part II (see pp. 110-112). By interpreting laws of economics as instruments constructed, like laws of nature, for the purpose of controlling the environment, operationalism challenges the whole predetermined structure of social and natural order assumed by essentialism and, along with it, the whole habit of acquiescing in that structure. It demonstrates that, however complex the problems involved, men can approach economic experience, including our particular form of economic order, as an area of life on which to operate for the purpose of correction and organized development.

Essentialists also fail to appreciate clearly enough that their theory, no less than any other, is the product and expression of a historic period. Hence, as we have emphasized above, the laws, axioms, rules, and principles that they hold to be pre-existent and universal prove upon more scrupulous inspection to be the articulations and rationalizations of a definite cultural period—the constructions primarily of a middle class striving earnestly to establish a solid foundation for economic, scientific, political, and other practices required by a dynamic realignment of cultural forces.

The historic manner in which philosophy is utilized to provide this foundation, a highly important although subtle relationship, has not, to this point, been adequately emphasized. Two tendencies may be noted: first, philosophy may assume a realist-scientific form or an idealist-religious form; second, it may assume an objective and worldly form or a subjective and personal form. Expressed in other terms, the search for a given and uniform reality is a search for a harbor of security—in some cases, in the pre-established reality of nature or God; in others, in the pre-established being of the natural or spiritual person. The appeal of the latter has been the sanction it provides for the individual who is struggling for new rights and new power—particularly the individualistic middle-class businessman. The appeal of the former, of an objective world of law and order, is that it provides a harbor large and deep enough to include and protect all such men as well as the multitudes who are dependent upon them.

Indeed, a history of modern philosophy might be largely written around the disputes over these two harbors of security. Such a history would need to point out, more clearly than has been done, that both the objective and the subjective, the worldly and the individualistic, forms have assumed the same premise of an antecedent, uniform set of principles, laws, and axioms, which presumably establish the supremacy and indisputability of their own point of departure. *Both are finally absolutistic.* Each one, because it is absolutistic, has often embraced and justified the other by its own favorite laws and axioms. The "subjectivist" (Berkeley, for example) builds an objective Supreme Being out of the substance of self; the "objectivist" (Hobbes, for example) builds a law-abiding, if still material, self from the stuff of physical nature. Each one often becomes a smooth *reflex,* reflecting the other as in a mirror: *the microcosm and macrocosm of modern philosophy are the intellectual symbols of a culture that is unwilling, or unable, to disavow the medieval belief in and reliance upon an unchallengeable and pre-established universe.*†

But the subjectivist and objectivist orientations are also symbols of the chronic instability of modern culture. Having no more ultimate basis than their own absolutism—the microcosmic or the macrocosmic—and, nevertheless, continuously suffering from the failure of economic and other institutions to provide a stable and peaceful order with full participation by the common man, these philosophies have ever swung from the subjective to the objective pole and back again. One can understand that, in their restless search for rest, men have tended to find justification for their behavior—often ruthless and anarchic—in some final, comforting authority transcending themselves. In our culture, however, this authority must also conveniently sanction such behavior by equating it with "freedom" or other "inalienable rights" endowed in the individual.

† This "reflexive" character of modern philosophy, as an expression of modern culture, is examined more fully in Theodore Brameld, *A Philosophic Approach to Communism,* pp. 128ff., 159, 197ff., 200ff.

The issue is admittedly complex, for the ramifications of modern culture and philosophy are themselves complex. Nevertheless, the essence of the third major concealment may be simply stated: *the whole doctrine of a pre-existent and indubitable reality becomes a powerful cultural device to reinforce attitudes of compliance either with objective institutional arrangements or subjective wishes and habits or both.* To teach, for example, that economic practices are governed by laws as impersonal and inviolable as the laws governing the stars is only to nourish a convenient belief in the righteous inevitability of those institutions and wishes.‡

To teach, however, that no such laws exist—that laws are intellectual tools constructed by men, that by means of these tools men gradually learn to shape and reshape a stubborn cultural environment by operating upon it as engineers operate upon the equally stubborn surface of the earth—to teach this is to threaten the "established" order. To the cultural conservationist this is sufficient grounds for attacking any philosophy of education that dares to propose such a heresy.

Summary of Beliefs about Essentialism

Although essentialism, as a theory and program of education, developed to maturity before progressivism, it is considered here mainly in its current formulation. It is, thus, regarded as a leading alternative to the most conspicuous theory of our generation—that is, to the present-tempered, experimental philosophy of "later liberalism," and therefore to progressivism as the educational expression of that philosophy. Our overview of essentialism has emphasized those constructive principles that are regarded by its advocates as both a reply to and substitute for the weaknesses and confusions of progressivism—the first of the three main roads to education-and-culture considered in this volume. Today essentialism (often identified by other terms) is experiencing a strong resurgence not only in education but even more in scholarship and among intellectuals. Indeed, among many of the latter it is now more fashionable to repudiate than to defend progressivist-liberal ideals and to express a sophisticated conservatism that is not necessarily identified with any formal philosophy.

‡ See Randall, *op. cit.*, pp. 323ff.

If its contemporary import is to be understood, essentialism—as the second road—must be observed in its historic context. Most of its leading exponents are still strikingly devoted disciples of the two major systems of philosophic thought—idealism and realism—that emerged in the Renaissance and attained their mature formulations between the early part of the eighteenth and the latter part of the nineteenth centuries. The expressions into which each system matured are extremely diverse and not always internally consistent, with the consequence that essentialism, which includes both idealism and realism, abounds with eclectic elements.

Despite their differences, however, idealist and realist philosophies alike are deeply concerned with the three chief areas of belief: reality, knowledge, and value. And all three, after many qualifications are taken into account, converge around one common belief—namely, that reality in both its more personal and its more objective expressions is governed by uniform, permanent, and antecedently determined regularities, procedures, principles, and axioms of all truth, all goodness, and all beauty. Idealists find in this belief the "reason for being" of a spiritual universe, while realists usually associate it with a more material, machine-like universe. Although, in certain writings, some exponents of both positions find the individual more important than the law-abiding universe of which he is an integral part, they most often seek to integrate him, his knowledge and his conduct, within the whole of that universe.

Philosophers of education in every modern century beginning with the fifteenth-century Erasmus may be broadly identified with the essentialist movement. Today, however, they cannot, even if they wish to do so, disregard the influence of recent developments in philosophy and psychology. Their theories of learning, for example, often incorporate functional, organismic tendencies with strong democratic implications. At the same time, despite such modernizing and the attractions of "later liberalism" for some of them, they remain admirably loyal to the idealist and realist belief that truth must be measured by the exactitude of correspondence with prior structures, facts, events, and causes, that is, with spiritual or physical relations and laws. Thus, when appraised in terms of their total impact their curriculum proposals, for example, are found to be based primarily on inherited subject matters in content and sequence and to be tested by quantitative techniques borrowed from the exact sciences. Finally, their conception of the school's role in society, although influenced by recent developments of democratic tendency, is to emulate patterns of control of the wider cultural environment—line-staff administration, local school autonomy, training of skilled and obedient workers, discipline by the mature over the immature, and a dominant leadership to formulate and carry out policy.

The significance of essentialism in our own culture can be fully appraised, however, only as the great systems of modern philosophy are placed in the setting of more than four centuries of history—centuries marked by both destructive turbulence and momentous accomplishments, of which by far the most destructive and momentous is the rise of a new type of economy. This gigantic and powerful economy, which came to be called capitalism, has required new political institutions to support its expansion and to sanction the authority of its promoters. Equally, if less obviously, capitalism requires the continuous cooperation of the economy with science, religion, morality, *and* education. The school thus comes to serve, both theoretically and practically, as one of the key underpinnings of modern culture. For not only does it train leaders to control and workers to function under its socio-economic institutions but—of even more importance—it cultivates habits of devotion to and compliance with those institutions. Viewed in this historical perspective essentialist education may be seen to have served the culture well. Indeed, on the basis of its own premises it was and still is "good" education, having made permanent and constructive contributions to society and to the development of education. The success of realism in analyzing educational processes in terms of scientific canons, for example, has advanced such fields as educational psychology, and the idealist stress upon selfhood has helped to provide a more friendly school atmosphere for individual child development.

But essentialism, although a dynamic force in the earlier stages of modern history, becomes a conserving force as the culture that formerly nourished it and to which it has since been loyal and grateful strains toward further sweeping change. In a crisis-culture such as our own, therefore, essentialism performs primarily the role of protecting the culture against the encroachments typified by progressivism. The performance of such a role is an educational symptom of a great cultural lag—the results of which are various concealments frequently not recognized as such even by essentialism's sincere proponents. Thus, the social heritage is often glorified for its own sake and without discrimination. Learning becomes largely an acquiescent process of corresponding with, by responding to and re-presenting, the selective stimuli of those who control the schools in the interests of their own entrenched patterns of authority. And the belief that both individual self and objective world are governed by predetermined uniformities and mandates becomes a subtle, sometimes inadvertent, but still potent means to instill habits of conformity with what has been and hence is assumed still to be both inevitable and right.

PART FOUR

PERENNIALISM

Education as Cultural Regression

CHAPTER 10

Philosophic Foundations of Perennialism

The "Regressive Road to Culture"

RECALLING THE FRAME OF REFERENCE BY MEANS OF WHICH PHIlosophies of education are being appraised in this volume, we raise this central question as we embark upon an interpretation of perennialism: How does our third major theory propose to deal with the world crisis confronting contemporary man?

In answering this question earlier, we said that perennialism beckons us to follow a "regressive road." It sees no other sure way through the impasse of our time but to return to the common principles that so largely shaped the attitudes and habits of ancient and medieval culture. Our use of the term "regressive" has no invidious connotations but merely suggests that *the perennialist reacts against the failures and tragedies of our age by regressing or returning to the axiomatic beliefs about reality, knowledge, and value that he finds foundational to a much earlier age.*

Perennialist theory thus makes a distinctive and influential contribution to both the theory and practice of culture-and-education today. When a civilization is severely disturbed by turmoil, bewilderment, and cross-purposes, when the need for moral and intellectual as well as economic security becomes both acute and chronic we then find many citizens among us who seek anchorage in the safe harbor of the remote past. Such a civilization is ours.

The chief motivational force of perennialism is not, however, solely or even largely nostalgia for values long remembered and revered. It is rather a strong conviction, bolstered by extraordinary philosophic acumen, that the core beliefs of ancient-medieval culture apply as vitally to the twentieth century after Christ as they did to the thirteenth century after Christ or the fifth century before Christ. Hence, from the very beginning of our study we need to appreciate that the perennialist would oppose the very frame of reference so important to our own interpretation of his philosophy. He insists that the supremely proper principles of concern to philosophy have no relation, *per se,* to cultural origins or effects; on the contrary, since they are axiomatic, timeless, and spaceless, such principles transcend all history and therefore all cultures within history. It is precisely because they have these qualities that they can serve as a reliable guide to any period, including our own. They are, indeed, the *only* reliable guide.

Our study also requires an understanding of why perennialism is even more hostile to progressivism than is the philosophy of cultural conservation studied in Part III. For, although essentialism is allied to perennialism and joins it in vehemently counterattacking the progressivist-liberal outlook, such characteristics as an eclecticism and an eagerness to accommodate itself to the industrial-scientific era force essentialism to admit virtues in that outlook that perennialism is reluctant to admit. Perennialism is less eclectic and less apologetic than essentialism, and, with some exceptions, it is more internally unified as a philosophy. Its major premises and conclusions are more completely opposed to the naturalist, evolutionary approach of progressivism. Hence, any concessions that perennialism makes to either of these philosophies of education are invariably made on its own premises, never on theirs. To be sure, it supports most essentialist criticisms as far as they go (for example, it also repudiates the adequacy of functional learning), but it insists that they fail to go far enough and, even more important, that they are poorly grounded because essentialism is often quite as unsatisfactory philosophically as progressivism itself.

Although no serious student of education can afford to disregard or disrespect the great significance of perennialism, we shall nevertheless be compelled to form a negative evaluation of it. Granting its very rich contributions to the history of philosophy and to the experience of Western civilization, we shall adjudge perennialism to be in theory and therefore in practice not only an unsound but a dangerous road for our culture any longer to follow.

It is unsound because, among other reasons, it would turn the clock of history backward. Dissatisfied even with much of the modern heritage that essentialism aims to conserve, perennialism resuscitates the spirit, if not the substance, of an earlier heritage. Its admiration for broad aspects of the medieval culture suggests that it is a reflection, after all, of historic habits and institutions, of definite time and place. In regarding as largely irrelevant the environmental influences that continue to shape its character, perennialism asks us to accept it as a cultural guide without having carefully considered its own cultural derivations. When we consider these derivations we must severely question the appropriateness of a philosophy that reached its highest formulation many centuries ago.

Perennialism is not only unsound but also dangerous, threatening our contention that the revitalization of democracy is the most pressing obligation facing contemporary mankind. Despite his occasional defense of liberal or even radical ideals, despite his opposition to such autocratic systems as fascism, despite his occasional forthright defense of academic freedom and other human rights, despite his sympathy for the common man, the typical perennialist cannot be genuinely democratic. Were his philosophy to be widely adopted either in politics or in education, democracy would cease. Whether in its place there would arise an aristocracy of high-minded directors of the masses of plain people or whether the very nature of his doctrine would open wide the door to corruption of authority is an option we might not enjoy facing. It is, however, one we would have to face because it would be inescapable.

But this anticipates the criticism of perennialism to be developed in Chapter 12. In Chapters 10 and 11 we present an exposition and interpretation of perennialism which parallel those of the two preceding Parts.

Historic Backgrounds

The general character of perennialist thought

If we define the term "perennial" to mean "everlasting" in a sense analogous to a species of flower that blooms continually season after season, then we may more clearly understand the general character of perennialist thought.* As suggested in our brief preview above, its core belief is precisely a kind of "everlastingness." It recognizes that individual persons, like individual experiences and individual flowers, come and go, bloom and wither with the passage of seasons and years. But the patterns or forms common to all things recur and remain identical as patterns or forms century after century, era after era—indeed forever.

To discover and characterize these common recurrences becomes the most important undertaking of which any civilization is capable. Without them human beings are rootless, hapless victims of circumstance. With them they are not only able to withstand the buffetings of chance and change but are also able to look upon their own lives and the lives of others with a serene awareness of inner significance and outer stability.

Fortunately, a philosophy of everlastingness is already available to us. To find it, however, we need to restore and apply to twentieth-century culture the metaphysics, logic, esthetics—in fact, virtually all the basic beliefs—of three great thinkers who stand above all others: Plato, Aristotle, and Aquinas.

Reliance upon these thinkers does not imply that perennialists bow to every word of their theories or that other thinkers are unimportant. As in the case of the individual flower, some of the "petals" and "leaves" of, let us say, Aristotelianism are unique to its own author and to the period of history that gave it birth, but its central principles, as a species of thought, transcend these uniquenesses and may be applied to any era. In addition, other thinkers, ranging in time from Augustine to Maritain, have helped to enhance the supremacy of the great triumverate and to widen the scope of perennialism itself.

We must also note, as we have of progressivism and of essentialism, that the leading contemporary spokesmen for this third philosophic outlook are not at all completely in accord. In some respects, their differences merely express the dynamic quality of perennialism, thus supporting their contention that it is far from being the static or sterile doctrine that its critics often claim it is. In other respects, the differences are symptomatic of possible elements of eclecticism even within this highly coherent body of thought. Despite their denunciations of any other eclectic posi-

* The phrase *philosophia perennis* was coined by Leibnitz. See Aldous Huxley, *The Perennial Philosophy*, p. vii. Jacques Maritain also refers to his philosophy by this term; see his *An Introduction to Philosophy*, p. 100.

tion (one reason, as we noted above, for their dissatisfaction with essentialism) and despite their own insistence upon irrevocable certainty as the necessary basis of any sound culture, perennialists have not reached unanimity as to the full conditions of such certainty. The differences have become especially sharp between those who emphasize the religious-theological beliefs of Aquinas and those who try to maintain a primarily secular point of view.

The one central belief upon which agreement among perennialists is universal is that, if our sick culture and our still sicker education are to be restored to health, we shall need first to restore to their positions of prestige and guidance the greatest "doctors" of all time. With their help, far more than with that of any others, we can hope to diagnose accurately our deep troubles and to construct a curative program that will prevent the chaos and death now threatening to devastate the earth.

The Greek Heritage: Plato and Aristotle

The few pages here allotted to historic backgrounds cannot even begin to reproduce the vast landscape of ideas swept by the searchlight minds of the Greek philosophers and by their successors. We therefore merely sketch in a few of the most relevant beliefs of Plato and Aristotle, returning to them frequently throughout this Part, and refer the student for elaboration to the immense critical literature available in many languages.†

Plato. Like Socrates, his immortal, half-mythical teacher, Plato was concerned above all else to strip the superfluous, the secondary, the transitory from the inner core of reality, truth, and value. It seems plausible that he was impelled to this search because everywhere about him he perceived a cultural decay induced by doubt, immorality, sophistry, and wars —evils that threatened the very survival of his beloved Athens.

It had been Socrates' chief contribution to insist upon scrupulous, relentless examination of beliefs by exposing their inconsistencies and fallacies and by developing more defensible formulations, which men could respect because they had thought them through. Plato built his

† See histories of philosophy cited in preceding chapters; B. Jowett (trans.), *The Dialogues of Plato,* 2 vols.; W. D. Ross and J. A. Smith (eds.), *Works of Aristotle;* R. McKeon (ed.), *Selections from Medieval Philosophy,* Vols. I, II; A. C. Pegis (ed.), *The Basic Writings of St. Thomas Aquinas,* 2 vols.

own system by this "Socratic method"—while analyzing more deeply the means of ascertaining how, in the midst of conflicting standards, men may follow the path of virtue.

Of all the dialogues in which the Platonic system is pieced together, none compares either in length or depth with the *Republic.* Here the author reached his highest peak of speculative vision and offered his most mature formulations. He believed that the only certain way of building a society at once stable and just is to determine the precise status, within the whole, of each person and each class according to his or its proper capacity. Those with most wisdom and virtue will occupy leading positions at the top; those with least, at the bottom; and the mediocre, in between. At the bottom are placed slaves and artisans; in the middle, soldiers; at the top, the small class of "philosopher-kings," who, through many years of arduous education and training, have proved their superiority in resisting temptations of evil and in living according to the highest good.

It is the exploration of the meaning of this highest good, without which men are unsure of their standards, that becomes the central problem of the *Republic.* The problem is solved by the famous doctrine of "Ideas," anticipated by Plato in earlier dialogues. Platonic "Ideas" are not to be confused with the "ideas" that men develop and discard as they engage in their everyday affairs: the latter are fleeting, temporal, particular, whereas the former are permanent, eternal, universal. Once grasped they become the only sure way by which daily events, passing impressions, fickle opinions can be measured, classified, and evaluated. What is, perhaps, most important to Plato, Ideas provide leaders with moral and political criteria, the most inclusive of which, justice, becomes also the highest good of men living in an association organized according to their worth.

Plato was at heart a practical man who was strongly committed to his principal beliefs. But he couched much of his thought in such poetic, even mystical, language that it is not always easy to distinguish between the literal and the metaphorical aspects of his philosophy.

Aristotle. It is against these poetic and perfectionist qualities in Plato that Aristotle rebelled most strongly. More prosaic and precise, more objective and strategic than Plato, Aristotle devoted his mature life of thought to tempering the extremes of his teacher. Especially did he rebel against Plato's frequent efforts to lure mere mortals away from this world of travail to the "heaven above the heavens," where all fleshly ills and guilts, all confusions and temptations are resolved in the transcendent calm of spiritual contemplation. Although he did not at all succeed in freeing his thought of the Platonic doctrine, Aristotle wished to provide, in such works as the *Ethics* and the *Politics,* sound rules of conduct which men might learn to trust. Thus, the *Politics* proposes a limited constitutional rule over willing subjects, suggesting the "polity" as a compromise between Plato's concept of a stern aristocracy of philosopher-kings and such "inferior" political forms as democracy.

Although the relation between such axiological considerations and his underlying ontology is perhaps not so systematic nor so obvious as in Plato's philosophy, nevertheless, the relation is there. For Aristotle, Platonic Ideas tend to be much too ideal, much too perfect, to be useful. Hence, it is necessary to bring them back into direct, organic relation with the ideas and experiences of daily life, with feelings, pleasures, pains, individual things and events.

The ingenious device he created for this purpose is frequently called *hylomorphism* (*hylo* derived from the Greek word meaning "matter" and *morphism,* from the Greek word meaning "form"), a theory of form *within* matter, ideas *within* things, souls *within* bodies. By the use of this device, Aristotle attempted to resolve the Platonic dualism of form *and* matter, ideas *and* things, soul *and* body, to which he so strongly objected. In contrast to the concept of two worlds of spiritual perfection and material imperfection, the Aristotelian world is a single cosmic order of *increasing* perfection—a hierarchy of lower and higher forms, patterns, and ideas. Near the base of his ontological pyramid one finds the greatest proportion of mere matter and, hence, the smallest proportion of form. Near the apex one finds the greatest refinement of spiritual form and, hence, the least matter. At the very peak of the pyramid, form is so completely free from the contaminations of mortal experience that it defies full human comprehension. Called the Unmoved Mover, it becomes a kind of deity which, although it does not itself change, eternally draws all lower forms toward it, somewhat as a magnet attracts iron filings in their own patterned field. The inner tendency of reality is, thus, toward greater and greater *actuality* (that is, purity of form) and away from mere *potentiality* (that is, impurity of matter). Most levels of experience with which we are familiar are a fusion of actuality and potentiality, which Aristotle called *substance*.

Human beings themselves afford the best example of substance, for they seldom actually are what they are potentially capable of becoming. Their ideas are often dormant and cloudy rather than vital and clear; their development toward actuality is more or less retarded by the relatively formless stubborn "mud" of their earthly existence. Nevertheless, some men do succeed in rising far above the level of their physical natures. As they do so their spiritual selves become increasingly dominant, their thoughts abstract more and more from the particularities of everyday life, and they approach, although they never completely attain, that state of rarified actuality of which the Unmoved Mover is the final end and final form.

We may conclude from this brief analysis that despite Aristotle's propensity for prosaic, realistic, practical attitudes, his philosophy emerges less as a departure from Plato's than as a fascinating elaboration of it. The this-worldly emphasis, although much stronger than in Plato, is, nevertheless, counterbalanced by a kind of spiritual-intellectual beatitude or other-worldly perfection attainable only by entering into the realm of the *super*-human and *extra*-natural. Even Aristotle's famous ethical doctrine of moderation—the Golden Mean—is supplemented by his deep conviction that the highest good is contemplation for its own sake. Likewise, his theory of political compromise concedes that the moderate, middle-class polity is less ideal and therefore less real and less good than the pure aristocracy or even than the monarchy ruled by the leader-thinker.

THE MEDIEVAL HERITAGE: FROM THE STOICS TO AQUINAS

The Reign of Faith. During the long era bounded by the decline of Greek civilization and the rise of modern civilization, philosophy, in the sense of critical examination and reformulation of basic beliefs, was overshadowed by faith. The prevailing tone was one of uncritical devotion to whatever beliefs might be assumed and inculcated as important, finished, indubitable.

At no time, however, was philosophy entirely dormant; at no time after the creative Greek period, even during the Dark and the Middle Ages, were thoughtful men content with a life of blind obedience to dogma and absolute authority.‡ The Roman period, for example, had

‡ See Etienne Gilson, *The Unity of Philosophical Experience;* and *The Spirit of Medieval Philosophy;* Hugh Miller, *An Historical Introduction to Modern Philosophy,* Chaps. 9, 10.

roduced such able thinkers as Epictetus and Marcus Aurelius, both of vhom lived during the first two centuries after Christ. They expressed n a more highly developed form the theory of Stoicism that had germi-ated in Greece, a theory holding the universe to be a predetermined vhole within which man functions successfully only as he acquiesces in hat whole. In the third century Plotinus revised Platonism in such a vay as to give it a more explicitly religious character. With such con-epts as "God" and "soul" becoming more predominant concerns it is not urprising that the fine mind of Augustine should, in the early fifth cen-ury, have intepreted reality in strongly dualistic terms—spiritual and naterial, soul and body, good and evil, heaven and earth, salvation and lamnation. The longing for the life hereafter, for the "City of God," vhich Plato had already predicated in nontheological terms and which Paul had infused with theological ardor, now captivated the Western vorld. For about ten centuries, *a thousand years and more,* philosophy oncerned itself chiefly with elaborating and justifying Christian tenets and the medieval mores reinforced by them.

From the ninth to fourteenth centuries this concern crystallized in he important intellectual movement called *scholasticism.* Its central aim was to demonstrate, among kindred beliefs, the existence of God and the assurance of immortality. Anselm, in the late eleventh century, was espe-cially skillful in such argumentation, demonstrating, for example, that we cannot possibly doubt God if we are willing to reason the matter out, because God is by definition a perfect being from Whom no attribute can be excluded and Who therefore includes existence as necessary to that very perfection. But scholasticism was not a completely systematic philoso-phy, having evolved through several stages which reflected successively the influence of Plato and neo-Platonism, of Aristotle, and, in the period of its slow decline, of such thinkers as William of Occam, who challenged its central postulates. Judged by its permanent influence, however, the Aristotelian period of scholasticism was by far the most important.

Aquinas. The chief protagonist of this period was Thomas Aqui-nas, "the angelic doctor" of the thirteenth century. His philosophy brings together in one encompassing outlook, without emasculating the essential qualities of either, Aristotelian and Christian principles. Although he very largely accepted the teachings of the immortal Greek, he insisted that beyond the substances of soul-body, or spirit-matter, lies a realm of faith which rational judgment cannot sufficiently explore. Both realms—

the "rational" and the "revealed"—are legitimate and, indeed, indispensa
ble to any whole individual or any whole civilization. Thus, although th
existence of God or the soul may be demonstrated by scholastic argu
ments, such arguments might weaken the more important immediate
self-sufficient faith in God. So, too, with ethics: we can and should buil
moral rules out of the stuff of dynamic experience, but surmountin
these rules are the supernatural virtues—faith, hope, charity—derived no
from experience but from the spiritual fountainhead.

In full perspective, Aquinas is found to remain true to the ancient
medieval tradition. Perhaps already clairvoyant about the stirrings of
culture standing near the threshhold of revolution, he was eager t
analyze more fully the perplexing issues of human life and destiny
Nevertheless, he was able to preserve authoritarian creed at the same
time that he sought to revitalize and redignify philosophy as the art o
critical reflection. Following Aristotle, Aquinas postulated pure form
intellectual and spiritual, as the compelling power, the final end, beyon
all matter. Following Plato and Augustine, he interpreted man-on-eart
as primarily preparation for man-in-heaven.

Partly because he never disparaged or ignored man-on-earth and be
cause he also recognized the importance of the daily life of work, pleas
ure, creation, and association, he has commanded a host of followers in
the centuries of the modern era—a host probably numerically larger than
the following of any other philosopher in Western history. Even in
our own time the philosophy of Aquinas continues to have many ad
herents, for it can comfort and persuade men who wish to justify *both*
the reflective and the dogmatic, *both* the earthly and the divine.

Perennialism in Modern Thought

The Waning of Perennialism. From Aquinas to our own generation—a span of about seven centuries—the essence of his great system
has been accepted as the official philosophic doctrine of one of the most
venerable and powerful institutions of all history, the Roman Catholic
Church (referred to below as the Church). Both Plato and Aristotle
have also commanded their quota of secular followers among modern
thinkers. We may recall that Platonism permeates indirectly or directly
all systems of objective idealism from Leibnitz to Croce. Likewise, the
Aristotelian belief in a universe organized in ascending levels of eternal

orms within matter and nature was held by most biological scientists ntil after Darwin's experimental disproof of the fixity of plant and nimal species.

But from the fourteenth century onward, the ancient-medieval vorld-view was steadily superseded by philosophies that sought to adjust heir conceptions to the jolting events that heralded new industrial and olitical arrangements (see pp. 264-269). Although essentialism, the ffspring of perennialism, did not so much repudiate the old absolutism f its parent philosophy as substitute new absolutisms (idealistic or ealistic), the substitutions have been sufficiently original and refreshing o justify the claim that modern thought is far from being a mere reworkng of Greek or scholastic thought. Science, art, economics, religion, and ducation all found it more and more difficult to fit their expanding nowledge and experience into the framework of a closed universe and revealed faith. Even within institutions of learning controlled by organzed religion, perennialism in its original formulation continued to wane.

The Waxing of Perennialism. In the course of the past half-cenury or so, however, the perennialist philosophy has been marked by a evival under such labels as neoscholasticism and neo-Thomism. Indeed, n some quarters it has recently become so vigorous as to support its own ontention that, however dormant they may appear during some historical eriods, its principles are truly perennial. Today it commands the alleiance of a growing roster of intellectual leaders who, although by no neans committed to all of its beliefs, nevertheless find many of them sufficiently congenial to justify our classifying them as perennialists.

Thus, two eminent French perennialist thinkers—Etienne Gilson nd Jacques Maritain—have achieved international distinction for their nodern elaborations of this ancient philosophy. In addition to years of teaching in America, Maritain has served as ambassador to the Holy See, has been a prominent figure in UNESCO, and is so often regarded as the leading perennialist thinker of our day that we shall rely more heavily upon him than upon any other in the sections that follow.†

Three contemporary writers of poetry or prose should also be cited, although, unlike Gilson and Maritain, they are neither professed philosophers nor systematic Thomists—Aldous Huxley, Hilaire Belloc, and

† Maritain's writings are a major source of the exposition below, but we wish also to acknowledge our special indebtedness to *Nature, Knowledge and God* by Brother Benignus.

T. S. Eliot. In *The Perennial Philosophy* (the title is revealing) Huxle acknowledges his indebtedness to Maritain, but his beliefs reflect the sti deeper influence of Oriental absolutism. Finally, we must not fail mention the anti-Soviet Russian philosopher Nicolai Berdyaev, who d serves to be more widely known for his regressive brilliance expresse in a kind of "modernized" Platonism.‡

Because American devotees of perennialism, with the exception those in clerical orders, are best known for their accomplishments i education, we defer primary attention to them until the next chapte We should, however, note here, because of his contributions to othe fields, one influential and outspoken philosopher among them, Mortime J. Adler, who, although a non-Catholic, has been warmly welcomed b the Church both in its publications and its conferences.* Says Adle "Aristotle and St. Thomas have answered more philosophical question than any other thinkers in the European tradition." [1] In this judgmen his French colleague Gilson more than concurs: "The three greates metaphysicians who ever existed [are] Plato, Aristotle, and St. Thoma Aquinas." [2]

Turning now to beliefs about reality, truth, and value, we elaborat the principles associated especially with perennialism's ancient an medieval founders, but our treatment will be derived most directly fro the formulations of such contemporary disciples as those listed above

Perennialist Beliefs about Reality

It is necessary only to recall the hostility of perennialism to such a experimentalist position as progressivism in order to infer that no ontolog that bears close resemblance to that position can be regarded by th perennialist as sound. What men need above all, says the perennialist, i

‡ See Huxley, *op. cit.;* Hilaire Belloc, *Essays of a Catholic Layman in Eng land;* T. S. Eliot, *The Idea of a Christian Society;* Nicolai Berdyaev, *Freedom an the Spirit.*

* For a brief statement of Adler's conception of philosophy, see his essay i R. Heywood (ed.), *The Works of the Mind.*

ne guarantee that *reality is universal*—that *it is everywhere and at every* *noment the same*. This is a guarantee that can be fulfilled only by laying are the harmonious forms that always lie, even though they may be oncealed, beneath the material crust of changing events and fleeting leas.

Individual Thing, Essence, Accident, Substance. To understand ne import of the perennialist view of reality requires familiarity with everal important building blocks of the perennialist ontology.

In typical Aristotelian fashion we begin not with arid abstractions emote from the concrete and the visible but with simple *individual* *nings* perceived everywhere about us: stones, grass, dogs, people, in neir wide array of shapes, sizes, colors, activities.

Although in our daily lives we never escape from such physical mbodiments, we should recognize that they are but paths to the inner anctuary of existence—to what the philosopher calls their *essence*. What important about individual things is not their multiplicity and variety ut their essential nature. If we are thoughtful, we do not say, for example, that a friend is characterized above all by a special talent, such as kating, or by a common attribute, such as eating; rather, we search for ne quality that makes him most intrinsically human. We find that he lone, among all objects of reality including the brute animal, is able to ngage in the kinds of practice we call deliberation, demonstration, and peculation. This discovery enables us to state that, in essence, man is a easoning animal. We do, of course, view our friend in a wide variety of articular ways: we like to watch him skate and we like the neckties he vears. But he would still be characterized in the same way—by his rationality—if he never skated in his life or if he never wore neckties. These are is *accidents* and not his *essence*.

Nevertheless, really to understand the ontology of our friend, we nust return to the study of him as an individual and therefore as a whole uman being. Regarded in this way, his essence is still the most important discovery we can make about him—so important as to constitute the leepest reality of his nature. But when we behold him with our senses, ve still see him, accidents and all, *as* an individual. So, likewise, do we ee all other things, from mountain peaks to mice. To recall here the Aristotelian sources of this fascinating theory, we can see things simultaneously *both* in their particular, accidental, and material characteristics *and* in their universal, truly essential, formal, and spiritual, characte istics. This union of the two aspects of an individual is the meaning c *substance*—a fusion of matter *and* form.

Teleology. Let us recall again that one of the most importar properties of substance, for Aristotle, is its tendency to move upwar out of its own potentiality toward its maximum actuality. The perennia example is the oak-from-acorn. The actual form of the species, oak, re mains potential in the acorn until the proper conditions for unfoldin occur. The individual thing, the particular oak, then takes the shape tha has been latent within the seed.

This example introduces us to the principle of *teleology*, which w have not treated explicitly above, despite its use in varied forms by certai other philosophies, especially by objective idealism (see pp. 217-220). To say that reality is teleological is simply to say that it is inherentl purposeful—that not only is it governed by an end which determine its predominant means but it is destined eventually to attain that en by its own inevitable course. This does not mean that all individua things do actually attain their own ends. An oak tree does not grow fror every acorn. Individual men as human beings, a church or a nation a a historic institution, seldom approach the full actuality of which the are capable.

Even so, if we look at reality in broad enough perspective, its direc tion clearly appears: the City of God, in Augustine's terms, will inevi ably arrive. In terms of this doctrine, then, we may explain why, of th four main "causes" operating in reality—matter as *material cause*, mc tion as *efficient cause*, form as *formal cause*, and end as *final cause*—th last is the most fundamental. Moreover, the final cause fuses with th other three causes in the sense that matter, motion, and form are presen together in the purposeful substances of individual things. This is t say that the changes (motions) occurring in any given material object— for example, that budding rose on yonder bush—are induced by its hylc morphic character, that is, by its form, which is also its own end.

The fourfold classification of causes under imperial authority of th final cause is pure Aristotelianism, but neo-Thomists prefer to state suc principles as this teleological one in language familiar to moderns. Thus in discussing war and peace, Adler holds "an optimistic view o history" and predicts that eventually we shall achieve a peaceful world He confesses the "probability" that it will not occur for about five hun ɪred years but that it *will* occur is not at all improbable. World peace is higher, a more real, end than national sovereignty and conflict; we may herefore assume that it is a certainty in the same sense that final cause s a certainty. How could it be otherwise so long as "ultimate ends are lways potentially present in the means, for the means are the ends in he process of being realized. . . ."? [3]

The Supernatural. Whereas such neo-Thomists as Adler usually ocus, however broadly, upon the mundane, other neo-Thomists are more oncerned with what they regard as the ultimate and supreme end of eality. This end lies beyond even a peaceful world, for it is *super*-mundane, *super*-natural—it is, in other words, God Himself. But God, as pure Spirit, pure Actuality, pure Form, is so utterly devoid of substance that, lthough reason is in some ways helpful, we cannot conceive of Him n any adequate way except by a faith which is above reason and is filled with mystery.

Indeed, we cannot grasp the import of teleology itself except by faith nd by dogmas, such as the dogma of the Trinity, which radiate from it. Despite all the philosophic equipment of modern perennialism, as exhibited by Maritain, for example, the supernatural reality is always present, repeatedly called upon as the final determinant upon which all else depends.†

It is on the issue of supernaturalism, of course, that ecclesiastic perennialism deviates from lay perennialism. Indeed, the creed and dogmas of the Church, which radiate to and from this supernatural reality, are considered so crucial to its members that Churchmen vigorously nsist upon their separation from other philosophers whom we have included as perennialists.‡

Realism versus Nominalism. The teleological approach to reality may be epitomized in the distinction between two terms familiar to every student of historic philosophy: *realism* and *nominalism*.

Realism as a perennialist doctrine requires careful analysis to avoid confusion. Realism in its *modern* sense, as applied to essentialism (see pp. 206-207, 214-216), refers to the priority and externality of the world's contents—an interpretation also acceptable, up to a point, to *medieval* realism. Essentialist and perennialist realists both believe that there is

† See Jacques Maritain, *Ransoming the Time*, Chap. 8.

‡ See Joseph McGlade, *Progressive Educators and the Catholic Church*, pp. 129-134.

a genuine objectivity about whatever exists; both, therefore, repudiat such doctrines as subjective idealism, which insist upon the primar reality of inner thought.

Except for these common premises, however, the two theories ar more often in disagreement than in agreement. Whereas realists in th tradition of Locke consider most real the physical world of multiple ele ments (objects, events, data), those in the Aristotle-Aquinas traditio consider the universality, the form, *among* elements to be most real— reality recognized through the individual's reason but never identifie with such reason.

Now it was the attacks of Occam and others upon this Thomis type of realism that weakened scholasticism and prepared the way for a modern philosophy of science. Under the banner of *nominalism,* th view gradually took root that the ideas people hold are nothing mor than the *names* with which we label things in nature. Thus, the specie rose has no reality of its own, for there is no objective pattern that em braces individual, living roses. At most there is only the word "rose" wit which we label them. The nominalist theory was in a sense the pre cursor of a pluralistic materialism which was brought to prominence b such thinkers as Hobbes and reached one of its most extreme formula tions in orthodox behaviorism. In this respect, therefore, nominalism resembles modern realism more than it does the medieval realism agains which it is aligned.

Let us not suppose that the issue between Occamist nominalism and Thomist realism is now of interest merely to antiquarians of philo sophic lore. On the contrary, it reappears in many guises today, occa sionally expressed even in its classic terminology. As one writer has ob served, the defeat of Thomist realism "in the great medieval debate wa the crucial event in the history of Western culture; from this flowed those acts which issue now in modern decadence." For when Occam "propounded the fateful doctrine of nominalism, which denies that uni versals have a real existence," he raised the issue of "whether there is a source of truth higher than, and independent of, man; and the answe to the question is decisive for one's view of the nature and destiny of humankind." [4]

But if the "source of truth" is so important, then epistemology as well as ontology has a place in the perennialist mosaic of beliefs. To this theme we now turn.

Perennialist Beliefs about Knowledge

TRUTH, SELF-EVIDENCE, AND REASONING

What Is Truth? Actually we have already been using epistemology. For the perennialist holds that only as we *know* can we apprehend the basic meaning of reality at all; that is, we cannot apprehend it unless we resort to faith and revelation—and the "unless" is finally paramount. As rational animals, however, we are able to achieve considerable understanding of ourselves and our world.

Beginning again with our perceptions of individual things, we proceed gradually to demonstrate the truth about them. *Truth,* indeed, may be defined as the conformity of thought to things; not, however, to temporal things as they appear to the naked eye, as some essentialists believe (see pp. 225-226), but rather to things as they eternally *are,* to their very being—their essence.* Since awareness of truth is ultimately awareness of essence, philosophy should first elucidate the principles by which this twofold, but really single, task can be achieved.

What Is Self-Evidence? Perhaps the most important of such principles is *self-evidence.* If we are willing to look for them diligently, the perennialist believes we shall discover propositions which convince us completely merely by their precision. They spring, as it were, from their own logical perfection and cannot possibly be denied by anyone honestly willing to consider them. An example is the self-evidence of sheer existence, of sheer being. We must accept this proposition, for *to reject it would be to reject the existence even of our rejection;* this is an impossibility if we think about existence at all.† Another example, on a somewhat different plane, is the self-evidence of mathematical axioms. Such simple rules as those of multiplication disclose to us that three times three always results in the same product.

We do not, of course, know *all* the self-evident propositions that it is possible to know, any more than we ever complete our search for essences. We do infer that, inasmuch as we have discovered some, we shall discover more. In any case, it is upon self-evident propositions that

* See Maritain, *An Introduction to Philosophy,* p. 180.

† For an example of this kind of reasoning on a more sophisticated plane, see Gilson, *The Unity of Philosophical Experience,* Chap. 12.

we can confidently proceed to build an edifice of reliable knowledge.

The term *first principles* is applied to those propositions that are at once so abstract and self-evident that, temporarily at least, we can apprehend them apart from all material content. The principle of being or existence, noted above, is one. Probably the most important first principle of all is that of causality. From this principle—namely, that everything has a cause—philosophers can proceed to "prove" the existence of God as the First Cause of all being.

The study and establishment of first principles is the great task of *metaphysics*—the "science" of speculation or intuitive reason. But we must not infer from its abstract character that this most profound of disciplines is remote from the world of reality. On the contrary it is concerned precisely with what is *most* real—pure form, pure essence, pure Idea. The meaning of the Greek term *meta,* "after," helps to elucidate the task of *meta*physics: it is the search for that which comes *after* we have perceived things in the variety of their immediate appearance—the search for their ultimate reality.

What Is Reasoning? The discovery of truth is also aided by the laws of reasoning, for logical definition and demonstration proceed in terms of these laws. Most of the laws of reasoning, first stated by Aristotle, are still employed not only by perennialists but by students taught by the typical logic textbooks used in philosophy courses today.

Perhaps the most familiar laws of reasoning are those of the *syllogism,* which state the established logical relations among major premise, minor premise, and conclusion. To cite one example: if we accept the premise that all men are rational animals (and we cannot possibly deny it as a first principle) and if we recognize that Mr. Smith is a man, we conclude that Mr. Smith must be a rational animal. This is the classic example of *deduction,* and it serves as an ever-present model hovering in the background of the logical arguments of scholastic thinkers. The major premise is invariably, although sometimes only implicitly, traceable to some first principle which either is held by metaphysics to be true or is simply a revealed dogma. The minor premise and the conclusion are then related to the major premise by a chain of rigid links, which constitute inviolable syllogistic laws.

The logic of perennialism, like every other important division of this philosophy, is dependent upon its beliefs about reality—not only upon its beliefs about thought. For this reason we should be careful to note that, despite the emphasis upon deduction, an important role in logic is also played by *induction,* that is, building general judgments by noting resemblances among particular data. This role is important because, as we have observed, perennialism by no means denies the particulars of reality but strongly insists that these particulars, as we sense them in individual things, are the starting point of all human efforts to understand the world.

We can better appreciate the role played by induction if we distinguish Francis Bacon's conception of it from that of Aristotle. For Bacon (and for many others—Dewey, for example), the general judgments we build up by studying specific data are, literally, outcomes; they are not implicit in the data and hence are not conclusive until we reach them inductively. For Aristotle and his followers, on the contrary, induction is primarily a device necessitated by our mortal limitations. We move clumsily, slowly toward general judgments only because in our potential state we are unable to recognize the universality that, in essence, is always present. Because we are human, we cannot move at once to the actuality, to the form, of things. In this sense, induction is an aid to facilitate our approach to the truth: by its help we achieve a clearer understanding of the major premises, the universals, which are always the source and goal of logical operations. Only when we are finally in a position to move confidently forward from these premises *deductively,* however, are we able to understand any concrete thing or event by virtue of its membership in the prior, encompassing whole.

The issue is resolved by Aquinas in a few words when he insists that "though the act of sense-perception is of the particular, its content is universal. . . ."[5] This is so even though we do not recognize the content explicitly until we have engaged in the inductive process by beginning with particulars.

The sciences and philosophy

Having followed the argument to this point, we can now appreciate the chief relations and distinctions between the sciences and philosophy as fields of knowledge.

The Sciences as Knowledge. The sciences (biology, physics, sociology, and others) are concerned with what has ingeniously been called "empiriological analysis" ‡—that is, analysis of individual things and events at the level of experience and nature. This kind of analysis is useful; indeed, the perennialist should become as familiar as possible with it and with the facts it determines.

Scientists exemplify the inductive method at work. Although they also utilize deduction, their special concentration is on examining and experimenting with data and, thus, on reaching conclusions or general judgments, which are regarded by perennialists as knowledge on a relatively lower level.

Philosophy as Knowledge. But just as induction is subordinate to deduction, so the sciences are subordinate to philosophy—above all, to philosophy's own highest "science" of metaphysics. In this valuation the term "ontological analysis" is useful since it indicates the kind of analysis that produces knowledge of self-evident first principles and that proceeds by its own laws of reasoning.

The precise relations between the several sciences and philosophy, although often complex when delineated by scholastic methods, should not cause us difficulty in our interpretation. For, although empiriological and ontological analysis are helpful to each other and although both ascend in a kind of continuous and orderly hierarchy of knowledge, philosophy at the top depends solely upon its own canons, not at all upon the sciences, for its conclusive demonstrations or discoveries. Up to a point and so long as they remain in their allotted territory, independence may also be granted to the sciences: they operate according to their own canons—of induction especially. But as soon as they venture into areas beyond these canons, they too find need for philosophic guideposts—for such first principles as causality. Accepting these principles as established, they can proceed with confidence. Thus, "the premises of scientific syllogisms are either self-evident truths or rest thereon . . ." says Adler.[6] In this respect the sciences are vastly more dependent upon philosophy than it is upon them.

Indeed, for perennialism the historic achievements of such a science as chemistry are, at best, temporal illustrations of the nonhistoric, that is to say, nontemporal, principles of philosophy. Regardless of the changes, corrections, proofs, disproofs that occur in the chemist's labora-

‡ See Maritain, *Scholasticism and Politics*, p. 33; Yves Simon, "Maritain's Philosophy of the Sciences," *Thomist* (quarterly), Maritain Volume.

tory, the principles of philosophy remain impervious to either change or correction by the methods that circumscribe the chemist's own results. Such principles are in a real sense *knowledge,* whereas the scientist's conclusions are at best only probable and therefore of the same species as *opinion.*

Perennialist Beliefs about Value

The sphere of ethics

> The nature of a man's being determines the nature of his actions; and the nature of his being comes to manifestation first of all in the mind . . . A man's being is his potential energy directed towards or away from God; and it is by this potential energy that he will be judged as good or evil . . . We see then that, for the Perennial Philosophy, good is the separate self's conformity to, and finally annihilation in, the divine Ground which gives it being; evil, the intensification of separateness, the refusal to know that the Ground exists.[7]

These sentences from Aldous Huxley, clothed in Aristotelian-Thomist terminology, summarize quite well the general axiological approach of perennialism. They imply a number of beliefs outlined above and suggest that not only knowledge but values, too, are grounded in a teleological and supernatural reality. As Adler expresses it, "Anything has as much goodness as it has being." [8] Also, the deep cleavage between perennialist and progressivist ethics is underscored, in Huxley's view, by the secondary importance of action. For Dewey the reverse proposition would be much more correct: the nature of a man's actions determines the nature of his being. Most revealing for ethics itself, Huxley maintains in the quotation that human goodness is determined by the actuality —by the spirituality of form—which man attains as he emancipates himself from the material, the corporeal.

The Hierarchy of Virtues. We have learned that it is characteristic of perennialism to recognize the importance, within limits, of natural experience. Neo-Thomists are fond of speaking of ethics, esthetics, and politics as branches of "practical philosophy," which is, to be sure, on a lower stratum than "speculative philosophy" but is nonetheless philosophy. In short, these branches are also concerned with universal principles, albeit principles of practice in ethical conduct, esthetic creation, and political organization.

But the highest good for Neo-Thomists is still what it is for Huxley: union with God. Just below this highest level is the life of reason, for in speculation we come as close as thinkers can to such a union. On the practical level, however, perennialists would doubtless continue with Aristotle to regard happiness as the most important value—happiness defined as maximum fulfillment of individual capacities in relation to other individuals.

The meaning of practical philosophy is illustrated by the perennialist's recognition that pleasures are a legitimate part of earthly happiness. The ascetic propensity of Platonism is thus counteracted by a deeper appreciation of emotions and appetites, which, however, should never be indulged excessively; when they are, man's material nature is sure to dominate over his spiritual nature. Passion must always be kept under the strict control of reason, with the life of reason itself considered the highest of all pleasures—indeed, the highest happiness. Here is a worldly ideal which, though very difficult to achieve, is sufficiently practicable so that a few men, at least, may hope to attain it to a high degree.

By referring directly to Aristotle's brilliant design for ethics, we can more systematically organize this analysis.* Let us observe that for Aristotle, as to a very great extent for his present-day disciples, there are two main classes of virtues: first, the "intellectual," second, the "moral." These virtues are arranged in a hierarchy, in which moral virtues, built by habit formation, are at the bottom and intellectual virtues, built by "teaching," are at the top.

The lower type belongs to the "irrational" part of man, although it also partakes of the rational. (Note again the implied hylomorphic principle.) Aristotle lists the virtues of moderation as standing midway between the extremes. Courage, for example, is the mean of foolhardiness and cowardice; modesty, the mean of bashfulness and shamelessness.

The higher, or intellectual, virtues belong to the "rational" part of man. Among these, intuitive or speculative reason is first in the hierarchy. But both prudence and art are also included among the intellectual

* See Aristotle, *Ethics*.

virtues because, although they stand at the level of human action and production, they are likewise subject to rational controls. Prudence, for example, is most concerned with individual conduct. It therefore commands the special attention of men as they go about their daily lives, for it establishes the rules by which they act morally while also acting vigorously and practically. The prudent man is properly self-interested and therefore clever; he is the "individual thing" of reality acting out his ethical role. Nevertheless, because he also deliberates about the universal forms that hide behind his particular actions—because he is "substance" —his aspiration is to be truly philosophic and hence purely rational about those actions.

The sphere of esthetics

We turn now directly to art as another important "intellectual virtue" of concern to practical philosophy. Probably no perennialist of our time has as successfully as Maritain restated and applied to the arts of today and tomorrow ancient-medieval ideas in this sphere.

"The Man of Learning," says Maritain, "is an Intellectual demonstrating, the Artist is an Intellectual operating, the Prudent Man is an intelligent Man of Will acting well."[9] By the "Intellectual operating," he means that the artist impresses his forms upon matter in order to give them in actuality the meaning that is in them potentially. The matter upon which the artist operates may be stone, paint, or such symbols as musical notes or words. Indeed, as Adler emphasizes, the artist of words may write not only poetry or fiction but on occasion a book of logic or grammar. He thereby creates a "liberal art," an art of reason, as distinguished from such "servile arts" as medicine, which deal mainly with things or bodies extrinsic to man's essence—that is, to his rationality.†

Beauty is the highest value of esthetics in the same way that the supreme good of speculative reason is the highest value of ethics. Also like speculative reason, it is in a sense self-evident, that is, it is intuited directly rather than demonstrated logically. Beauty differs, however, from other forms in the respect that we behold it with an immediate *delight.* There is something ecstatic about pure beauty—so much so that, in its

† See Mortimer J. Adler, *Art and Prudence,* pp. 432-436. In this work Adler acknowledges his great indebtedness to *Art and Scholasticism* by Maritain. See also Maritain, *Art and Poetry;* and *Creative Intuition in Art and Poetry.*

presence, philosophy finally fails us. Only a state of grace can fully appreciate that

> God . . . is the most beautiful of beings, because . . . His beauty is without alteration or vicissitude, without increase or diminution: and because it is not like the beauty of things, which have all a particularized beauty . . . He is beautiful by Himself and in Himself, absolutely beautiful.[10]

Such language is reminiscent of the famous doctrine of "Platonic love" —the love of the spiritual—which in Plato's *Symposium* is identified with love of pure beauty unsullied by passion.

But the art of everyday life is very much concerned with things—indeed it is the one intellectual virtue that is chiefly so concerned. Moreover, it involves pleasure, for we experience a pleasurable emotion when we hear fine music or witness fine drama. As Aristotle insisted, however, there is another and even more important value in such enjoyment: the value of *catharsis*. By participating vicariously in the passions of the actor on the stage, the spectator in the audience releases his own tensions and so, when he leaves the theater, finds himself better able to regulate his personal life. Such purgation, says Adler, "temporarily relieves the burden of ever-present passion, and thus aids reason in its office of discipline and control." [11] Man may thus derive a rich value from listening to music or watching a motion picture.

Other interesting distinctions and definitions might be introduced were we able to proceed further with esthetic theory. We need now, however, to consider the third and final branch of practical philosophy.

The Sphere of Politics

Differences Among Perennialists. Extensive surveys of perennialist philosophy are still being written with virtually no reference to politics—an omission which tempts the conjecture that its disciples sometimes become so engrossed with eternal things that such a worldly activity scarcely warrants careful consideration.‡ This is not, however, a completely accurate statement, for the world crisis of our time has very deeply disturbed a few of the leading perennialists. Moreover, as opposing phi-

‡ See Louis de Raeymaeker, *Introduction to Philosophy;* Brother Benignus, *op. cit.;* Huxley, *op. cit.*

losophies have become established in vigorous cultural institutions (communism, especially), the most powerful organized expression of perennialism (the Church) has become increasingly articulate about such practical issues as war and peace, economics, and politics.

Nevertheless, it is difficult to generalize about the present-day political thought of perennialist leaders. Differences are sometimes so acute that the terms "left wing" or "right wing" may be applied even to perennialists. Belloc and Berdyaev, for example, hold political views on the extreme "right," while Adler and Maritain would, by comparison, be considered politically "left."

A philosophic reason for these differences is the status of politics within the perennialist hierarchy of beliefs. Situated on the relatively low level of the practical, politics is rather removed from, although still related to, the ruling axioms of metaphysics. In this respect politics is roughly analogous to the sciences; epistemologically it lies somewhere between opinion and pure truth, just as axiologically it partakes of both the moral and the intellectual virtues. But it is still capable of intellectual analysis and thus of the development of sound, because philosophic, principles.

A final reason for differences among present-minded perennialists is that those who are friendly to the forces of democratic expansion may experience a certain discomfort in reconciling such friendliness with Aristotle's or Thomas's preference for aristocratic monarchy. Nevertheless, we may find Maritain vigorously and openly endorsing as the best political order a conception which he calls "democracy." In this conception he and such allies as Adler reach further than their venerated masters. Since we are especially concerned with the legitimacy of this endorsement, let us turn once more to Maritain's views.

Political Personalism. The term "political personalism" is used to epitomize Maritain's outlook. It is the wholly developed person, dignified to himself and to others, rather than the individual who is but a part, that is considered to be the great purpose of political life.* This concept is developed as the "true humanism"—a humanism which "tends to render man more truly human and to make his original greatness manifest. . . ."[12]

By the whole person Maritain obviously assumes a core perennialist

* See Maritain, *The Person and the Common Good;* and *Christianity and Democracy,* pp. 68, 78.

belief. Man is integrally both material and spiritual; but he becomes fully himself in the degree that he rises to the heights of reason and purpose always latent within him. Such an effort is really successful only under divine guidance—under the magnetic pull, we may say, of deified Form. In this sense political personalism also rests upon theological, supernatural grounds and supports Maritain's firm contention (developed also by the right-wing Anglican T. S. Eliot in his widely read works†) that the ideal society must be Christian at heart or fail.

A Christian society cannot be maintained either by fascism or communism. It cannot be maintained by the former primarily because the state swallows up the person and, also, discriminates among persons on such false grounds as race. Nor can it be maintained by the latter because that too is totalitarian and, even more, because it rests upon the iniquitous philosophy of materialism. But fascism and communism are not alone in this failure, for Maritain applies the same judgment to that truncated kind of humanism which, in the name of democracy, limits itself to a merely "anthropocentric" conception of man by insisting that you and I are socially self-sufficient, earthly individuals. Rousseau, Comte, and Dewey are all repudiated because they commit this grievous fallacy.

Nevertheless, it is not to be denied that Maritain, in contrast to some perennialists, has earnestly sought to reconcile his philosophy with the revolutionary events of our century and to use it in behalf of the humane values accepted by the most ardent advocates of a radically socialized order. Occasionally he goes so far to the left as to insist that capitalism as an economic system has largely outlived its usefulness; that the working class has become the most important single force in shaping the destiny of humanity; that considerable collectivization of industrial processes is now urgently needed; that the people should properly be the determiners of public policies and their chosen leaders the "vicars" of their interests. All such proposals are considered under the general category of the secular or "temporal city," and Maritain carefully points out that within this kind of regime it is necessary to tolerate many differences in religious allegiance, including even the difference of those individuals who swear to none.

Nevertheless, the temporal city is finally subordinate and secondary to the spiritual order—it is "on a lower plane." In his attempt to bring the two "cities" into juxtaposition, Maritain utilizes his fine scholastic

† See Eliot, *op. cit.*; and *Notes towards the Definition of Culture.*

training to draw innumerable fine distinctions. They are distinctions which in all likelihood are symptomatic of considerable personal as well as intellectual suffering induced by the struggle between his devotion to complete Thomism, on the one hand, and his sensitivity to contemporary issues and dangers, on the other. He speaks of the secular state "as an end and principal agent—but not . . . the final end or . . . the highest principal agent." He insists that the "spiritual and temporal planes" are "clearly distinct"—yet "they are not separate." He regards Church and state as independent of each other but willingly admits that the Church not only should discern its own political interests but, as the "deposit" of revealed truths, is entitled to direct temporal affairs "from above." Conversely, the state even has the "duty" to "assist the Church in the free accomplishment" of its mission (which is, of course, to promulgate its absolute and unchallengeable doctrine). Despite his own preference for "democracy," he is able to say that the Church, as a church, "is compatible with all forms of government worthy of man." We can understand from this relative valuation of Church and state why Maritain seems to accept without reservation the authority of papal pronouncements, even referring to them repeatedly in firm support of his own arguments.‡

Maritain touches upon so many other significant questions in the political sphere and shows such extraordinary comprehension of philosophies such as Marxism (toward which he is nonetheless hostile) that this presentation can merely sample his thought as accurately as possible. In closing this chapter we should, however, note two other qualifications. The first is that through the years Maritain himself has somewhat modified his political views, so that one cannot always be sure in a given criticism that one is expressing his *current* view. The second is that Maritain is much further "left" than many others who proclaim their devotion to perennialist precepts.*

If, indeed, there is any validity in the progressivist view that the ultimate and most reliable test of beliefs is their active consequences, we may conclude that Maritain is politically a rather atypical perennialist. In its recent history, the hierarchy of the Church has in practice much more often aided political regressivism (its role in the Spanish Civil War

‡ See Maritain, *True Humanism,* pp. 100, 158, 180ff., 230, 170f., 288f., 293, 172; *Christianity and Democracy,* p. 37; *Ransoming the Time,* p. 206.
* See Simon, *op. cit.*

is a glaring example) than it has supported Maritain's objectives.† By the test of consequences one might contend that Belloc is more representative of the dominant perennialist position when he expresses grave doubts about majority rule as the basic criterion of democracy or when he places the Church above the popular majority even to the point of insisting that, in moral choices, the faithful should if necessary "resist the civil law and obey the law of the Church." ‡

Notes

[1] Mortimer J. Adler, *Problems for Thomists*, p. 3.

[2] Etienne Gilson, *The Unity of Philosophical Experience*, p. 317.

[3] National Society for the Study of Education, *Forty-first Yearbook*, Part I, "Philosophies of Education," p. 226. See also Adler, *How to Think about War and Peace*, Chap. 14.

[4] Richard M. Weaver, *Ideas Have Consequences*, p. 3.

[5] Quoted from Brother Benignus, *Nature, Knowledge and God*, p. 392.

[6] Adler, *Art and Prudence*, pp. 238, 242.

[7] Aldous Huxley, *The Perennial Philosophy*, pp. 179, 224. Copyright 1945 by Harper and Brothers and reprinted with their permission.

[8] "Philosophies of Education," *op. cit.*, p. 242.

[9] Jacques Maritain, *Art and Scholasticism*, p. 20.

[10] Maritain, *Art and Scholasticism*, p. 31. Copyright 1933 by Charles Scribner's Sons and reprinted with their permission.

[11] Adler, *Art and Prudence*, p. 204. See also Maritain, *op. cit.*, p. 65.

[12] Maritain, *True Humanism*, p. xii.

† See Paul Blanshard, *American Freedom and Catholic Power*, Chaps. 2, 3, 11.

‡ See Belloc, *op. cit.*, pp. 68, 80, 84.

CHAPTER 11

The Perennialist Pattern of Educational Beliefs

THE QUALIFICATIONS WITH WHICH ESSENTIALIST BELIEFS ABOUT education were treated in Chapter 8 also apply in considerable measure to perennialism. We shall not contend that perennialism's educational beliefs are always completely consistent with its philosophic substructure. Thus, we recognize that every Platonist, Aristotelian, or Thomist is not necessarily a consistent or self-avowed educational perennialist, although all of the latter are almost certain to be one or more of the former.* Also, we do not propose to deal with the educational beliefs of perennialism in exhaustive fashion, either in their theoretical or practical significance. Our study is limited to their more general features.

The Sweep of Perennialist Education

ANCIENT-MEDIEVAL BACKGROUNDS

Considering the overwhelming contribution of Plato, Aristotle, and Aquinas to the perennialist world-view, we may assume that their atti-

* For a recent example of deviants, see the "classical realist" theory of Harry S. Broudy in *Building a Philosophy of Education* and of John Wild in "Modern Philosophies and Education," *Fifty-fourth Yearbook*, Part I, National Society for the Study of Education.

tudes toward education are also influential. That this is the case is demonstrated by the fact that a large proportion of the outstanding proposals by perennialists of our own day are derived directly from these three masters.†

Plato. The educational beliefs of Plato are adjuncts of his aristocratic position in politics and hence are even more immediate adjuncts of his pivotal doctrine of Ideas. This is the doctrine, we may recall, that finds the essence of reality, knowledge, and value to consist of eternally existing patterns—the archetypes of all particular things, truths, and goods. Since a just social order is really possible only as these Ideas become the standards by which we are governed, the single most important objective of education is to train leaders to recognize and to apply them in every possible way.

The *Republic,* particularly, outlines a program of education to this end. Since this program continues almost from birth to the age of fifty years, we might suppose that it is an ancient recognition of the popular current view that people can learn continuously throughout life. But Plato showed little interest in training the majority of the people. His program so rapidly weeds out the "unfit" that only a few continue into the later years. Until the age of twenty, the student concentrates on music, gymnastics, the three R's, and military training, from twenty to thirty on mathematics and science, from thirty to thirty-five on philosophy, and from thirty-five to fifty on practical experience in society, where moral and intellectual stamina is rigorously tested. The artisan class receives least education because it is least competent. (The huge class of slaves beneath the artisans is simply ignored.) Those who qualify as soldiers are almost all selected by the time they are twenty; those best suited for secondary offices in the state, by the time they are about thirty. Study of philosophy—the all-important subject—is therefore confined to an elite who, over a five-year period, acquire knowledge of first principles and who, after a prolonged period of practice, are then, and only then, ready to rule as philosopher-kings.

The Platonic psychology pervades this entire program. Man is endowed with three capacities: appetite, will, and reason. Education should consider all three—hence the emphasis on gymnastics and music, espe-

† See John S. Brubacher, *A History of the Problems of Education,* pp. 98-103; R. Freeman Butts, *A Cultural History of Education,* pp. 75ff.; J. Donald Butler, *Four Philosophies and Their Practice in Education and Religion,* Chap. 13.

cially in the earlier years, as aids respectively to the physical and energetic, or "spirited," qualities of human nature. But reason requires the most exact training if it is to rule effectively over both qualities and if each is to exercise its proper function in relation to the other two.

This "tripartite soul" likewise corresponds to a "tripartite society." Artisans are those in whom appetite is strongest; soldiers, those in whom will is strongest; leaders, those in whom reason is strongest. The just society is measured by the correctness of the hierarchical order of these classes, in the same way that the just man is measured by an analogous order of his psychological traits. In this sense education is "good" in so far as it establishes justice both in political institutions and in human beings.

Aristotle. Our contention above that Aristotle is fundamentally a Platonist (see p. 294) is supported by the extent to which his writings reinforce Plato's major educational principles. He does not, of course, literally repeat them. Yet in his insistence that the cultivation of reason by means of the sciences—and especially by philosophy—is the single most important task of education, and in his conception of such training as having the political purpose of wise leadership, he is in complete agreement with his teacher.

Aristotle is more original than Plato in his emphasis upon habit formation as the primary purpose of elementary schooling. In this respect, he foreshadowed the view of various essentialists, for he holds that obedience to moral rules, to tradition and law, is properly and most easily inculcated during the earliest years. Ontologically, he implies that children require firm guidance because of the dominance in their natures of matter and motion over form and purpose—a dominance that may recede as their actuality comes to prevail more fully over their potentiality. This theory suggests that the teacher possesses more actuality than his pupil. Thus, being closer to virtue, he is properly entitled to serve as the latter's mentor.

Also distinctive in Aristotle is the emphasis upon happiness as a goal of good education, although even in this emphasis the Platonic influence is noticeable. Not only does Aristotle stress the concomitant cultivation of the several components of human nature—the physical and emotional as well as the intellectual—but he finally agrees that the highest happiness is a life of speculation. In his delineation of man as a hylomorphic being, however, Aristotle sometimes conceives of happiness in a more rounded or balanced fashion. Indeed, it is in terms of this conception that some perennialist educators try to adapt the progressivist conception of the "whole child" to their learning and curriculum programs without doing violence to their own principles.

Aquinas. The skill with which Aquinas incorporated Aristotelianism within his own medieval-Christian system of beliefs is nowhere more aptly illustrated than in his views on education. The purpose of education is to draw the dormant capacities of the learner from their hiding places within him so that they will become active and real by his consciousness of them. The teacher's role is primarily to instruct, in the sense of giving aid to the susceptible human substance, and, above all, to help the learner to reason clearly and to intuit first principles. In this task, learning through words becomes more fruitful than learning through the senses, for "words are symbols of intelligible content . . . ,"[1] that is, of essences.

An interesting analogy may be drawn between the teacher and the physician. Just as the latter assists sick or wounded organisms in their inherent tendency to heal themselves, so the former assists ignorant man in his inherent tendency to become wise. Were the tendency not already present, neither physician nor teacher could possibly succeed, for neither can create what is not potentially existent. Both in this sense are agents of reality, the teacher acting as a direct channel to the mind of the student from the final source of reality—the divine headwaters of Truth.‡

It follows, as we should expect, that the distinctive emphasis in the medieval philosophy of education, in contrast with the Greek, is its *theocentricism:* its preoccupation with a supernatural God. Its ultimate concern is not with education for this life but for the afterlife. Despite the sinfulness of men, Aquinas finds hope for their redemption by the aid of the Church and its official advocates. In order to avail himself of this help, man must above all cultivate those supernatural virtues that have to do, respectively, with "knowledge" of God, desire for God, and love of God. These virtues crown the intellectual and moral virtues that serve as proper ends of learning on the merely profane, or earthly, level.

Such Thomist views found solid support in the historic structure of medieval education. Although secular control continued to operate

‡ See Robert Ulich, *History of Educational Thought,* pp. 94f.

to some extent, the Church was certainly the most important agency of learning over an era of several centuries. Under it, elementary and secondary schools emphasized the rote study of Latin, taught some music and arithmetic, and enforced discipline by frequent corporal punishment. The first universities emerged in the twelfth and thirteenth centuries, and with them teaching slowly gained the status of a profession, eventually achieving immense prestige. (Aquinas himself was a professor at the University of Paris.) The typical university curriculum consisted of the "seven liberal arts"—subsumed under the *trivium* (grammar, rhetoric, and logic) and the *quadrivium* (arithmetic, geometry, astronomy, and music). To these, other studies were gradually added, especially Aristotelian "science," ethics, politics, and metaphysics, all of which were strictly prescribed under faculties licensed by the Church. The astonishing import of this curriculum for contemporary perennialist education will soon become clear.

Perennialist education in modern times

The Persistence of Medieval Beliefs. The medieval theory and practice of education have remained influential down through the centuries. Even today, the organization of our most modern universities shows marked resemblance to their medieval predecessors. Learning through words, advocated so strongly by Aquinas, is a widely accepted practice, and there is little doubt that the study of Latin, still required in many secondary schools, is a medieval inheritance.

Nevertheless, despite the persistent influence of perennialism, few theorists have made additional contributions to its original formulation until very recently. To be sure, medieval ideas about education carried over into modern culture in many ways, just as they carried over into education and the whole of modern philosophy. Thus Comenius and Pestalozzi, for example, reflected, at least indirectly, the strong absolutist spirit of Thomism. But, except within parochial circles, the historian is hard pressed to find educators in the original medieval tradition who exerted much influence during the centuries following its height of influence and power. An exception, perhaps, was the Catholic leader Cardinal John Henry Newman, whose *The Idea of a University*, published in 1852, continues to be quoted frequently, even today, for its eloquent defense of perennialist higher education. In America, probably the most eminent Catholic educator during the nineteenth and early twentieth centuries was Bishop John L. Spalding. His beliefs about education, always in the framework of his faith, are still a good index of the beliefs of the more farsighted Church leaders.*

Contemporary Perennialists. The American revival of interest in perennialism in the past two decades derives less from Catholic than from lay educators. In the 'twenties and early 'thirties, a new movement in behalf of classical education, expressed under the old name of "humanism," attracted wide attention. Although not directly grounded in any one philosophic tradition, its exponents included the Thomist Louis J. Mercier and the intellectualist Norman Foerster, both of whose views on university education reveal the influence of Newman and anticipate those of the best-known perennialist in contemporary American education, Robert M. Hutchins.†

Indeed, future historians who write about our extraordinary century may give more credit to Hutchins than to anyone else for the movement referred to in the preceding chapter as neoscholasticism or neo-Thomism. Although he does not formally attach either label to himself, and although less well equipped philosophically than his intimate associate Mortimer J. Adler (to whom he gives major credit for his own "education"), he is able, as former Chancellor of one of the world's greatest universities, the University of Chicago, and subsequently as a high official of the affluent Ford Foundation, to extend his influence widely. This influence is illustrated not only at Chicago, where he introduced, in the face of bitter faculty opposition, a number of "reforms" (some of which were modified after his departure), but still more in other programs and institutions. The most famous of the latter is St. John's College, in Annapolis, Maryland, which he helped to reorganize with the cooperation of two former Chicago colleagues, Stringfellow Barr and Scott Buchanan, who became its first administrators. Adler, after many years on the Chicago faculty, now heads the Institute of Philosophical Research, San Francisco, which is heavily supported by the Ford Foundation. In addition, other scholars—Mark Van Doren and John U. Nef are

* See Merle Curti, *The Social Ideas of American Educators,* Chap. 10.

† See Louis J. Mercier, *The Challenge of Humanism;* Norman Foerster, *The Future of the Liberal College;* Robert M. Hutchins, *No Friendly Voice; The Higher Learning in America; Education for Freedom;* and *The Conflict in Education.*

outstanding examples—have advocated a program of learning based more or less upon perennialist principles.‡

Most Church leaders have enthusiastically welcomed the current rise of perennialism within secular circles. Jacques Maritain, particularly, has written admiringly of Hutchins, Nef, and others. His own writings on education, to which we refer below, are characteristically broad and appreciative of other points of view, although they also strongly reflect the supernatural and revelatory aspects of Thomist doctrine. Among Church specialists in the philosophy of education we name five who have received especial recognition from their non-Catholic colleagues—William F. Cunningham, William J. McGucken, J. D. Redden, F. A. Ryan, and Edward A. Fitzpatrick.† All of them, along with other Catholic educators, would, of course, emphasize their differences rather than agreements with secular perennialists. Indeed, these differences, judged in the context of their theological creed, are far-reaching. Nevertheless, when viewed in broad educational perspective, Church and secular perennialist educators also share so many common principles that our analysis below of perennialist beliefs about learning, curriculum, and educational control must be derived from the writings of both groups.

Perennialist Beliefs about Learning

Let us recall that perennialist views, despite the demand for unity, are by no means wholly unified. The Platonist, for example, would not be expected to agree on every point with the Aristotelian nor with the Thomist. Nevertheless, just as the beliefs of Plato, Aristotle, and Aquinas are basically much more similar than dissimilar, so the range of agreement among their disciples is likewise strikingly wide. It is upon this broad area of agreement that we turn our spotlight.

‡ See below for references to writings of these leaders.

† See William F. Cunningham, *The Pivotal Problems of Education;* William J. McGucken, *The Catholic Way in Education* and his chapter in "Philosophies of Education," *Forty-first Yearbook,* Part I, National Society for the Study of Education; J. D. Redden and F. A. Ryan, *A Catholic Philosophy of Education;* and Edward A. Fitzpatrick, *How to Educate Human Beings.*

Mental discipline: the focus of learning

All perennialists concur in the proposition that exercising and disciplining the mind is one of the highest obligations of learning—or, more strictly, is paramount in the *higher* learning. Accordingly, they insist that any theory and program of education that in general ranks vocational skill, overt action, interest, or similar concepts over mental discipline for its own sake has clearly put last things first and first things last. Behind this standard—central and explicit in the writings of some advocates, more implicit in the writings of others—lies the elaborate psychological apparatus with which we have become briefly acquainted in our survey of perennialist beliefs about knowledge and related beliefs about reality and value. Learning theory is but a restatement in a different context of more basic philosophic theory.

Rationality and Freedom. Let us consider, as a key example, the perennialist contention that man is distinct in kind as well as in degree from all other animals. The scientific evidence provided by Darwin and by subsequent evolutionists—that man has descended from lower species—is completely irrelevant because, in last analysis, man's distinctiveness is "proved" not by science but by speculative reason. The rationality common to all men is self-evident; one cannot reason against the existence of such rationality without using reason. This is a first principle that would be true at any conceivable time or place in which man attempted to consider rationality at all. Thus, by deduction, we proceed from the major premise that man is universally rational to the conclusion that any particular man whom we may meet is likewise rational.‡

But the principle of rationality generates out of its own self-evident clarity a second highly important principle, namely, that of freedom. The mechanism of metaphysics and logic used by perennialists in order to convince us that they believe in freedom is much more elaborate than this brief statement can suggest. For example, consideration of freedom leads to the age-old problem of "free will" and eventually to the solution offered by theology: man has the will, if he will but exercise it, to save himself from the damnation that his fallen state of sinfulness continually threatens.

The concept of freedom in which we are most interested, however, is the freedom that can be cultivated by education: the power to act

‡ See Mortimer J. Adler, *Art and Prudence*, pp. 252-256.

voluntarily, which depends, in turn, upon the power of reason itself. Since, according to perennialism, the authority of reason is the only possible source of freedom, it follows that the supreme purpose of education is to perfect that authority as far as possible. In this doctrine lies an important meaning of liberal education: to "liberate" man by helping him to become his essential self—a self which, distinct from the brute, is a *rational* animal and therefore free. All learning must be dedicated to this end of man's maximum actualization.*

Learning to Reason. How is man to undertake so difficult a task as learning to reason? To anticipate our discussion of the perennialist curriculum, we may say that he must begin with correct habit formation during his first years of schooling. The skills of reading, writing, and computation are so necessary that they might easily take precedence over all else. But these are chiefly preparatory. Learning to reason, in the strict sense, becomes a major objective of secondary and college education—an objective attainable only by continuous exercise in the related disciplines of grammar, logic, and rhetoric. We begin to achieve the greatest power, to reason, as we learn how to relate words to one another so that they acquire clarity and order—as, further, we learn how to communicate inwardly, with ourselves, and outwardly, with others. In this effort, semantics is helpful, but we can find most of the required rules about the "meaning of meaning" in such thinkers as Plato, Aristotle, and Aquinas.

Just as we do not assume that all semanticists are equally accurate, neither do we assume, say perennialists, that all logicians can teach us to reason. The logical theory of Dewey, for example, has done inestimable harm to education by identifying the reasoning process almost exclusively with experimental problem solving. Actually, not only is problem solving limited merely to the area of discovery and research but the "knowledge" it produces, being largely inductive and therefore only probable, is of a distinctly lower order than that which may be obtained by employing the "critical faculty" of reason proper.†

We reach the conclusion that learning how to reason, in the highest sense, consists in learning how to philosophize as we develop the intel-

* See Jacques Maritain, *Freedom in the Modern World.*

† See Adler, *How to Read a Book,* pp. 82, 43-47. Adler admits that most of his rules are obtained from a "medieval commentary" (p. 97). See also Richard M. Weaver, *Ideas Have Consequences,* Chap. 10.

lectual virtues. By means of metaphysics, reason, as man's highest natural attainment, ascends even above logic and becomes purely intuitive, completely disengaged from experience. Reason, says Maritain, is "visible only by means of abstraction and universal concepts. . . ."[2] In this rarefied atmosphere, and only in it, man becomes for the moment utterly free. But it is a freedom obtainable only at the cost, paradoxically, of prolonged mental discipline.‡

Learning to live: the perennialist recipe

Mental discipline, although it stands at the apex of the pyramid of learning, does not constitute the whole pyramid. Aristotelian perennialists, especially, are quick to insist that they are equally concerned with the substance of the student and therefore with the material, or bodily, as well as with the spiritual, or rational, part of his nature.

Concessions to Contemporary Psychology. Because of this concern, Aristotelian perennialists incorporate, to their own satisfaction, many doctrines of modern psychology. Despite his charge of the "inductive sterility" of much psychological research, Adler, for example, accords a limited recognition to the importance of recent experiments in reading and in psychoanalysis. Cunningham goes so far as to accept, rather eclectically, certain findings of the realist Thorndike and such important psychological concepts of progressivism as interest and motivated learning. Maritain, with characteristic breadth, suggests work experience as desirable learning experience, and he is insistent that, up to a point, elementary education should encourage the free play of imagination, the "kind of bounding, temperamental, and lucid freedom" that is natural to the child.* Even Hutchins has been known occasionally to approve the methods of progressive education, as has Van Doren.†

But the significance of a remark made in the chapter above should be recalled: *whatever concessions perennialism makes to psychology or to other fields are always made on its own premises, never on theirs.*

‡ See Etienne Gilson, *The Unity of Philosophical Experience,* pp. 313f.

* See Maritain, *Education at the Crossroads,* pp. 45f., 60f. For a more recent statement of his philosophy of education, see his chapter in "Modern Philosophies and Education," *op. cit.*

† See Adler, *How to Read a Book,* pp. 77f., 120; "The Order of Learning," *Moraga Quarterly,* September 1941; *What Man Has Made of Man,* pp. 89f., 201; Cunningham, *op. cit.,* Chap. 7; Hutchins, *No Friendly Voice,* pp. 127f.; Mark Van Doren, *Liberal Education,* pp. 91f.

Since this is so, the reader of such treatises as Hutchins' *The Conflict in Education* and Van Doren's *Liberal Education* should not be seduced by their sophisticated persuasiveness until he is certain of their major premises. He should be careful, also, not to isolate specific passages for approval until he has determined that they are valid indices to those premises.

Returning to our analysis, we may say that the perennialist recipe for learning to live, in the sense of expressing richly one's whole nature, is flavored far more abundantly with one ingredient than with any other—namely, learning to reason. Therefore, learning to live, in any morally defensible fashion, becomes impossible except under the authority of the thoroughly educated—meaning the metaphysically equipped—mind. The Thomist goes beyond this doctrine by insisting that both learning to live and learning to reason are but two steps on the path to eternity. Hence, in addition to such "universal human needs" of life as health, family, economic security, leisure, and knowledge, there is the superlative need of that "divine security" that absolute faith alone can satisfy. Thus, McGucken states forthrightly that "the thing of ultimate importance is not here but hereafter. This world has genuine value only in so far as it leads to the next." [3] Psychologically, this last and crucial step is well accounted for by the same core principle that accounts for others—by man's hylomorphic, teleological being, which ever drives him, however faltering his progress, toward expression of the essence abiding within him. Learning, in short, is the development of substance: the purification of man's actuality and thus of his spirituality.

That such a typical Aristotelian interpretation can be translated without too much difficulty into a Platonic interpretation is illustrated by Cunningham. He divides human nature into the main parts of (1) cognition, or knowing, (2) affection, or feeling, and (3) conation, or doing—a division not too unlike Plato's "tripartite soul" of reason, appetite, and will—and attempts to demonstrate that all three are compatible with contemporary psychology. In terms of learning, for example, all three must be recognized if we are to educate richly for living; accordingly, we learn from Freud, for example, when we concern ourselves with the affective part of man, just as we learn from Watson or Dewey, for example, when we deal with the conative. Also, the affective and conative are still integral with the whole; man is really a "somatopsychic" (a body-mind) organism, as Gestalt psychology has rediscovered and as medical diagnosis is beginning to comprehend. Nevertheless, despite this integrality, the cognitive remains primary and dominant, just as it does in Plato. Reason must rule or we shall wallow in the evil of our lower nature, matter will overshadow form, potentiality will fail to become actual, and the "acorn" of our beings will shrivel instead of rising to the giant "oak" of our full spiritual capacities.‡

Learning Through Teaching. Perennialists today seem to find quite beyond compare the analogy between the art of teaching and the art of medicine which was immortalized by Aquinas. Thus, Maritain insists that each art aims to magnetize the spontaneous inclination of the human organism both to be healthy and to learn—an analogy that reminds us of the role of Socrates.* Just as the "gadfly of Athens" sought to disturb the tranquillity of his listeners by persistently challenging their vague, half-formed beliefs and by pointing out contradictions and comparisons, so the teacher today is effective when he performs a similar role. Lectures also can be helpful, to be sure. But even these are never for the sake merely of conveying information; they are also to provide enlightenment by interpreting and pointing up implications in the subject matter. When the teacher thus functions as physician of the soul, we have an example, in its precise sense, of what Adler calls "learning by instruction." It is distinguished from "learning by discovery" because in the latter no teacher is needed—the student learns by himself if he knows how to read actively and creatively. Each type of learning can, of course, reinforce the other; it is obvious that learning by instruction should stimulate the self-education of learning by discovery.†

The teacher, according to the perennialists, is, then, not at all a mere "conveyor belt" of information between world and mind—a recognition which distinguishes perennialist theories of learning from many essentialist theories. Indeed, the teacher is himself a learner to the degree that his own capacity for self-discovery is increased as he instructs others. Nevertheless, the teacher ought to exert "moral authority" over his pupils because, if he is professionally qualified, he is properly superior to them. As Adler indicates in precise Aristotelian terms, he "must possess actually whatever the person being taught possesses only potentially and hence is

‡ See Cunningham, *op. cit.*, Chaps. 3, 6; "Philosophies of Education," *op. cit.*, pp. 276f.

* See Maritain, *Education at the Crossroads*, pp. 30-33.

† See "Philosophies of Education," *op. cit.*, p. 213; Adler, *How to Read a Book*, p. 31; Van Doren, *op. cit.*, pp. 171-174.

able to learn."[4] Some perennialists have gone so far as to insist that the teacher must have "perfect" knowledge.‡

We summarize the perennialist approach to learning and teaching with a significant quotation from Maritain. It should enable us to test our skill in detecting subtle overtones of words which, taken out of context, might apply to philosophies completely in conflict with his.

> What is learned should never be passively or mechanically received, as dead information which weighs down and dulls the mind. It must rather be actively transformed by understanding into the very life of the mind, and thus strengthen the latter, as wood thrown into fire and transformed into flame makes the fire stronger.[5]

Perennialist Views of the Curriculum

Because perennialism, like other philosophies of education, has practical effects on the schools today, its views of the curriculum are affected by current practices while at the same time it steadily reconditions those practices. Two main levels are surveyed: (1) elementary and secondary education; (2) the higher learning and adult education.

The elementary and secondary levels

Education as Preparation. One of the most revealing differences between progressivism and perennialism—a difference which serves to highlight the latter's special emphasis—is in their respective attitudes toward "education as preparation." Whereas Dewey and his associates vigorously reject the doctrine that schooling is preparation for some later period of life, many perennialists frankly insist that schooling in the early years is precisely that. Their underlying belief is that the child is still primarily potential rather than actual; hence, the first task of education is to prepare him for his maturity, his life of reason, by guiding him toward that maturity.*

‡ See M. H. Mayer, *The Philosophy of Teaching of St. Thomas Aquinas* p. 65.

* See "Philosophies of Education," *op. cit.*, p. 219.

Here we have a philosophic justification for the attack upon those elementary schools that fail—as perennialists often say they do—to teach the three R's adequately and thus fail to give the child the rudimentary skills without which he cannot in later years act rationally. On this issue, although proceeding from somewhat different premises, certain perennialists argue in the manner of certain essentialists. Nef, for example, insists that a certain amount of unpleasantness in learning is good for the child's morale.† Van Doren, in language reverberative of ancient authorities, attaches great importance to the memorization of passages: "There should be no school in which the young mind fails to receive, like seeds destined to germinate in later years, a full sowing of sentences great men have spoken. . . ." [6] Buchanan goes still further, urging a good deal of rote memory in learning almost all subjects.‡

It is true that one can find perennialists—curiously, perhaps more often among parochial educators than among secular ones—who have tried to reconcile the progressivist type of "activity curriculum" with their own principles. Some have gone so far as to insist that their schools are the most "progressive" of all. Maritain occasionally invites such an interpretation, as does the Catholic "humanist" Mercier in his regard for direct experience, for integration of subject matters, and for the study of human needs.* More conspicuous, however, is their Aristotelian stress upon habits that can be toughened into permanent human possessions only by continuous exercise and familiarity with right content.

And what is "right" content? Most important on the elementary level is "reading, writing, and figuring," with some consideration, in Hutchins' scheme, for history, geography, literature, science, and a foreign language. As Hutchins puts it in his first book, the educator must above all avoid the concept of the elementary school as in any sense "an agency of social reform." In a book published seventeen years later, he even proposes that elementary education "not bother inexperienced children with what are called the social studies." §

Equally important for some perennialists is character training in

† See John U. Nef, *The United States and Civilization*, p. 299.

‡ See Scott Buchanan, "The Crisis in Liberal Education," *Amherst Graduates' Quarterly*, February 1938.

* See Maritain, *op. cit.*, pp. 31f.; Mercier, in Lyman Bryson, Louis Finklestein, and R. M. MacIver (eds.), *Goals for American Education;* L. J. O'Connell, *Are Catholic Schools Progressive?*

§ See Hutchins, *No Friendly Voice*, pp. 66, 114; *The Conflict in Education*, Chap. 3; and *The University of Utopia*, pp. 56f.

the early years. This may be discovered, upon careful inspection, to be another term for training in the moral rather than the intellectual virtues —the latter, as with Aristotle, being more properly the subject of later education. Reading is heavily stressed throughout—especially reading of such classics as the Bible, which, in Nef's elementary program, occupies as paramount a position as any commonly advocated even among Church leaders.‡

The Secondary Curriculum. The principles of the elementary curriculum discussed above are also applicable to secondary education. Although the dividing line between the two levels varies for different perennialists, one finds extraordinary unanimity in their proposal that almost all adolescents engage in a program of "general education" or in trade and skill training, with one type or the other open to every normal young person between the ages of twelve and twenty.

The students who receive most attention (the percentage ranges from less than forty for Mercier to approximately one hundred for Maritain, Barr, and Hutchins) are those eligible for general education.* For those under the age of about sixteen, the stress by several perennialists is upon foreign languages—Greek and Latin as well as modern tongues. For those between the ages of sixteen or seventeen and twenty, the stress is, first, upon the related disciplines of logic, rhetoric, grammar, and mathematics—the master keys of reasoning—and, second, upon the "great books" of all time.

This unanimity of general purpose should not be taken to imply, however, that all perennialists are agreed upon the best plan for general education. Just as we have found differences among progressivists and among essentialists, so, too, perennialists sometimes differ vigorously. Cunningham's *General Education and the Liberal College,* probably the best summary of contemporary thinking among Catholic experts, offers a plan for general education which is characteristic of his breadth of mind and his eagerness to consider criticisms and proposals from educators of other orientations. It is significant of the differences among perennialists that he finds much that is unsatisfactory in the great-books program associated especially with Hutchins and Adler.

Nevertheless, it is this program that, more than any other, has

‡ See Nef, *op. cit.,* pp. 298f.; Hutchins, *No Friendly Voice,* p. 66.
* See Maritain, *op. cit.,* p. 64; Mercier, *op. cit.;* Nef, *op. cit.,* pp. 305f.; Hutchins, *The Conflict in Education,* p. 88.

brought perennialist education to public attention. For nearly all leaders of this allegiance, the most certain means to sound general education for every educable citizen is careful reading of the most important, most perennially influential, works of the leading minds of history.

The St. John's Program. Every student of the lay college St. John's (where this proposal has actually been implemented since 1937 and subsequently only slightly modified) becomes acquainted during a four-year course with a fairly large proportion of those classics which perennialist leaders have selected as "great." † (The list, consisting recently of more than one hundred titles, is amended from time to time.) During each of the four years, the reading program is chronological, beginning with the Greeks (Plato and Aristotle, especially) and extending to such contemporaries as Freud and Whitehead. Many of the books are philosophic, as is to be expected, but works of scientists (Newton, for example) and artists of literature (Shakespeare, for example) are also prominent. Teaching occurs usually in seminars of approximately twenty students, with at least two leaders present to serve as "Socratic" questioners, interpreters, and suggesters during the "conversations."

In addition to the central seminars on the great books, all students study mathematics, science, and language for four years each. These required courses are arranged in more or less immediate relation to the great books, for the two kinds of studies are intended to supplement each other. Thus, Greek, German, and French—each of which is studied for one year—are employed more for their mental discipline than as skills of practical communication. (For example, the year devoted to German is concerned in part with grammar, in part with reading such works as Kant's *Critique of Practical Judgment* in English, some practice being afforded in translating passages from the original.) Similarly, science courses are designed to study and demonstrate classic discoveries and experiments in chemistry and physics as these are described in the works of a Lavoisier or a Galileo. Regular open lectures by outside authorities or by St. John's professors complete the curriculum. There are no electives.

Is the Great-Books Program Perennialist? Since it is obvious that beliefs of the authors of the great books are by no means always in harmony with perennialist beliefs (they are sometimes at opposite poles),

† See St. John's College catalogues of recent years. The author's visit to the College, mentioned under "Aids to Learning" for this chapter, has also influenced this interpretation.

he question arises whether a program such as that of St. John's is a good example of the perennialist philosophy of education. This question s peculiarly pertinent in view of the fact that one of its own leaders, John S. Kieffer, although himself a professed Platonist, has insisted that he College is not dominated by any single theoretical position. Likewise, its president, Richard D. Weigle, denies that the College may be properly classified as perennialist.‡ A few recent curriculum revisions uggest the possibility of somewhat greater eclecticism than previously obtained.

Nevertheless, the fact that such men as Adler, Hutchins, Van Doren, and Maritain have all lauded the program in the highest terms —speaking of it as "the only college in the country" that is moving in the right direction and even as "the greatest college in the world"—is significant, although not conclusive, evidence of a positive answer to our question.* More conclusive is the fact that Hutchins' own prescription for general education, which is based upon secular beliefs consistent with hose reviewed above, is a literal formula for the St. John's curriculum. Although he has on occasion tempered his characteristic tone by admitting alternative possibilities, his pivotal principle is typically Aristotelian: "In general education we are interested in drawing out the elements of our common human nature; we are interested in the attributes of the race, not the accidents of individuals . . ."—attributes which are "the same in any time or place." Moreover, since the "truth is everywhere the same," (Aquinas is cited as authority for this self-evident principle) therefore "education should be everywhere the same." † Not only is this prescription completely harmonious with Adler's position (in discussing his own experience the latter often says "Mr. Hutchins and I") but it is nowhere unharmonious with public statements of such perennialist leaders as Van Doren, Barr, and Buchanan.§ Indeed, Hutchins reaffirmed this prescription in a book published after he had left the University of Chicago: "The aim of an educational system is the same in every age and in every

‡ In communication with the author. See John S. Kieffer, "Inaugural Address," *Inauguration of John Spangler Kieffer*.

* See Adler, "Liberalism and Liberal Education," *Educational Record*, July 1939. The second quotation is credited to Van Doren in publicity material issued by St. John's.

† Hutchins, *The Higher Learning in America*, pp. 61-87. See also Hutchins, *The Atom Bomb and Education*, p. 10.

§ See Adler, *How to Read a Book*; Buchanan, *op. cit.*; Stringfellow Barr, "The Education of Freemen," *New Republic*, August 31, 1942.

society . . . : it is to improve man as man . . . [who also is] the same in every age and in every society. . . ."[7]

We may justifiably assume, therefore, that Hutchins and his associates wish the great books to be read not merely for the mental discipline provided—although this is important—but also for the distillations of transcendental truth that they allegedly contain. The fact that scientific treatises appear quite frequently in the list of great books may be justified on one or both of two grounds: first, that these, too, contain first principles which may be explicated through learning by instruction and by discovery and, second, that they offer contributions to those sub-philosophic levels of knowledge obtainable by "empiriological analysis." Similarly, works on ethics or politics by a Mill or dramas by an Ibsen are included because they help the reader to understand the two great intellectual virtues of practice: prudence and art.

Church educators would, of course, deny that any program that fails to give priority to a study of theology could possibly be perennialist in their sense. We re-emphasize and respect this distinction, again calling attention, however, to the many common beliefs of Church and secular perennialists. Once more Maritain may be the strongest spokesman of the former, for he is convinced that teachers who encourage study of the "heritage of philosophical wisdom . . . may always hope, indeed, that by virtue of its very truth, the philosophy which they think to be true as I do Aristotelian and Thomistic philosophy, will gain momentum among their fellow men, at least in the generation to come."[8]

The Higher Learning and Adult Education

The University Curriculum. In some respects, our outline of perennialist "general education" has anticipated the treatment of higher learning and adult education. Our example, St. John's, is a liberal arts college offering the bachelor's degree. For Hutchins and other sympathizers, however, its organization is a compromise forced upon it by the prevailing American pattern. Actually, general education should, according to Hutchins, be relegated to the junior college, which is usually classified as in the field of secondary education. The "higher learning" proper should begin after general education has been completed—and then only for those students who, at the age of about twenty-one, have clearly demonstrated their superior ability.

Perennialists are scathing in their denunciation of the present university for its eclecticism—its disorganized accumulation of courses and requirements, its duplications, its emphasis on education for money making and other kinds of merely utilitarian training.* They would correct these evils by an "ordering principle," the model for which they candidly derive from the medieval university. To be sure, the latter found its own ordering principle in theology, whereas today's perennialists (excepting Churchmen) would find theirs in metaphysics or speculative philosophy —in what Hutchins has called "the intellectual love of God."[9] Indeed, Hutchins' own writings belie his claim: "I am not here arguing for any specific theological or metaphysical system. . . .";[10] for it is clear in the perspective of his ideas that he argues very often for at least one specific metaphysical system—the Aristotelian. Indeed, when he speaks of the necessity of "divine aid" and of faith in "the fatherhood of God,"[11] one wonders if there are very consequential distinctions between his views and those even of the clerical Thomist.

Hutchins' *The Higher Learning in America* advocates that the reorganized university contain three, and only three, divisions: philosophy, the natural sciences, and the social sciences. Since we are interested mainly in common principles, which pervade the second and third of these, we should observe them in their organic relationship to the first. For example, the social sciences are inescapably concerned with practical philosophy, with ethics and politics, which in turn derive from metaphysics proper.

The former Chancellor of the University of Chicago also includes a place for fact-finding research in his educational scheme for the higher learning. Such experience is as indigenous to it as matter is to the Aristotelian pyramid of reality, which is its ontological archetype. But just as the level of facts and sense data in the latter is inferior to the level of reason and form, so the collector of information is inferior to the seeker of self-evident first principles. Accordingly, "research institutes" should be established on the fringe of the university; its members, who would hold nonfaculty status, would be helpful in providing material to illuminate such principles.

Finally, Hutchins would permit the establishment of "technical institutes" for training in the "routines" connected with such learned

* See Hutchins, "Double Trouble," *Saturday Review of Literature,* July 17, 1948; and *The Conflict in Education.*

professions as law, teaching, and medicine. But, since these profession would also emphasize the intellectual and moral virtues, the greatest and most important part of the education necessary for them would be offere to pre-institute students by the faculty of the university proper. All uni versity students would already have had a general education of the typ advocated for the junior college. This would make it possible for then to concentrate in the university upon those principles of philosoph (ethics for the prospective lawyer is an illustration) held to be mos important to their intended specializations. Throughout the entire educa tional plan, only slightly qualified in later writings, experimental scienc is accorded a subordinate position, because "all the most important ques tions of human existence" cannot and "do not yield to scientific inquiry." For the same reason, the division of philosophy, despite its claim o "philosophical diversity," apparently does not include representatives o scientifically-oriented positions, such as positivism or pragmatism, sinc they are unworthy to be considered philosophies.†

The Hutchins plan for higher education is modified in certain re spects by other perennialists, just as is the plan for general education Maritain and Cunningham, for example, stress theology more heavil than does Hutchins.‡ Nef has emphasized the need of higher educatior for small cloistered groups of scholars, artists, and carefully chosen gradu ate students to work independently within the universities. His enthu siasm for Hutchins' ideas and efforts, guided by his own philosophic beliefs, makes clear that his high valuation of the contribution of such groups proceeds from fairly orthodox perennialist premises. Simila premises underlie another of Nef's proposals admired by Maritain— namely, that master's and doctor's degrees should be awarded on the basis of a threefold knowledge: philosophy in its several main divisions the "essential nature" of two or more scientific disciplines, and training in history.*

In many perennialist discussions of the higher learning, as well a of general education, the medieval university is frankly held up as a model.§ Thus, the terms "quadrivium" and "trivium" are revived a

† See Hutchins, *The Conflict in Education,* pp. 79, 55; *The University o Utopia,* Chap. 3; and *The Higher Learning in America,* Chap. 4.

‡ See Maritain, *op. cit.,* pp. 82-86; Cunningham, *op. cit.,* p. 421.

* See Nef, *op. cit.,* pp. 272-278; Robert B. Heywood (ed.), *The Works of the Mind;* Nef, *The Universities Look for Unity,* p. 38; Maritain, *op. cit.,* p. 81.

§ See Van Doren, *op. cit.,* p. 128; Hutchins in William F. Cunningham *General Education and the Liberal College,* pp. 4-5.

appropriate captions under which their proposals are classified, and Hutchins has written: ". . . no universities since the Middle Ages have been able to duplicate the accomplishments of those that existed then." [12]

Adult Education. Perennialists have always been concerned with adult education. In recent years Catholics, for example, have established a number of programs for trade unionists, in the hope of exerting a greater influence upon the labor movement. We might reasonably contend that the regression toward *secular* perennialism in American education began in New York, during the 1920's, with a number of adult-education "experiments" in which Adler and Buchanan participated. It is understandable, then, that the most publicized development since the reorganization of St. John's has been the further development of the perennialist program by a strongly backed venture in adult education organized around the great books.

Although the literature issued by the Great Books Foundation, of which Hutchins was an organizer and which receives considerable support from the Ford Foundation, makes little reference to a particular philosophy of education, there are valid grounds for believing that it is saturated with perennialist predilections. For example, the original procedure recommended for organizing adult learning groups had already been outlined by Adler several years earlier in his *How to Read a Book* ‡ —an Aristotelian entertainment for laymen. Moreover, within the limits of an adult program, the typical series of courses (conducted in more than a thousand American communities) contain a chronology and content very close to those followed by St. John's. Plato is studied with greater concentration than any other thinker, although many works of Aristotle and Aquinas are also read. Indeed, the only writer that compares with them in frequency of selection is Shakespeare. While still at Chicago, Adler helped to train leaders of study groups by lecturing on such neo-Thomist themes as "knowledge and opinion" and "immortality of the soul." Since then, he has remained a member of the board of directors of the Great Books Foundation. The conclusion is unavoidable that he, Hutchins, and their followers continue to apply to adult education no less than to the higher learning their conception of "an ordering principle."*

To be sure, adult groups functioning in local communities cannot always be depended upon to proceed consistently within the perennialist

‡ See Adler, *How to Read a Book,* pp. 97, 357ff.
* See Hutchins, *The Conflict in Education,* p. 75.

framework. Assurance that they will do so, however, is strengthened by the expert guidance their leaders receive from professional trainers in the Foundation, most or all of whom, it may be assumed, are in agreement with the premises upon which it was organized. Their ultimate hope is that the kind of adult learning they advocate will reach enough superior adults throughout the world to neutralize the pernicious effects of earlier schooling. Perhaps in time such adults, having attained metaphysical wisdom, will then insist upon reorganizing not only the education of their children but civilization itself.

"If we want to help save the world within the next few years, we must attend to the education of adults, for only they will have the influence within that period to affect the course of events." [13] This is Hutchins, speaking to the people of England by radio.

Problems of Social and Educational Control: The Perennialist Solution

"THE TWILIGHT OF CIVILIZATION"

The World of Events. One of the deep concerns of perennialists is with the difficult and crucial question of how the institution of education can be organized and controlled so as to exert the best and strongest possible influence upon the world of concrete events. That theorists of neo-Thomist persuasion are concerned about such events is philosophically implied by the life-centered aspects of Aristotelianism and directly expressed by such remarks as that of Hutchins quoted above.

Indeed, few educators today are more outspoken in their conviction that, to employ the title of a Maritain tract, we are already deep in "the twilight of civilization." Most American perennialists, indeed, cannot be compared with him in respect to the acumen with which he has analyzed faults in the political, economic, and cultural scene. To be sure, Hutchins has, on occasion, warned of the dire threat to human survival which his own university helped to generate by its experiments with atomic energy. He has expressed clearly his strong distaste for "witch hunts" and extreme "anti-communism" and has, for this expression, received wide acclaim from educators who otherwise reject his ideas. He has also made public condemnations of contemporary social practices ranging from the ruthless wastage of soil to compulsory military training and inadequate housing.† Such former colleagues as Nef have likewise discussed frequently the extraordinary array of "evils" in our culture. Finally, Hutchins, Barr, and Adler, in addition to a number of scholars who could scarcely be classified philosophically with them, have prepared a "preliminary draft for global federation," which is based on a strong conviction, again anticipated in some detail by Adler, that national sovereignty is now so obsolete that only a world union of governments can possibly solve the terrible disease of war.*

The Cause and Cure of the Cultural Crisis. To what extent perennialists would unite in specific solutions to the major problems confronting our midcentury is less relevant to our present interest than their very considerable agreement on the most common cause of these problems. Maritain on the social "left," Adler, Hutchins, and perhaps Van Doren somewhere "left of center," Nef somewhere "right of center," although not so far on the extreme "right" as the Englishmen Belloc and Eliot—all agree that *the cause is the spiritual-intellectual bankruptcy of modern man.* This bankruptcy already began to appear with such early heralds of modern science as Occam and Bacon. It was aggravated by such individualists as Rousseau and culminated in the pragmatists James and Dewey. While agreeing that the "material," particularly the economic, levels of life are not at all satisfactory, perennialists repeatedly contend that these levels are of minor importance. Thus, we may reasonably presume that Hutchins speaks as a true representative when he writes that:

> We are concerned, not with a rearrangement of material things, but with a moral and spiritual reformation. . . . Man is a moral, rational, and spiritual being. He needs material goods; unless he has them he cannot survive. But he does not need them without limit. *Preoccupation with material goods will hinder and not assist his progress toward his real goal,* which is the fullest development of his specific powers.[14]

† See Hutchins, *The Atom Bomb and Education.*

* See Robert M. Hutchins and others, "Preliminary Draft for Global Federation," *Saturday Review of Literature,* April 3, 1948.

From this Aristotelian keynote, we can understand why most perennialists are so frequently ambiguous when they discuss such "material" problems as they casually touch upon. Hutchins never offers a clearly outlined proposal to solve, for example, a concrete problem such as inadequate housing, about which he feels sad, tending rather to be exceedingly demagogic in his stated preferences either for various methods which make free enterprise work or for methods which admit the failure of free enterprise. His defense of academic freedom, itself derived from the perennialist conception of freedom, is more forthright than that of most educators. Nevertheless, it is not so unqualified as to allow him to accept honor for his service to academic freedom from a teachers' union accused of "Communist leanings." Nef's economic proposals, despite his status as an economic historian, are scarcely less vacillating or innocuous. Adler is usually content to limit his discussions of "means" and "actions" to asserting their importance by interesting abstract phrases, but he seldom outlines a possible practical application. Indeed, with the exception, in some degree, of Maritain, the best known perennialists are either dubious or simply silent about such concrete but controversial economic objectives as the democratic socialization of our major instruments of production. They tend to agree with Hutchins that a program of education devoted to such an objective would be "even worse than the one that springs from John Dewey and the earlier progressives." For, among other educational evils, it would "subordinate" the intellect to a clear-cut social purpose that is not, in fact, determinable.†

Belief in World Order. It is true that some lay perennialists have, in recent years, overcome their hesitancy to discuss at least one social issue—internationalism. Their proposed world constitution, although still ambiguous in its economic principles, nevertheless demonstrates that, when social purposes meet with their approval, they are able to justify the feared "subordination" of intelligence. Perhaps it also provides a sample of the eclectic tendencies which even this exceptionally un-eclectic philosophy sometimes reveals.

Their pronouncements show no obvious eclecticism, however, on the issue of the ends that are implicit in their desired world order or of the

† See Hutchins, *No Friendly Voice,* pp. 129, 67; Hutchins' speech before Modern Forum, Los Angeles, 1946; Nef, *The United States and Civilization,* Chap. 10; Adler, *How to Think about War and Peace,* p. 284; Hutchins, *The Conflict in Education,* Chap. 3, where he also criticizes the "reconstructionalists" for believing in social reform through education.

means best suited to attain it. The ends are expressed in a preamble to the constitution, which, although unavoidably abstract in language, is certainly interpreted in their own philosophic sense by the neo-Thomists among its coauthors. (Consider such a statement as, "the advancement of man in spiritual excellence and physical welfare is the common goal of mankind.") The means are not stated by the framers of the proposed constitution, but they are systematically although still vaguely considered in seven pages of Adler's three-hundred-page book *How to Think about War and Peace*.‡ Except for such relatively sparse instances, the entire weight of the perennialist "strategy" is carried by Hutchins' oft-reiterated demand for a "moral, intellectual, and spiritual revolution."[15] This demand underlies the plea for world government which Hutchins makes in his Aquinas lecture, *St. Thomas and the World State* (delivered before the Aristotelian Society of Marquette University) in which he refers to St. Thomas's *Treatise on Law* as "the greatest of all books on the philosophy of law" and the supreme guide to world peace.[16] This demand also underlies Nef's invocation to Americans, particularly, to dedicate themselves to "international justice" by loving "righteousness" in accordance with a philosophy derived mainly from the Greeks.* Here, then, is the task—the one important task—of education. If it can be effected in time, then may we hope, as we stand in the chill evening twilight of civilization, to glimpse the rays of dawn.

The centrality of leadership

The attainment of the required "moral, intellectual, and spiritual revolution" is the responsibility of two institutions, the Church and the university. Whether the Hutchins group would, if pressed, admit with the theologians that the Church is ultimately the more important of the two, we cannot say. But they are unequivocal in their insistence that the university must provide strong leadership for the "revolution."

The Criteria of Control. In considering leadership, we return directly to the issue of social and educational control. For, granting that men must bring rational and ethical order to the world, we ask: Who is to determine its principles? Who is best qualified to decide finally who shall control? Who shall direct whom? As perennialists themselves insist,

‡ See Adler, *How to Think about War and Peace*, Chap. 23.
* See Nef, *The United States and Civilization*, p. 12.

we cannot restore order in the culture if each man is left to be his own arbiter, for we have seen that a kind of immoral anarchy has resulted from individualistic, "anthropocentric" interpretations of freedom. We cannot restore order, either, by imposing the tyranny of such a system as fascism. What, then, is the source of those principles that alone can guarantee that the required controls will be grounded in "justice" and "righteousness"?

This question leads us to the heart of perennialist education. We can find the principles, say the perennialists, only in philosophy—not in any philosophy, however, but in that one that has been found to consist of a systematic, positive structure of beliefs about reality, knowledge, and value. More specifically, since we are here concerned with the practical spheres of society, economics, and politics, we can obtain reliable criteria in these areas of life only through the moral and intellectual virtues. And, as we have said, these virtues are in turn derived from metaphysics—hence from an intuitive awareness of eternally real first principles.

The supreme purpose of the university becomes, therefore, the education of those who can engage in this high philosophic pursuit, whose objective is not merely philosophizing for its own sake but philosophizing in order to create leaders who *know* with certainty what justice and righteousness *really* are. We can even detect a paradox in this proposal: the best way to solve the great problems of society is to turn our backs upon them—to develop leadership by immunizing our minds from the confusions and accidents of experience and purifying them by immersion in the distilled essence of such Ideas as Truth, Goodness, and Beauty.

This is essentially what Adler means when he points out that the only philosophy of education that is capable of creating educational leadership worthy of the name is the one that is concerned "with the educational *ideal*, with answering the question: 'What is the best education *absolutely*, that is, for any man according to his essence?' "[17] Adler's position is that the philosophy of education formulates final principles but, as philosophy, is uninterested in decisions or specific actions on the plane of practice.

Varying Emphases Among Perennialists. Perennialists are not always in agreement, however, in their conception of leadership as it relates specifically to the problem of control. The world constitution mentioned above places ultimate authority in the electorate, not in its officers. Maritain, especially, has professed a deep faith in the capacity of ordinary people to solve their problems according to their own best judgment, a faith that leads him to find in working and farming people the single greatest reservoir of future social hope. In holding that ". . . the man of common humanity is not possessed of a less sound judgment and less equitable instincts than those social categories which believe themselves to be superior . . . not because he is more intelligent but because he is less tempted . . . ,"[18] Maritain meets directly the underlying issue of control. His position is that, ultimately, "common humanity" is more likely to know its own interests than is any single person or any minority. This is a position, however, that even he cannot reconcile, except by scholastic logistics, with such beliefs as the infallibility of the Church, its final superiority to the state, and the unimpeachable authority of the hierarchy which issues the Church's mandates. Since "all authority derives from God as from its primordial source . . ." it follows that a leader "can establish a genuine *right* to be obeyed" only as his "supreme ordinating Law" is derived from "the Cause of being. . . ."[19]

In considering the issue of leadership and control, we recall that most American perennialists are agreed that general education should be freely available to the largest possible majority. They do not, however, express clear-cut reasons for this belief—although one practical reason is that there are insufficient employment opportunities for those under the age of twenty. More characteristically neo-Thomist is Hutchins' assertion that general education is desirable for all when it develops the "intellectual power" and the "humanity" which every citizen has "in common" with his fellows.† But such assertions as this certainly do not adequately indicate the kind of confidence in the judgment of ordinary people that is characteristic of Maritain. What they do indicate, if we trace the perennialist plan back to its base, is *the Aristotelian belief in hylomorphism as it bears upon the schools*—the belief that every human being tends to develop from matter to form, from potentiality to actuality, from appetite to reason, but that most of us succeed in doing so only imperfectly.

The perennialist conception of the distribution of power in society is well stated by Eliot. While denying that he is defending aristocracy, he nevertheless insists upon the principle of hierarchy:

> What is important is a structure of society in which there will be, from "top" to "bottom," a continuous gradation of cultural

† See Hutchins, "Double Trouble," *op. cit.*

> levels: it is important to remember that we should not consider the upper levels as possessing *more* culture than the lower, but as representing a more conscious culture and a greater specialisation of culture. . . . The levels of culture may also be seen as levels of power, to the extent that a smaller group at a higher level will have equal power with a larger group at a lower level . . . and in such a society as I envisage, each individual would inherit greater or lesser responsibility towards the commonwealth, according to the position in society which he inherited —each class would have different responsibilities.[20]

In this statement we may perceive perhaps the strongest of reasons for the kind of program of general education that the perennialists have developed. The potentially highest men, few in number, are most likely to be discovered in the process of providing for all the opportunity to blossom intellectually in the fertile soil of the great books. General education will thereby select and prepare those few who are fit for the higher learning and so for the fundamental and necessary leadership of superior minds.

In this perspective, we can appreciate why Nef should propose that a large percentage of the young be trained for practical work rather than for a future intellectual or professional life: *"the majority of our citizens . . . are concerned neither with education nor with the creative life. . . ."*[21]

Hutchins on Philosopher-Kings. Let us grant that perennialists, however divergent in their proposals for general education, are all concerned with the good life, as they conceive it, for the masses of men. Even so, two crucial aspects of this conception must be recognized. The first is that, for secular perennialists, only the university is capable of creating the intellectual, moral, and spiritual elite necessary for the survival of civilization. The second is the affinity between such a conception of an elite and the ancient-medieval philosophy of leadership from which it directly derives.

Hutchins himself frankly avows this affinity. He believes not only that the higher learning should be a "privilege" not a "right" and should be limited strictly to those with demonstrated "ability" and "interest" but also that there should be *"far fewer"* students over the age of twenty (that is, beyond the level of general education) than are now enrolled in universities. Further, he finds in Plato's philosopher-king his own model for the university administrator and the symbol of his ideal leader. This rare person is a true aristocrat of the mind and spirit, to be selected by no less an ordeal than the *Republic's* long program of education and training for potential possessors of Ideas—the philosopher-kings. Hutchins carefully summarizes the stages of this ordeal. For it is "the kind of scheme which is called for if the administrator is to have the moral and intellectual qualities which the times demand." [22]

Thus the most conclusive and consistent answer to the question "Who is to control whom?" might be epitomized as "He who is best qualified to do so." We may grant as generously as possible a great range of ramifications and concessions to current conditions and experiences. Nevertheless, the ultimate answer of perennialists is crystal clear. It is, in essence, the answer of Plato.

Control within the schools

Control by Lay Perennialists. The perennialist conception of leadership, as we have described it, helps us to understand how education, as an institution, is to be controlled. Strong authority must be vested in those competent to control—the reason, perhaps, why Hutchins and his associates seem curiously indifferent to or at least silent about the trend among school administrators to broaden the base of student-teacher-parent participation. Their sparse comments on such questions seem to indicate that they regard them as of secondary importance—no doubt a matter of mere means, on the low level of opinion. As a consequence, one finds it as difficult to determine precisely their position on such controversial matters as the unionization of teachers as to determine their position on economic questions.

Perhaps the closest perennialist approximation to a democratic view of school administration is Hutchins' remark that the administrator should "get others to join him in the search for the end and try to lead all his constituency to see and accept it when it has been found." [23] Although this view might invite widespread discussion by the constituency of the university, it in no way violates the conviction elsewhere implied that, since administrators indoctrinated in Platonism-Aristotelianism already know what the end of education should be, it becomes their obligation to instruct others in their own superior knowledge. The fact, moreover, that he and his colleagues at St. John's advocate a completely nonelective and carefully systematized curriculum suggests that they regard the kind of cooperative, inductive teacher-pupil planning proposed by progressivists as superfluous—superfluous because philosophically unsound.

Control by Clerical Perennialists. The theories of certain Catholic educators, indeed, are more akin to this kind of planning than their secular colleagues, just as they are more akin to the activity curriculum. Thus, a document of the Commission on American Citizenship, sanctioned by the Church, contains a number of suggestions for widening social and educational controls which, on the surface, seem quite compatible with the most advanced democratic principles.† Cunningham, in his proposals for general education, also reveals a concern for democracy and especially for student participation in the formulation of educational policy. "We maintain," he writes, "that the student should be given the widest latitude in rights and responsibilities consistent with his potentiality. We know that he is not equipped to dictate policies of the curriculum, but he should be able to conduct, under guidance, most of the extracurricular activities." [24] It is also notable that some American pioneers of teachers' unions, such as Margaret Haley, were Catholics and that Bishop Spalding expressed far more sympathy with organized labor as a force for democratizing economic power than Hutchins and most other school administrators have ever expressed.‡

Nevertheless, we must face the question of whether these differences between religious and secular leaders are actually as sharp as they at first appear. Regardless of how liberal a theoretical position in behalf of "self-discipline" and "self-activity" within the school Catholic educators seem willing to accept, we must also remember that *the source of authority and discipline lies elsewhere—that is, "over ourselves."* * Such an authority decrees, for example, that coeducation is undesirable, just as systematic sex education is undesirable.§

Even more significant is the evidence that parochial schools in practice completely lack democratic administrations. Ownership of schools is not vested in those who support or attend them but in ecclesiastic officials, and financial support is exacted from the Church membership

† See Commission on American Citizenship, *Better Men for Better Times.*
‡ See Curti, *op. cit.*, pp. 242f., 366f.
* See Cunningham, *Pivotal Problems of Education*, p. 221 (italics supplied).
§ See *ibid.*, pp. 180, 185, 205.

without consultation as to budgets or policies. Obviously, leaders also seldom consult the teaching force, a large percentage of which consists of nuns who have dedicated themselves to the authoritarian creed of the Church under the inviolable rule of its mandates.

Although the attitude of clerical perennialism is officially hostile *to* public education, the Church is not averse to using the resources *of* the public. A strong campaign has been conducted for several years to guarantee a full share of federal funds for the use of parochial schools. Catholic writers have persistently sought to prove that the founders of the United States—James Madison, particularly—never intended that religious schools should be denied public support.† Although the Supreme Court has thus far opposed Catholic efforts to break down the traditional separation of church and state, many individual states of the Union do provide tax-paid services to parochial schools, ranging from bus transportation to the purchase of textbooks.‡ There is also some evidence that the Church has, in certain communities, endeavored to win appointments to administrative and teaching positions in public education, for the express purpose of increasing its control in local communities and in the classroom.* (That public school teachers of Catholic faith often attempt to be objective and to refrain from indoctrinating their beliefs is, however, indisputable.) Probably the Church's main argument in favor of federal aid is that Church parents are taxed twice—once for public and once for parochial education—despite the fact that, in most localities, their children are free to attend public schools. At least they are free except for the fear that, if they do attend, they and their parents will not receive the full blessings of their faith.

Behind all its militant efforts to maintain and strengthen control over education is the absolute dictum of perennialism that man should subordinate himself to a power superior to himself.§ This power is, of course, a supernatural God, recognized and accepted through divine grace. Its institutional voice is the Church itself. Therefore, control is properly vested in those most certain of the principles that determine the method and the content of good education. From a perennialist point of view,

† See James M. O'Neill, *Religion and Education under the Constitution.*

‡ See V. T. Thayer, *The Attack upon the American Secular School;* and *Public Education and Its Critics,* Chap. 2.

* See Paul Blanshard, *American Freedom and Catholic Power,* Chaps. 4, 5.

§ See Cunningham, *op. cit.,* Chap. 16; and *General Education and the Liberal College,* pp. 30, 37-42.

this is how and why the Church, as well as the university, should lead the way to the necessary "revolution."

Notes

[1] Quoted from John S. Brubacher, *A History of the Problems of Education,* p. 108.

[2] Jacques Maritain, *Education at the Crossroads,* p. 46.

[3] Quoted from National Society for the Study of Education, *Forty-first Yearbook,* Part I, "Philosophies of Education," p. 273.

[4] *Ibid.,* p. 213. See also Mark Van Doren, *Liberal Education,* p. 173; Maritain, *op. cit.,* p. 33.

[5] Jacques Maritain, *Education at the Crossroads,* p. 50. Copyright 1943 by Yale University Press and reprinted with their permission.

[6] Van Doren, *op. cit.,* p. 95.

[7] Robert M. Hutchins, *The Conflict in Education,* p. 68.

[8] Maritain, *op. cit.,* p. 73.

[9] Hutchins, *No Friendly Voice,* p. 67.

[10] Hutchins, *The Higher Learning in America,* p. 105.

[11] Hutchins, *The Atom Bomb and Education,* pp. 13-14.

[12] Hutchins, *The Conflict in Education,* p. 100.

[13] Hutchins, *The Atom Bomb and Education,* p. 7.

[14] Robert M. Hutchins, *No Friendly Voice,* p. 44. Copyright 1936 by the University of Chicago Press and reprinted with their permission (italics supplied). See also Hutchins, *The Conflict in Education,* Chap. 2.

[15] Hutchins, *The Atom Bomb and Education,* p. 9.

[16] Hutchins, *St. Thomas and the World State,* p. 38.

[17] Quoted from "Philosophies of Education," *op. cit.,* pp. 228f.

[18] Maritain, *Christianity and Democracy,* p. 78.

[19] Maritain, *Scholasticism and Politics,* pp. 103ff.

[20] T. S. Eliot, *Notes towards the Definition of Culture,* p. 47. Copyright 1949 by Harcourt, Brace and Company and reprinted with their permission.

[21] John U. Nef, *The United States and Civilization,* pp. 304-307, 315 (italics supplied).

[22] Hutchins, "The Administrator," *Journal of Higher Education,* November 1946.

[23] *Ibid.*

[24] William F. Cunningham, *General Education and the Liberal College,* p. 233.

CHAPTER 12

A Cultural Evaluation of Perennialism

THAT PERENNIALISM, AS THEORY AND PROGRAM OF EDUCATION, is also a theory and program for contemporary culture is readily admitted by its proponents. It is admitted, however, only in terms of their own definition of the precise relation of education to culture. We have observed that perennialists persistently point out that civilization is now caught in an age of crisis, which places upon the higher learning, especially, a solemn responsibility. But we cannot infer from this attitude alone that the perennialist's diagnosis of that crisis or his corrective proposals are identical with those of any other major alternative. Indeed, they tend to be diametrically opposed.

Assuming the same general limitations that applied to our evaluation of progressivism and essentialism, this chapter contends:

1. that perennialism, taken as a whole, so deeply reflects specifiable cultural conditions that, notwithstanding its denials, even its most ultimate principles fortify just such conditions; and
2. that it must finally be judged in terms of whether or not the kind of culture of which it is the philosophic advocate is ultimately a desirable culture.

This thesis is developed first by considering the cultural context of perennialism, and secondly by developing two evaluations that derive from that context: the mind as escape and the perennialist challenge to democracy.

The Cultural Context of Perennialism

Plato and Aristotle: citizen-aristocrats

That the hardy perennials—Platonism and Aristotelianism—took root in the cultural soil of Greece was no mere accident of time or circumstance. The political and economic soil of Athens provided the needed seedbed, and the social climate of the fifth and fourth centuries B.C. was very favorable to sustain its tender philosophic plants.

Added to these assets of soil and climate were others that favored the prospect that Platonic-Aristotelian beliefs would sprout, blossom, and produce generations of their species. First, there was the rich fertilizer of waste, blood, and bone that war always supplies in abundance. Ancient Greece was torn by violent conflicts, both in foreign wars, notably with Persia, and in civil strife, especially between the city-states of Athens and Sparta. Second, the way had been well prepared for cultivation of the cultural soil. War again had helped, turning over the earth almost too continuously, but thus preparing it for fresh plantings and new germinations of belief. Still more important were the fruits provided by a long preceding period of creative interest in drama, literature, architecture, and other arts and in such intellectual disciplines as logic and mathematics. For example, the worship of a magical power in numbers by Pythagoras and his disciples was exploited by Plato and Aristotle in their creation of a more sophisticated but nevertheless absolutist and finally supernatural philosophy of nature and man. All these and still other events and achievements cultivated a cultural climate favorable to perennialist beliefs.

Contrary to the picture of Plato and Aristotle that too many scholars have drawn, they were, both as human beings and as citizens, deeply affected by this environment.* Far from being isolated within ivory towers of rarefied wisdom, both were men of action, both were embroiled in the turmoil of corruption and violence chronic to their time. Plato himself, according to one account, was sold into temporary slavery; even

* Our discussion of Plato and Aristotle relies heavily upon K. R. Popper, *The Open Society and Its Enemies;* Richard H. S. Crossman, *Plato Today;* W. Jaeger, *Paideia: The Ideals of Greek Culture;* Alban D. Winspear, *The Genesis of Plato's Thought;* George H. Sabine, *A History of Political Theory.* See also histories of philosophy and education cited above.

if this fact cannot be verified, it is known that he traveled widely and that he worked closely with the rulers of Syracuse as well as of Athens. Aristotle also traveled throughout much of the civilized Western world of his time. He tutored Alexander the Great and, like Plato, was directly associated with the most powerful political leadership of his age. So involved was he that, after Alexander's death, he was forced to flee or suffer the fate of Socrates, who had been martyred for his beliefs.

Democracy versus Aristocracy in the Greek Culture. Of even greater cultural significance to the perennialist philosophy they founded is the fact that both men looked out upon the conflicts about them from the point of view of a powerful aristocratic class. We cannot, of course, measure precisely the extent to which their personal class status was responsible for their consistent support of the aristocratic outlook or for their equally consistent rejection of all other points of view. We must recognize, too, that scholars continue to debate the cultural role they played as well as the wider meanings of their profound doctrines.† From all that we have learned since their time about cultural motivations of belief, however, we have no reason to suppose that Plato and Aristotle, alone among thinkers, were immune to such motivations. On the contrary, if we judge them by such fruits as the *Republic* and the *Politics,* we may justifiably infer that the closed aristocratic circle, in which they were charter members and from which their families and friends benefited, strongly influenced both their criticisms and their proposals.

Thus, Plato and Aristotle found unsatisfactory all three types of rule which intermittently prevailed in the countries and cities about them. They disliked the tyrants who for a time controlled Athens as much as they disliked those of Syracuse. They disliked the oligarchy, which placed control in "uncouth" commercial classes. They disliked the democratic order, which had reached its widest circumference under Pericles, just before Plato was born.

If tyranny was denounced as the worst of the three, it is also easy to understand why democracy might have been considered even more responsible, in the long run, for the troubles of Athens. The democratic structure of government had been expanding continuously throughout the fifth century. The aristocracy exercised progressively less power and the popular assembly, consisting of artisans, merchants, small farmers,

† For an interpretation opposed to that of Popper *et al.*, see Ronald Levinson, *In Defense of Plato.*

and sailors, progressively more. During this period, the Athenians had been engaged in imperialist struggles, and, although temporarily victorious, they had passed their peak of success more than a generation before Plato's lifetime. Thus, Plato came to manhood during a period when past glories overshadowed present attainments. Even more significant for his developing thought, his whole impressionable youth was spent in an atmosphere of bloody struggle within Greece. The long Peloponnesian War against Sparta ended when Plato was twenty-five, with the humiliation and defeat of Athens. For him and the younger Aristotle to have inferred a cause-effect relation between violent strife and democratic control is quite understandable—and especially when we recall that the class within which they moved was forced by this control into a subordinate position. No doubt, the Greek aristocrats of this period criticized Pericles and other democratic leaders as bitterly as twentieth-century American and English upper-class citizens almost unanimously disapproved of such leaders as Franklin Roosevelt and Clement Attlee.

That democratic forces were actually responsible for the decline of the Athenian Empire is, nevertheless, a highly dubious contention. Historians differ on this question of responsibility, perhaps more today than ever before, just as they differ today on the responsibility of Roosevelt and his New Deal policies for America's entrance into World War II or for other contemporary cultural problems. It may, however, be cogently argued that, in both historic situations, *it was not the too-rapid increase in power of the common people that produced the difficulties of the two cultures but, on the contrary, the much-too-slow increase.* We must recall that, despite the remarkable economic, artistic, and scientific achievements of Athenian culture, the fruits of these achievements were denied to the greater part of the population. We must also recall that the Athenian economy could expand only to the limits set by the slave labor force, upon which it finally depended. This limitation not only stunted its democratic growth but also blocked its commercial expansion and military power. The American democracy, too, has been circumscribed by scarcity, by insecurity, by feeble popular participation in economic policies, and by inadequate political power for tens of millions of citizens.

The Platonic Formula. The relevant point in our analysis, however, is *not what we are now able to understand about ancient Greece but what Plato and Aristotle themselves must have understood.* If we recall that they believed in the inevitable course of history but nevertheless disapproved the course Greece had been following, we can perhaps appreciate the significance of Plato's master design for a class-structured society. Whether this society, like the real Athens, depends upon a great pool of slave labor is a point on which interpreters differ; certainly the *Republic* does not explicitly disavow slavery. In any case, Plato does construct a three-level order of artisans, soldiers, and philosopher-kings. With the philosopher-kings in supreme authority and with the army and navy to enforce its decisions, the Platonic pattern is thus entirely consistent with the desired status of the author and his class. Not only does it propose to place an aristocracy in power—to be sure, an aristocracy of talent rather than blood—but also it aims to restore peace and unity by means of the ingenious formula that "justice" will emerge in the culture when each member of his respective class functions according to his nature. Thus it leads to the harmonious acceptance by all classes of a hierarchical political order.

Plato's "republic" was not at all the mere speculative dream of a poet-perfectionist. Although he recognized the practical difficulties of instituting such a state, we must not overlook its resemblance, in certain political and educational features, to the real Sparta—a state which had demonstrated its temporary superiority of power over Plato's Athens by the dreadful test of war and which was controlled by an entrenched class of rich, hereditary landowners who ruled with the collaboration of a strong military clique. This ruling class not only disciplined itself sternly and rigidly (whence the term "Spartan," which we still use) but it disciplined those beneath it even more relentlessly, and often cruelly. Its educational program, too, was mainly an instrument of the state to inculcate habits of strict obedience and sacrificial service.

To be sure, Plato sought to improve upon the Spartan system. We may recall that in the *Republic* the soldiery is relegated to a level below that of the supreme rulers, the philosopher-kings. He recognized and feared the narrow callousness of the typical military character. Also, he hoped, by his psychological-political theory of tripartite harmony of parts (see p. 317), to create a spirit of willing rather than coerced obedience to the corporate whole; he was too keen not to perceive that continued, stable, and absolute rule is possible only if the lower, as well as the upper, classes support such rule. Moreover, it is probable that he founded his famous Academy for the training of scholars partly if not primarily in the hope that it would produce leaders purified of the military and economic ruthlessness that contaminated the leadership both of Sparta and Athens. And it seems to have been historically established that he sought to apply parts of his program in Syracuse, where his influence with Dionysius II was at one time strong, thus evidencing his own belief in its practicability.

The Aristocratic Bias. To what extent Plato and Aristotle were patriotic and to what extent subversive citizens of Athens is thus seen to be a controversial question. To those who have allowed Plato's intriguing dialogues to shape many of their judgments of Greek culture, such a question is perhaps shocking. But one fact we must never forget: both Plato and Aristotle largely opposed the progressive and experimental forces in Athens personified by the popular assembly, as well as the beliefs and efforts of such pro-democratic philosophers as Protagoras and Democritus. This is so despite the fact that both men loved many aspects of their culture (they could scarcely have failed to recognize that the democratic reign of Pericles was also the "golden age" of creative achievement in Greece); despite evidence in such later dialogues as the *Statesman* and the *Laws* that Plato modified his extreme aristocratic views; and despite Aristotle's even greater willingness to accept some of the strengths of Greek democracy. The fact still remains, however, that their political philosophies are marked throughout by a strong aristocratic bias. Indeed, Aristotle reveals his discipleship to Plato in no field more strongly than in politics.

Just how much the influence of the two philosophers hastened the ultimate collapse of Athenian democracy and finally of Greek civilization cannot, of course, be measured. Certainly their charge against the "democracy" of their day—that it produced a society governed by excesses of "freedom" and "variety" and of equality "to equals and unequals alike"—was devastating.‡ Through the centuries, and finally expressing itself in perennialist movements of our own day, it has continued to be one of the most persuasive and, to democratic ideas and practices, one of the most destructive influences in history. This judgment has been no more vigorously confirmed than by the historian Arnold Toynbee:

> . . . the Hellenic Utopias [notably, Plato's and Aristotle's] . . . were conceived at Athens in the schools of philosophy that arose in the age immediately following the Peloponnesian War. The

‡ See Plato, *Republic,* Book 8.

negative aspiration of these works is a profound hostility to Athenian democracy . . . The first concern of the Athenian post-war philosophers was to repudiate everything that for two centuries past had made Athens politically great. Hellas, they held, could only be saved by an alliance between Athenian philosophy and the Spartan social system. In adapting the Spartan system to their own ideas they sought to improve upon it in two ways: first by working it out to its logical extremes and secondly by the imposition of a sovereign intellectual caste (Plato's 'Guardians'), in the likeness of the Athenian philosophers themselves. . . . In their condonation of caste, in their *penchant* towards specialization and in their passion for establishing an equilibrium at any price, the Athenian philosophers of the fourth century B.C. show themselves docile pupils of the Spartan statesmen of the sixth. In the matter of caste the thought of Plato and Aristotle is tainted with that racialism which has been one of the besetting sins of our own Western Society in recent times.[1]

Aquinas and the Medieval Pyramid

Not for well over a thousand years did democracy again loom, even dimly, as a natural and cultural ideal to attract seriously the masses of mankind. The Platonic ideal of two worlds—the inferior, corrupt world of earthly experience and the superior, perfect world of spirituality—slowly enveloped Europe in the strange, occasionally grotesque disguises of theology, dogma, and superstition. Whatever philosophy remained (partially excepting the work of Plotinus, Augustine, and a few lesser men) was wrapped in the heavy trappings of sect, creed, and ritual.

The Thirteenth Century: An Overview of Its Culture. Nevertheless, developments in the thirteenth century after Christ prove that the light of reason had never been totally extinguished. This fact supports the hypothesis (which we consider more fully below) that so long as men can breathe they will sooner or later struggle to combat the forces in their culture that frustrate their most basic urges, including the urge to think through and then act upon their problems.

The thinkers of this period were concerned, above all, with a twofold task. On the one hand, their time demanded that they interpret medieval civilization to itself and provide a rationale which would give meaning and justification to its most powerful political, economic, and religious institutions. On the other hand, they were motivated in this effort by the restlessness of men too long confined by the strait jackets of dogmatism, absolutism, and a static economy. In meeting these two demands, their rationale was both defensive and clairvoyant: *defensive* in the face of forces symptomatic of social change, *clairvoyant* in recognizing that, notwithstanding the philosophers' valiant efforts, these forces would continue to grow until they finally replaced the medieval order by some other way of life, perhaps a very different one.

Any brief characterization of the thirteenth century and of the centuries we call the Middle Ages unavoidably oversimplifies the complex facts. Nevertheless, it is accurate to state that one of its most characteristic features was the pyramidal arrangement of religious and secular levels into which the culture was organized. The Church itself was structured in ascending levels of authority—faithful masses at the base; simple clergy and monastic servants closest to the masses; above them, various orders of officials, such as bishops and archbishops; and finally, at the apex, the supreme pontiff. The economic order of feudalism may also be pictured in ascending levels—serfs at the base; professional soldiery above them; lords of the manor still higher; and, at the apex, the kings. As still a third way, medieval culture might be conceived as roughly analogous to the class structure in the *Republic:* the class of "commoners" lowest; next, the baronage or land-holding class with its coterie of knights and soldiers; highest, the priesthood with its presumed superior wisdom and spiritual authority.*

Such pyramidal classifications should be regarded as merely operational, designed to help clarify for us the meaning of the Middle Ages. That no such neat patterning actually existed throughout Europe is proved by the fact that individual communities were usually very small, widely scattered, sometimes quite autonomous, and frequently in conflict. Moreover, religious, political, and economic authority was sometimes vested locally in one person or one group. Thus, in many places the Church, by controlling the land, served literally as landlord over the multitude of serfs. Also, in any region, the lord might function as king.

Regardless of discrepancies between the unity of its theoretical design and the plurality of its historic facts, this much seems to be characteristic of medievalism: so far as order existed, it was to be found in

* See John H. Randall, Jr., *The Making of the Modern Mind,* p. 60.

a crude, organic spirit of reciprocity which pervaded those who belonged within it. The lord, for example, considered himself obligated to his serfs for military protection; his serfs, in turn, were obligated to provide him with a generous share of their produce. To be sure, this reciprocity was not one of equality: all positions in the hierarchy of the culture were strictly class stratified. Nevertheless, one can find some sense of corporate wholeness in such an order, in the manner that one can find it in the interdependence, however hierarchical, of communicants within the universal Church.

Thomism as Rationale. Now it was precisely this half-expressed sense of corporate wholeness upon which Aquinas fastened his philosophic attention. By articulating its principles into the brilliant philosophic synthesis we have come to call Thomism, he rendered the great practical service of strengthening both the idea and the fact. Let us restate the salient features of Thomism, noting how, by virtue of their role in the medieval drama, they acquire richer significance (see pp. 294-296, 318-319).

We may recall that the great accomplishment of Aquinas was to bring the inherited theological and practical system of Christianity into unity with Aristotelianism, thereby justifying both faith and reason without sacrificing either. He was able to demonstrate, to his own satisfaction and that of countless followers, how every individual thing within reality is itself related to all other things through common substances—how these substances, in turn, unfold in a spiral-like pattern from the less pure to the more pure, from the more material and potential to the more spiritual and actual. In such an absolute but dynamic and purposeful plan of the universe, a hierarchical order of ascending levels of form is acceptable and desirable because it is inevitable. Also in such a plan, although higher forms are related to lower ones in the sense of common membership in one total system, the lower are inferior in worth to the higher.

In Thomism we thus observe a perfect *ontological* justification for *axiological,* and therefore political, harmony. It is a corporate harmony of unequal but interrelated members not fundamentally different, after all, from Plato's "just" harmony of classes. But Thomism crucially amends Platonism by incorporating Aristotle's teleological principle of the "Unmoved Mover," which is suggestive of the Christian God of divine wisdom, goodness, and omnipotence.

Thomist political theory is broad and flexible enough to allow its adherents, down to our own day, to accommodate various practices to it. Thus, the principle that God is the final judge can be used, as it has often been used, to justify the exercise of absolute authority by rulers who insist that they alone are attuned to God's will. Aquinas himself, however, insisted that political authority should be limited by law and that even revolution against a tyrant might conceivably be justified. Following Aristotle's political beliefs, Aquinas here revealed a willingness to adopt a moderate position between the extremes of tyranny and democracy.

Nevertheless, Aquinas, like Aristotle, felt an ultimate dissatisfaction with such moderation. Law, for example, proves to be much less simple than our common understanding of the word itself. Instead of one kind of law, he considered four—eternal, natural, divine, and human. All are properly authoritative on their own levels of hylomorphic reality, but all are traceable to a single fount which is the law of God.† Likewise, although he provided a place for legitimate secular power, he admitted when pressed that the authority of the Church and its rulers was, in crucial circumstances, supreme.

Thus, it seems altogether legitimate to compare Aquinas with Plato and Aristotle, not only for their many similarities in philosophic thought but also for similarities in their roles as men of practice, as leading citizens of their respective eras. It is true that Plato and Aristotle were, to a great extent, critics and foes of the democratic tendencies that had *already* developed in their culture whereas Aquinas, more strictly, was a critic and foe of democratic tendencies that were to emerge only *after* his time. Nevertheless, it is not unlikely that he, too, detected in his day certain current dangers to long-cherished beliefs and institutions. Plato and Aristotle were alarmed by instabilities in their culture, especially by the decline of aristocracy. Aquinas saw all about him the increasingly rapid development of cities and towns, of commerce and guilds, of the mobility of population—all tokens of expanding, although still nascent, gropings toward power and freedom, toward greater self-expression by growing numbers of people. It is no more possible, of course, to determine exactly how far these events shaped the philosophic formulations of Aquinas than it is possible to measure the correlations between culture and thought in Aristotle. Certainly one discovers in both (and even to some

† See George H. Sabine, *A History of Political Theory,* Chap. 13.

extent in the more reluctant Plato) a readiness to accommodate themselves to impending forces of change while trying to hold fast to their strong allegiance to the old.

In his theory of a corporate culture united by divine and absolute law, Aquinas becomes the supreme apologist of his age. His *Summa Theologica* is not only the greatest philosophic portrait of the greatest medieval century; it is the summation of a millennium.

Perennialism in its Contemporary Milieu

Is Perennialism Obsolete? Our demonstration of the compatibility (although not precise cause-effect relations) of perennialist beliefs with the two cultural eras that witnessed their conception, birth, and maturation should prepare us to consider whether perennialist beliefs are compatible with our own crisis-culture.

A superficial view might suggest a negative answer. As noted above (see pp. 264-266), the centuries following the thirteenth were marked by revolution against corporate authoritarianism in both religious and secular spheres. The rise of industrialism with its middle-class power structures, the establishment of modern science with its experimental methods of regulating both nature and man, the spread of democratic movements and the concomitant restatement of principles governing democracy and education—all of these and the many attempts to test them in the laboratories of national practice are evidences of the modern revolution. As a consequence, the perennialist approach to culture had come, in the nineteenth and twentieth centuries, to be widely regarded as obsolete—as the fascinating interpretation of an era which had long since been consigned to the limbo of historic memory.

On sharper scrutiny, however, this conclusion is seen to be unfounded.

Power of the Church. The impact of Thomism on modern culture has been perpetuated by the long-established institution that so deeply reveres it. Even though the influence of the Church has seemed to wane through much of the modern era, its dominance over vast multitudes has certainly not waned. It is so solidly entrenched in some countries, such as Italy, Spain, and Ireland, that its political and economic power seems often to be more decisive than that of the national government. Even in predominantly Protestant countries, such as the

United States, the Church exerts great pressure in politics, in education, and in popular arts, such as the motion picture.‡

Down to our generation, Thomism has remained not only one of the most influential philosophies, one of the great credos of human life and destiny, but also a doctrine exercising great institutional power.

Medieval Absolutism Perpetuated. In addition, the apparatus of medieval authority, with its many nuances of belief and conduct, has not been completely discarded in the modern era. As we observed in our cultural evaluation of essentialism, the history of Western man since the fourteenth century has been marked by a significant effort to recrystallize institutional forms so that the new requirements of secular authority for the industrial age would still justify strict controls over most people and most practices.

We observed that, among all their diverse and subtly qualified contributions, the philosophies of idealism and realism—with their accompanying social, economic, religious, and educational rationales—have been especially useful to this objective. By such assumptions as that of a preexistent and law abiding universe, they cultivate precisely those habits of mental and moral acquiescence that tend to conserve dominant practices. In performing this task both the spiritual and material types of essentialism borrow freely from Greek and medieval thought: Platonism, for example, has richly contributed to all of the influential expressions of objective idealism, including contemporary expressions; Aristotelianism has affected various forms of modern realism.

Thus, although perennialists frequently criticize essentialists for encouraging easy conformity and adjustment,* as well as for eclecticism or empirical compromise with evolutionary and other modern beliefs, these two groups still find it less difficult to establish a friendly *rapprochement* with each other than with such nonabsolutist, nonauthoritarian philosophers as the progressivists. At the same time, the very weaknesses of essentialism (weaknesses symptomatic of a culture that has failed to solve its own problems—depression, war, demoralization, frustration) offer the perennialists their great opportunity for influence. Although it might be argued that these same weaknesses are also characteristic of perennialism, its advocates think otherwise. Drawing upon the achievements of modern thought, science, and education, perennialism unites into one complete

‡ See Paul Blanshard, *American Freedom and Catholic Power.*
* See Robert M. Hutchins, *The Conflict in Education,* Chap. 1.

ystem a theory of absolute reality, knowledge, and value and a consoling, nvincible faith. Never before in our era has this momentous philosophy een so strategically equipped to exploit both the successes and failures f its closest ally.

The Regressive Synthesis. Even disregarding the support this allince affords, we may say that perennialism is one important expression f contemporary culture because it still offers one of the most revered aths to the amelioration of a deep cultural crisis.

As in all periods of crisis, many men among us today seek a haven here their bewilderments or uncertainties, their lack of conviction or irection, can be resolved and corrected. One of the most alluring ways) security, moreover, is to rise above individual and social problems—to nd succor in a realm of perfection, which presumably transcends the truggle and crassness that reflective, forthright actions always demand. f such a haven also provides a secondary place for rich experience and articipation with our fellow men, so much the more is our sense of bligation satisfied and our conscience assuaged. Just as Plato looked ostalgically backward to the closer approximation of perfection which e imagined to have existed in the aristocracy of pre-democratic Athens, ut just as he carefully incorporated in his *Republic* such accomplishnents of his own culture as Spartan discipline and Socratic dialectic, so erennialists twenty-five centuries later also look backward while coneding and accepting certain contemporary achievements and ideals.

This subtle, although regressive, synthesis—today exemplified so rilliantly by Maritain, so practically by Hutchins—has a double appeal. Vhile it offers intellectual and emotional anchorage in the remote and stensibly more nearly perfect past, it also insists upon its modernity. Iutchins' support of international government, to cite a significant exmple, seems to accord with the advanced thinking of our time. But even his ideal is strikingly consistent not only with that of Aquinas but also vith that of the medieval Dante who, in accord with the Thomist archelief in corporate unity, advocated a "spiritual empire" for the world of is time. Where, indeed, could Hutchins and his colleagues find a more oble formulation of their international principles than in this excerpt rom Dante himself?

> The human race, therefore, is ordered well, nay, is ordered for the best, when according to the utmost of its power it becomes

> like unto God. But the human race is most like unto God when it is most one, for the principle of unity dwells in him alone . . . But the human race is most one when all are united together.[2]

We conclude, then, that the significance of perennialism for our times is to be evaluated in relation to its cultural context, just as its significance for earlier periods must be evaluated in relation to their context. In all three major periods—ancient, medieval, and modern—it is to be regarded as a philosophic interpretation of and program for the culture as an organic whole. Yet, just as the perennialist interpretation of the medieval period (that of Aquinas) incorporates the achievements of the ancient period (that of Plato and Aristotle), so today perennialism incorporates certain developments of the seven centuries since Aquinas. Its leading exponents are much too sophisticated to ignore, for example, such a modern development as the industrial technology. They recognize that their only hope of becoming dominant once more is to be flexible and sensitive to contemporary public opinion and social interest.

Role of the Common People in Three Periods of History. Nonetheless, despite its many concessions to recent history, the contemporary expression of perennialism still strikingly resembles both of its earlier expressions. In all three, it reacts subtly (at times almost despite some of its advocates) against the democratic forces of the respective eras. In all three, its basic orientation and major premises compel it finally to stand *against* the drive of the common people to make all final policy decisions and *for* the alternative power of a higher authority to whom the people should properly and finally bow.

Let us consider successively the historic roles of the common people in the ancient, medieval, and modern cultures. In Greece, we observed that artisans, sailors, and similar groups had gained rapidly in power during the period preceding Plato and Aristotle but that such instruments as the popular assembly were beginning to weaken by the time the *Republic* was composed. In the thirteenth century after Christ, a new and disturbing restlessness among the people was doubtless perceptible to Aquinas, although their characteristic attitude remained submissive. Now, in the twentieth century, the people are in a position somewhat similar to that of both earlier cultures. Especially during the past two centuries, they have increasingly demanded and won their rights; but they continue to chafe from frustrations and oppressions which deny them the complete ulfillment of those rights. Like the followers of Pericles, they have tasted emocratic privilege and found the flavor good; but, like the new city wellers of late medieval Europe, they envisage far greater privileges than hey have ever yet enjoyed.

In this kind of setting, the contemporary perennialist is faced with n even more difficult task than those of his predecessors. While pro-essing devotion to "democracy," he is compelled by his own doctrine not only to doubt the success with which ordinary citizens have controlled heir lives and institutions in the immediate past but also, as we shall bserve below (see pp. 365-378), to question their ultimate capacity or successful self-government in the period that lies ahead. Because of he greater confidence and experience of the common peoples of the earth, both in their *record* and in their *expectations,* the contemporary perennialist is more likely to fail than were either of the earlier peren-nialists, when their influence was stronger.

The Mind as Escape

Mere demonstration that contemporary perennialism is a cultural regres-sion analogous, in our age of crisis, to the perennialism of previous ages is not sufficient to prove that it is an undesirable philosophy. The most extreme judgment that might thus far be adduced is that its claim to be finally and purely immune to cultural forces is untenable.

Indeed, many perennialist advocates would probably admit that our interpretation above has given an impression of the value of their beliefs, for it has emphasized the contemporary need for revitalized premises and purposes similar to those "superior" beliefs that governed the Greek and medieval cultures. We must, therefore, address ourselves directly to the issue raised above in discussing the role of the world's common peoples: Is the insistence of perennialism that the people should conform to a higher authority than themselves a *desirable* choice for our own culture?

The Perennialist Theory of Mind: Recapitulation. Let us approach this issue by recapitulating the perennialist theory of mind. It is ex-pressed within the context of a theory of reality which itself serves as a rationale for a culture in which the corporate unity of all classes is the

ideal. In other words, perennialism presents a system of relations betwee
lower and higher levels of status whose pattern resembles a pyramid—
hierarchy of ascending orders of knowledge and goodness. Near the ape
of the pyramid is mind itself—the beacon by which alone, except by th
help of sheer faith, we can hope to find our way through the jungles o
lust, hatred, and selfishness which beset mortal beings on every hand.

The distinctive quality of mind is its capacity to grasp "first prin
ciples," which are ultimately found "true" by the test of "self-evidence.
That only the exceptional human intellect can reach such "metaphysical
heights of "ontological analysis" is not sufficient argument against posit
ing such an achievement as man's supreme mundane goal. For man, a
a "teleological" being, has as his end such purity of speculation that th
"form" contained within the "matter" of every object of nature can b
revealed to him by the excellence of his mind. By the same token, hi
"hylomorphic" character draws him upward through the "moral virtues'
toward that "intellectual virtue" which is, with one exception, the highes
attainment of truth: the virtue of "wisdom." The one exception is "reve
lation" of the supernatural, wherein even mind loses its identity in th
mystical being of God.

We have observed how this whole system of belief is carried ove
into educational principles. Mental discipline, "freedom" as pure ra
tionality, teaching as "instruction" and "discovery," schooling as "prepara
tion," the "great books" program for college students and adults, th
centrality of "metaphysics" in the university—all such proposals ar
harmonious with the philosophic formulation of perennialism. How
then, shall we appraise them?

Affinities of Perennialist and Essentialist Education. Several aspect
of our appraisal have been considered above in our evaluation of essential
ism. Notwithstanding significant deviations, ranging from subtle over
tones to first principles, it is clear that contemporary perennialists do no
repudiate such educational consequences of their philosophy as acqui
escent learning. Their perpetuation of much of the faculty psychology,
upon which this kind of learning is based, their effort (as at St. John's
College) to store minds with the wisdom of the classics, their insistence
upon memorizing and intense study of grammar—these and other practices explain clearly why some essentialists, although finding areas of disagreement, applaud Hutchins and Adler.†

† See National Society for the Study of Education, *Forty-first Yearbook,* Part
I, "Philosophies of Education," pp. 123f.

We can understand, also, why the kind of socio-economic groups ho approve essentialist schools tend also to approve enthusiastically erennialist programs. A college education devoted mainly to mastering he ideas of other ages may reasonably be assumed to be a "safe" education. It discourages direct study of the controversial problems of our time n the ground that these are either trivial or that they can be solved only y following a long, circuitous route through the great minds of the past. urther, despite its greater concern for logic and other mental skills, we ave seen that perennialism is not always averse to those mental and noral habits conditioned by "passive mentation." On the contrary, in so ar as these habits discourage the young from active participation or esponsibility in educational policy making and curriculum planning, hey encourage deference to those of superior status (teachers, clergynen, or civil officers) and thus help to perpetuate patterns of entrenched ower.

The Leader's Mind: Its Import. Although perennialists, like essenialists, are sufficiently friendly to traditional formulas for elementary and econdary schooling so that they, too, sometimes appear to be allies of ultural conservation, nevertheless, conservation is not their sole *ultimate* im. In addition, they insist upon certain basic *changes* in the culture—hanges required by the failures of both the liberal-progressivists and the onservative-essentialists, changes which can and should be implemented *rimarily* by the training of wise leaders. Such training cannot be chieved by essentialist methods. Hutchins, for example, insists upon the rimacy of the Socratic method of learning, in which the teacher funcions as physician of the soul.‡ Thus, the precise character of the minds" possessed by these leaders becomes of immediate, practical imortance, for they are to guide the people toward the promised land.

Although experimental methods are by no means disregarded by ll perennialist educational programs, it is significant that the clue to he desired "mind" lies elsewhere. Such methods are so distinctly secondry and subordinate that the kind of "mind" progressivists, for example, egard as the object of good education is likewise secondary and subordiate. The primary and dominant mind, as conceived by the perennialists, s capable of engaging in metaphysics and of attaining intellectual virtue. t alone can grasp those first principles which, being self-evident, beome the master keys to every human experience, every institution of ulture, every subject of the curriculum.

‡ See Hutchins, *op. cit.*, pp. 95f.

Retreat Within. Are we now prepared to contend that the perer nialist concept of mind in its most "real" form is also a form of escape A partial answer is that it retreats *into itself*. In terms of his deepe premises, the perennialist completely denies the necessity—on the level o ontological analysis and the purest intellectual virtue (by far the mos important level)—of employing experimental, cooperative testing or o checking its "pure" knowledge against the knowledge of other people.

To be sure, on the level of empiriological analysis and the mora virtues, such comparative testing may take place. Nevertheless, discoverie of the highest speculative mind are discoveries *of* itself, *by* itself, *withi* itself. Since it provides its own sanction *for* itself, it has no need, on thi metaphysical level, to reach into the realm of social or natural experienc —that is, to bring its principles into the laboratory for public inspectio and approval. It provides its own authority by the unsullied purity of it own intuition.

Retreat Without. But there is an even more important escap mechanism in this extraordinary theory of mind. We may epitomize i as a kind of *outward* retreat. All perennialists since Plato tend to tur not only subjectively to inner speculation for guidance but also objectivel to an outer absolute, ideal conception of the universe and hence of th culture that belongs within that universe. Such a conception retreats i two ways: first, away from the present into the more or less remote pas where it finds much of its basic theory; and, second, away from th responsibility of openly and publicly examining or achieving cultura aims by experimental methods of verification, and toward a realm of time less perfection.

The first aspect of outward retreat has been illustrated by peren nialist beliefs in corporate unity and hierarchical authority (rephrasec of course, to suit modern situations) as key principles of social order. Both beliefs were central philosophic and practical purposes of medieva culture.

The second aspect has been variously illustrated. One illustration i the belief that the basic purposes of culture are implicit within the telec logical, hylomorphic character of reality itself and that they cannot, there fore, *really* be denied or doubted however much we may try to do sc Another illustration is the belief that men must rely upon an elite that i

* See Jacques Maritain, *True Humanism*, pp. 115, 156.

ubject, ultimately and exclusively, only to its own unimpeachable au-
hority. Still another illustration is the belief that such authority springs
rom the same fount of eternal being and wisdom as do the subjective
elf-certainties of each superior mind. All such illustrations point to a
imilar conclusion: there is a transcendental, perfect universe ruled by
livine law to which men may turn from their own troubles with the
ssurance that they can depend upon it ultimately to guide and comfort
hem.

Both kinds of retreat, the inward and the outward, are reciprocal
arts of one encompassing philosophic system. No disciple of Aristotle
vould accept the contention that the self-evidence attained by specula-
ion has the form only of subjective thought within the field of *epis-
emology* alone. It is a form likewise of *ontology;* hence, in contrast with
he nominalist doctrine that thoughts are merely words (see pp. 301-
302), the self-evidence of thought is always of the very fiber of objective
eality itself. If minds are especially high forms of this reality, then they
ave the superior right to reveal these forms to themselves in their own
ntellectual purity. The purposes of mind thus become the purposes of
he universe, including culture; *the one supports the other, according to
onvenience.* But they are alike in their assumption that no infallible test
an be found for either, except the self-evidence of their own highest
rinciples. It is these to which men must finally retreat and upon which
ll education must finally build.

The Perennialist Challenge to Democracy

THE SANCTION OF AUTHORITY

We have now arrived at two major judgments. First, perennialism, con-
idered as an important type of cultural bulwark, rather than merely as
 form of pure erudition, strikingly supports those political and economic
rrangements in which the common people find guidance in an aristocracy
f presumably wise and virtuous leaders. Second, the supreme authority
f these leaders centers in the finality of *their own* wisdom and virtue;

it is a finality which depends, above all, upon the self-evidence of *inn* speculative principles and of *outer* universal-cultural purposes, both e compassed under the one absolute of knowledge—reality—value.

These two judgments imply a third—a harsh but logically determine inference. Granted the beauty and fertility of its contributions to Wester civilization, perennialism is, in last analysis, a serious challenge to th democratic conception of culture. It is a challenge because its own cruci beliefs are inimical and dangerous to that conception.

Democracy Defined. One pivotal belief distinguishes democrat purposes from the perennialist purposes we have been studying: the b lief that the majority of people in any organized society should be the so sovereign authority over the whole of society; conversely, no single in dividual or minority group should hold sovereign authority in any or ganized society. Closely related to this belief is the important belief i the fallibility, temporality, and finiteness of judgments made by the majo ity in its own behalf. Since decisions of the majority are always liable t error, as well as to changed circumstances which may compel a chang in judgment, they require continuous criticism, continuous checking c evidence and introduction of new evidence, continuous experiment testing of all important facts and proposals, and continuous public test mony among as many dissenting and consenting groups as possible.

Such a conception of democracy attained one of its earliest practic expressions in Periclean Athens. It was revived in the Renaissance cu ture by such men as Locke and was adapted to the needs of the ne middle classes as they successfully rose to power. It was made mor dynamic and flexible between the eighteenth and early twentieth cen turies by liberal thinkers and leaders ranging from Rousseau and Mi to Dewey and Holmes. It has been widened and deepened still furthe by more radical thinkers and leaders, such as Paine and Marx, Veble and Laski, and by the increasing strength of mass movements througho the world. Today it threatens the civil and ecclesiastic power of eco nomic and political minorities, and it attacks, on a scale unprecedente in history, the complex tangle of special interests and privileges.

Opposition to Democracy. Throughout the two thousand yea during which democracy has struggled for supremacy over alternativ conceptions of economy and culture, it has met bitter opposition fro minority power-groups and from the intelligentsia who are their spoke men. During that time the opposition has often successfully submerge democratic beliefs and habits which, even when they have had practical effects, have been restricted or denied in various ways. The history of essentialism in philosophy, education, and culture is one long illustration of such restriction or denial.

In such a setting, perennialism is then to be regarded as still another illustration. Although some of its exponents may earnestly believe they are not opposed to democracy, just as most essentialists insist they are not, nevertheless, perennialism is often impelled, willingly or unwillingly, to support undemocratic theory and practice. It is impelled both by its own beliefs and by the cultural structures and habits that these beliefs reflect and bolster.

Self-evidence: a philosophic and social critique

Self-evident to Whom? This cultural interpretation is supported by further scrutiny of the perennialist insistence upon the self-evidence of first principles. Although these are to be used for the "good" of all people, the perennialist fails to provide any way by which we can safely trust them to be so used—any way, that is to say, except by the presumed intellectual integrity and purity of those who maintain that they are in possession of such self-evidence.

Let us state the point differently. Perennialism identifies something called "freedom" with something called "rationality," thereby insisting again upon its devotion to "democracy" (see pp. 322-323). But since "rationality" proves, at its highest and most real, to be another name for metaphysical speculation, "freedom" becomes the freedom of a few to pronounce final injunctions of truth or value in such a way that the rest of the people are "free" also only in so far as they obey these injunctions.

If, however, first principles are really as self-evident as perennialists hold, should they not be self-evident to all who are equally competent to judge them philosophically? If a proposition is self-evident, should it be subject to logical argument at all? If it can be challenged, even denied by such argument, how can it also claim to be self-evident? Such questions are persistently raised among many philosophers recognized by their professional colleagues as thoroughly competent in logical analysis. These philosophers disagree so completely with such philosophers as Adler, and insist so vehemently that principles self-evident to him are not at all self-evident to them, that we are forced to question the presumed universality or dependability of these principles.

We may consider, as one illustration of their disagreement, Adler's categorical assertion that the two following "propositions" are completely self-evident: "corporeal substances differ essentially or accidentally, according as they are individuals of different species (having diverse natures) or as they are numerically distinct individuals having the same specific nature"; and "the good is convertible with being. . . ."[3] Any non-Aristotelian philosopher would at once insist that there is nothing at all self-evident about either of these propositions—unless it be that neither one *is* self-evident! The first involves an array of assumptions about the structure and process of reality which every evolutionary, experimental philosophy of science rejects. The second involves equally dubious assumptions about ontology in its relations with axiology—assumptions tending to confuse two types of belief which, while perhaps related, are far from necessarily identical.

Moreover, even such highly abstract first principles as were noted in our brief exposition of perennialist beliefs about knowledge are challenged by logicians holding alternative views. Thus, the principle of causality has been examined by many philosophers who have reached quite different conclusions regarding its meaning—some even doubting that it has any meaning. Others have cogently argued that the use of the principle of causality to "prove" the existence of God exposes the perennialist himself to inconsistency: if *everything* has a cause, do we actually add anything to our knowledge by assuming a First Cause, which is an exception to the principle of causality, and calling this exception "God"?

The self-evidence of mathematical principles is also frequently challenged. One of the most familiar disagreements derives from the alternative point of view that every mathematical system is a series of logical relations, starting from premises which are themselves arbitrarily assumed. Hence, it is possible to predicate varying or even opposed starting points, as do Euclidean and non-Euclidean geometry, and to proceed from these through different chains of logical relations to different mathematical results. Such a point of view clearly does not deny that starting points are needed in mathematics or in any other discipline; it does deny the perennialist dogma that these starting points are either eternal or real in any meaningful sense. In the language of deductive logic, it denies that ontological or other major premises are ever final or universal.†

Our position in regard to this issue of self-evident principles is well epitomized in the following statement by two American philosophers:

> . . . the history of human thought has shown how unreliable it [self-evidence] is as a criterion of truth. Many propositions formerly regarded as self-evident . . . are now known to be false. Indeed, contradictory propositions about every variety of subject-matter . . . have each, at different times, been declared to be fundamental intuitions and therefore self-evidently true. But whether a proposition is obvious or not depends on cultural conditions and individual training, so that a proposition which is "self-evidently true" to one person or group is not so to another.[4]

The Dangers of Self-evidence plus Power. The consequences of the principle of self-evidence, as applied to democracy, are disastrous. *The philosophy of perennialism would vest ultimate control over culture in those who, by definition, cannot be contradicted because they are their own supreme authority.* And it would do so without having convinced anyone except its own apologists that its highest principles, upon which that authority finally depends, are beyond error. As Gilson states it, "Reason has not to prove any of these [first] principles, otherwise they would not be principles but conclusions. . . ."[5]

Indeed, perennialism requires only one more device to ensure that the "wise" judgments of its leaders will be respected and obeyed—the device of *power*. Opposed by a power sufficiently prepared to support the leaders' judgments—as was Plato's military class or the armies of medieval theocratic states—it would be exceedingly difficult for others, whose minds might lead them to different judgments, to challenge that support successfully. Actually, dissent is often and conveniently silenced under the name

† The examples of self-evidence and its criticism are necessarily simple; readers further interested in this problem should consult such sources as those cited in footnotes and, in addition, Robert H. Beck, "Neo-Thomism and Rational Humanism in Educational Philosophy," *Harvard Educational Review*, Winter 1949. See also debate between Paul Schilpp and Mortimer Adler, "Are There Absolute and Universal Principles on Which Education Should Be Founded?" *Educational Trends*, July-August 1941; John Dewey and others, "The New Failure of Nerve," *Partisan Review*, January-February and March-April 1943; R. W. Sellars, V. J. McGill, and Marvin Farber (eds.), "Aristotelian Philosophies of Mind" in *Philosophy for the Future;* and Herbert Feigl in "Modern Philosophies and Education," *Fifty-fourth Yearbook*, Part I, National Society for the Study of Education.

of falsehood, immorality, heresy, treason—as the pages of history, with their profusion of torn and bloody epitaphs, tragically record.

In short, a self-evident "wisdom" that is *enforceable*—however benevolent it may be and however virtuous Plato's philosopher-kings aimed to be—is an exceedingly dangerous privilege. It is especially dangerous when threatened by the taint of corruption by which great power is always threatened. Frequent though the mistakes of democratic judgment may be, they are open to the therapy of public analysis, testing, consent, and correction. To be sure, democratic judgments are not infallible. But neither are they irremediable. The import of the choice between them and perennialist judgments is unmistakable.

Revelation and Democracy. The critique we have offered of self-evidence on the level of reason applies still more forcibly on the level of revelation. On that level, the tenuous efforts of the "intuitive" mind to make itself plausible to other minds are no longer considered indispensable: religious communion with God can replace philosophic communion among men. Nevertheless, for this very reason, the revelatory and mystical are held to be still more real, still more true and good than the speculative and metaphysical. This is so because the rare mortal who wins such divine companionship is himself closest to divinity. Therefore, he is very properly the authority over ordinary men who, contaminated as they are by matter and passion, can at least enjoy vicariously through him the aura of spiritual blessedness.

Thus, the essence of democracy is denied again by the highest of all their guiding principles. Yet, this principle, even if it is not directly incorporated into the educational theory and practice of lay advocates, is often tacitly sanctioned by them (see pp. 332-333, 337, 339). Certainly, parochial education becomes in this context the very antithesis of democratic education, for it indoctrinates students in the belief that the ultimate guidance of their lives is to be sought, not in their own natural capacities, in their own shared judgments, but in a supernatural Being Whose orders are most safely entrusted to His hierarchy of earthly representatives. On these grounds alone it is surprising that any perennialist should argue that the truths or values in which he believes "are not logically assumed in advance to be true nor are they taught without solid consideration of alternatives." [6] The theories of self-evidence, of revelation, and of indoctrination all contradict this statement.

Maritain reflects the authentic tradition with typical forthrightness. He discusses "mixed questions," *including education,* which should be considered "primarily and above all, not in reference to the temporal order and the good of the earthly city" but in reference to the spiritual order and "the good of souls. . . ." Actually democracy, "more than any other regime," requires the absolute authority of God; and no leader deserves to be obeyed unless he derives his own authority from "the sovereignty of the Cause of being. . . ."[7]

"Equality" and Perennialism. How, then, shall we meet the contention that perennialism can still claim to be democratic in the sense that it finds all men to be "equal before God"? Everyone recognizes, of course, the contribution to the ideal of brotherhood of the simple beliefs of Jesus and the Judaic tradition. Similarly, no one denies that some members of the Church and some philosophers of Thomist preference are concerned with enhancing this ideal.

One does fail, however, to find clear evidence that such concern follows consistently *from* that philosophic preference. History demonstrates that perennialism has supported and still supports various political systems, some of them rigidly authoritarian. Moreover, Maritain himself has affirmed that the Church is not obligated to support democracy more than it does other "worthy" systems of rule (see p. 313).‡

What is the meaning of the doctrine that men are equal before God? * The question is: *In what sense are they equal?* In the sense that all human beings are equally human? Perhaps, but this circular statement tells us nothing at all; so, too, are all animals equally animals. Are men equal in the sense, then, that they should share equally in determining all policies by which their lives will be governed justly? Clearly *no,* if we judge either by the record of two millenniums of Church control or by the theory of self-evident and revelatory justice.

Are men equal, then, in the sense that all men should seek and pray equally for eternal salvation? Clearly *yes* if the highest aim and measure of this life is the hope of afterlife. But, because the hope of afterlife is precisely such an aim and measure (certainly for all Church educators), equality on earth becomes at best a question of secondary interest; the Church readily supports national regimes officially opposed to equality as a political and economic end; and Maritain characterizes the Church as the "perfect society organized in accordance with its own

‡ See Maritain, *Ransoming the Time,* pp. 41, 206, 214f.
* See Sidney Hook in Dewey and others, *op. cit.*

appropriate . . . hierarchy, in which authority comes from above to teach souls and lead them to salvation."[8]

Role of the Majority: The Perennialist View and Its Refutation

Perennialist Attitudes Toward the Majority. The last stronghold of the perennialists' defense against the contention that their doctrine is ultimately a negation of democracy might be their insistence that they do recognize the role of the majority as legitimate and important. It is on this issue more than on any other that differences between "left wing" and "right wing" perennialists are most pronounced (see pp. 336-338)—the right wing revealing skepticism of and sometimes contempt for common citizens; the left wing revealing greater confidence in them and, hence, in the hope of increased privileges and powers for them. We have noted that such differences are defended on the ground that perennialists may differ about social philosophy, which stands on the comparatively low plateau of the moral virtues. These will necessarily produce differences of opinion that are not possible on the high level of the intellectual virtues.

Regardless of their varying positions on the social, economic, or political scale, perennialists should not be satisfied with so facile an answer. To insist upon it puts them in the position of doubting their own ability to reach clear, governing principles on the social level of experience. This is a doubt that is inconsistent with their argument that it is exactly on the social level that such principles are now so desperately needed. A far stronger answer—one which left-wing perennialists, at least, would emphasize—is that ordinary men, who constitute the majority of any culture, deserve the right to join in determining social policies for the simple, but fundamental, reason that even they are potentially capable of rational judgments. Stated more precisely, all men, being hylomorphic, *could* ideally become rational enough to govern themselves, even if actually they have not thus far learned how to do so. But if they could, then could not democracy, as rule by the majority, also succeed? And does not admission of this possibility demonstrate that perennialists are not, after all, opponents of democracy? Does it not also follow that, theoretically, perennialists do not necessarily advocate stratified cultural structures? Even though it must be admitted that the two greatest cultures of which this philosophy was the rationale were heavily stratified, no man is condemned by his nature to occupy one level of culture throughout his life. Therefore, any man may, if he sufficiently exercises the faculties of will and intellect, rise to the heights of reason and wisdom—nay, even of revelation.

Here we have the major premise, more or less frankly admitted, that underlies perennialist programs of general education such as those of St. John's and the Great Books Foundation.† Only when this kind of education becomes the universal pattern will the latent powers of mortal men be aroused sufficiently so that the majority may be equipped in the only way that has real significance—in behalf of *actual* rather than *potential* rationality. It is a solemn obligation of all civilized societies to ensure that it does become the pattern.

This is the perennialists' last stronghold of defense. Unfortunately, it, too, totters under the impact of examination. Several of its most glaring weaknesses are summarized below.

Perennialist Education Judged Unsound. We are not convinced that the kind of education typified by study of the great books—however much it is supported by logic, rhetoric, mathematics, or even by such practical virtues as prudence—will enable most citizens to judge intelligently or act effectively. Since, by perennialist definition, the scientific method is an inferior way to acquire knowledge, perennialists would hold that any educational program, including a program such as that of St. John's, cannot be judged by experimental canons. Although no way is available to prove by the canons of such scrutiny that it is unsound, neither is there any way by which perennialists can prove that it is sound. We must, therefore, finally accept the judgment of Van Doren and other advocates—themselves no doubt intuitively certain of their own self-evidence—that it is superior education. Debate is terminated, just as it is terminated in politics or religion, by the wisdom or revelation of the "superior" few.

If, however, we are willing to compare empirically the effects of the perennialist curriculum with the effects of the "new education," if we are willing to study both kinds of education by setting up control groups and by evaluating scientifically the competences and attitudes emerging from both—then we can infer their effects at least experimentally upon actual living in the contemporary world. In the higher learning, to be sure, such comparative studies are altogether too few in number. Also,

† See Hutchins, *op. cit.*, Chap. 5.

for the sake of strict accuracy, let us recall that some parochial schools have tried to utilize and even to experiment with methods resembling the progressivist method.‡ On the whole, however, a growing body of scientific evidence supports the conclusion that primary and secondary programs which are dominated by perennialist beliefs fail to educate people to govern themselves in the meaning of the democratic process as defined above.

To select one of many illustrations, the Eight-Year Study of the Progressive Education Association (although it compares progressivist and essentialist rather than strictly perennialist education) demonstrates that acquiescent learning, based upon "mental storehouse" and faculty psychologies, fails to teach even skills and facts more effectively than do modern methods.* Such learning is vastly less successful in developing critical awareness, community responsibility, and other qualities indispensable to social participation and cooperative action.

Again, the assumption of some perennialists that the kind of mental discipline acquired through the study of foreign languages or mathematics *transfers* to other logical skills has not been verified, and even most realist essentialists now question its validity.

Lack of Concern for Democratic Processes. Whether perennialist education best prepares average citizens for democratic rule may also be questioned by its relative disregard of the basic *processes* by which such rule must always operate. That Hutchins and other perennialists, even when they approach acceptance of democratic *ends,* are usually either vague or inadequate in discussing democratic *means*—indeed, the whole complex problem of social control—has been an important contention of the preceding chapter.

The great-books program perhaps illustrates the point most graphically. To be sure, students occasionally *read about* majority control in Mill's essay *On Liberty* or other classics. Some perennialists also admit, however charily, a limited value in the activity curriculum, inductive learning, and other life-centered aspects of progressivist theory. But we search in vain through such institutions as St. John's for democratic learnings that are equal to the learnings derived from active *sharing* in the problems and policies of teacher-pupil planning. We find only

‡ See L. J. O'Connell, *Are Catholic Schools Progressive?*

* See W. M. Aikin, *The Story of the Eight-Year Study;* Ernest O. Melby and Morton Puner (eds.), *Freedom and Public Education,* pp. 227-247.

aughty indifference to the political and economic struggles of surround-ıg communities or to student-faculty participation in such struggles. Vork experience is obviously not considered educational experience. And ıere is very little firsthand or even secondhand familiarity with the great ssues and conflicts *of our own time,* as seen and practiced by *contem-orary* statesmen, artists, social scientists, business and labor leaders—or hilosophers.

With almost no regard for or practice in the means by which real ıdividuals can organize and improve their condition, the belief of peren-ialists in the right of every man to rise above his stratum becomes little ıore than a pious wish. It is a wish only too reminiscent of the individ-alist tradition of self-exertion, which essentialists so frequently applaud. y neglecting analysis of and action against economic or other cultural onditions and forces that block the freedom of people to rise by their wn efforts, the perennialist program of education disregards those proc-sses and strategies that might sustain, by *forthright demonstration,* its erbal disavowals of a stratified culture.

The lively current issues of public concern that are sometimes dis-ussed by seminar groups are seldom grounded in careful research or elevant scientific data. Equally seldom are problems with a cultural bear-ıg studied by experimental analysis and testing of hypotheses. Hence, he method of Socratic conversation, although by far the most attractive eature of the St. John's and adult programs, does not establish that the rogram meets the criteria of democratic learning implied by full presenta-ion of evidence, full communication of that evidence, and maximum greement as well as action upon such evidence and communication. Im-licit in it, rather, is a kind of pseudo-Platonic hope that eternal Ideas of ruth, value, and reality lurk somewhere in the background of each eminar discussion—patiently awaiting that enunciation by which, alone, ational answers shall at last be deduced.

Disparagement of Science. Our next justification for questioning erennialism's professed concern for majority rule has already been im-lied, namely, its disparagement of science. If perennialist apologists be-rudgingly accord recognition to experimental methods, they nevertheless reat science, along with its educational allies, as the scapegoat largely esponsible for mankind's contemporary troubles.

It is unnecessary to analyze further the weakness of perennialist rguments against scientific method and its social effects. Although we

may question the adequacy of that method as thus far exercised, ou
doubts call not for the weakening of science but for its strengthening. Fo
example, we can not fairly accuse it of causing the present crisis in world
affairs so long as has not been systematically applied to the intra- or inter
national conflicts and tensions chronic to that crisis. Indeed, if we are to
fix the blame at all, supernatural religion and secular absolutisms—with
their concomitants of superstition, escapism, dogmatism, and mysticism
—are much more vulnerable. For centuries it is these attitudes, not the
scientific method, that have most often influenced and determined
the course and outcome of both social and personal affairs.†

We do need to consider further, however, the role of science in the
operation of democracy—more precisely, the role of science in building
majority consent with respect to all fundamental policies of public wel
fare. Such a role is exactly the antithesis of what we have called "mind
as retreat without." In a democracy, cultural problems are not faced,
purposes and programs are not fashioned, by retreating into the remote
past or into an absolutism dependent upon transcendental principles. On
the contrary, they are derived inductively from common interests, they
are subjected to factual scrutiny and open testimony, and they are finally
tested in cultural laboratories under the best available experimental conditions. Throughout this process, democracy operates to the degree that the
majority of citizens not only express their common judgments on every
public policy but also are informed of the techniques required to make
those judgments operative. They themselves are not experts in these techniques; this would be impossible. But they must strive to understand and
approve the character and conditions of the general procedure and to
express their willingness to be guided by it in deciding finally whether
the product it creates satisfies their widest interests.

In these terms, democracy still remains a hypothesis which has been
far from adequately tested. But certainly it cannot be tested by any system
of beliefs that denies the decisive importance of social experiment by
denying the adequacy or ultimate dependability of scientific knowledge.
Nor can it be tested by an educational philosophy or program which
endorses that denial.

The Elite and the Majority. Finally, democracy may be justifiably
suspicious of the importance and the prestige perennialism attributes to
an intellectual elite. We cannot recall too often the ancient and medieval

† See Dewey and others, *op. cit.*

ructures of autocratic-aristocratic relations from which perennialists orrow so many of their own dominant beliefs. We cannot disregard that ıeir program for the higher learning is designed almost entirely for the enefit of an exceptional few who survive the rigors of general education nd for whom even that education is largely intended as a proving round. We do not forget that Hutchins' pattern for university adminis- ation was borrowed directly from Plato himself. We stress again that, ı their regard for a supernatural outlook consistent with the Thomist iew, lay perennialists lend support to the belief of all members of the Church (not the least of whom is the democratically-tempered Maritain imself) that "*Man craves for a power superior to himself to whom he an pay homage and under the shelter of whose authority he finds ecurity.*" [9] We must recognize the historic fact that this power, although llegedly emanating from God, has been exercised for many centuries y a rigidly authoritarian and powerful elite—by a hierarchy whose own nandates are frequently regarded as the highest court of appeal, stand- ng even above civil government.‡

The conclusion is inescapable. Although the perennialist may affirm hat the majority is rational *potentially*, the whole practical weight of the erennialist program, certainly in education, denies the expectation that he majority is likely to become rational *actually*. If this were not the case, ne would expect such an educator as Hutchins at least to imply that he need for universities limited to an elite would eventually be super- eded by universities for the majority of people. Or Maritain might inti- nate that perhaps, sometime, ecclesiastic absolutism will be superseded y completely democratic controls within the Church itself. Neither sug- gestion, of course, has been made. On the contrary, both are absurd, in he sense of being incongruous with the whole "spirit and substance," the whole elaborate system of premises and deductions which constitute the Platonic-Aristotelian-Thomist *Weltanschauung*. Thus our response to such democratic suggestions as are still sometimes offered—Adler's world government, for example, or Maritain's more equitable economic system —is to regard them, in the perspective of their total outlook, as ambiguous, inconsistent, eclectic, or simply as subordinate to their more definitive and finally undemocratic framework of beliefs.

What is decisive is that the kind of education that perennialists pro-

‡ This doctrine seems to have been reaffirmed by Pope Pius XII in 1954. See New York *Times,* November 4, 1954.

pose *for* the majority is not primarily education for responsible, vigorou participative rule *by* or *of* the majority. It is rather a scheme by which th average citizen, relegated properly if not inevitably to lower rungs of th ladder of culture, can be sufficiently sensitized to the "wisdom" of grea minds and, through them, to the authority of self-evident truth and revela tion, so that he will respect and revere that authority. In this context Adler's remark is especially revealing: "A democracy, in short, depend on men who can rule themselves because they have the art of bein ruled. . . . The democratic ruler must move us by rational persua sion."[10] This statement is the pivotal assumption of perennialist socia theory. Certainly, most men cannot become philosopher-kings, but through universal education of the kind proposed, they can join willingl in a harmony of membership in a corporate whole. They can be com forted by their sense of unity in a cultural pyramid whose apex point toward God Himself. They can thereby "really" share in the mainte nance of that kind of "justice" whose core is always finally self-evident to their nearly divine leaders.

Summary of Beliefs about Perennialism

Perennialism, as a philosophy of education, is rooted in a philosophy of culture. Its central position is regressive in the precise sense that it reacts against such characteristic beliefs of our present democratic culture as science and majority control in favor of a constellation of beliefs characterizing great cultures of past ages. In this regression, it draws most heavily upon three thinkers—Plato, Aristotle, and Aquinas—revising their principles only superficially, often merely by expressing them in terminology more appropriate to the twentieth century. Differences between clerical and secular perennialists arise in the area of theology—the former upholding the supremacy of the Roman Catholic Church and its interpretations of perennialist doctrine. Nevertheless, the two wings of perennialist philosophy recognize at least as many common principles, if judged by cultural and hence educational consequences, as do the realist and the idealist wings of essentialist philosophy.

Perennialist beliefs about reality pivot around the doctrine of hylomorphism: the unfolding of everlasting or perennial forms which

e potentially within matter. This doctrine is developed with great com-
lexity through many related principles, among the most important of
hich are teleology (belief in the inherently purposeful character of all
eings) and supernaturalism (belief in the existence of a realm of abso-
ıte spirit, which finally controls all lower realms).

Beliefs about knowledge are strictly consistent with these principles
f reality. Knowledge rises in ascending levels of purity, from the sheer
gnorance of material passion through intermediate levels of empirical
nethod and opinion to that level of rare achievement of reason and spirit
where self-evident first principles and, still higher, revelation stand as the
upreme accomplishments of man.

Beliefs about value rise also in an increasingly more nearly perfect
eries—the "moral" virtues being subordinate to the "intellectual." Art
nd prudence are characterized by both the moral and the intellectual
irtues. Politics, although concerned primarily with the moral virtues,
s nevertheless also inspired by the intellectual-spiritual fountainhead of
netaphysics and extra-natural intuition.

Perennialist education is a unified development of its own deepest
hilosophy. Even the particular educational proposals of contemporary
hinkers are often astonishingly similar to ancient-medieval proposals.
earning, for example, is typified by the kind of mental discipline that
uarantees the maximum unfolding of man's more or less latent ration-
lity, while teaching is best characterized by the assistance it gives man
n this developing. This does not mean that perennialist educators are
lways unconcerned about emotional or other kinds of experience; rather,
uite consistently with their belief in man's many-sided nature, they may
orrow from progressivist and other modern practices. They are careful,
owever, to point out the signal limitations of this kind of education.
They return always, therefore, to the key principle—learning is ultimately
ot *doing* but *reasoning*—and hence to the supreme importance of eduation of the mind and spirit.

We may understand from this doctrine why perennialist curriculums
ften closely resemble essentialist emphases upon learning by correspond-
nce, upon mental substances, and upon similar beliefs. But in the peren-
ialist programs for junior colleges, adult education, and higher learning
great books are central to the first two, training of intellectual leaders
o the third) its proposals are more original.

In their approach to social and educational control, perennialist educators are concerned chiefly with fomenting a "spiritual and intelle tual revolution." With rare exceptions, programs of control, processe and means might seem ambiguous or innocuous were we to forget tha they are held to be relatively unimportant by comparison with the nee for "rational" training of the many and philosophic-religious leadershi by the few.

In evaluating this profound and influential philosophy of educatio we must recall primarily not only that it is derived directly from aristo cratic, hierarchical patterns of culture but also that it proves to be bot interpreter and archapologist for just such patterns. In final analysis, th crisis that contemporary perennialists find so threatening to our ow civilization is to be met by restoring the kind of beliefs most characteristi of and fundamental to both ancient and medieval cultures, adapted t modern conditions.

We criticize these beliefs on two principal grounds. First, they pr vide a conception of mind as escape from direct, cooperative, and publi attack on the great problems of our day. Second, they constitute a genuin threat to democracy itself.

The first criticism reveals that perennialist education, like essentiali education, encourages the development of acquiescent personalities amon the majority of the people—personalities more suited to following orde than to criticizing or approving them. The elite mind of the intellectua minority, depending most crucially upon a presumed capacity to discove self-evident first principles, is able to retreat, for the sanction of its ow authority, either inward to itself or outward to some transcendent realm

The second criticism follows from the conception of democracy a that form of society in which the majority of the people, conditioned b minority criticism or dissent, are the final determiners of public policy This conception was not only opposed by the most influential Greek an medieval thinkers; it is decisively opposed today by all consistent peren nialists, however earnestly some of them may express sympathetic atti tudes toward democracy. Such opposition is revealed by their insistenc upon leadership endowed with the capacity to recognize self-evident, o revelatory, "truths" and "values"—leadership which, by definition, canno finally be challenged, especially not when supported by power. It is re vealed also by their belief in an "equality before God" which is mor concerned with equality in heaven than with equality on earth. It is re ealed, finally, by a theoretically and practically vulnerable program of ducation for the majority.

Although such a program seldom subjects itself to scientific methods f appraisal, the evidence that results when such methods are employed ends progressively to discredit it. The program provides little if any eduational practice in self-government. The actual processes of democratic truggle and participation, and of cooperative determination of the ends f democratic culture, are minimized or ignored. The role of data acumulation, communication, controlled testing, and agreements about ublic proposals are frequently belittled. Indeed, the experimental determination of policies in terms of wide public interest is treated as largely rrelevant to sound general education. The whole program rests, finally, ipon the unimpeachable reason of a political or ecclesiastic elite—an lite whom the majority shall be taught to trust with confidence. For ipon its brow rests the sovereign crown of supreme wisdom and virtue.

Thus is the Platonic formula of "justice" reincarnated to fit our imes. Perennialism offers a theory and program of great brilliance and ersuasiveness. But it is a theory and program that cannot be accepted by ny student, teacher, or citizen who prefers, in place of its kind of security nd escape, the privilege of sharing cooperatively, equitably, publicly in he adventure of building a world-wide democratic culture.

Notes

[1] Arnold J. Toynbee, *A Study of History,* p. 183. Copyright 1947 by Oxford Jniversity Press and reprinted with heir permission.

[2] Quoted from John H. Randall, Jr., *The Making of the Modern Mind,* p. 06. See also George H. Sabine, *A History of Political Thought,* p. 257.

[3] Quoted from National Society for he Study of Education, *Forty-first Yearbook,* Part I, "Philosophies of Education," pp. 244f.

[4] Morris R. Cohen and Ernest Nagel, *An Introduction to Logic and Scientific Method,* p. 131. Copyright 1934 y Harcourt, Brace and Company and reprinted with their permission.

[5] Etienne Gilson, *The Unity of Philosophical Experience,* p. 314.

[6] Joseph McGlade, *Progressive Educators and the Catholic Church,* p. 120.

[7] Jacques Maritain, *True Humanism,* p. 293; and *Scholasticism and Politics,* pp. 103ff.

[8] Maritain, *Ransoming the Time,* p. 199.

[9] William F. Cunningham, *The Pivotal Problems of Education,* p. 221 (italics supplied). See also Maritain, *Scholasticism and Politics,* pp. 103ff.

[10] Mortimer J. Adler, *How to Read a Book,* p. 369.

EPILOGUE

CHAPTER 13

Prospects for American Education

THE THREE GREAT THEORIES AND PROGRAMS OF EDUCATION that we have reviewed and appraised are the most influential educational theories in the American culture of our time. Although we might study various other theories and programs which are not subsumed consistently or wholly under the wide operational categories of progressivism, essentialism, or perennialism, we must recognize that no others have, to date, exerted a comparable influence.

We do not imply, however, that American education will inevitably continue to function solely on the basis of one or more of these three philosophies. That it *may* continue to do so for a long period of time, that each *may* be modified in major or minor ways, or that one or another of the three *may* overwhelmingly dominate the other two is certainly conceivable. Indeed, the ardent advocate of each is convinced that his is most deserving of support, and the advocate of at least one of the three—the perennialist—is convinced by his very premises that his, and only his, *must* prevail: the absolute metaphysical system upon which perennialism is built assures its ultimate, if belated, victory. Such absolute assurance is likewise typical of some essentialists, especially if they are governed by the beliefs of objective idealism. The philosophy that is least doctrinaire, because of its empirical and nonteleological assumptions, is the progressivist: despite its radiant optimism and its liberal hopes, it can logically offer no guarantee of the final emergence of the kind of culture and the kind of schools it values most highly. The future, it holds, is always contingent and therefore unpredictable.

In this tentativeness, we find ourselves in agreement with progressivists. But we would insist even more vigorously than they that it is unsound to assert that American education is confined to a choice among or even a combination of the chief philosophies that now so largely overshadow all less influential claimants. We are especially doubtful about their adequacy because of the chronic condition of our crisis-culture. A culture which is torn, as we have found ours to be torn, by wide and deep conflict, which suffers "schisms of the soul" as well as schisms of the body politic, is a culture which gives no assurance that it will, in the future, necessarily continue to follow any of the roads it has followed in the past. Also, the history of revolutionary periods—and ours is a revolutionary period—proves that the social, economic, moral, religious, and educational attitudes and practices that emerge from cultural upheavals always differ from our expectations. Sometimes they are infinitely worse, occasionally better, but invariably they are different.

It is not at all impossible, indeed, that the American culture, bound as it is to the fate of the rest of the world, will sooner or later succumb to totalitarian power. Whether this power, should it conquer America, will resemble more the Russian type or the prewar German or Italian type, or whether it will assume native colorations and labels distinct from either of these, no one can foretell. Certainly we should be grossly naive to assume that an American totalitarianism is impossible. Our country can no longer afford to bask in its earlier complacent mood of invincible self-confidence and self-sufficiency. Oceans are too narrow, flight too swift, weapons too destructive.

Nor can America safely disregard the interpretations of distinguished scholars that Western culture as a whole has passed the zenith of its creativity and might. We do not imply that the deep pessimism of Oswald Spengler is fully justifiable—if for no other reason than that *The Decline of the West* is littered with historical errors. We do not imply that Pitirim Sorokin, in *The Crisis of Our Age* and in his other works, logically and historically supports his impassioned faith that the Western world is about to undergo a "spiritual" rebirth which will alter the whole character of our hitherto "materialistic" culture. We do affirm that, if we compare such diverse interpretations with a number of others (Arnold Toynbee's is most prominent), we find a striking consensus on one basic theme: the Western world is experiencing cataclysmic change out of which can only arise a transformed way of life.

However wrong or right the future will demonstrate these prognostications to be, one outcome does seem certain: the kind of educational philosophy and practice that await mankind will, at every stage, express and serve the interests of the future culture. Should an American adaptation of totalitarianism rise on the ruins of our contemporary democracy, we may be certain that the schools will be harnessed to its purposes. Should a "spiritual" culture supplant our allegedly "materialistic" one, the schools will serve its purposes. So, too, will they serve the purposes of a pattern of human existence that may be radically different from either possibility.

In thus re-emphasizing the first premise of our interpretation—the premise that education is always and inescapably the agent of the culture by which it is fashioned and endowed—we must, however, equally re-emphasize that education is not thereby to be viewed solely as a *passive* agent. In some cultures, especially absolutist or totalitarian cultures, it may, for a time, seem predominantly passive; in others, it may not even seem so. The American culture, most notably perhaps, has never regarded education as the mere automatic transmitter of accepted routines. From the earliest years of our history, Jefferson and other leaders have conceived education to be the greatest of all the *active* agents of a democratic people. All major educational philosophies continue, although from disparate points of view, to uphold this conception.

Most anthropologists, moreover, lend the prestige of their discipline to such a conception of the basic role of education. In the first place, we should recall that "culture" is an operational concept designed to encompass all characteristics of the environment constructed by human beings living in societies. It is not, as a few other anthropologists still tempt us to believe, a self-contained, autonomous level of nature, independent of real persons. Rather, both in what it means and in what it does, culture is that body of experience that man himself has fashioned. In short, not only would there be no culture without men who analyze and define its innumerable attributes; there would be no culture, either, without men who actively modify and create, as well as transmit, the complex attitudes and habits, organizations and processes that embody these attributes.

In the second place, anthropologists regard education not merely as a matter of classroom instruction, of teachers and schools, but as an indigenous cultural experience. True, in some sophisticated cultures, it is embodied in special institutions, built for special educational activities and designated as such. But, even where this happens to occur, education is not limited to these institutions. Education is operating, at least as richly and usually much more richly, as men absorb, apply, modify, perpetuate, improve, strengthen, and reshape the means and ends of believing, acting, and living that are the stuff of culture.

Viewed comprehensively, education, then, is never solely or permanently passive. Rather, it is active as participation in cultural experience (although varying in time, place, and intensity) is active. Since man does not and cannot transmit culture through his genetic structure, education—that is, the capacity to learn from and to teach other members—is the inclusive process through which any member of a culture is able to transmit it at all. But man never *merely* reproduces culture; he utilizes it, too, and thus he sometimes discovers different ways of doing what his predecessors did, of demonstrating these ways to those who follow him, and thus of molding the culture itself.

Education, in sum, is the chief institution through which culture, entirely the creation of men, maintains dynamic continuity. It stabilizes the patterning of social experience and, in this sense, always reflects that patterning. But education also makes possible the great or small innovations, the cumulative readjustments without which, in the long career of cultures, stability either degenerates into sterility or finally explodes into chaos and destruction.

Thus far in this Epilogue we have attempted to establish three major points. The first is that the most prominent American philosophies of education, although they may continue to dominate the majority of schools, will not inevitably do so. A crisis-culture such as ours stimulates possible alternatives, some of them less desirable, some conceivably more so. The second point is that, because education is inherent in the life of every culture, it will also act as the agent of whatever kind of cultural patterning emerges in the future. The third point is that education, although always intrinsic to and the servant of its respective culture, never permanently plays only a passive role. In different degrees and ways, it guides and shapes at the same time that it serves.

The broad frame of reference that is now constructed prepares us to recapitulate our assessments of the three philosophies. Each of them, as the active agent of different periods and conceptions of culture, has performed its function often effectively and always conscientiously. Each, in its present form, is indebted to the other two, having adapted features of the others. All of them recognize, for example, the necessity of an education for every normal individual. All are in favor of more generous support for American public schools. All believe that children of every class and race should know how to read, write, and compute; should learn and respect our rich traditions; should acquire vocational skills; should understand something about the sciences and arts; should recognize the rules of conduct ordained by contemporary social life. All three philosophies reject either Communist or Fascist totalitarian education.

Nevertheless, if we refer briefly to the Prologue, where we considered four exemplary issues of the great educational debate now waging in America, we may observe that—sometimes only slightly and sometimes very sharply—the chief philosophies also conflict.

Let us consider, first, the issue of support-and-control of the public schools. Notwithstanding their common demand for considerably greater financial support, they fail to agree either on how this support should be obtained or by whom it should be controlled. Progressivists appear to be more united than the other educational philosophers on the proposition that federal funds are now required. Nevertheless, their "later liberal" political philosophy, beset as it is by tensions between means and ends, between present and future, between individuality and sociality, does not admit a clear consensus on the degree and kinds of necessary control over such funds. Essentialists appear to be less in accord on even the need for substantial federal support. Despite important deviants within their ranks, a stronger loyalty to the "early liberal" tradition causes them to resist, in principle, current trends away from that tradition and toward more centralized, collective power and responsibility. Perennialists, perhaps because they do not consider the issue of federal aid and control to be "philosophic" at all—it is, at best, merely "empirical"—tend to be silent or ambiguous rather than specific. Not completely so, however. The ecclesiastic wing is extraordinarily articulate in its opposition to federal aid that would exclude parochial schools; and, in countries where the Church is politically powerful, governmental controls which strengthen its hold on both private *and* public education are officially supported. We may also suppose that secular perennialists would not reject federal aid or control under all conditions: so long as either is governed by their axiological canons of corporate harmony and justice, they could and should logically approve.

The related problem of authority within schools and colleges is met in equally divergent ways. Progressivists are by far the most explicit in their support of practices that would widen participation and decision making by all members of the educational community. Yet, their authorities on school administration are often singularly vague in their formulations of guiding policies, and even their philosophers are more divided than united on such questions as teacher affiliation with organized labor. Essentialists, although their stronger eclectic tendencies may encourage progressivist policies among some supporters, more frequently apply to education the line-staff type of authority characteristic of modern industry. Some perennialists, too, occasionally advocate greater popular participation than has been their typical practice. Nevertheless, both their historical record and their basic theory make it difficult if not impossible for them to challenge hierarchical patterns of control—patterns which of course govern every institution of the Church and which also seem inherent in the doctrine of leadership espoused by non-Church spokesmen.

On the issue of curriculum-and-learning progressivists tend to be aligned against proponents of both other theories. Because they conceive the educative process as the myriad experiences of individuals who learn only as they live these experiences, the curriculum becomes the channel through which flows every significant cultural event. And learning, in turn, becomes a continuous, interested effort not only to enter fully into the stream of culture but to meet by the method of intelligence the problems that every culture constantly engenders. Essentialists typically regard the process and product of learning as a transmission of the cultural heritage. Although some (especially idealists) interpret learning more creatively, even they do not highlight the progressivist idea of experimental change so much as they advocate a kind of spiritual self-awakenng. Essentialist proposals for the curriculum may be said to derive mainly rom the social and/or religious heritage and their methods of learning to est upon a philosophy of mind that sets it in a predominantly reflexive ather than functional relation to that heritage. Perennialists, too, may egard the primary aim of learning to be a creative one—in their case, of ourse, creative in the sense of metaphysical thought which occurs mainly n the higher learning. But their hylomorphic premises imply political nd social consequences different from those of the progressivists and ssentialists—namely, an aristocracy ruled by philosopher-kings (or the- ocratic rulers) and possessed of those "intellectual virtues" (or revela- ory faith) upon which any cultures that aspire to greatness must finally lepend.

Academic freedom is supported by all three theories. All resent with greater or lesser indignation the meddling of demagogues who promote heir own ambitions by damaging or destroying reputations and careers. Again, however, because philosophic interpretations of freedom vary, concepts of academic freedom also tend to vary. So, too, do the cultural ffects of these interpretations.

For the progressivist, freedom centers in the interactive and thus social effort of individuals to cope scientifically with the endless obstacles confronting their lives. Thus, freedom is the opportunity to explore, to question, to examine, to improve. Academic freedom is a crucial aspect of this wider freedom: without it, good education in any culture simply cannot function. Nevertheless, one recalls the tendency of certain progres- sivists to qualify this abstract ideal in the face of concrete cultural events —particularly to deny to some of those who oppose their philosophy of freedom the unqualified right to maintain their differences in academic life. It is a tendency induced, as we suggested above, partly by the very flexibility of their ontological, epistemological, and axiological beliefs; partly, also, by "later liberal" attitudes and habits which saturate these beliefs.

Academic freedom tends to be conceived by essentialists as a species of "universal freedom" grounded in the laws of history, nature, or God —or possibly all three. Their reverence for the Constitution, for example, is based on a belief in "natural rights," which derive from "natural law" —a reverence which, grounded on other ontological premises, is also felt by perennialists. But neither type of philosophers always zealousl defends academic freedom when it departs too far from their respectiv premises. Essentialists often effectively, although not always deliberately equate laws of universal freedom with policies of academic freedom con genial to the ideologies of middle-class groups. Perennialists of clerica allegiance are rarely, if ever, willing to permit advocates of "heresies," such as atheists, humanists, and Protestants, to teach philosophy or an of its branches in their schools and colleges: freedom thus becomes th right to indoctrinate *their* ideas of value, reality, and truth. Secular peren nialists are not, of course, so rigidly bound to doctrine. Thus, we agai emphasize, certain representatives have been in the forefront of the con temporary American battle for intellectual freedom. Even in regard t their position, however, a serious qualification must be observed: in s far as freedom becomes the rational activity of discovering and impartin "self-evident first principles," it becomes, precisely by virtue of such "self evidence," an unchallengeable freedom. And that which is unchallenge able is always, if given power of enforcement, politically and henc culturally perilous to that self-correcting, public process which is th genius of democracy.

And now let us consider the issue of the community in its relations with the school. Although vacillating and sometimes inconsistent on the question of one of the community's dominant institutions—organized religion—progressivists do believe that exposure to other cultural institutions, and even to pressure groups, affords rich learning experiences inside the school. Also, they zealously provide opportunities for students of all ages to join widely in group activities outside the school. Essentialists and perennialists generally offer less support to student participation in community activities. Their stress upon mental discipline, formal subject matters, and other principles derived from opposing educational, hence philosophic as well as cultural, assumptions are not conducive to developing an active partnership of school and community in the progressivist sense. But they do welcome other types of partnership. We may observe, for example, the ties that may be traced between essentialist programs for schools and traditional interests of power groups approving those programs. We may observe, too, the consummate skill with which leaders of the Church affect political decisions (released time for religious education, for example) when their own educational interests are deeply involved. Still more intimate if also more complex are the historical relations of all three philosophies with that all-encompassing community—the culture itself.

We now epitomize these historical relations.

Progressivism is the theory and practice of an American culture in the process of growing up. It is a philosophy that is liberal in character. It prides itself on tolerance, continuity, progressive experimentation. It expresses the adventuresome spirit of a youthful nation. It recognizes the reciprocity of "how" and "what," of methods and goals. But, to recall the words of the brilliant pragmatist, George Herbert Mead, it finds "the ideal phase of politics and business . . . in the process rather than in their objectives . . . [in] the end in terms of the means. . . ."

Essentialism is the philosophy and program of an American culture subtly but resolutely dedicated to the conservation of patterns that were born in the Renaissance and achieved maturity by the nineteenth century. It is a philosophy much more European in its origins and essential spirit than is the progressivist philosophy. Hence, it is concerned less with a way of life that would cultivate experimental growth as the supreme good, than with adjustment to and acquiescence in already prized axioms and/or institutions of the inherited way of life.

Perennialism derives ultimately from an era still more ancient than the essentialist—the Greek and medieval. It is a philosophy of American culture deeply disturbed not only by the kind of cultural instabilities often sanctioned by progressivists but even by the kind of stabilities often sanctioned by essentialists. It believes that Americans will restore the one defensible kind of cultural stability only when they are prepared to regress to, while translating and refining for their own age, those timeless, spaceless principles of truth, value, and reality by which alone any culture may be divinely or at least virtuously led.

We find in the simultaneous and powerful appeal of all three of these philosophies a clear symptom of culture-crisis. Each point of view wins large numbers of devoted followers, erects schools and colleges, educates millions of children and adults, is effective not only in self-defense but in exposing weaknesses in other points of view. We would be inaccurate to affirm that this competition of ideas and institutions is an unmitigated good. That it is in many ways an enriching and stirring experience for the people of America is undoubtedly true. But in so far as it is organically related to other "schizophrenic" symptoms, of conflict, bewilderment, and divided loyalties, it may also aggravate these symptoms.

Such a danger is further aggravated by the fact that all three of these philosophies emerge as in various respects deficient cultural-educational alternatives. Let us grant again their gigantic influence and continuous vigor. Let us grant, too, that American education has benefited and can continue to benefit from their insights and accomplishments. One may still, however, properly inquire whether any of these philosophies sufficiently resolves the four issues reviewed above. Do they resolve the issue of support-and-control, of curriculum-and-learning, of academic freedom, of community-and-school? Clearly, they do for some Americans. But here judgments are usually conditioned by whether one or another of their inclusive outlooks has already, more or less explicitly, persuaded their adherents. If, for example, the regressivist-perennialist attitude toward freedom is your general preference, then its approach to a specific issue, such as academic freedom, is probably also your preference. Or, if the liberal-progressivist approach to cultural change is convincing to me, then its functional approach to learning is also likely to be convincing to me.

The crucial issue, however, is that such solutions do not invariably convince either you or me. And perhaps, as we have sought to demonstrate in Chapters 6, 9, and 12, they fail to convince precisely because we realize that they are not merely educational but are, far more fundamentally, cultural solutions. Perhaps, for example, the perennialist doctrine may be seriously questioned because, in wide enough perspective, it reveals itself to be incompatible with the ideal of that fully democratic culture that the common peoples of America and other nations may still, if they wish, erect. Perhaps the essentialist philosophy is open to grave doubt because, in equally wide perspective, it proves to be a way to perpetuate beliefs, practices, institutions that mirror a stage in Western industrial democracy that is now rapidly declining. Perhaps, finally, the progressivist philosophy is vulnerable because it represents the transitional period of an adolescent culture—because it is a philosophy which is unwilling or unable to perceive that its own hypothetical, methodological character blocks the road of a culture confronted, as ours is now confronted, with the imperative of reformulated commitments, strategies, and goals.

This over-all evaluation is itself as controversial as the educational ssues with which it deals. Nevertheless, it does support our contention hat the possibilities for American education are not confined to these alternative philosophies. Not only may any or all three, while retaining their core assumptions, be amended in ways now unforeseeable; not only is our culture and thus our education susceptible to totalitarianism or, as some philosophers of culture predict, to a long period of decadence; not only, as suggested in Chapter 2, are many Americans attracted by skepticism, eclecticism, or some other inadequate level of belief—but still another alternative philosophy must be explored, a philosophy of culture-and-education possessing many of the richly constructive aspects of the three contenders now most dominant but differing from all of them in its radically *re*-constructive character. Recognizing the difficulties chronic to these contenders, recognizing further the precarious and swiftly moving time in which we live, we should seriously consider the potentialities of this fourth alternative.

Are its outlines already discernible? We believe that they are. It is a philosophy that borrows profusely from its predecessors and contemporaries but particularly from progressivism—the youngest, most pliable, most inherently American of the major philosophies of education. It is a philosophy, however, that strives to remove the ambiguities and resolve the inconsistencies that inhere in progressivism. Should it evolve into another powerful contender for our educational allegiance, it will be one that welcomes—nay, insists upon—scrupulous criticism, comparison, and correction of its own deficiencies. It is a philosophy, moreover, that recognizes the debits and the assets, the fears and the hopes of our crisis-culture. In its vigorous commitment to radically democratic means and radically democratic ends, it firmly opposes totalitarian means and ends. It is international as well as intercultural in processes and objectives, and, for this reason, it strives not merely for good schools but, even more, for good communities. It is also a philosophy that aims to stir imagination, create intellectual and emotional excitement, and galvanize the loyalty of students, teachers, parents—indeed, all citizens committed to its principles. It draws deeply on the psychological and social sciences. And, finally, it is a philosophy that implements the full significance of the anthropological hypothesis that education is, if accurately understood, the *active* agent of culture.

As may be recalled from Chapter 3, we have provisionally termed this emerging theory the "reconstructionist" philosophy. Some of its characteristics have been implied in various chapters of this volume, but systematic study of its underlying beliefs and of its ensuing educational proposals are better provided in a companion work. Our main task here has been a prior but necessary one. In the degree that this task has been accomplished we have, it is hoped, convinced the reader of the superlative importance of our chief prevailing philosophies of education in providing the foundations of American schools; we have shown, also, that these philosophies are powerful interpretations of and programs for the culture. To judge each in turn as patiently as possible and only then to choose, to modify, or to reject becomes a personal and professional responsibility of the highest order.

Appendix

AIDS TO LEARNING

and

WHAT TO READ

for Chapters 2 through 12

Chapter 2

AIDS TO LEARNING

1. A class discussion of the meaning of "philosophy" is held *before* students read Chapter 2. How do their acquaintances use the term in everyday conversation? What, hitherto, has the term meant to these students? After Chapter 2 has been studied, another discussion brings out similarities and differences between the text's conception of the term and their own, with the aim of achieving as much consensus as possible as to the clearest meaning.

2. Each member of the class prepares a descriptive list of educational issues in addition to the four selected for treatment in Chapter 1. With this list as a resource, the class considers how these additional issues, as well as the four, may reveal *philosophic* beliefs as defined in Chapter 2.

3. Part or all of the class visits an instructor in economics, or a leading businessman in the community, or invites such an individual to visit the class. He is requested to indicate his most *basic* reasons for believing in a particula system of economic enterprise. Students prepare for the meeting by agreeing upon what beliefs to watch for, especially the degree to which they conform to the kind exemplified in the final topic in Chapter 2 (pp. 41–43). Without openly agreeing or disagreeing with the speaker, they question him, following his presentation, with a view to determining the basic foundation of his convictions.

4. Further examples of the main terms introduced in this chapter are suggested either in written or oral form. These include: ontology, epistemology, axiology, cosmology, metaphysics, logic, semantics, ethics, hedonism, esthetics,

socio-political theory, monism, pluralism, dualism, empiricism, naturalism, idealism, transcendentalism, materialism, absolutism, conservatism, regressivism, liberalism, radicalism, eclecticism, skepticism, and agnosticism. The *Dictionary of Philosophy* edited by Runes would be a handy reference while students are becoming familiar with technical terms. *Who's Who in Philosophy* edited by Runes, Denonn, and Winn would also be useful both for terminology and scholarly records of many contemporary thinkers.

WHAT TO READ

If philosophy is a new field for students in this class, they will find it helpful to read the discussion of its meaning in any one of the standard encyclopedias. One of the best for this purpose, as well as for understanding many of the other major concepts used in this book, is the *Encyclopædia of the Social Sciences.* Popular interpretations of philosophy include Will Durant's *The Story of Philosophy* and Harold Larrabee's *What Philosophy Is.*

One of the clearest histories of philosophy for beginners is Hugh Miller's *An Historical Introduction to Modern Philosophy. A History of Philosophical Systems,* edited by Ferm, also contains useful chapters on Oriental philosophy and rich bibliographical sources. One of the most brilliantly written studies is Bertrand Russell's *A History of Western Philosophy.* For American philosophers, consult *A History of American Philosophy* by Herbert W. Schneider; *Contemporary American Philosophy,* two volumes, edited by Adams and Montague; and *Men and Movements in American Philosophy* by Joseph L. Blau.

Introductions to philosophy, and to its major branches, would enrich further the meanings of the major terms introduced in Chapter 2. Among the introductory texts most widely used in the colleges of America during the past quarter-century are: *Types of Philosophy* by W. E. Hocking; *Introduction to Philosophy* by G. T. W. Patrick; *Ethics* by John Dewey and James H. Tufts; *An Introduction to Logic and Scientific Method* by Morris R. Cohen and Ernest Nagel. A useful discussion of "tasks and opportunities" is found in *Philosophy in American Education* by Brand Blanshard and others. Recent introductions include *The Way of Philosophy* by Philip Wheelwright; *The Meaning of Philosophy* by Joseph G. Brennan; *The Compass of Philosophy* by N. P. Stallknecht and R. S. Brumbaugh; *Philosophies Men Live By* by Robert F. Davidson; and *The Spirit of Philosophy* by Marcus Long. In ethics, consult *Ideals of Life* by Millard S. Everett.

Selections from the writings of some of the great philosophers may be found in *Readings in Philosophy* edited by Randall and Buchler; *Basic Problems of Philosophy: Selected Readings with Introductions* edited by Bronstein, Krikorian, and Wiener; and *Classic American Philosophers* edited by Fisch. The book by Wheelwright, above, also contains selections.

To obtain some idea of the kind of philosophic issues now being discussed, consult the following periodicals: *Journal of Philosophy, Ethics, Journal of the History of Ideas, Review of Metaphysics, Thomist, Philosophy of Science, Philosophical Review, Philosophical Studies,* and *Mind* (English publication).

References in educational philosophy will be listed under "What to Read," especially for Chapters 5, 8, and 11. Students who would like some preliminary acquaintance with the major points of view to be considered in this volume, as well as with other views, may consult *Goals for American Education* edited by Bryson, Finkelstein, and MacIver, especially Chapters 1, 8, 9, 11, 12, 13, and 18; *A First Course in Philosophy of Education* by E. V. Sayers (contains useful bibliography); and, most important, National Society for the Study of Education, *Fifty-fourth Yearbook,* Part I, "Modern Philosophies and Education."

Students interested in examining some of the evidence for the issues discussed in Chapter 1 may consult *The Battle for Free Schools* edited by Brameld and *Public Education Under Criticism* edited by Scott and Hill.

Chapter 3

AIDS TO LEARNING

1. The term "culture" is one of the most fruitful terms to have entered into wide usage, especially in philosophy and the social sciences, during the past quarter-century. Since it is also fundamental to this volume, careful analysis of its meaning, with abundant illustration, would be helpful to subsequent study. By discussion, compare the popular idea of the term with the anthropological meaning. Is there any similarity between them?

2. Consider the evidences of our "schizophrenic" culture discussed on pages 53–61. How far do they seem to characterize our time fairly? What other examples might be added to the six? How do the six overlap? See "What to Read" below.

3. Another fundamental term in this volume is *revolution.* What does it mean? (See *Encyclopædia of the Social Sciences.*) How far does the class agree that ours is an age of revolution? What other evidence could be marshaled for or against the contention?

4. Consider the several "levels of belief" discussed in Chapter 2 (pp. 22–24) and in Chapter 3 (pp. 70–74). Students should find it interesting to write a brief "philosophic autobiography" of the levels on which they have found themselves thus far in their own lives, supporting their self-interpretations with reports of experiences that caused them to change from one level to another or to decide upon the level where they now find themselves. These essays could be returned to their writers near the end of the course with a view to reconsidering them in the light of further learning.

WHAT TO READ

The greatest need here is acquaintance with some of the literature dealing with crisis-culture. The literature is, of course, enormous. Students in the social sciences should recommend books they have found provocative and relevant to the problems discussed in this chapter.

One of the best popular overviews is Hans Kohn's *The Twentieth Century*. A random sampling of books on the theme includes Lewis Mumford, *The Conduct of Life;* Pitirim Sorokin, *Social Philosophies of an Age of Crisis;* F. S. C. Northrop, editor, *Ideological Differences and World Order;* Arnold J. Toynbee, *A Study of History;* D. W. Brogan, *The Price of Revolution;* Karl Mannheim, *Diagnosis of Our Time;* Wilhelm Röpke, *The Social Crisis of Our Time;* José Ortega y Gasset, *The Revolt of the Masses;* David Riesman, *The Lonely Crowd;* Bertrand Russell, *New Hopes for a Changing World;* Robert Dahl and Charles Lindblom, *Politics, Economics, and Welfare;* William O. Douglas, *An Almanac of Liberty;* Norbert Wiener, *The Human Use of Human Beings;* Ernst Cassirer, *The Myth of the State;* Harrison Brown, *The Challenge of Man's Future;* and George Orwell, *Nineteen Eighty-four*.

Some familiarity with anthropology is very helpful. In addition to *The Science of Man in the World Crisis* edited by Linton and *Man and His Works* by Melville Herskovits, consult Clyde Kluckhohn, *Mirror for Man;* Ruth Benedict, *Patterns of Culture;* Julian Huxley, *Man in the Modern World;* Alfred L. Kroeber, *Anthropology;* and John Gillin, *The Ways of Men.* The most thorough analysis of the concept "culture" is in Kroeber and Kluckhorn, *Culture: A Critical Review of Concepts and Definitions.* A useful treatment of the relations of philosophy and culture is found in George Geiger's *Philosophy and the Social Order.*

To gain some idea of current discussion in the social sciences, consult such periodicals as these: *American Sociological Review, Journal of Educational Sociology, Social Forces, Journal of Social Issues, American Economic Review, Monthly Labor Review, Science and Society, Annals of the American Academy of Political and Social Science, Review of Politics, American Political Science Review, Foreign Affairs, American Anthropologist, Journal of Social Psychology.*

It is highly desirable that students in this course read a *good* daily newspaper (for example, the New York *Times*) and a regular commentary on current events (for example, *Nation, Newsweek, New Republic, Reporter, Progressive, New Statesman and Nation, Time,* and *U.S. News and World Report*).

Chapter 4

AIDS TO LEARNING

1. Students are strongly urged to visit schools exemplifying each of our three major types of educational theory. It would be interesting to go a step

further and visit *two* of each type studied in this part—one after the appropriate chapter on philosophic beliefs has been studied, the other after the succeeding chapter on educational theory. Each visit would aim to detect the underlying beliefs upon which practice functions (for example, the values held by teachers or administrators; or the principles of social control which determine how much or how little participation by teachers and students is permitted). The first visit, however, would utilize philosophic concepts that are only *implicitly* educational in large part, while the second would use those that are more *explicitly* so. A comparison of findings, after the two trips have been completed, would enable students to determine whether they detected more significant beliefs after having the advantage of additional study provided by the pertinent chapter on educational theory.

If the trips are to be as fruitful as possible, they should be carefully planned by the instructor and students together. The kinds of beliefs to look for in classrooms; the kinds of questions to ask administrators or teachers; the organization of student visitors into teams of four or five—these are necessary components of preliminary planning. If the entire class cannot conveniently make both trips, perhaps half might make the first and half the second. (This proposal is developed further in the "Aids to Learning" for Chapter 5.)

2. Invite an instructor from the department of philosophy in this institution or a nearby one to visit the class for an informal discussion of pragmatism and of some of its leading American exponents today.

3. Practice outlining an "act of thought" (pp. 104–107). A written example from actual experience might be requested of each student, followed by criticism of those exemplifying well or badly the process of problem solving. Dewey's own illustrations in *How We Think* might be helpful here.

4. How accurately does Dewey's theory of democracy describe actual democratic practice today? Does the theory seem adequate? How is it rooted in pragmatic beliefs about reality and knowledge, as well as about value? How far does it agree with the liberal level of belief described in Chapter 3, page 73?

WHAT TO READ

Books listed in the footnotes are most useful. It is important to read some of the source material—especially the writings of Charles Peirce, William James, and John Dewey. The beginning student will find *Chance, Love, and Logic* by Peirce, *Pragmatism* by James, and *Reconstruction in Philosophy* by Dewey as readable as any of their philosophic writings. Probably the best sampling of writings by these three men is in *Classic American Philosophers* edited by Fisch.

A fresh approach to the general psychological point of view of progressivism is Hadley Cantril's *The "Why" of Man's Experience,* based on pioneering research. (See also Earl Kelley's *Education for What Is Real.*) For a clear statement of the progressivist philosophy of science, with special emphasis on semantics, read Anatol Rapoport's *Operational Philosophy.*

Chapter 5

AIDS TO LEARNING

1. Note the suggestion in Chapter 4, "Aids to Learning," item 1, that schools be visited for the purpose of detecting the underlying beliefs that govern everyday practice. This experiment in "applied philosophy" should be tried again here by visiting a second progressivist school. Each visiting team of students should discuss their findings and should present them before the class, indicating the extent to which members of each team agree or disagree on what they observed. Some things to look for:

   a. Were the *professed* beliefs of administrators and teachers in the school consistent with their practices?
   b. Did the teachers and administrators seem consistent with one another in their statements of belief?
   c. Did the students show awareness of the philosophic bases of their school?
   d. Was the *learning* process consistent with underlying theory?
   e. Was the *curriculum* organized in accordance with underlying theory?
   f. Did the pattern of *control* in the school seem harmonious with underlying theory?
   g. Were there any conspicuous signs of *eclecticism* in the theory and/or practice of the school?
   h. Did the school seem to be guided by a clearcut, meaningful *philosophy*?

2. Select five or six of the leading educational periodicals (see "What to Read" below) and read a variety of current articles with a view to detecting some of the philosophic beliefs underlying them. To what extent are the articles governed primarily by progressivist beliefs? To what extent do they show signs of being eclectic? To what extent is it impossible to be certain of the philosophy of the writer?

3. Invite a progressivist who is outstanding in the schools or colleges of the community to visit the class. Ask him to clarify some of the concepts discussed in this chapter about which uncertainty has been expressed by one or more students.

4. Review the several *Yearbooks* of the John Dewey Society. What are their major themes? How far are they expressions, in one form or another, of progressivist beliefs? What are some of their major recommendations? To what extent do they deal with genuine "frontier" movements in education?

WHAT TO READ

Many of the most important books in the progressivist theory of education are listed in the footnotes. Some reading in these is highly desirable.

Several of the more outstanding are listed again here, and a few others are added:

John Dewey, *Democracy and Education, Experience and Education,* and *Education Today;* William H. Kilpatrick, *Philosophy of Education* and *Selfhood and Civilization;* Boyd H. Bode, *How We Learn;* John L. Childs, *Education and Morals;* Joseph K. Hart, *Education in the Humane Community;* R. Bruce Raup, *Education and Organized Interests in America;* Harold Rugg, *American Life and the School Curriculum;* Horace Kallen, *The Education of Free Men;* V. T. Thayer, *Public Education and Its Critics;* Earl Kelley and Marie I. Rasey, *Education and the Nature of Man;* George S. Counts, *Education and American Civilization;* William H. Kilpatrick, editor, *The Educational Frontier;* William O. Stanley, *Education and Social Integration;* Kenneth D. Benne, *A Conception of Authority;* Harold Taylor, *On Education and Freedom;* and Richard B. Ballou, *The Individual and the State: The Modern Challenge to Education.*

Some of the leading educational periodicals, which should be consulted throughout this course, include *Educational Theory* (by far the most important for our purpose), *Progressive Education, New Era* (English publication), *Educational Leadership, Childhood Education, Journal of Higher Education, School and Society, Educational Forum, N. E. A. Journal, Harvard Educational Review, Educational Record, American Teacher, Education Digest, Journal of Educational Research, Journal of Educational Sociology, Education, School Review,* and *Social Education.*

For a recent statement of the general progressivist position by an academic philosopher, read "An Experimentalist Approach to Education" by G. Geiger, in National Society for the Study of Education, *Fifty-fourth Yearbook,* "Modern Philosophies and Education." See also "Aims of Education for Our Age of Science: Reflections of a Logical Empiricist" by Herbert Feigl, in "Modern Philosophies and Education."

Textbooks in educational philosophy that give extended attention to progressivism include John S. Brubacher, *Modern Philosophies of Education* (rev. ed.); Stella Henderson, *Introduction to Philosophy of Education;* John P. Wynne, *Philosophies of Education;* Rupert Lodge, *Philosophy of Education;* John T. Wahlquist, *The Philosophy of American Education;* Harry S. Broudy, *Building a Philosophy of Education;* and E. V. Sayers, *A First Course in Philosophy of Education.* See also William H. Kilpatrick's *Source Book in the Philosophy of Education* and the collection of writings by many educational theorists in *Eclectic Philosophy of Education* edited by Brubacher.

Histories of education upon which this chapter, as well as Chapters 9 and 12, depend heavily are listed in the footnotes, page 125. We wish especially to recommend *A Cultural History of Education* by R. Freeman Butts, *A History of the Problems of Education* by John S. Brubacher, and *History of Educational Thought* by Robert Ulich. See also *The Development of Modern Education* by Frederick Eby.

For an excellent treatment of curriculum development from a progressivist point of view, see *Fundamentals of Curriculum Development* by B. Othanel Smith, William O. Stanley, and J. Harlan Shores.

Chapter 6

AIDS TO LEARNING

1. After careful study of this chapter, a role-playing session should be conducted to bring out some of the criticisms made of progressivism, together with the views of the progressivists. (For this purpose, it is well to consult a guide to group dynamics, such as *Human Relations in Curriculum Change* edited by Benne and Muntyan.) Each role player represents a character in the community who stands for one of the major positions indicated on pages 170–178. He should not, of course, limit himself to the points made there but should bring in whatever criticisms or views of progressivism he has heard in his own experience. Following the session, which should occupy about half an hour, the class considers the issues raised and tries to reach consensus about their meaning.

2. This chapter depends upon a conceptual structure on three levels (see pp. 163–168). Draw a diagram representing this structure, and show how the levels support one another.

3. In what ways can it be said that President Franklin Roosevelt was a political symbol of "later liberalism"? Was President Harry Truman a more or less adequate symbol than was Roosevelt? How do their political policies seem compatible with the educational policies of John Dewey? Are there any important differences between their *basic* beliefs and his? If so, do these differences outweigh the similarities?

4. Invite a community leader regarded as an outstanding liberal to meet the class for informal discussion. Try to bring out his basic assumptions, and compare these with liberalism-progressivism as interpreted in this chapter.

WHAT TO READ

Students in modern history should be invited to help the class become better acquainted with the development of "early liberalism" and "later liberalism." Indispensable is Harold Laski's *The Rise of Liberalism.* Charles and Mary Beard's *The Rise of American Civilization,* especially the latter part, is important for background. Crane Brinton's *Ideas and Men* and Merle Curti's *The Growth of American Thought* emphasize intellectual and social forces. See also Arthur M. Schlesinger, Jr., *The Age of Jackson,* Joseph Dorfman, *The Economic Mind in American Civilization,* and Karl Polanyi, *The Great Transformation.*

The most important research thus far conducted in progressive education is the Eight-Year Study. The complete study is published in five volumes—Progressive Education Association, Commission on the Relation of School and College, *Adventure in American Education* edited by Aikin. It deserves careful attention.

Many footnote references are useful for further reading. The critique of progressivism by I. B. Berkson in *Education Faces the Future,* Chapters 10,

11, and 15, has been helpful in writing this chapter. See also his *Preface to an Educational Philosophy.*

The attack on progressivism is treated in a number of books cited in the footnotes. The most comprehensive collection of materials is in *Public Education Under Criticism* edited by Scott and Hill. The two most widely read books by critics are Arthur Bestor's *Educational Wastelands* and Albert Lynd's *Quackery in the Public Schools.*

For an overview of progressivism in its American development, see Harold Rugg's *Foundations for American Education,* Chapters 17 and 18. See also his *The Teacher of Teachers,* containing helpful reading guides to many problems raised in this volume.

Chapter 7

AIDS TO LEARNING

1. Refer to the first suggested "Aid to Learning" for Chapter 4. This time two trips, if possible, should be made to essentialist type of schools. Follow and supplement the trip suggestions made above.

If it is too difficult for the entire class to attempt such trips, teams could be organized so that everyone makes at least one trip during the course and reports back to the class.

2. What are the philosophic beliefs underlying the textbooks, lectures, etc. offered in educational psychology in the institution where this course is being taken? An attempt to answer this question could be made after interviewing instructors or attending two or three classes for the purpose of detecting governing beliefs. Is educational psychology offered primarily from an organismic point of view, a behaviorist point of view, a connectionist point of view, or some other—for example, an eclectic point of view? (This question might be considered again after studying Chapter 8.)

3. Can we find important exponents of the idealist position, generally expressed, in the life of the local community? What is the fundamental position of the devout Christian Scientist, for example? It would be interesting to interview such persons, seeking to compare their beliefs with those presented in this chapter. Can we also find important local exponents of realism (for example, businessmen or politicians whose beliefs approach those of Sumner or Spencer)?

The main purpose of such an interview should be to detect underlying beliefs, *not to argue, challenge, or disagree.* Interviewers should be extremely careful in this respect, not only in this interview but in all others suggested throughout the following chapters. Role-playing interviews before the class could help to improve techniques.

4. What contemporary novelists, painters, dramatists show realist or idealist assumptions in their work? Are there good examples of recent movies

that bring out these assumptions? If so, members of the class might attend one, bearing in mind a set of esthetic concepts by which to appraise what they see. Further reading in esthetic sources is desirable as preparation.

WHAT TO READ

The history of modern philosophy is the most important single source, especially John H. Randall's *The Making of the Modern Mind.*

Acquaintance with the main streams of modern thought is so desirable that, if at all possible, the student should read at least briefly in primary sources. The Library of Classics, the Great Books Foundation series, and the Modern Student's Library are excellent, as are a number of volumes in the Modern Library and Everyman's Library. See the selections suggested under "What to Read" for Chapter 2. Especially important would be at least brief acquaintance with Spinoza, Descartes, Hobbes, Locke, Berkeley, Hume, Kant, and Hegel; for these, along with a few others, were the intellectual giants who laid the foundations of essentialism as a philosophy of education, as we know it today. Excellent selections from Josiah Royce are to be found in *Classic American Philosophers* edited by Fisch.

For recent intelligent examples of conservationist points of view toward contemporary American culture, read Alan Valentine's *The Age of Conformity,* Russell Kirk's *The Conservative Mind,* and Peter Viereck's *The Shame and Glory of the Intellectuals.*

Chapter 8

AIDS TO LEARNING

1. Note the suggestion for an experiment in "applied philosophy" in item 1 of "Aids to Learning," Chapter 5. If at all possible, try the same experiment here, adding to the criteria by class discussion before the visit takes place.

2. Note suggestion 2, Chapter 5. Utilize essentialist, instead of progressivist, beliefs as instruments of critical judgment.

3. Note suggestion 3, Chapter 5. Many members and officers of the National Education Association and of state associations are more or less explicitly essentialists. Many would, however, also profess some degree of progressivist or perennialist beliefs. Try to determine whether your consultant is *primarily* an essentialist or an eclectic, or something else and whether the policies he supports in practice seem to accord with his theory.

4. Review some of the recent yearbooks of the national educational organizations—for example, the National Society for the Study of Education. Look for underlying beliefs. To what extent are they consistently essentialist? To what extent eclectic? Every writer builds his presentation on assumptions

about reality, knowledge, value. Try to "read between the lines" to detect what these assumptions are.

WHAT TO READ

Some important contemporary essentialist writings should be read directly, if at all possible. Among idealist writings, Robert Ulich's *Fundamentals of Democratic Education* and *The Human Career* are among the most scholarly. Michael Demiashkevich's *An Introduction to the Philosophy of Education,* especially Part III, is a good example of the conservationist implications in essentialist education. A helpful comparison between progressivism and essentialism is afforded by Herman H. Horne's *The Democratic Philosophy of Education,* a page-by-page analysis from an idealistic viewpoint of Dewey's *Democracy and Education.* See also Horne's *The Philosophy of Christian Education.* More recent than any of these is Gordon K. Chalmer's *The Republic and the Person,* although his idealist premises are more implicit than explicit.

Among realists, perhaps the best known in Frederick S. Breed; see his *Education and the New Realism.* See also his chapter in the *Forty-first Yearbook* of the National Society for the Study of Education, "Philosophies of Education," and compare with Horne's chapter. Good bibliographies are provided at the close of both. William C. Bagley's *Education and Emergent Man* may be supplemented by his *Education, Crime, and Social Progress.*

An interesting presentation by contemporary academic philosophers of idealist and realist views of education is found in "Modern Philosophies and Education," *Fifty-fourth Yearbook* of the National Society for the Study of Education. Read "A Liberal Christian Idealist Philosophy of Education" by Theodore M. Greene and "An Ontological Philosophy of Education" by James K. Feibleman. Compare the latter with John Wild's "classical realism" in the same volume.

The Harvard Report, *General Education in a Free Society,* and Ross Finney's *A Sociological Philosophy of Education* provide excellent opportunities to observe eclectic tendencies in essentialism, while judging the parts by the *over-all* philosophic position.

Two recent pseudo-essentialist statements are Mortimer Smith's *Diminished Mind: A Study of Planned Mediocrity in Our Public Schools* and Bernard I. Bell's *The Crisis in Education: a Challenge to American Complacency.* Both books demonstrate how an essentialist may be quite as concerned with the crisis of our times as an exponent of another position—he may even seem to be "radical" in his pronouncements—and yet may operate from a conservative level of fundamental beliefs when these are judged in their cultural context. For a more entertaining argument from essentially similar premises, see the second edition of Albert Jay Nock's *The Theory of Education in the United States.* All three are worth reading.

W. E. Hocking's *Types of Philosophy,* Rupert Lodge's *Philosophy of Education,* John T. Wahlquist's *The Philosophy of American Education,* and J. Donald Butler's *Four Philosophies and Their Practice in Education and*

Religion are good examples of conventional classifications—pragmatism, idealism, realism, etc.—with minimum regard for the cultural settings of these philosophic points of view.

For many examples of essentialist ideas, consult selections in *Eclectic Philosophy of Education* edited by Brubacher.

Chapter 9

AIDS TO LEARNING

1. Examine a number of the widely used textbooks in educational philosophy, principles of education, and allied courses to determine whether the criticism under our first topic in this chapter (pp. 263–264) seems justified. If these textbooks consider the cultural context of their theories, how fully do they do so? How far do they help the student to choose among alternative theories? What bases or criteria of choice are suggested, if any?

2. In parallel columns, make a list of similarities between idealism and realism as these may be manifested in common educational practice (for example, the "correspondence theory of truth" with its concomitant of learning the "essentials" given to the mind by a pre-existent world). Then make a list of differences between idealism and realism as these may be manifested in typical educational practice (for example, the more optimistic spirit of the typical idealist teacher). In making the list, try to translate the concepts provided by both Chapters 7 and 8 into concrete examples. Which list seems to you to have the heavier weight—the similarities or differences? How far does the list support the general interpretation of this chapter that, in terms of educational *consequences,* the similarities have much more importance than the differences?

3. To what extent have the members of this class been subjected to "acquiescent learning" in their educational careers (see pp. 272–273)? To what extent do other schools in the local community emphasize this kind of learning? To what extent does it seem to serve a "conserving function" in the economic and political life of the community?

4. Examine some of the editorials in current newspapers and popular magazines, or listen to a political speech or two on the radio. Watch critically for the use of such words as "freedom" or "duty" or other common "essential" virtues. Try to detect the cultural context of these terms. What *kind* of "freedom," for example, is meant: that which agrees with the values of our inherited "free enterprise" order, or some other? Note the quotation from Horne, Chapter 7, page 249, and the discussion of the " 'Social Heritage' as Concealment," pages 275–277. How far does the editorial writer or the radio speaker mean something similar to this, how far something different? If he uses the term "liberty," does it seem to connote "early liberalism" or "later liberalism," or some other?

WHAT TO READ

As indicated in the footnote on page 265, further reading in the history of modern culture is highly desirable here. Consult the *Encyclopædia of the Social Sciences* for excellent references, especially at the conclusion of the important articles on "Liberalism," "Technology," "Industrialism," "Capitalism," and "Science."

Books of special value are Max Weber, *The Protestant Ethic and the Rise of Capitalism;* R. H. Tawney, *Religion and the Rise of Capitalism;* Thorstein Veblen, *The Place of Science in Modern Civilisation and Other Essays;* John H. Randall, *The Making of the Modern Mind,* especially Book III; Charles Beard, *The Economic Interpretation of the Constitution of the United States;* Merle Curti, *The Growth of American Thought;* Edwin R. A. Seligman, *The Economic Interpretation of History;* and Crane Brinton, *Ideas and Men.*

For further direct support of our interpretation of essentialism as a cultural-philosophic movement, see especially Harold J. Laski's *The Rise of Liberalism,* John Dewey's *The Quest for Certainty,* and Jerome Frank's *Fate and Freedom.*

Chapter 10

AIDS TO LEARNING

1. Refer again to the first suggested "Aid to Learning" for Chapter 4 and Chapter 7. In the present case, a trip to a parochial school or college—or possibly to St. John's College, Annapolis, Maryland, is called for. (The latter trip is not impossible for Eastern students. Some twenty-five students and the author were welcomed as overnight guests of the College in conjunction with their study of perennialism. The procedure was similar to that suggested above—an experiment in "applied philosophy.") Note suggestion 1 in "Aids to Learning" for Chapter 11.

2. Invite a lay or clerical spokesman for perennialism to visit the class. Discuss with him the meanings of the most basic concepts presented in the chapter. Try to determine whether he would agree or disagree in his political beliefs with, let us say, Maritain. How far would he wish to modify the original formulations of Aristotle and Aquinas?

3. It would be helpful here to illustrate the cluster of technical terms that have accumulated in the course of the past seven chapters. Make a list of the terms that seem most important, and try to clarify each by an example. Thus: you and I are *teleologists* if we believe that the course of history is moving toward some sort of final perfection—perhaps a "classless society," such as the Communists believe in, or a "city of God," such as Catholics believe in.

4. Because of the central importance of *hylomorphism* to this chapter,

students should seek maximum clarity as to the similarities and differences between it and, for example, the theory of evolution. For this purpose, teams could interview two or three perennialists in a nearby Catholic college and then interview two or three biologists or other natural scientists who hold a purely naturalistic view of the kind studied in Chapter 4, pages 101–103. Without necessarily using the technical terms of the perennialist philosophy, try to determine the beliefs of each "interviewee" on this problem by asking for examples. Report findings to the class for comparative discussion.

WHAT TO READ

As in the case of both progressivism and essentialism, a primary need is for some acquaintance with the great masters of philosophy. For perennialism, this means, of course, Plato, Aristotle, and Aquinas before all others. Among contemporaries, Jacques Maritain and Etienne Gilson are most important.

Parts, at least, of Plato's *Republic* should be read, and of Aristotle's *Ethics*. The best recent edition of Aquinas is probably *Basic Writings of St. Thomas Aquinas*. (See footnotes, p. 291).

Maritain's thought may be sampled in any of his writings cited in this chapter. Perhaps as popular and "liberal" a tract as any is his *Christianity and Democracy*. A simple exposition of his over-all theory is his *An Introduction to Philosophy*. Gilson's thought is profoundly developed in his *The Unity of Philosophical Experience* and *History of Christian Philosophy in the Middle Ages*.

Inexpensive editions of many of the great books (discussed in Chapter 11 but relevant here) are obtainable from the Henry Regnery Company, Chicago.

Chapter 11

AIDS TO LEARNING

1. Note again the suggestions for a second trip to a perennialist type of school (see "Aids to Learning," Chapters 5 and 10). A fairly easy trip in the larger cities might be arranged to one of the great-books classes for adults. Call the public library to determine whether such classes are scheduled, or write the Great Books Foundation, 37 South Wabash Avenue, Chicago 3, Illinois. This trip could complement the previous one and would be most useful if the previous one had been made to an elementary parochial school.

2. Part or all of the class could give a demonstration of a great-books seminar, either after the above visit or after studying pages 330–332 and making a careful study of the catalogue and other literature from St. John's

College. A student should act as "Socratic" leader, using one of the "great books" listed in Chapter 10.

3. Compare essentialism with perennialism by making a list of similarities and differences; then, by class discussion, try to reach consensus as to whether similarities outweigh differences, or vice versa.

4. Arrange a debate between two teams of two members each—one team representing Hutchins and Adler, the other Dewey and Kilpatrick. This would give opportunity for role playing and for reviewing progressivist beliefs.

WHAT TO READ

Perhaps the most influential perennialist volume in education during the past twenty years has been Robert M. Hutchins' *The Higher Learning in America.* Mortimer J. Adler's *How to Read a Book* is an ingenious demonstration of how Aristotelian-Thomist beliefs about education can be restated for popular reading in the twentieth century. Hutchins' *The Conflict in Education* and *The University of Utopia* are more recent statements of his general point of view. The most important educational treatise by Jacques Maritain is *Education at the Crossroads,* although a more recent interpretation is his "Thomist Views on Education," in National Society for the Study of Education, *Fifty-fourth Yearbook,* "Modern Philosophies and Education."

Both lay and clerical views of perennialist education will be found in the *Forty-first Yearbook* of the National Society for the Study of Education, "Philosophies of Education," chapters by Mortimer J. Adler and William J. McGucken. The clerical view is probably best stated in William F. Cunningham's *The Pivotal Problems of Education* and in J. D. Redden's and F. A. Ryan's *A Catholic Philosophy of Education.* See also Edward Leen, *What Is Education?;* Joseph McGlade, *Progressive Educators and the Catholic Church;* Scott Buchanan, *Essay in Politics;* and readings in *Eclectic Philosophy of Education* edited by Brubacher.

Chapter 12

AIDS TO LEARNING

1. Hold a debate on "Plato Today," utilizing Richard Crossman's book of that title or K. R. Popper's *The Open Society and Its Enemies* as a resource against Plato and Ronald Levinson's *In Defense of Plato* as a resource on the opposing side. How widely are Plato's beliefs about leaders still held today? To what extent do they still seem defensible? To what extent should his general ideas about education be adopted today, especially for the training of leaders?

2. A role-playing session brings out the views of the perennialist on adult education by having a character advocate establishment of a great-books program in the local community. He calls upon the imaginary director of an adult-education program who is a strong progressivist. The advocate tries to convince the director of the need in terms of a "moral, intellectual, and spiritual revolution."

3. Invite to the class or interview the president, dean, or some other top administrator of a local college or university for the purpose of determining his basic beliefs about higher education. Watch for agreements or disagreements with Hutchins. Try to determine his basic assumptions and to evaluate them in terms of the cultural context in which he operates. Is he primarily a perennialist, an essentialist, or a progressivist, or does he fit none of these frames of reference?

4. Restudy the paragraphs headed, "Role of the Common People in Three Periods of History," pages 360–361. By class discussion, try to decide in what ways *subsequent* pages of the chapter support our evaluation of the perennialist's attitude toward the common people. Why is this issue fundamental for our time?

WHAT TO READ

For cultural as well as philosophic support of our interpretation of Greek culture, and the role played especially by Plato, see Volume I of K. R. Popper's *The Open Society and Its Enemies.* John Wild's *Plato's Theory of Man* takes a view of Plato sharply different from Popper's, as does Ronald Levinson's *In Defense of Plato.* For rich background and interpretation of both ancient and medieval political thought, George H. Sabine's *A History of Political Theory* is especially helpful.

For a clerical critique of our general evaluation of perennialism, see Chapter 5 in Joseph McGlade's *Progressive Educators and the Catholic Church.* McGlade's criticisms have been considered in the writing of this chapter.

Perhaps the richest additional resource, however, is in the original perennialists listed under "What to Read" for Chapter 10. In Plato, Aristotle, and Aquinas we have the best possible examples of the kind of learning advocated by proponents of the great-books program.

BIBLIOGRAPHY

This bibliography does not pretend to cover the entire field of educational philosophy. It is merely a compilation of all works cited in the text, footnotes, end-of-chapter notes, and "Aids to Learning and What to Read."

Adams, G. P., and William P. Montague (eds.), *Contemporary American Philosophy* (2 vols.), Macmillan, 1932.

Adler, Mortimer J., *Art and Prudence*, Longmans, Green, 1937.

———, *How to Read a Book*, Simon and Schuster, 1944.

———, *How to Think about War and Peace*, Simon and Schuster, 1944.

———, "Liberalism and Liberal Education," *Educational Record*, July 1939.

———, "The Order of Learning," *Moraga Quarterly*, Sept. 1941.

———, "The Philosopher," in R. B. Heywood (ed.), *The Works of the Mind. See* Heywood.

———, *Problems for Thomists*, Sheed and Ward, London, 1940.

———, *What Man Has Made of Man*, Longmans, Green, 1937.

———, and Paul Schilpp, debate. *See* Schilpp.

Aikin, W. M., *The Story of the Eight-Year Study*, Harper, 1942.

Aquinas. *See* Thomas Aquinas.

Aristotle, *Nicomachean Ethics* (trans. by Welldon), Macmillan, 1927.

———, *Works* (ed. by Ross and Smith), Oxford University Press, London, various dates.

Bagley, William C., *Education, Crime, and Social Progress*, Macmillan, 1931.

———, *Education and Emergent Man*, Nelson, 1934.

———, "An Essentialist's Platform for the Advancement of American Education," *Educational Administration and Supervision*, Apr. 1938.

———, "The Significance of the Essentialist Movement in Educational Theory," *Classical Journal*, Mar. 1939.

Ball, Lester B., and Harold G. Shane, "The New AEF Policy in Review," *Progressive Education*, Apr. 1948.

Ballou, Richard B., *The Individual and the State: The Modern Challenge to Education*, Beacon Press, Boston, 1953.

Barnett, H. G., *Innovation: The Basis of Cultural Change,* McGraw-Hill, 1953.

Barr, Stringfellow, "The Education of Freemen," *New Republic,* Aug. 31, 1942.

Beard, Charles, *The Economic Interpretation of the Constitution of the United States,* Macmillan, 1913.

———, and Mary Beard, *The Rise of American Civilization,* Macmillan, 1930.

Beck, Robert H., "Neo-Thomism and Rational Humanism in Educational Philosophy," *Harvard Educational Review,* Winter 1949.

Bell, Bernard I., *The Crisis in Education: a Challenge to American Complacency,* McGraw-Hill, 1949.

Belloc, Hilaire, *Essays of a Catholic Layman in England,* Sheed and Ward, London, 1931.

Benedict, Ruth, *Patterns of Culture,* Houghton Mifflin, 1934.

Benignus, Brother, *Nature, Knowledge and God,* Bruce Publishing Co., Milwaukee, 1947.

Benne, Kenneth D., *A Conception of Authority,* Bureau of Publications, Teachers College, Columbia University, 1943.

———, and Bozidar Muntyan (eds.), *Human Relations in Curriculum Change,* Dryden, 1951.

Berdyaev, Nicolai, *Freedom and the Spirit,* Centenary Press, London, 1935.

Berkson, I. B., *Education Faces the Future,* Harper, 1943.

———, *Preface to an Educational Philosophy,* Columbia University Press, 1940.

Bestor, Arthur, *Educational Wastelands,* University of Illinois Press, 1953.

Bidney, David, *Theoretical Anthropology,* Columbia University Press, 1953.

Blanshard, Brand, and others, *Philosophy in American Education,* Harper, 1945.

Blanshard, Paul, *American Freedom and Catholic Power,* Beacon Press, Boston, 1949.

Blau, Joseph, *Men and Movements in American Philosophy,* Prentice-Hall, 1952.

Bobbitt, Franklin, *How to Make a Curriculum,* Houghton Mifflin, 1924.

Bode, Boyd H., *Democracy as a Way of Life,* Macmillan, 1939.

———, *How We Learn,* Heath, 1940.

———, *Modern Educational Theories,* Macmillan, 1927.

———, *Progressive Education at the Crossroads,* Newson and Co., 1938.

Bradley, F. H., *Appearance and Reality,* Oxford, 1930.

Brameld, Theodore, "Absolutism and Democracy," *Educational Forum,* Mar. 1939.

——— (ed.), *The Battle for Free Schools,* Beacon Press, Boston, 1951.

———, *Toward a Reconstructed Philosophy of Education,* Dryden, 1956.

———, *A Philosophic Approach to Communism,* University of Chicago Press, 1933.

Breed, Frederick S., *Education and the New Realism,* Macmillan, 1939.

Brennan, Joseph G., *The Meaning of Philosophy,* Harper, 1953.

Brickman, William W., "Essentialism Ten Years After," *School and Society,* May 15, 1948.

Bridgman, P. W., *The Logic of Modern Physics,* Macmillan, 1927.

Brightman, Edgar S., *A Philosophy of Religion,* Prentice-Hall, 1940.
Brinton, Crane, *Ideas and Men,* Prentice-Hall, 1950.
Brogan, D. W., *The Price of Revolution,* H. Hamilton, London, 1951.
Bronstein, Daniel J., Yervant H. Krikorian, and Philip P. Wiener (eds.), *Basic Problems of Philosophy: Selected Readings with Introductions,* Prentice-Hall, 1947.
Broudy, Harry S., *Building a Philosophy of Education,* Prentice-Hall, 1954.
Brown, Harrison, *The Challenge of Man's Future,* Viking, 1954.
Brubacher, John S. (ed.), *Eclectic Philosophy of Education,* Prentice-Hall, 1951.
———, *A History of the Problems of Education,* McGraw-Hill, 1947.
———, *Modern Philosophies of Education* (2nd ed.), McGraw-Hill, 1950.
Bryson, Lyman, Louis Finkelstein, and R. M. MacIver (eds.), *Goals for American Education,* Harper, 1950.
Buchanan, Scott, "The Crisis in Liberal Education," *Amherst Graduates Quarterly,* Feb. 1938.
———, *Essay in Politics,* Philosophical Library, 1953.
Burtt, E. A., *The Metaphysical Foundations of Modern Science,* Doubleday, 1954.
Bury, J. B., *The Idea of Progress,* Macmillan, 1932.
Butler, J. Donald, *Four Philosophies and Their Practice in Education and Religion,* Harper, 1951.
Butts, R. Freeman, *A Cultural History of Education,* McGraw-Hill, 1947.

Cantril, Hadley, *The "Why" of Man's Experience,* Macmillan, 1954.
Cassirer, Ernst, *An Essay on Man,* Yale University Press, 1944.
———, *The Myth of the State,* Yale University Press, 1946.
Catalogue of a Loan Exhibition of Drawings and Paintings by John Steuart Curry, Lakeside Press, Chicago, 1939.
Chalmers, Gordon, *The Republic and the Person,* Henry Regnery, Chicago, 1952.
Childs, John L., "Communists and the Right to Teach," *Nation,* Feb. 26, 1949.
———, "Democracy, Education, and the Class Struggle," *Social Frontier,* June 1936.
———, *Education and Morals,* Appleton-Century-Crofts, 1950.
Clapp, Elsie R., *Community Schools in Action,* Viking, 1939.
Cohen, Morris R., and Ernest Nagel, *An Introduction to Logic and Scientific Method,* Harcourt, Brace, 1934.
Cole, G. D. H., *Europe, Russia and the Future,* Macmillan, 1942.
Commission on American Citizenship, *Better Men for Better Times,* Catholic University of America, Washington, D.C., 1943.
Counts, George S., *Education and American Civilization,* Bureau of Publications, Teachers College, Columbia University, 1952.
Crossman, Richard H. S., *Plato Today,* George Allen and Unwin, London, 1945.
Cunningham, William F., *General Education and the Liberal College,* B. Herder Book Co., St. Louis, 1953.
———, *The Pivotal Problems of Education,* Macmillan, 1940.
Curti, Merle, *The Growth of American Thought,* Harper, 1943.

Curti, Merle, *The Social Ideas of American Educators,* Scribner's, 1935.

Dahl, Robert A., and Charles E. Lindblom, *Politics, Economics, and Welfare,* Harper, 1953.

Darwin, Charles, *The Origin of Species,* Modern Library, 1936.

Davidson, Robert F., *Philosophies Men Live By,* Dryden, 1952.

Demiashkevich, Michael, *Introduction to the Philosophy of Education,* American Book, 1935.

Dewey, John, *Art as Experience,* Minton, Balch, 1934.

———, *Characters and Events,* Holt, 1929.

———, *Democracy and Education,* Macmillan, 1916.

———, *Education Today,* Putnam's, 1940.

———, *Essays in Experimental Logic,* University of Chicago Press, 1916.

———, *Experience and Education,* Macmillan, 1938.

———, *Experience and Nature,* Open Court Publishing Co., Chicago, 1925.

———, *Freedom and Culture,* Putnam's, 1939.

———, *How We Think* (rev. ed.), Heath, 1933.

———, *Human Nature and Conduct,* Modern Library, 1930.

———, *Individualism, Old and New,* Minton, Balch, 1930.

———, *Intelligence in the Modern World. See* Ratner, Joseph (ed.).

———, *Liberalism and Social Action,* Putnam's, 1935.

———, *Logic: Theory of Inquiry,* Holt, 1938.

———, *My Pedagogic Creed,* Personal Growth Leaflet 19, National Education Assocation, Washington, D.C., N. D.

———, "Philosophy," *Encyclopædia of the Social Sciences,* Macmillan, 1935.

———, *Philosophy and Civilization,* Putnam's, 1931.

———, *The Philosophy of John Dewey. See* Schilpp, Paul A. (ed.).

———, *Problems of Men,* Philosophical Library, 1946.

———, *The Quest for Certainty,* Minton, Balch, 1929.

———, *Reconstruction in Philosophy,* Holt, 1920.

———, and James H. Tufts, *Ethics* (rev. ed.), Holt, 1932.

———, and others, "The New Failure of Nerve," *Partisan Review,* Jan.-Feb., Mar.-Apr., 1943.

Dorfman, Joseph, *The Economic Mind in American Civilization,* Viking, 1946.

Douglas, William O., *An Almanac of Liberty,* Doubleday, 1954.

Dreiser, Theodore, *An American Tragedy,* Boni and Liveright, 1925.

———, *Jennie Gerhardt,* Liveright, 1926.

Durant, Will, *The Story of Philosophy,* Simon and Schuster, 1927.

Eby, Frederich, *The Development of Modern Education,* Prentice-Hall, 1952.

Edwards, Newton, and Herman G. Richey, *The School in the American Social Order,* Houghton Mifflin, 1947.

Eliot, T. S., *The Idea of a Christian Society,* Harcourt, Brace, 1940.

———, *Notes towards the Definition of Culture,* Harcourt, Brace, 1949.

Encyclopædia of the Social Sciences, Macmillan, 1935.

Essentialist Committee, "Summary of Theses," mimeographed pamphlet, N. D.

Everett, Millard S., *Ideals of Life,* Wiley, 1954.

Feigl, Herbert, and Wilfrid Sellars (eds.), *Readings in Philosophical Analysis,* Appleton-Century-Crofts, 1949.

Ferm, Vergilius (ed.), *A History of Philosophical Systems,* Philosophical Library, 1950.

Finney, Ross L., *A Sociological Philosophy of Education,* Macmillan, 1928.

Fisch, Max H. (ed.), *Classic American Philosophers,* Appleton-Century-Crofts, 1951.

Fitzpatrick, Edward A., *How to Educate Human Beings,* Bruce Publishing Company, Milwaukee, 1953.

Foerster, Norman, *The Future of the Liberal College,* Appleton-Century, 1938.

Frank, Jerome, *Fate and Freedom; a Philosophy for Free Americans,* Simon and Schuster, 1945.

Fromm, Erich, *Man for Himself,* Rinehart, 1947.

Geiger, George, *Philosophy and Social Order,* Houghton Mifflin, 1947.

Gillin, John, *The Ways of Men,* Appleton-Century, 1948.

Gilson, Etienne, *History of Christian Philosophy in the Middle Ages,* Random House, 1955.

———, *The Spirit of Medieval Philosophy,* Scribner's, 1936.

———, *The Unity of Philosophical Experience,* Scribner's, 1937.

Great Books Foundation Editions (series of classics), Henry Regnery, Chicago.

Green, T. H., *Prolegomena to Ethics,* The Clarendon Press, Oxford, 1929.

Hart, Joseph K., *Education in the Humane Community,* Harper, 1951.

Hartshorne, Charles, and Paul Weiss (eds.), *Collected Papers of Charles Sanders Peirce,* Harvard University Press, 1931–1935.

Harvard Committee on the Objectives of Education in a Free Society, *General Education in a Free Society,* Harvard University Press, 1945.

Hayek, F. A., *The Counter-Revolution of Science,* Free Press, Glencoe, Ill., 1952.

———, *Individualism and Economic Order,* University of Chicago Press, 1948.

Heidbreder, Edna, *Seven Psychologies,* Appleton-Century, 1933.

Henderson, Stella, *Introduction to Philosophy of Education,* University of Chicago Press, 1947.

Herskovits, M. J., *Man and His Works,* Knopf, 1948.

Heywood, R. (ed.), *The Works of the Mind,* University of Chicago Press, 1947.

Hobhouse, L. T., *Liberalism,* Williams and Norgate, London, 1911.

Hocking, W. E., *Science and the Idea of God,* University of North Carolina Press, 1944.

———, *Types of Philosophy,* Scribner's, 1939.

Hoover, Herbert, *The Challenge to Liberty,* Scribner's, 1934.

Horne, Herman H., *The Democratic Philosophy of Education,* Macmillan, 1932.

———, *The Philosophy of Christian Education,* Fleming H. Revell, 1937.

Hulburd, David, *This Happened in Pasadena,* Macmillan, 1951.

Hutchins, Robert M., "The Administrator," *Journal of Higher Education,* Nov. 1946.

Hutchins, Robert M., *The Atom Bomb and Education,* National Peace Council, London, 1947.
———, *The Conflict in Education,* Harper, 1953.
———, "Double Trouble," *Saturday Review of Literature,* July 17, 1948.
———, *Education for Freedom,* Louisiana State University Press, 1943.
———, *The Higher Learning in America,* Yale University Press, 1936.
———, *No Friendly Voice,* University of Chicago Press, 1936.
———, *St. Thomas and the World State,* Marquette University Press, Milwaukee, 1949.
———, *The University of Utopia,* University of Chicago Press, 1954.
———, and others, "Preliminary Draft for Global Federation," *Saturday Review of Literature,* Apr. 3, 1948.
Huxley, Aldous, *The Perennial Philosophy,* Harper, 1945.
Huxley, Julian, *Man in the Modern World,* Chatto and Windus, London, 1947.

Jaeger, W., *Paideia: The Ideals of Greek Culture,* Oxford, 1939.
James, William, *The Meaning of Truth,* Longmans, Green, 1909.
———, *Pragmatism,* Longmans, Green, 1907.
———, *The Principles of Psychology* (2 vols.), Holt, 1890.
———, *Talks to Teachers on Psychology,* Holt, 1900.
John Dewey Society, *Fifth Yearbook,* "Workers' Education in the United States," Harper, 1941.
———, *Sixth Yearbook,* "Mobilizing Educational Resources," Harper, 1943.
———, *Tenth Yearbook,* "Democracy in the Administration of Higher Education," Harper, 1950.
———, *Twelfth Yearbook,* "Educational Freedom in an Age of Anxiety," Harper, 1953.
———, *Thirteenth Yearbook,* "American Elementary School," Harper, 1954.
Jowett, Benjamin (trans.), *The Dialogues of Plato. See* Plato.
Judd, Charles H., *Education and Social Progress,* Harcourt, Brace, 1934.
Jungk, Robert, *Tomorrow Is Already Here,* Simon and Schuster, 1954.

Kallen, Horace M., *The Education of Free Men,* Farrar, Straus, 1949.
Kandel, Isaac L., *Conflicting Theories of Education,* Macmillan, 1939.
Kattsoff, Louis A., *Elements of Philosophy,* Ronald Press, 1953.
Kelley, Earl C., *Education for What Is Real,* Harper, 1947.
———, and Marie I. Rasey, *Education and the Nature of Man,* Harper, 1952.
Kieffer, John S., "Inaugural Address," *Inauguration of John Spangler Kieffer,* St. John's College, 1947.
Kilpatrick, William H. (ed.), *The Educational Frontier,* Appleton-Century, 1933.
———, *Foundations of Method,* Macmillan, 1925.
———, *Philosophy of Education,* Macmillan, 1951.
———, *Selfhood and Civilization,* Macmillan, 1941.
———, *Source Book in the Philosophy of Education,* Macmillan, 1923.
Kinsey, Alfred C., and others, *Sexual Behavior in the Human Female,* W. B. Saunders, Philadelphia, 1953.
———, *Sexual Behavior in the Hu-*

man Male, W. B. Saunders, Philadelphia, 1948.

Kirk, Russell, *The Conservative Mind,* Henry Regnery, Chicago, 1953.

———, *A Program for Conservatives,* Henry Regnery, Chicago, 1954.

Kluckhohn, Clyde, *Mirror for Man,* McGraw-Hill, 1949.

Kohn, Hans, *The Twentieth Century, A Midway Account of the Western World,* Macmillan, 1949.

Koopman, G. Robert, Alice Miel, and Paul J. Misner, *Democracy in School Administration,* Appleton-Century, 1943.

Krikorian, Y. H. (ed.), *Naturalism and the Human Spirit,* Columbia University Press, 1944.

Kroeber, A. L., *Anthropology,* Harcourt, Brace, 1948.

———, and Clyde Kluckhohn, *Culture: A Critical Review of Concepts and Definitions,* Peabody Museum, Cambridge, Mass., 1952.

Larrabee, Harold, *What Philosophy Is,* Vanguard, 1928.

Laski, Harold, *The American Democracy,* Viking, 1948.

———, *The Rise of Liberalism,* Harper, 1936.

Leen, Edward, *What Is Education?* Sheed and Ward, 1944.

Levinson, Ronald, *In Defense of Plato,* Harvard University Press, 1953.

Lewin, Kurt, *Resolving Social Conflicts,* Harper, 1948.

Library of Classics, Haffner Publishing Co.

Linton, Ralph (ed.), *The Science of Man in the World Crisis,* Columbia University Press, 1945.

Lodge, Rupert, *Philosophy of Education,* Harper, 1947.

Long, Marcus, *The Spirit of Philosophy,* Norton, 1953.

Lovejoy, Arthur O., *The Revolt against Dualism,* Open Court Publishing Co., Chicago, 1930.

Lund, S. E. T., *The School-Centered Community,* Anti-Defamation League of B'nai B'rith, New York, 1949.

Lynd, Albert, *Quackery in the Public Schools,* Little, Brown, 1953.

Lynd, Robert S., *Knowledge for What?* Princeton University Press, 1939.

———, and Helen M. Lynd, *Middletown, a Study in Contemporary American Culture,* Harcourt, Brace, 1929.

McGlade, Joseph, *Progressive Educators and the Catholic Church,* Newman Press, Westminster, Md., 1953.

McGucken, William J., *The Catholic Way in Education,* Bruce Publishing Co., Milwaukee, 1934.

McKeon, Richard P. (ed.), *Selections from Medieval Philosophy* (2 vols.), Scribner's, 1929–1930.

Malinowski, Bronislaw, *Freedom and Civilization,* Roy Publishers, 1944.

Mannheim, Karl, *Diagnosis of Our Time,* Kegan Paul, Trench, Trubner and Co., London, 1947.

Maritain, Jacques, *Art and Poetry,* Philosophical Library, 1943.

———, *Art and Scholasticism,* Scribner's, 1933.

———, *Christianity and Democracy,* Scribner's, 1945.

———, *Creative Intuition in Art and Poetry,* Pantheon Books, 1953.

———, *Education at the Crossroads,* Yale University Press, 1943.

———, *Freedom in the Modern World,* Scribner's, 1936.

———, *An Introduction to Philosophy,* Longmans, Green, 1930.

Maritain, Jacques, *The Person and the Common Good,* Scribner's, 1947.
———, *Ransoming the Time,* Scribner's, 1941.
———, *Scholasticism and Politics,* Macmillan, 1940.
———, *True Humanism,* Geoffrey Bles, London, 1939.
———, *The Twilight of Civilization,* Sheed and Ward, 1943.
Mayer, Frederick, *Essentialism,* Russell F. Moore, 1952.
Mayer, M. H., *The Philosophy of Teaching of St. Thomas Aquinas,* Bruce Publishing Co., Milwaukee, 1929.
Mayhew, K. C., and A. C. Edwards, *The Dewey School,* Appleton-Century, 1936.
Mead, George H., *Mind, Self, and Society,* University of Chicago Press, 1934.
———, "The Philosophies of Royce, James, and Dewey in Their American Setting," *International Journal of Ethics,* Jan. 1930.
Mead, Margaret (ed.), *Cultural Patterns and Technical Change,* UNESCO, Paris, 1953.
Meiklejohn, Alexander, *Education between Two Worlds,* Harper, 1942.
Melby, Ernest O., and Morton Puner (eds.), *Freedom and Public Education,* Frederick Praeger, 1953.
Menninger, Karl, *Man against Himself,* Harcourt, Brace, 1938.
Mercier, Louis J., *The Challenge of Humanism,* Oxford, 1933.
Meyer, Adolph, *The Development of Education in the Twentieth Century,* Prentice-Hall, 1929.
Mill, John Stuart, *On Liberty,* Longmans, Green, 1913.
Miller, Hugh, *An Historical Introduction to Modern Philosophy,* Macmillan, 1947.
Modern Student's Library, The (series of classics), Scribner's.
Montague, William P., *The Ways of Knowing,* Macmillan, 1925.
———, *The Ways of Things,* Prentice-Hall, 1940.
Morris, Charles, *Paths of Life,* Harper, 1942.
Morrison, Henry C., *Basic Principles in Education,* Houghton Mifflin, 1934.
Mumford, Lewis, *The Condition of Man,* Harcourt, Brace, 1944.
———, *The Conduct of Life,* Harcourt, Brace, 1951.
———, *In the Name of Sanity,* Harcourt, Brace, 1954.
Myrdal, Gunnar, *An American Dilemma,* Harper, 1944.

National Education Association, Educational Policies Commission, *The Structure and Administration of Education in American Democracy,* National Education Association, Washington, D.C., 1941.
National Society for the Study of Education, *Forty-first Yearbook,* Part I, "Philosophies of Education," Public School Publishing Co., Bloomington, Ill., 1942.
———, *Fifty-fourth Yearbook,* Part I, "Modern Philosophies and Education," University of Chicago Press, 1955.
Nef, John U., *The United States and Civilization,* University of Chicago Press, 1942.
———, *The Universities Look for Unity,* Pantheon Books, 1943.
"New Failure of Nerve, The." *See* Dewey, John, and others.
Newman, John Henry, *The Idea of a University,* Longmans, Green, 1947.
Nock, Albert Jay, *The Theory of Education in the United States,*

Harcourt, Brace, 1932.
Northrop, F. S. C. (ed.), *Ideological Differences and World Order,* Yale University Press, 1949.
———, *The Meeting of East and West,* Macmillan, 1947.

O'Connell, L. J., *Are Catholic Schools Progressive?* B. Herder Book Co., St. Louis, 1946.
O'Neill, James M., *Religion and Education under the Constitution,* Harper, 1949.
Ortega y Gasset, José, *The Revolt of the Masses,* New American Library, 1950.
Orwell, George, *Nineteen Eighty-four,* Harcourt, Brace, 1949.
Otto, Max C., *The Human Enterprise,* Appleton-Century, 1940.
———, *Things and Ideals,* Holt, 1924.

Patrick, G. T. W., *Introduction to Philosophy,* Houghton Mifflin, 1927.
Pegis, Anton C. (ed.), *The Basic Writings of St. Thomas Aquinas. See* Thomas Aquinas.
Peirce, Charles S., *Chance, Love, and Logic,* Harcourt, Brace, 1923.
———, *Collected Papers. See* Hartshorne, Charles, and Paul Weiss (eds.).
Perry, Ralph Barton, *Present Philosophical Tendencies,* Longmans, Green, 1912.
———, *Realms of Value.* Harvard University Press, 1954.
Plato, *The Dialogues* (trans. by Jowett; 2 vols.), Random House, 1937.
———, *The Republic* (Modern Student's Library Ed.), Scribner's, 1928.
Polanyi, Karl, *The Great Transformation,* Rinehart, 1944.
Popper, K. R., *The Open Society and Its Enemies,* George Routledge and Sons, London, 1945.
Powdermaker, Hortense, *Hollywood, the Dream Factory,* Little, Brown, 1950.
Progressive Education Association, Commission on the Relation of School and College, *Adventure in American Education* (5 vols.), Harper, 1942–1943.

Rader, Melvin, *A Modern Book of Esthetics,* Holt, 1935.
Radin, Paul, *Primitive Man as a Philosopher,* Appleton, 1927.
Raeymaker, Louis de, *Introduction to Philosophy,* Joseph F. Wagner, 1948.
Randall, John H., Jr., *The Making of the Modern Mind* (rev. ed.), Houghton Mifflin, 1940.
———, and Justus Buchler (eds.), *Readings in Philosophy,* Barnes and Noble, 1946.
Rapoport, Anatol, *Operational Philosophy,* Harper, 1953.
Ratner, Joseph (ed.), *Intelligence in the Modern World: John Dewey's Philosophy,* Modern Library, 1939.
Raup, R. Bruce, *Education and Organized Interests in America,* Putnam's, 1936.
———, Kenneth D. Benne, George E. Axtelle, and B. Othanel Smith, *The Improvement of Practical Intelligence,* Harper, 1950.
Redden, J. D., and F. A. Ryan, *A Catholic Philosophy of Education,* Bruce Publishing Co., Milwaukee, 1942.
Riesman, David, *The Lonely Crowd,* Doubleday, 1953.
Rogers, A. K., *A Student's History of Philosophy,* Macmillan, 1907.
Röpke, Wilhelm, *The Social Crisis of Our Time,* University of Chicago Press, 1950.

Ross, W. D., and J. A. Smith (eds.), *Works of Aristotle. See* Aristotle.

Royce, Josiah, *The Spirit of Modern Philosophy,* Houghton Mifflin, 1892.

Rugg, Harold, *American Life and the School Curriculum,* Ginn, 1936.

———, *Foundations for American Education,* World Book, 1947.

———, *The Teacher of Teachers,* Harper, 1952.

———, and Ann Shumaker, *The Child-Centered School,* World Book, 1928.

Runes, Dagobert D. (ed.), *Dictionary of Philosophy,* Philosophical Library, 1942.

———, Lester E. Denonn, and Ralph B. Winn (eds.), *Who's Who in Philosophy,* Philosophical Library, 1942.

Russell, Bertrand, *Education and the Good Life,* Boni and Liveright, 1926.

———, *A History of Western Philosophy,* Simon and Schuster, 1945.

———, *New Hopes for a Changing World,* Simon and Schuster, 1951.

———, *Selected Papers,* Modern Library, 1927.

Sabine, George H., *A History of Political Theory,* Holt, 1937.

Santayana, George, *The Realm of Essence,* Scribner's, 1927.

Sayers, E. V., *A First Course in Philosophy of Education,* Holt, 1952.

———, "Social Patterns and Educational Goals," *School and Society,* July 3, 1948.

Schilpp, Paul A. (ed.), *The Philosophy of John Dewey,* Northwestern University Press, 1939.

———, and Mortimer J. Adler, "Are There Absolute Universal Principles on Which Education Should Be Founded?" (debate), *Educational Trends,* July-Aug. 1941.

Schlesinger, Arthur M., Jr., *The Age of Jackson,* Little, Brown, 1945.

Schmeckebier, Laurence, *John Steuart Curry's Pageant of America,* American Artists Group, New York, 1943.

Schneider, Herbert W., *A History of American Philosophy,* Columbia University Press, 1946.

Scott, C. Winfield, and Clyde M. Hill (eds.), *Public Education Under Criticism,* Prentice-Hall, 1954.

Seligman, Edwin R. A., *The Economic Interpretation of History,* Columbia University Press, 1924.

Sellars, R. W., V. J. McGill, and Marvin Farber (eds.), *Philosophy for the Future,* Macmillan, 1949.

Simon, Yves, "Maritain's Philosophy of the Sciences," *Thomist* (quarterly), Maritain Volume, Sheed and Ward, London, 1943.

Smith, B. O., and others, *Fundamentals of Curriculum Development,* World Book, 1950.

Smith, Mortimer, *Diminished Mind: A Study of Planned Mediocrity in Our Public Schools,* Henry Regnery, Chicago, 1954.

Sorokin, Pitirim, *The Crisis of Our Age,* Dutton, 1941.

———, *Social Philosophies of an Age of Crisis,* Beacon Press, Boston, 1951.

Spengler, Oswald, *The Decline of the West,* Knopf, 1932.

Stallknecht, N. P., and R. S. Brumbaugh, *The Compass of Philosophy,* Longmans, Green, 1954.

———, *The Spirit of Western Philosophy,* Longmans, Green, 1950.

Stanley, William O., *Education and Social Integration,* Bureau of

Publications, Teachers College, Columbia University, 1953.
Sumner, William Graham, *Folkways,* Ginn, 1906.

Tawney, R. H., *Religion and the Rise of Capitalism,* Harcourt, Brace, 1926.
Taylor, Harold, "Education as Experiment," *Antioch Review,* Summer 1949.
———, *On Education and Freedom,* Abelard-Schuman, 1954.
——— (ed.), *Essays in Teaching,* Harper, 1950.
Tenenbaum, Samuel, *William Heard Kilpatrick,* Harper, 1951.
Thayer, V. T., *The Attack upon the American Secular School,* Beacon Press, Boston, 1951.
———, *Public Education and Its Critics,* Macmillan, 1954.
Thomas Aquinas, *Basic Writings* (ed. by Pegis), Random House, 1945.
Thompson, Laura, *Culture in Crisis,* Harper, 1950.
Thorndike, Edward L., *Selected Writings from a Connectionist's Psychology,* Appleton-Century-Crofts, 1949.
Toynbee, Arnold J., *A Study of History,* Oxford, 1947.
Turner, Frederick Jackson, *The Frontier in American History,* Holt, 1921.
Tylor, Edward B., *Primitive Culture* (5th ed.), J. Murray, London, 1929.

Ulich, Robert, *Conditions of Civilized Living,* Dutton, 1946.
———, *Crisis and Hope in American Education,* Beacon Press, Boston, 1951.
———, *Fundamentals of Democratic Education,* American Book, 1940.
———, *History of Educational Thought,* American Book, 1945.
———, *The Human Career—A Philosophy of Self-Transcendence,* Harper, 1955.

Valentine, Alan, *The Age of Conformity,* Henry Regnery, Chicago, 1954.
Van Doren, Mark, *Liberal Education,* Holt, 1943.
Veblen, Thorstein, *The Place of Science in Modern Civilisation and Other Essays,* Viking, 1919.
———, *The Theory of the Leisure Class,* Modern Library, 1934.
Viereck, Peter, *The Shame and Glory of the Intellectuals,* Beacon Press, Boston, 1953.

Wahlquist, John T., *The Philosophy of American Education,* Ronald Press, 1942.
Warner, W. L., and P. S. Lunt, *The Social Life of a Modern Community,* Yale University Press, 1941.
Washburne, Carleton, *A Living Philosophy of Education,* John Day, 1940.
Weaver, Richard M., *Ideas Have Consequences,* University of Chicago Press, 1948.
Weber, Max, *The Protestant Ethic and the Rise of Capitalism,* George Allen and Unwin, London, 1930.
Werkmeister, W. H., *A History of Philosophical Ideas in America,* Ronald Press, 1949.
Whitehead, Alfred N., *The Aims of Education and Other Essays,* Macmillan, 1929.
Whyte, L. L., *The Next Development in Man,* Holt, 1948.
Wild, John, *Plato's Theory of Man,* Harvard University Press, 1946.

Winspear, Alban D., *The Genesis of Plato's Thought,* Dryden, 1940.
Wynne, John P., *Philosophies of Education from the Standpoint of the Philosophy of Experimentalism,* Prentice-Hall, 1947.

Index

INDEX